T0374654

DOES SKILL MAKE US HUMAN?

Does Skill Make Us Human?

MIGRANT WORKERS IN 21ST-CENTURY QATAR AND BEYOND

Natasha Iskander

PRINCETON UNIVERSITY PRESS

PRINCETON & OXFORD

Published by Princeton University Press
41 William Street, Princeton, New Jersey 08540
6 Oxford Street, Woodstock, Oxfordshire OX20 1TR

press.princeton.edu

All Rights Reserved

Library of Congress Control Number 2021940598
ISBN 978-0-691-21757-4
ISBN (pbk.) 978-0-691-21756-7
ISBN (e-book) 978-0-691-21758-1

British Library Cataloging-in-Publication Data is available

Editorial: Meagan Levinson and Jacqueline Delaney
Production Editorial: Jill Harris
Cover Design: Karl Spurzem
Production: Brigid Ackerman
Publicity: Kate Hensley and Kathryn Stevens
Copyeditor: Cindy Milstein

Cover image: Scaffolding construction being erected in Central Doha, Qatar. Photo: Gavin Hellier / Alamy Stock Photo

This book has been composed in Miller

10 9 8 7 6 5 4 3 2 1

For Magdi Rashed Iskander,

father and friend

CONTENTS

DOES SKILL MAKE US HUMAN?

Introduction

THE MEN RAN. They ran in the clothes they had: jeans and flip-flops, or work boots. Some men, their feet cut up, abandoned their plastic sandals on the side of the road and ran barefoot on the hot pavement. They ran in the heat of the afternoon—with temperatures well into the mid-80s°F and the air humid. They ran past the police lined up on the side of the road. In places, they ran past tables with bottled water, but the water had been left out in the sun and was hot and undrinkable. They ran for a long time—maybe hours. Their jeans chafed their skin. Their lungs burned, and their muscles cramped. A few collapsed. Many tried to step off the road, to stop running and rest, but they were forced back, yelled at that they needed to finish the race.

The men, many thousands of them, had been press-ganged to run the Qatar Mega Marathon 2015, organized in Doha as an attempt to set a new world record for the race with the most runners.[1] The race's official website advertised the marathon as a protest against the bad press that Qatar had received after being awarded hosting rights for the 2022 World Cup. It billed the event as a "decisive response to the campaign waged by the sector of envious haters on the success of Qatar to host the 2022 Fédération Internationale de Football Association (FIFA) World Cup, and to their false allegations of persecution of workers and residents in our beloved country."[2] Despite these efforts, enrollment in the race was low. Even after the organizers scaled back to a half-marathon and postponed the event from National Sports Day on February 2 to March 27—when the weather was much hotter, and each year hotter than the last—only a few hundred runners voluntarily registered.[3] To make up for the shortfall of participants, the organizers conscripted construction and factory workers. At the end of race, the organizers announced that thirty-three thousand runners had participated.[4] They fell many thousands short of the record.

The race was held on a Friday, the only protected rest day for workers. Buses picked the workers up in the early morning from their labor camps in the industrial area, a segregated zone in the desert where they were lodged. The Al Sadd Sports Club, which organized the race, later admitted that it had asked companies to encourage workers "with decent jobs" to take part, but insisted that participation was voluntary and appropriate running gear was made available to anyone who wanted it.[5] Many of the workers bused to the marathon route would likely not have known that they would be expected to run a race. But all of them would have found it difficult to refuse. These workers were migrants. They worked in Qatar under a sponsorship system that gave their employers the ability to deport them without notice and for any reason. The photographs and footage of the race show South Asian and African men, massed at the starting line, wearing identical white T-shirts and running bibs marked with contestant numbers.

Still, some of the migrants refused to participate.[6] The start time was delayed until 2:00 p.m., and workers who refused to run were ordered to remain on the buses that brought them, where they had already sat for the entire day in the heat, without water or food. When the club spokesperson was asked about the decision to confine workers to their buses, he said, "We wanted to keep the course clear, and for the course to look presentable." He conceded that he pressed workers in the race to "keep going" because a world record was at stake. "I spoke to them very politely," he added. "They are human as well, right?"[7]

When I read the press coverage of the Mega Marathon, I was reminded of a field trip I had made to a construction site for an oil and gas facility in Qatar just a few months before. I was in Qatar studying workplace practices in the construction industry and the process through which workers developed skill on-site. As part of my fieldwork, I went to observe construction on a liquefied natural gas (LNG) train, where workers were building a section of the plant where natural gas would be pushed through a network of pipes and then cooled into a liquid so that it could be shipped around the world. The construction site in Qatar's northern desert was massive. Tens of thousands of workers from different trades worked concurrently on different elements of the structure. Like other construction sites I visited in Qatar, it was frenetic and crowded. In many places, workers bunched up as they waited to walk through the narrow passageways marked out by scaffolds and ramparts. Throughout the day, I shadowed different trades—mostly scaffolders and welders.

In the afternoon, I went to one of the on-site welding workshops. Located in a large hangar-like structure, the workshop was a vast, multipurpose space: small subcomponents of the structure were welded in one corner, training to improve welding skills took place at another end of the hangar, and quality control and the verification of the integrity of welded seams took place in another quadrant. The Turkish director of the welding center, Mehmet, would later describe it to me in elegiac terms. "This place is like my paradise. I have twenty-five years working as a welder. [Welding] is something that comes into your body. It's like your blood. I can just look from outside at the finished product, and I can see how the welder is doing. Even from the sparks, I can see his philosophy. I can see whether he is moving slow or fast, how much he understands the work."

The LNG train required welding that was flawless. The materials that would be pushed through the train's maze of pipes were highly volatile and flammable. To assess the welding quality, the center used an X-ray system. "Visual testing is not enough, even on the best seams," explained Mehmet. Radiographic testing was essential because even slight discontinuities in the internal structure of the weld could have consequences that were catastrophic. "There are many factors. If you weld in the high heat, the seam won't have integrity. If you are not confident, the seam won't have integrity. If we see even one problem, we retrain," added Mehmet. Natural gas and the potential for explosion meant there was no margin for error, and the center continually tested and reinforced the expertise of its workers, who were already incredibly adept.

Ordinarily, the center was busy and cacophonous, with hundreds of welders, supervisors, and apprentices at work. But the day I first visited, it was empty. There were two supervisors at the desks in the office at the entrance, a few workers were sweeping the floor, and a couple of others were quietly doing maintenance on machinery. The scaffolding manager who accompanied me that day asked where everyone was. "Sporting match," answered one of the supervisors.

The company had scooped up hundreds of men from the welding hangar and sent them to this sporting event—perhaps a soccer game; the supervisor was unsure. Someone in the government had made the request. The company had supplied the workers to fill the bleachers in the audience so that the international press would not report an empty stadium in a country that wanted to position itself as a global sporting destination.

This kind of conscription of construction workers was commonplace in Qatar, although this was the first time I had observed it directly. By and large, companies viewed it as a tax, a request that disrupted production, but with which they had no choice other than to comply. Companies bused their workers from labor camps to the sporting facility where the workers would be used as props. The workers would be treated as bodies, press-ganged into whatever activity was required, perhaps in the heat, perhaps without sufficient access to water, food, or rest. The welders missing from the training center were also, undoubtedly, used in this way. And in the process, their humanity, like that of the migrants forced to run a half-marathon in flip-flops, was turned into something that was no longer clear or certain, something that was open to question. "They are human as well, right?"

Work, Workers, and the Politics of Skill

In 2010, Qatar won, somewhat improbably, the hosting rights for the 2022 FIFA World Cup for soccer. The Qatari government began channeling hundreds of billions of dollars of state revenue toward reinventing itself as a global destination for sports and culture. It commissioned state-of-the-art stadiums, tourism facilities, and infrastructure for the games, and recruited hundreds of thousands of men—mainly from South Asia, the Middle East, and Africa—to build the structures.

As the country began the buildup to the games, the international press and human rights organizations turned a spotlight on the working conditions experienced by the migrants on construction sites in Qatar. The reports were damning; they identified numerous instances of forced labor, low or withheld pay, debt bondage, injury, and death. The reports pointed to the regulations that governed the employment of migrant workers in Qatar as the enabling cause for the patterns of exploitation they documented.[8] Migrant workers were in Qatar under the country's *kafala*—or sponsorship—system, which bound migrants to their employers, who were defined as sponsors in Qatari law. Under the kafala system, migrants were prohibited from changing or quitting their jobs, even in cases of abuse or the nonpayment of wages. They could be deported at any time and, for a while, were barred from leaving the country without their employer's permission. The image of the construction worker, dressed in blue overalls, became the symbol of the exploited migrant in Qatar, a visual shorthand for the conditions produced by a labor relation that resembled bonded labor and slavery.

I wanted to reach behind this image of the exploited construction worker and understand how the conditions that were reported had been produced. Most of the reporting and research on work in Qatar, and more broadly, throughout the Persian Gulf, was inferential. Research took place at work's edge; workers were often interviewed outside the worksite, and their testimonies about the working conditions they faced were used to make assumptions about how the structure of work produced labor violations. To be sure, restricted access to worksites made this research approach necessary. For the most part, the Qatari government and the companies it contracted barred observers from conducting research on active construction sites. Yet this indirect research strategy also reflected a broader move in social science research away from the study of work and its content, and an assumption that the features that define work—the delineation of jobs, content of the tasks required, and occupational profiles along with the hierarchies they reflected—were, in established industries like construction, basically stable.[9] The nature of work in construction was treated as well understood, and construction jobs in Qatar were presumed to be roughly similar to construction jobs everywhere. As a result, the chronic and egregious labor violations were attributed not to the content of jobs—not to the way work was organized, tasks were assigned, and supervision was applied—but instead to the regulatory framework—to the laws—that bound workers to their employers and set the floor for minimal working conditions.

Laws, like the kafala system, may set the terms of employer behavior and specify the outer bounds of labor exploitation, but work is the arena where the conditions of work are defined.[10] Practices that people engage in at the worksite shape the content of work and structure the power relations between employer and worker. I wanted to examine the on-the-job work practices taking place at construction sites all over Qatar in order to understand how the power relations outlined in the kafala system were enacted at the worksite. How did the content of work, patterns of labor exploitation at the worksite, and forms of worker resistance play out within the parameters defined by the kafala system? What did these labor relations reveal about the consequences of bondage for production, work, and the migrants who were, formally and contractually, bound to their employer?

To get at these questions, I focused on skill and practices of skill development. Skill is the marrow of production; all forms of production require competence and ability, both from the people who produce and from the organization that orchestrates their efforts. Skill is therefore necessarily at the core of all work and work relations. As a result, an attention to skill and skill development can highlight the lived experience of working and the power dynamics at the worksite. Skill is where worker autonomy, and worker expressions of initiative and creativity, chafe at workplace structures of control. Skill is visible in the coordination of effort and action; the expression of skill at the jobsite shows whether the organization of work is the product of managerial command or worker collaboration. Whether skill is recognized at the worksite, and whether those who enact or manage it receive credit for that skill, reveals a company's ethos and political culture. Skill illuminates the contours and patterns of labor practices at the worksite, and brings the conventions and routines of hierarchy, dominance, and power—as well as the strategies to challenge them—into focus.

On the Qatari construction sites I visited, skill was *the* core principle around which work was organized, and to a degree far more pronounced than on construction sites I had observed in other settings around the world. Construction projects in Qatar functioned as vast training systems, and building practices doubled as vehicles through which hundreds and thousands of workers on-site developed specialized trade skill. Most of the migrants recruited to build Qatar's state-of-the-art structures arrived with minimal construction experience, if any, and the many workers who migrated from rural areas arrived with little exposure to the kinds of buildings they had been drafted to build. To make up for this shortfall in skill, construction companies invested heavily in training their workforces. They structured every aspect of their production processes to promote on-the-job learning, organizing their workflows to build skill stepwise, designing their supervisory systems to deepen competence in specific technical areas, and selecting their building materials to match the skill of their workforce. Many also set up specialized vocational training centers on-site for trade skills, like the welding hangar I visited at the LNG plant. Workers met these top-down interventions with apprenticeship networks of their own. Informal practices of teaching and learning ran through every single workplace interaction.

The training systems on-site enabled workers to acquire robust and often highly advanced trade skill quickly. Workers who hadn't climbed a scaffold before their arrival in Qatar learned within months how to build towering grids, self-standing, elaborate, and sometimes rising so high that they shattered world records. Others developed cutting-edge skill in steel fixing, and workers who had never seen a construction document before working in Qatar learned how to turn diagrams on paper into arched and asymmetrical columns of rebar and wire. Still others learned how to build and install massive wooden frames that would hold liquid concrete until it congealed into deep foundations for Qatar's skyscrapers and the tunnel walls for Doha's new metro system. In these trades and others, workers quickly developed the expertise required to build the technically complex projects slated for construction in Qatar: stadiums with radical and gravity-defying architectural designs; ultra-modern installations for fossil fuel extraction and processing; luxury developments on archipelagoes reclaimed from the sea; and high-rise structures on waterfront land so saturated by underground water that the foundations had to be designed like boat hulls.

And yet when I asked managers and supervisors on construction sites about their workers, they invariably described them as unskilled. They identified their companies' advanced technical expertise as the most important asset their firms brought to the construction process and described the strategic investment they made to develop construction skill in their workforce. Managers and supervisors perceived their workers' skill clearly and precisely and assessed it repeatedly over the course of a project as they structured their training interventions for the advanced construction techniques required, and yet, quite jarringly, they routinely and indiscriminately dismissed their workers as unskilled, disparaging them as "poor quality," "unproductive," or simply and most derisively, "bodies." Even Mehmet, the supervisor who had waxed so eloquently about welding expertise, discounted the competence of the welders in his crew: "The technique belongs to the [building] design" and not to the workers who welded it.

As these managerial comments made clear, the meaning of skill on Qatari construction sites did not map onto actual observed ability. If skill was not about competence, what was meant by the term "unskilled"? What aspects of work, labor relations, and power structures on-site did it reflect? How did the representation of skill relate to the structure of the work and working conditions that migrants faced? And what it did reveal about the political standing of workers and the political rights they could access? How did their representation as "unskilled"—as bodies that were unable to acquire skill—connect with, and even legitimate, the conditions of bondage under which they had migrated and were employed?

To answer these questions, I needed to look at the valence of skill beyond the worksite and consider how skill was invoked in broader political discussions about the role of migrant workers in the Qatari economy. In government policy, public pronouncements, the local press, and even international advocacy reports and initiatives—spaces outside the worksite—migrant construction workers were also widely portrayed as unskilled laborers. Their function in the economy was described as providing brute labor power for a labor-intensive industry. Their skill, so obviously visible in Doha's gleaming skyline and its modernist developments, was downplayed or denied altogether. Skill, as a descriptor used to shunt migrant construction workers into the category of unskilled, had only a tangential relationship to the actual ability of the workers it portrayed. Skill was a political concept in Qatar, the organizing lexicon of a political language, and as a political language, skill was not a matter of competence but a matter of power.

To understand how representations of skill functioned as a political language, I needed to understand how the characterization of construction workers as unskilled shaped their political status as migrant workers in Qatar and how that political standing fostered the conditions—often extreme and exploitative—under which they worked. Stated differently, I needed to understand how the representation of migrant workers as unskilled in Qatar—representations used to describe workers with, as the organizer of the Mega Marathon put it, "decent jobs"—meant that those workers could be press-ganged into activities outside work, where they would be forced to use their bodies in ways that were painful and physically damaging. I needed to understand why a welding contractor that valued the skill of its welders, invested in the development of their expertise, and appreciated the nuance and creativity they brought to their work—"their philosophy," as Mehmet put it—would deliver them to events where they would be treated as props, and undoubtedly be subject to conditions that were difficult, shaming, and injurious. I needed to understand how the experience of being treated as a mere body—or even the possibility of that experience—shaped workers' expression of competence, their assertion of the autonomy that is so critical to skillful practice, and their ability to imagine working with dignity.

For workers represented as unskilled, the politics of skill also had significant and tangible consequences that were felt outside the worksite. "Unskilled" migrants were subject to a set of policies that consigned them to second-class status. Bureaucratic roadblocks and migration controls, such as the Ministry of Interior's energetic antiabsconding campaign against "runaway" workers who quit their jobs, drastically narrowed their ability to access the already limited rights that the legal system afforded foreign workers. Workers classed as unskilled were confined, as a matter of urban policy, to peripheral zones of the city and excluded from most public spaces. Their physical mobility was monitored, sometimes through personalized GPS sensors, and constrained.

The living conditions in the labor camps, where most workers were lodged, were poor, and the workers' access to services such as health care and basic infrastructure was substandard.

The measures and politics applied to so-called unskilled workers occurred within the framework of the kafala system, but despite many of the claims made in international press coverage, they were not an automatic product of that legal structure. All foreigners in Qatar, regardless of the skill level ascribed to them, were covered by the same legal code. The kafala system did not distinguish among migrants, whether by country of origin, class, or profession; all migrants, whether executives, professionals, architects, doctors, nurses, maids, or construction workers, were bound to their sponsor in the same way. The kafala system specified the legal bonds that subjugated migrants to their sponsor—but the politics of skill in Qatar shaped how sponsors used the rights and powers afforded to them under the kafala system. Skill politics shaped the forms of exploitation that workers faced.

In reinforcing the subjugation of supposedly unskilled workers, the political language of skill did more than just set the stage for worker exploitation. It did more than degrade the political standing of unskilled workers, subjecting them to state control and leaving them open to employer mistreatment. Its effect was far more penetrating than this. The political language of skill shaped every aspect of work in Qatar—large and small, abstract and material, subjugating and empowering. It determined how companies operated, and how they approached skill, skill development, and skill use. The political representation of skill shaped the function of skill—technical competence—as the organizing logic for the industry. Political interpretations of skill overrode concerns with profit, growth, and even solvency.

The political language of skill, spoken and sharpened in spaces outside the worksite, told a story that became manifest at and through work. The politics of skill determined how companies operated, shaping the broader business parameters of construction like the ratio of capital to labor in production, profile of the technology used, and management of workflow. At the worksite, skill narratives deeply inflected the specific labor relations that emerged, bending the power relations between employer and worker. Workplace routines, hierarchies, and forms of control all reflected the broader politics of skill, but even more fundamentally, these politics shaped how skill was perceived and understood at the worksite, and influenced how competence was appraised and developed. Whatever forms of effective worker resistance did emerge in this restrictive context were articulated in opposition to the political language of skill. The most effective modes of resistance were strategies that sought to disrupt the political distinction between the skilled and unskilled. Even more profoundly, the politics of skill mediated workers' relationship to their own physicality, and in many cases, undercut their ability to perform their work safely, without bodily injury to themselves or others. Ultimately, the politics of skill informed the economic value and social meaning of construction jobs for migrants, and shaped the consequences of migration for the communities and countries to which migrants returned.

The reason that the political language of skill had such a powerful effect on work and production was not because it was concerned with skill but instead because it was concerned with personhood. Because the political rhetoric around skill had little to do with actual competence, its advance into the work-site was never stalled by the reality of the way that skill was practiced on-site. But its effect on work was profound because it was used to define the political subjectivity of workers. Not only did this political language allocate different rights to agency, bodily integrity, and freedom from coercion based on whether workers were described as skilled or unskilled, but it created uncertainty about whether those portrayed as unskilled had access to the full experience of their own humanity. "They are human as well, right?" was the question that the organizer of the Mega Marathon had asked about the workers press-ganged into his race. Could skill, as an expression of intelligence and agency, be skill, in fact, if the workers enacting it did not have access to the full personhood necessary to enact it? Or would it rather become automated action that an employer could appropriate and direct? If the humanity of workers was unclear, was coercion necessarily a form of "power over," or was it instead the simple direction of labor power, as a raw material input, to production needs? If workers were bodies and not skillful agents, did it matter that their freedom of movement was restricted and they were compelled to use their bodies in ways that went against their wishes, through measures like forced overtime, or even forced participation in races and sporting events? By creating uncertainty about the humanity of workers, the political language of skill generated questions like these, and turned work into a place where workers were separated from their skill, divided from their agency, and split from their bodies.

Skill as a Language of Power

The effect of skill as a language of power was ubiquitous in Qatar, but not unique to Qatar. The political language of skill is spoken in many different places, but across contexts, it uses the same logic to say much the same thing. Like all social categories, representations of skill structure economic and social interactions, political identities and coalitions, and power relations. These representations interact with other social categories, attaching themselves to signifiers of race, gender, and class, and amplifying the social hierarchies they produce.

As a political language, the representation of skill is impactful because it is believable. It seems to describe characteristics that are objective and observable, and less open to debate than other markers of social difference. We can have arguments about whether some people are skilled, and whether some

are more skilled then others, but the notion of skill itself, as acquired competence, seems credible and is generally shielded from political challenge. This
sense of realness is produced by the duality in the way skill is defined: skill is
represented at once as an attribute that grows out of personal initiative and
action, and an economic resource that can be measured and translated into
quantifiable—generally monetary—terms, as wage returns to skill.

These two faces make the politics of skill slippery and powerful. Slippery
because the assumption, in most political discourse, is that we can recognize
skill—we know it when we see it—and its role in economic production even
allows us to measure it. But when we try to pin it down to arrive at a more precise definition, perhaps to open it up to political contest, the many and diverse
expressions of expertise—practiced by many specific people in many specific
contexts—make it difficult to identify what it is that we mean exactly by the
concept of skill. And powerful because the representation of skill as an economic
resource opens up the possibility that some people might not have it. It lays the
groundwork for the category of unskilled. When skill as economic asset is overlaid with the idea that skill is the product of personal effort, the unskilled—the
have-nots in this politics—can be made responsible for their lack of skill.

For the most part, debates about skill fall between these two ramparts.
They tend to center on what constitutes skill and how to measure its value,
with skirmishes that focus on, for example, whether skill that involves abstract
cognition and is acquired through formal education is more valuable than skill
that is manual and developed through practice.[11] Similarly, policy debates
about skill tackle the institutional and political mechanisms through which
skill is made visible in the labor market, through credentialing, labor institutions, or other means.[12] But on some level, these debates are semantic. The
consequences of skill as a political concept have little to do with skill itself as a
measure of competence, its content, or its value. The implications of skill as a
political language do not hinge on whether the engineer is in fact more skilled
than the welder. Skill becomes a language of power through its ascription of
political rights and personhood, and its denial of rights and personhood to
those persons represented as unskilled—a descriptor, when deployed politically, that frequently has little relation to actual expertise.

To understand how skill functions as a language of political exclusion, we
have to look at the definition of skill that undergirds a politics of skill haves
and have-nots. For skill to be represented as something that some people possess and others do not, skill has to be defined as something distinguishable
from the everyday flow of human activity, as if it were an oil slick atop a flow
of water. Skill has to be exceptional, because its quality as something out of
the ordinary is what makes it identifiable and possible to assess. Moreover,
skill has to contain its own competence so that its value is held in the skill
itself rather than in the person exercising it. We have to be able to talk about
the expertise required to be a doctor, the skill required to be welder, and the

craft required to be a musician, as if it were self-standing and could be considered separately from the life of a practicing doctor, welder, or musician. As if, in Mehmet's language, skill could belong to the building rather than to the worker.

Or as Karl Marx might phrase it, as if skill belonged to the capitalist and not to the worker. Marx's theory of the alienation of labor offers an early window into the political logic that underpins the category of skill have-nots and its function in the organization of capitalist production. His definition of labor is expansive in its inclusion of skill. Marx calls labor "life-activity, productive life . . . life-engendering-life," and views it as the ultimate expression of human creativity, capacity, and the skillful enactment of imagination; labor is the practice through which human beings engage with the world around them. This skillful, purposeful, and generative activity is what distinguishes humans as a species—as a *species-being*, as he terms it, that is perpetually creating itself and the world around it. The expression of productive capacity is how people inhabit their identities as "free beings" who produce not only to meet their needs but also to fulfill their dreams, "in accordance with the laws of beauty." In capitalist systems of production, argues Marx, the owners of capital strip off this imaginative, skillful capacity when they appropriate workers' labor. Workers are "estrange[d] from the intellectual potentialities of the labor-process," and their labor is bent to "the shape of the powerful will of another, who subjects their activity to his aims." Workers are alienated from their labor—from the skillful, creative, and affective registers through which they enact themselves and their freedom—and are reduced to a degraded form of labor power. This debasement to skill have-nots, to people denied access to the productive capacities through which they enact their humanity, is at the core of the exploitation they suffer. Their labor "is therefore not voluntary, but coerced; it is forced labor."[13]

Once the generative fullness of labor is split in two, with labor power split from skill, then both labor and skill can be made abstract, depersonalized, and movable. Labor, stripped of its specific, contextual, and imaginative expressions, is reduced to a raw material that powers production processes designed and controlled by others. It is shucked out of specific persons and turned into "quantities of homogeneous human labor, i.e. of human labor-power," as Marx put it, measured only in units of time—hours and days—that are purchased with a wage. Skillful practice too becomes an abstraction; pulled out of the lived expression of the person enacting it, it becomes skill, a noun instead of a verb, generic and decontextualized. The tangle of contingent, imaginative, responsive practices become a fixed set of proficiencies that can be identified, isolated from other practices, and standardized. Skill becomes a self-standing ability—machinelike—made to run by the fuel of undifferentiated labor power.

Human capital is the most emphatic shorthand for this idea. Skill, as a form of capital, is an identifiable resource "out there" that can be bought, whether by investing in education, hiring workers who have themselves bought the expertise, or making the investment to develop it.[14] Skill, as human capital, is an asset distinct from the labor power of the practitioner, as if it were a tool—like a hammer—separate from the person using it and could be traded on the open market. And like all capital, skill is portrayed as fungible, independent of any context or persons. Knowledge can be introduced into the production process either through the skill of the worker or technology; both will generate returns on investment. According to this view of skill, it can be encoded in the building, as Mehmet claimed, rather than live as an expression of the welder's situated expertise and imagination.

But even in the most ruthless capitalist systems, even in the most orthodox Marxist accounts, this political representation of skill as distinct from labor requires some suspension of disbelief. To have any purchase, the notion that skill is self-standing has to allow for learning. The view of skill as an asset that can be separated out from the flow of human activity is can only function as a convention if it admits the process through which people acquire skill and draw it into their actions. This is because skill is in fact not a tool or machine. After all, a hammer is nothing more than an inert piece of wood and metal until a person picks it up and directs it at the nailhead. Skill is not a thing. It can only manifest as skillful practice and can only shape outcomes when actors enliven it through situated, imaginative, and intelligent responses to specific conditions. This means that the political definition of skill has to allow for the qualities of sentience that learning requires. It has to allow for the creativity and effort that go into the development of competence; it has to allow for the interpretative resourcefulness needed to apply as well as adapt those skills to situations that are diverse, contingent, and contextual. It has to allow for the process through which the person learns to imagine the arc of the hammer moving through the air, and adjust the movements of their arm, wrist, and hand to hit the nail on the head.

Moreover, because learning needs teaching, an acknowledgment of learning also requires the recognition of the social connections and interpersonal exchange that go into teaching and learning. But most of all, a definition of skill that allows for learning has to allow for agency. Learning cannot be forced; even under the most restrictive conditions, learning can only occur if the learner chooses to apply the imagination, attention, and initiative needed to develop skill and apply it in practice. Learning needs the exercise of will in response to a desire, and in this sense, learning is an expression of freedom.

This description of skill as a self-standing resource that is acquired and applied through learning is what makes the politics of skill so hazardous. It is why skill can be used as a political crowbar to pry people from their agency. If skill is an asset that some people have and some others do not, and if having skill is a product of the desire and purposive activity required to learn, then not having skill can be represented as not having the capacity for agentic creativity.

The absence of skill—being unskilled—can be equated with the absence of will, creativity, and sentience. If skill is an asset as fixed and external as a hammer, then the absence of skill can be invoked as proof that the unskilled person did not have the desire or capacity to learn how to use it. And if learning is an expression of freedom, then representing people as unskilled can easily slip into representing them as not having the desire or capacity for freedom. This is different than the representation of people as alienated from the generative, imaginative register of their labor, debased by an economic system that denies them the right to enact their birthright as free beings. The reason the politics of skill that allows for learning can be so pernicious is that the claim it makes is ontological: it is not that the unskilled are prevented from enacting the generative, agentic capacity of skillful practice; it is that their status as unskilled—as skill have-nots—indicates that they may not have that capacity to begin with. The legal restrictions or political dynamics that constrain the freedom of the unskilled become sidelined—and instead, unfreedom is recast as a reflection or even function of the basic character of the unskilled, and their fundamental inability to be free. Their humanity can thus be made uncertain and turned into a matter of question. "They are human as well, right?"

Skill Politics on the Body

This book explores the political language of skill—a language that inflects debates about labor market policy, immigration criteria, and wealth inequality and poverty. Ideas about skill enter political life stealthily, cloaked in claims of objectively observable attributes. Skill passes as a technical matter, protected from the kind of discussion and analysis through which the political dimensions of other social categories, such as race, gender, and national origin, are made visible and challenged.

My project is to make the political language of skill audible and make clear the ways that skill, as a language of power, is exceptionally powerful. As a language of power, skill is often tuned out, but the stakes for listening are high. Notions of skill structure basic political rights, and assumptions about skill run through the legal codes that protect rights to freedom, agency, and bodily integrity. As a marker of difference, skill shapes how we participate in social life and delineates and stratifies the social and political spaces to which we have access. The political definition of skill informs how we perceive and evaluate actual competence; it informs what we view as mastery and expertise. More fundamentally, it shapes how we learn and whether we are afforded the right to the imagination and interpersonal connection on which learning depends. The consequences of skill as a political language are also material: skill shapes how we experience our own bodies and even mediates our relationship to the natural environment, as our political definitions of skill and competence have begun to shape our response to the effects of global warming.

The politics of skill are so consequential, touching all part of our human existence, because of the ways they enlist the body. We use referents that are deeply corporal to assign value to skill, and determine who is skilled and who isn't. We define some skills as manual—the skill of a welder—and some skills as cognitive—the skill of an engineer—and appraise them based on their perceived distance from the body, privileging skill that seems further away from muscle and sinew. This is true even of skill viewed as valuable because of its embodied dimension. Tacit skill, defined as an ability that so fundamentally entangled with the body that it is impossible to fully describe with language or codify in any way, is celebrated when it provides the basis for skill that is characterized as conceptual and abstract. The tacit skill that enables the engineer to connect mathematical calculations to dreams of buildings that exist only in the mind's eye is judged, in social discourse and scholarly production, as more significant and far more sophisticated, than the tacit skill of a welder, and the embodied feel that allows them to adjust their speed or bend the angle of the blowtorch's flame to respond to changes in wind shear or cloud cover so that they can weld a perfect seam.

The political language of skill also draws on political portrayals of the body to hide and deny skill. As a long tradition of scholarship on gender and race at work has shown, representations of bodies as feminized and racialized fold skill into the body as a means to cheapen it. Gender and racial discourses entomb skill in the flesh of skilled practitioners and turn layered and creative skillful practices into an inert physical feature, or an innate bodily tendency over which the people who inhabit the bodies have no say and no control. Women's supposedly small and nimble fingers, for instance, become a stand-in for the skill that women garment workers develop.[15] The racialized representations of male bodies, and especially their dismemberment into their backs, arms, and stature, erase the skill required to complete the challenging physical tasks that the rhetoric justifies, whether in agricultural fields or mines, or on sped-up production lines.[16] And the skill involved in health care or childcare work is represented as an expression of women's caring instinct, especially racialized women.[17] Skillful embodied practice is not skill at all in these representations; it is just raw corporality. By subsuming skill in the body in this way, burying it beneath racialized and gendered descriptions of physiques and biology, denying its existence and value, these social discourses make it possible to shunt groups of people into the category of unskilled based on markers of social difference that have no relation to actual competence or expertise.

But the use of the body in the politics of skill is more than about devaluing skill or denying its presence. The power of skill politics comes from the definition of skill in opposition to the body—as a resource that is fundamentally superior to and irreconcilable with the body.[18] The distinction made between skill and the body—a version of the cartesian split between mind and body—is the grammar that the language of skill relies on to call into question the personhood of those defined as unskilled.[19]

For skill to be defined as a stand-alone resource that some people have and some others do not, it *has* to be located outside the body. It can't maintain its character as an asset that is identifiable, measurable, and alienable—an asset that can be lifted off the welder and attributed to the building—unless it is abstracted out of the body. This is because when skill is left in the body—when it is considered a form competence expressed through the body—the boundaries around it dissolve and it becomes a stream of practices. It emerges in its full aliveness, observable as creative responses to emergent conditions, moment-to-moment expressions of connection and relationship, and ongoing assertions of agency and imagination. Skill in the body is revealed to be as immanent, changing, and imaginative as the living embodied persons who practice it. The hammer becomes incidental and the swing takes center stage as movement, graceful and adaptive, responding moment to moment to the pull of gravity and feel of the wooden handle in the palm. Skill viewed in the body can't be delineated and fixed and cannot be possessed. And importantly, it cannot be alienated. It cannot be lifted out of the hand and credited to the hammer. It cannot be lifted off the welder and attributed to the building. Skill viewed as embodied practice only exists when it is enacted, brought into existence as corporal expressions of competence and potentiality in the moment. The skill of both the welder and engineer exists only when they are engaging with it, when they are manifesting it by acting, connecting, or simply imagining. Since skill is not a thing but rather a flow, it cannot be "had." An appraisal of skill as embodied, and thus as indeterminate and changing, makes the political fiction of skill haves and have nots impossible and even inconceivable. We all are, in a sense, skill have-nots until the moment we become skill haves by bringing skill alive through practice.

Because so much rides on the distinction between body and skill, the body is where the politics of skill turn brutal. If skill is not a machinelike asset out there, and is instead an expression of embodied moments of creativity, intelligence, and will, then the only way to draw a political distinction between skill haves and have-nots is to control the bodies of those classed as unskilled. The representation of some people as not having skill requires the discursive, regulatory, and even literal policing of the embodied practices through which those defined as unskilled express the skill they are not supposed to have.

In this way, the boundary between skilled and unskilled cuts through the body. We may use wage, occupation, years of formal education, and certification to talk about skill and the people who have it. In the everyday interactions of work and production, we may even recognize skill as a continuum, running without break from the novice to the master. But ultimately, when we define some people as "skilled" or "unskilled," we are talking about their bodies. We are talking about the extent to which their embodied existence is subject to political regulation and control. The body is where we draw the line through rich, multifaceted, layered, and relational expressions of competence to split people into two categories: the skill haves—the highly skilled, the knowledge workers, the innovators—whose full range of creative agentic expression is recognized and elevated, and the skill have-nots—the laborers, the workers, the poor and dispossessed—whose skillful actions are an unthinking product of their bodily traits. The body is also where we *enforce* the line between skilled and unskilled, and where the politics of skill slip into actions of physical coercion and degradation.[20] The method of those actions is as racialized and gendered as the bodies of the unskilled are represented as being, and reinforces their status as laboring bodies without the capacities associated with skill.[21] Once their full range of agentic and imaginative capacities are denied, and their personhood rendered questionable, then the unskilled can be forced to run marathon races in life-threatening heat.

This book listens to the language of skill and examines its political consequences as they played out in Qatar. It focuses on the lived experiences of the migrants working in the country's construction industry to understand the consequences of skill as a political language. But in some important sense, this book is not about Qatar; it is about the politics of skill. It takes place in Qatar because the language of skill was bellowed there. In Qatar's national development plans, geopolitical aspirations, laws, and the organization of society, the language of skill was spoken loudly and clearly. It takes place in Qatar also because people, companies, and governments from around the world came together there to develop new ways to speak about skill as well as repeat old understandings of who could be skilled and who could definitely not be. Global finance, hydrocarbon interests, firms, recruitment networks, and cultural institutions all used Qatar as a setting to refine the ways that the language of skill could be used to harden and normalize social divisions and hierarchies around class, race, and gender—and ultimately personhood. And finally, the book takes place in Qatar because as the earth began to warm, and the climate started to change, it was a site where the way in which the politics of skill defined the political and economic implications of those ecological changes was becoming evident.

The Politics of Migration and Skill in Qatar

Qatar is a small country, a diminutive peninsula appended to another peninsula, poking out into the Arabian Sea. In 2020, it had a total population of around 2.8 million, slightly larger than that of Houston, Texas.[22] But Qatar has had an outsized impact on both the global economy and imagination. It is a country of extremes, where models of global capitalism and migration have been pushed to their limit, and where the interaction between these two dynamics has amplified the politics of skill.

Qatar was the wealthiest country in the world per capita in 2018, topping US$130,000 per person (based on purchasing power parity).[23] Most of its revenue came from the production and export of oil and natural gas. That same year, Qatar ranked as the world's largest exporter of LNG, and the world's third-largest known natural gas reserves sat off the country's northern tip.[24] Qatar used its vast resources to reinvent itself as a global hub for sports, art, and elite culture. Its capital, Doha, boasted a skyline drawn by striking, futuristic skyscrapers, and as the country geared up for the 2022 World Cup using the slogan "Expect Amazing," it spent hundreds of billions on new developments and infrastructure. The construction activity was so frenzied that it changed local climate conditions in Doha. Qatar was already one of the hottest places on earth, and by 2020, was warming faster than any place outside the Artic.[25] Its development activities were only accelerating these changes; construction turned Doha into a heat island where summertime temperatures rose so high that Qatar began to pour air-conditioning into its outdoor spaces, cooling the stadiums, markets, and cultural centers designed to position it as a global destination.[26]

For Qatari elites, creating a version of the future out of glass and steel was a national project, but the people who were building this vision were all migrants. Nine out of every 10 people in Qatar were foreigners. In this respect, Qatar offers us the photonegative of the typical migration story: instead of a setting where migrants were the minority, workers in Qatar joined an economy where over 95 percent of the workers were foreign. In 2015, the midpoint of the research for this project, there were 1,955,627 people working in Qatar, but only a tiny fraction, 99,204 of them, were Qatari nationals, with most of them employed by their government.[27]

Migrants working in Qatar came from all over the world. The government of Qatar did not release data on the nationality of foreign residents—although it undoubtedly collected them—but estimates based on embassy reports and a review of official government statements capture the diversity of the population. More than ninety countries were represented among Qatar's two million foreigners in 2017. Migrants from South Asia and the Middle East made up the lion's share. India, Bangladesh, Nepal, Egypt, and the Philippines made up more than half of the migrants in Qatar, but the numbers of migrants from sub-Saharan Africa were growing fast.[28] This diversity was part of the lived experience of Qatar; languages, religions, customs, and cuisines jostled and blended together in everyday life. Everyone—police officers and bank tellers, shopkeepers and lawyers, doctors and teachers—was from somewhere else.

Permission to reside in Qatar was tied to employment, and any rights and protections that migrants had stemmed from their role in the economy. All migrant workers in Qatar were governed by the kafala system and legally bound to their sponsor, usually their employer. The bonds of the kafala system loosened over the past several years, especially since reforms in 2017, and most workers no longer required their employer's explicit consent to leave the country. Some were permitted, under limited circumstances and with regulatory approval, to change employers, and since late 2020, migrant workers could change jobs without their employer's permission. Even so, all migrants, irrespective of skill, profession, or nationality, remained employed under a system that tied their political rights to their economic function.

The kafala system was generally portrayed as the product of a specific—and Arab—cultural setting, but in fact, it was similar in its basic components to the regulatory structures that governed the employment of migrants around the world—and still do. Work visas in many countries—including the United States—tie migrants to their employers, and make it difficult as well as sometimes legally impossible for workers to challenge their working conditions or leave their jobs without jeopardizing their right to remain in the country. Just as in Qatar, these regulations reduce migrants to their economic function. They grant political rights only on a limited and often probationary basis, and in ways that are contingent on migrants' role in the economy. These regulations, however, generally do not distinguish migrants by skill; both highly skilled and unskilled workers are bound to their employers. In most countries, however, only a fraction of all migrants—sometimes smaller, sometimes larger—are governed by this kind of regulatory structure. In Qatar, by contrast, all migrants were covered by this regulatory framework. This means that 95 percent of the workforce was legally bound to an employer. Qatar had a robust and growing labor force, but it did not have a functioning labor market.

The presence of a labor force, but the absence of a labor market, made Qatar a useful place to observe the effects of the political language of skill. In settings with functioning labor markets, where workers can sell their own labor, the effect of the political language of skill occurs in a context that is noisy. This is because a functioning labor market is multivocal in that numerous voices, in chorus and competition, speak to the value of different kinds of skill. To be sure, marketplace bargaining over the value of specific skills is a deeply political process, structured by the economic imbalance of power between worker and employer, and contoured by racial and gendered discourses about the bodies of workers. The recognition and definition of skill is shaped by labor market institutions, such as worker and educational organizations, regulatory structures, and even societal norms. Still, workers' ability to commodify their own labor as well as choose *not* to commodify it, and withdraw from a profession or the labor market altogether if they are not compensated, gives them, individually and collectively, an avenue to make their skill visible—and make themselves visible as skillful practitioners. It gives them some ability to influence how their expertise is valued. By binding workers to their employers and snuffing out the emergence of a labor market, the kafala system in Qatar muted—or controlled for—some of the many voices, particularly worker voices, that determine the visibility and value of skill in the market, at the worksite, and in society. As a result, it became possible to observe more clearly how the politics of skill played out in areas that might have seemed beyond its reach: intimate spheres of personal connection, material experiences of the body, and responses to the earth and its ecological changes.

The relationship between the politics of skill and ties of bondage was also especially pronounced in Qatar because it had existed for a long time. For over a century, most of Qatar's residents had been foreign, and almost all had been tied to their employers through various iterations of regulatory bondage in which their political rights were tied to their employment. When Qatar, in 1984, defined the version of the regulatory framework that still, with a few amendments, governed migrants' status in the country in 2020, some four decades later, nonnationals already represented more than 85 percent of its workforce—a proportion far higher than almost any other country in the Persian Gulf.[29] Even as Qatar swelled to absorb large numbers of foreign workers, the kafala system prohibited migrants, with few exceptions, from establishing long-term residence in Qatar. The migrant population in Qatar had always been made up of workers, growing in response to the country's economic needs at any given moment in time.

Historically, the size of the labor force in Qatar was spurred by the construction industry, expanding in response to the country's periodic modernization and urban development drives. In 2020, almost half the workers in Qatar were directly involved in Qatar's massive construction projects. (As a point of comparison, construction generally represents between 5 and 10 percent of the workforce in most countries.) The workforce for the industry was entirely foreign. Out of the 785,075 workers employed in construction in 2015, only 1,643—or 0.002 percent—were Qatari.[30] The construction companies in Qatar were also thoroughly international. Over the decade from 2010 to 2020, firms from around the world rushed in to participate in the construction boom. The projects that the government has awarded to international firms, operating as joint ventures with Qatari firms as required by Qatari law, totaled more than US$120 billion in 2015.[31]

The projects commissioned by the Qatari government were more massive, cutting edge in their engineering, and radical in their design that ever before in the country's history. They required companies to pioneer new building approaches, materials, and technologies. The extreme heat in Qatar drove innovation too. Qatar experimented with new design strategies to shield residents from the intense heat, such as the application of paving material that reflected the sun's radiation or solar-powered cooling systems that drew on environmental conditions to modulate temperature.[32] Because of these buildings' complexity, their construction demanded advanced ability. Qatar's capacity to build its future as a hypermodern destination—to keep the promise that we should "Expect Amazing"—fundamentally depended on the skill of workers that the Qatari legal system confines to employment relationships of bondage. This tension heightened the political charge around the politics of skill in Qatar. To fulfill its modernist aspirations, Qatar needed the skill that migrants developed. At the same time, the regulatory structure the country used to govern migrant workers gave sponsors and employers enormous latitude to restrict the agentic creativity, embodied dignity and imagination, and freedom on which learning always depends.

Although Qatar's national development projects drove migration, the discourses that shaped the conditions that migrants faced in Qatar were as international as the array of companies operating there, as global as the financial flows that poured in and out of the country, and as encompassing as the World Cup games that the country was preparing to host.[33] The skill politics articulated in Qatar seeped out past the country's borders to enter global discussions about the rights of migrant workers and who should have the right to migrate to begin with. The political language classifying migrant workers as unskilled in Qatar joined the chorus of calls for the use of skill qualifications—"merit-based immigration"—to advance more restrictionist immigration agendas and use increasingly ruthless police measures against the bodies of those migrants defined as unskilled. The politics of skill spoken in Qatar inflected even those conversations that championed the defense of migrant workers. International campaigns to improve migrant working conditions, with their widespread adoption of the image of the overall-clad migrant as the symbol of modern slavery, slipped, however unintentionally, into discourses that echoed beliefs about unskilled migrant workers' limited capacity for agency. Global coverage of working conditions in Qatar argued over whether workers under the kafala system were free or unfree, but reports tended to pay less attention to the actual practices, rooted in the representation of migrants as unskilled, through which migrants' freedom was denied and their personhood rendered questionable. If political definitions of skill are another way of delineating freedom, then discussions about skill were fundamentally about freedom and unfreedom in Qatar and everywhere.

Research in Phases

The research for this project unfolded in several overlapping phases. With each phase, the reach of skill as a language of power became clearer. I began the fieldwork for this study in early 2013, when I traveled to Doha to examine the structures and practices that shaped work and working conditions in Qatar's construction industry.

In the first phase of my research, my goal was to learn what factors shaped work and working conditions for Qatar's migrant construction workers. I needed to understand how the construction industry was organized and the basic strategies it used to complete Qatar's massive development projects. I created an institutional map of the industry and the government actors that shaped its operations. I traced the stages of construction, from project conception through delivery. I started with the architectural design process, and followed projects through the tendering and bidding process. I looked at how projects were awarded, and how subcontracting chains, building permits, and materials requests were assembled once the contract for the project was secured. I analyzed how firms hired and managed their workforce, including recruitment strategies, methods for integrating workers on-site, and the management of migrant workers at the close of the project. I explored how formal and informal institutions regulated these processes, and looked at variations within the industry.

To sketch out this institutional map, I drew on a broad swath of interviews. I interviewed the actors and organizations that shaped how the industry operated, including representatives and managers of local and international construction companies, supply chain and logistics planning firms, specialized engineering firms, and government agencies and social service companies that addressed labor law and working conditions on jobsites, including consular representatives. I also interviewed the government and semigovernmental agencies that defined the urban plans and building strategies to position Qatar as a global destination, including the Qatar Foundation, a royal institution directing the development of Qatar's educational complex, and the Supreme Committee for Delivery and Legacy, charged with managing the construction of the stadiums and infrastructure for the 2022 World Cup.

To complement these informational interviews, I invited managerial staff from construction and consulting companies to roundtable discussions about industry dynamics, manpower management, and regulatory policies. In the interviews I conducted, my interlocutors had voiced sharp differences in opinion about the factors that shaped the industry and working conditions, and my hope in bringing managers together was to understand why. Over the course of the three two-hour roundtables I conducted, with a total of twenty-eight people, participants shared their frank assessments of challenges in the industry, especially those caused by government action, along with why the viewpoints that their colleagues expressed in the discussion were misguided.

The second phase of my research engaged more directly with work, workers, and work processes in the construction industry. In early 2014, I began the ethnographic portion of my research, spending time in the places that workers worked and lived. Ethnography is a method of inquiry that uses detailed and proximate observation to understand what people do in specific settings, why they act in that way, and how they interpret their own actions as well as those of others—and even how they understand themselves.[34] It requires a situational engagement from the researcher—a process of *being there*—and involvement in the flow of life of a place—sometimes termed "participant observation" in the technical literature. The researcher has to be responsive to the questions that the situation asks them to pursue—but they also have to remain attentive to the questions that the social context and power structures make inconceivable or impossible to ask.[35]

The first part of my ethnographic study was built on fieldwork at eight construction sites and three training centers. I also visited seven dormitories for workers—which in Qatar were called labor camps and were provided (and often closely monitored) by employers. Visits at each site lasted from several hours to several days. In selecting my research sites, I chose construction sites and affiliated labor camps that had good reputations in terms of their labor practices and production systems. I wanted to understand work and working conditions at firms that operated well, as opposed to at firms that made a habit of exploiting their workers to compensate for shoddy production practices. Also, patterns of workplace control or labor violations among firms widely considered to be industry leaders, locally and internationally, were likely suggestive of practices among industry laggards. This selection preference meant that the construction sites I visited were large, with several hundred to several thousand workers, and building projects commissioned by government or other institutional clients. Several—sometimes dozens—of firms operated on-site and were involved in the project through complex subcontracting chains. My research at these sites explored how production was organized, how different construction trades coordinated their work, how the training systems were designed, and how they incorporated informal practices of skill development. I looked at patterns of teamwork along with the ways that supervisors and workers structured their workflow. I asked about working conditions—shift schedules and pay scales—and living spaces—labor camps and sleeping quarters.

To deepen my ethnographic observation, I selected two sites for extended research. I spent hundreds of hours at these two sites, and followed them through much of 2014. At both sites, I focused on the processes through which migrant workers developed skill and expressed their mastery. I looked at learning processes and the kinds of exchanges they involved among workers. I explored how the many people involved in skillful practice on a site—workers, foremen, supervisors, engineers, and managers—interpreted skill, and how they valued the skill that was developed and shared. I examined how skill was used and controlled, and why expressions of competence were sometimes viewed as constructive and sometimes as insubordinate. Throughout, I was concerned with the interplay between skill and power.

The ethnographies of these two sites were spun out of a back-and-forth movement between interviews, formal and informal, and process observation. Through seventy-eight semistructured interviews and innumerable on-site conversations, I asked workers, foremen, supervisors, and engineers about work and skill. But I also followed them as they worked, watching how they enacted the skill they described and observing in action the kinds of teaching moments they recounted. This research dialectic was important because my interlocutors frequently found skill difficult to define. In part, this was because the kind of skill used in construction has a large tacit component, and drew on aspects of competence that were impossible to make explicit or spell out in any propositional or systematic way.[36] So while workers enacted their skill when they scaffolded, poured cement, or welded, they could not pinpoint how they knew what they knew.

But the people I interviewed also struggled to describe skill because skill was not a fixed asset, with clear outlines and content, that could be lifted out of context or practice. Skill was not like a hammer. Instead, the skill I observed on-site was a stream of practice made up of skillful action. It was the ongoing process of developing responses that were more refined, precise, and attuned to the environment that was constantly being rebuilt and transformed.[37] This meant that the people I spoke with couldn't fully apprehend skill—their own or that of others—in the abstract. For my interlocutors and me to arrive at a shared understanding of what was meant by skill—including its emotional, interpersonal, and political registers—we had to rely on an iterative process that moved between a description of skill, observation of skill in action, and then further reflection on skill using the observed skillful practice as a touchstone.

At both sites, I chose a subset of task areas to follow and shadowed workers completing these tasks. Task areas are elements like scaffolding, cement form building, and steel fixing. Shadowing workers allowed me to engage more closely with the materials used in those trades so that I could better understand the physicality of the work and the skill it required—the scaffolding tubes and planks, hoses and nozzles for cement, and wires and rebar for steel fixing. This also allowed me to concentrate on the engineering and managerial facets of these task areas. I spent hours poring over construction documents, manpower histograms, health and safety checklists, and the technical specifications of the equipment used for the task areas I selected.

The construction sites in Qatar were as cosmopolitan as the rest of the country and involved workers from many different nationalities. The sites I selected were no different. A manager at one of two sites decided to count the number of languages spoken among the workforce, and his informal tally was twenty-two. This linguistic diversity required me to conduct research in a variety of languages and work with translators. Research was conducted in eight languages, and five translators worked on this research project. Even so, there were many gaps. But this was useful too; it gave me insight into how workers worked together, how they taught and learned from one another, and how they forged ties of solidarity without the benefit of a common language, apart from the stripped-down English used on most sites.

The third phase of this research project focused on the processes through which migrant workers were recruited. This portion of the research took me outside Qatar to a selection of countries where recruitment took place. In Manila, Philippines; Kerala, India; and Kathmandu and Dhanusa, Nepal, I traced the recruitment networks that connected local communities to construction sites in Doha. I interviewed government officials, recruitment agency owners and staff, and staff at centers for vocational training and trade testing. I spoke with advocacy organizations, and people who hoped to migrate or had recently returned. The field trips for this third layer took place through fall 2015.

The final phase of the research for this project, through fall 2016, was a historical analysis of Qatar's kafala system. As the political valence of skill became clear through the layers of fieldwork, I wanted to explore whether and how skill had been woven into the regulatory structures that govern migration to Qatar. The kafala system in its contemporary form was a product of a century of global trade and regulatory exchange, and striated with imperial dictates governing the movement of people that set the parameters for the use of indentured labor. Archival research as well as the many careful historiographies on migration under the British Empire allowed me to trace how these historical currents structured the political definitions of skill built into the kafala system.

In this book, I have the changed the names of the people I spoke with, construction firms I visited, and many of the organizations that participated in this research project. To protect the confidentiality of people and organizations, I have also changed details that may be identifying, including but not limited to nationality, trade, and location. The importance of the commitment to confidentiality that is part of any academic research involving people was only underscored by the political sensitivities that attached to this project at various points in time. These political winds and the ways they buffeted my research—and specifically the ways they constrained my access to construction sites and migrant workers—are described more fully in the book's postscript.

This book is about the politics of skill, and how the power relations they produce shape work and working conditions. It is also, in important ways, about men. The workforce in Qatar's construction industry was male; in 2015, 99.5 percent—780,528 out of 785,087 people working in the industry—were men.[38] On all the construction sites, and in all the training centers and labor camps, I did not encounter a single woman. This, of course, had implications for how people responded to me, my female research assistant, and one of the translators who was a woman. The responses were complex and varied: for some, it made it easier to talk about skill and working conditions, and even share confidences, whereas it made others more guarded and reserved. In all cases, however, the experiences of workers were experiences they had as men. As a result, the politics of skill described in this account are inflected with gender politics. How skill was expressed, how the body was experienced, and how political definitions of personhood shaped subjectivity were all gendered. This means that while this book can offer a window onto how skill functions generally as a language of power—the mechanism through which it structures work and narrows rights to agency—it can't make definitive claims about how this language is spoken when it is used to define the role of women at work or in society. It does, however, mean that this book can, and does, speak to the politics of masculinity in Qatar and ways it gendered political representations of skill. It does engage with the gendered ways that men's bodies were racialized, controlled, and disciplined as well as the gendered practices through which men drew on skill to create connection, community, and shared imaginaries. The use of pronouns in this book—the deliberate and specific use of male pronouns and male-gendered nouns when the discussion considers the politics of skill as men experienced them—positions it in the rich and burgeoning conversation about gender in the Persian Gulf region and the way it structures labor relations there.[39]

A final point on notation and nations. While I am cognizant of the political valences attached to the terms "Persian Gulf" and "Arabian Gulf," this book uses them interchangeably. The term "Arab countries" is used colloquially—and sometimes in academic writing—as a stand-in for countries of the Persian or Arab Gulf region, but in my writing I use "Arab" to refer to all the countries in the Middle East and North Africa that view themselves as culturally Arab, and have also been subject to Orientalist representations, both historically and at present. Finally, this book takes Qatar as its focus, but Qatar, perhaps to a greater extent than many countries, has been shaped by regional and international political currents and conversations. Strategic jockeying in the region has both hemmed in and sharpened Qatar's development ambitions. The blockade that Saudi Arabia—joined by the United Arab Emirates, Egypt, and Bahrain—imposed on Qatar in 2017 had the most direct impact on the country's modernization plans and geopolitical alliances—all of which shaped its approach to the recruitment of workers, construction schedule, and labor relations. I detail those pressures when and where they elucidate the politics of skill that played out on Qatari construction sites as well as in the country's marathon races.

Skill through the Layers

The argument that runs through this book is that skill, as a language of power, shapes all aspects of economic and social life. It has certainly structured all facets of life in Qatar, and has, in many respects, been more influential in shaping working conditions than any specific labor relations at the workplace. This book traces the reverberations of skill as a political language, and shows how these reverberations structure social and economic life, at the many different levels in which that life unfolds. Each chapter—or essay—examines a different layer of life and considers how the politics of skill play out there. The analysis that runs through these chapters begins with skill as defined in political and regulatory structures, follows it through production and work as well as protest and resistance, and tracks it all the way down through its expression on the body and in relation to the earth.

The book's trajectory—from the more abstract to the more material— follows the path that the political language of skill uses to shape social and economic life. The chapters follow the language of skill from its clearest register down to more material contexts, where its sound is more blunted and blurred. Skill emerges most clearly and audibly as a political language in the spheres that are most overtly political, and where political discourses are marshaled to shape legal and institutional structures. As it moves into society, its expressions mix and merge with the actions involved in production, work, and protest, and the language of skill becomes more equivocal and ambiguous, though no less powerful. When the politics of skill reach into the body, they become interwoven with the experience of being embodied and become difficult to distinguish from the physical sense of self. And as they touch down to earth, the politics of skill shape responses to changes in the environment, but their effect is difficult to identify because the responses themselves are still emergent and evolving due to the unprecedented ecological shifts caused by global warming.

In exploring the effect of skill as a political language, the book makes a second but equally important claim: skill derives its power as a political discourse from its believability. Because skill as a political category is treated as if it were real and as a stand-in for measures of actual competence, the political consequences of its use fade into the background where we cannot see or do not look for them. Likewise, the way that ideas about skill inform our interpretation of social and economic life remains underexplored. As a result, an examination of how the politics of skill operate at different layers of social and economic life also brings to light the assumptions built into the frames that we use to analyze and understand life at those layers. The chapters, in their reflection on skill, engage the conceptual frameworks that guide inquiry at the layer they consider.

Regulation opens the book with an analysis of the way that the political language of skill has been codified into law throughout the development and history of Qatar's kafala system. The chapter traces how political definitions of skill shaped the political rights afforded to migrants and details the forms of bondage specified for their employment. Qatar is often represented as a place outside history, a lost stretch of desert that joined the modern world only after the discovery of oil and gas in the mid-twentieth century. In press accounts and academic writing, the kafala system too is portrayed as a cultural holdover from an earlier, isolated time. This chapter challenges this representation, and shows that the contemporary kafala system, along with ongoing efforts to reform it, was forged through more than a century of global economic exchange and political interconnection. It traces the kafala system's defining features, all of which stem from the distinction the British made between skilled and unskilled migrants when they governed the movement of indentured workers within the empire. The chapter investigates how this regulatory process was refined through wave after wave of international investment and engagement, and examines how international reform efforts, which led to a significant overhaul of the kafala system between 2016 and 2020, reproduced the tiered definitions of personhood and freedom associated with different categories of skill.

Production looks at the way that political definitions of skill shape and are shaped by economic systems. This chapter explores how the political division between skilled and unskilled migrants drives business strategy and the organization of production. More centrally, it shows that skill politics determine what buildings are built. Qatar adopted a high modernist approach to urban planning and embraced its method of imposing political values on society by building those values—concretely—into the buildings and plan of the city. Qatar's modernist structures and urban design reflected as well as enforced a sharp social divide between migrants classified as skilled and those classified as unskilled. It also enacted the modernist view of skill as the purview of a professional elite, imprinted and contained in the design of buildings and urban spaces. Ironically, this modernist approach to urban development increased the construction industry's reliance on the skill of the very workers who were segregated into marginal tracts of the city, and excluded from the very buildings and built spaces that they created.

Skill examines the embodied qualities of skill, and how power is expressed through the representation and control of skill. Construction on Qatar's building sites required skill that is deeply sophisticated but also deeply embodied, and this chapter documents the richness and complexity of the learning processes through which it was developed. Learning on-site grew out of many repeated moments of interpersonal connection, attunement, and creativity, and as a result, was an expression of agency. Managers and supervisors sought to control and appropriate workers' skill, but because the skill was embodied, this meant exercising physical control over the men who enacted that skill and the bodies through which they expressed their competence. In this way, labor relations on-site became a vehicle through which skill was used to deny the embodied qualities of agency and imagination required to enact it.

Protest considers the role of skill and learning as strategies of political resistance. Protests were illegal in Qatar, but they still happened frequently. Companies tolerated wildcat strikes and short-term work stoppages so long as they adhered to certain patterns and did not build solidarity among workers from different countries. As a result, these protests were ineffectual; they were hemmed in and disciplined by management, and any protest that broke through the limits imposed on labor action was cut short through the deportation of striking workers. In this context, the practice of learning—as a form of praxis—emerged as an important form of resistance to exploitation on-site. Learning became a vehicle through which workers consciously affirmed their agency in a work setting that denied them claims to agentic creativity and personhood, and reduced them to bodies. Workers used learning to strengthen their interpersonal relationships across nationalities. They used these cross-national social ties as the basis for tactical solidarity to challenge exploitative conditions and unsafe practices.

Body examines how the politics of skill shape the experience of the embodied self in the physical world. This chapter takes as its focus the heat injury suffered by workers on Qatari construction sites. Heat injury manifests, some-times immediately and sometimes with delay, as cardiac arrest and organ damage or failure. It also significantly, and sometimes permanently, disrupts cognition and interferes with the ability to direct physical movement. The politics of skill, expressed at Qatari worksites in the denial of worker agency and exercise of control over workers' bodies, heightened workers' exposure and vulnerability to extreme temperatures. They were pressed to work in heat conditions that were dangerous and damaging. The heat, through its effect on their bodies, also destroyed their access to the skillful practice, social connection, and emotional attunement they needed to protect themselves from extreme temperatures. This allowed the culpability for injury to be shifted onto workers, and the damage their bodies sustained was invoked to confirm the political representation of workers as unskilled.

Earth considers how political definitions of skill shape interpretations of the ecological environment and responses to the changes caused by global warming. This chapter looks at the recruitment of migrant labor and shows how companies in Qatar leveraged climate change damage in migrant sending areas to recruit workers at lower wages. Companies in Qatar preferred workers with the ability to learn—with absorptive capacity—over workers with demonstrated skill, including skill documented through certification. This preference for unskilled workers allowed companies to train workers in the specific skills required for a project, but gave them the scope to render those skills invisible too, and thus to deny workers their own agency and personhood. Companies in Qatar viewed climate-damaged areas as promising sources for workers with absorptive capacity because global warming had often only recently impoverished them. The residents in those communities still retained the benefits of the investments in human development—in education, nutrition, and health—they had made in more ecologically stable times; they retained especially the foundation that those investments established for the ability to learn. Skill politics in Qatar closed the cycle of climate damage: an industry emitting large amounts of carbon and bankrolled by hydrocarbon revenue capitalized on the damage caused by the use of fossil fuels to source learning at bargain prices. The final two chapters of this book underscore that the consequences of skill politics are not abstract or ideological but rather cause tangible material injury to the body and the earth.

The conclusion of this book argues that listening to the language of skill in Qatar can allow us to hear its discourse in places beyond that small peninsula—to perceive how it shapes political rights, definitions of personhood, and the material conditions of being alive everywhere. The book shows that listening to the political language of skill—slippery, powerful, and pervasive—matters because if we listen, we can also respond. If we listen, we can also contest the ways that the political language of skill shapes migration, work, and agency, now and in a rapidly warming world.

CHAPTER ONE

Regulation

HOW THE POLITICS OF SKILL BECOME LAW

ON DECEMBER 2, 2010, Sepp Blatter, president of FIFA, the world soccer federation, pried open a white envelope on a stage in Zurich. He announced in award ceremony style that the 2022 World Cup hosting rights had been awarded to Qatar. The small Gulf nation, widely seen as a dark horse in the race, had beat out bids from the United States, Japan, Korea, and Australia. As the Qatari delegation—visibly moved—leaped up and embraced one another, President Bill Clinton, heading up the delegation from the United States and seated in the front row at the ceremony, smiled wanly. The *Washington Post* reported that when he returned to the Savoy hotel, he smashed a mirror in rage at the outcome.[1]

At the close of the internationally televised ceremony, Blatter glossed the controversial decision as a brave new step for FIFA, saying, "We go to new lands. . . . [T]he Middle East and the Arabic world have been waiting for a long time." Hassan Al-Thawadi, the chief executive of the Qatar bid, echoed Blatter's sentiment, declaring, "We can allow history to be made while opening up the gates of communication between east and west. The Middle East will be put on a platform for everyone to see it as it truly is. And, more importantly, it allows the Middle East to interact with the rest of the world, so that any misconceptions that people here have about the west can be taken away."[2]

Labor and human rights organizations took Al-Thawadi at his word. Within months, they began issuing reports on labor abuses in Qatar. The International Trade Union Confederation (ITUC) published an exposé in May 2011 that detailed the working and living conditions of workers.[3] The labor organization warned of the intensified exploitation of migrant laborers in the run-up to the World Cup and estimated that four thousand workers would die as a result of labor practices in Qatar before the first ball of the 2022 games was kicked. The ITUC called for Qatar to be stripped of the games and promised that labor organizations around the world "would mobilize workers and football fans to target each of FIFA's football associations and the international body to stop the World Cup in Qatar if labor rights are not respected."[4] Human Rights Watch and Amnesty International followed with reports of their own, in 2012 and 2013, respectively, showing that abusive labor practices were endemic in Qatar, and particularly acute in the construction industry.[5] Media accounts of the poor treatment of migrant workers soon ran under the mastheads of major international newspapers and on cable news channels, with headlines that exposed Qatar's "World Cup 'slaves'"[6]

The catalog of abuses that these dispatches recorded was devastating. The reports highlighted the pervasiveness of wage theft and prolonged nonpayment of wages, enumerating cases where workers labored without pay for months at a time. They featured worker testimonies of forced labor and overtime, and management's habitual disregard of health and safety protections. More disturbingly, they described workers being recruited under false premises and trapped in a form of debt bondage, working to pay back the middlemen who charged them up to a year's wages for jobs in Qatar. They cited the widespread practice of passport confiscation and the physical intimidation that kept workers confined to the labor camps where they were housed.

The reports backed their allegations by documenting the effects of exploitation on workers' bodies. Many of the reports featured graphic depictions of worker injuries, illustrated in many cases by photographs of the damage— literal bodies of evidence of the effects of exploitation. Some organizations analyzed patterns of bodily harm to extrapolate specific forms of employer negligence. Amnesty International's 2013 report, for example, referenced the high rate of injuries to the head and spine (as compared to injuries to the lower extremities) as evidence that worker deaths and disabilities were caused by workers falling on their heads from accidents that could have been prevented with adequate safety measures and protective equipment.[7]

Damage to the body was not limited to the workplace. Human rights and press reports contained ubiquitous evidence of substandard living conditions. Their exposés featured videos and photos of housing facilities that were cramped, squalid, and lacking basic infrastructure. They showed small sleeping rooms where bunk beds were stacked floor to ceiling, and ten to fifteen men slept in shifts on planks or the floor on thin, disintegrating foam mattresses. Photographs documented the absence of air-conditioning units, and captured the filth of kitchen and bathroom facilities, where clogged sinks and urinals were filled with the sludge of human and kitchen waste. Other photos showed open septic tanks and sewage that had overflowed into the courtyard of housing facilities, and living spaces piled with trash, toxic construction materials, and debris.

FIFA soon found itself buckling under accusations that it was abetting manslaughter in Qatar. After much prevarication, Blatter finally conceded in 2014 that labor abuse in Qatar's construction industry was "unacceptable" and urged its government to introduce "fair working conditions." The sporting organization pressed the Gulf nation to adhere to the worker rights listed in the International Labor Organization's (ILO) core standards and eliminate all forms of forced labor. International firms building the infrastructure for the games fell in line and publicly pledged to elevate their labor policies to international best practices. The emir of Qatar soon entered the fray, declaring in an interview with CNN later that year that he was "personally hurt about the situation." He insisted that Qatar had stepped up the enforcement of protective legislation and instituted new regulations to ensure that employers paid their workers.[8]

Sharon Burrow, the general secretary of the ITUC, dismissed the commitment to reform as "empty promises," adding that "Qatar is a slave state. The discrimination, the racism, the denial of rights for 1.4 million migrant workers adds up to apartheid and a model of employment that is simply slavery."[9]

As headlines about "world cup slaves" amassed, commentators began to opine on the apparent contradiction between Qatar's regressive labor practices and the hypermodernity that it projected to the world. "Though Doha, the capital, looks uber-modern, with glittering skyscrapers and innovative architecture, its labor system is less forward-looking," observed the BCC.[10] "The plight of foreign laborers in the Gulf underscores a dark underside to the modern, glossy exterior the GCC [Gulf Cooperation Council] states like to showcase to the world," concurred Foreign Policy in Focus.[11] The implication was that the iconic buildings that drew Doha's distinctive skyline, so flamboyantly avant-garde in their architecture, represented development at its most dystopian: the most backward and brutish exploitation gilded with a thin veneer of modernity.

Many news outlets and human rights organizations pointed to the country's kafala system as the source of the "slavery-like" conditions. Kafala was the country's sponsorship system for the employment of foreign workers. Under the terms of the law that specified this system, all foreign workers had to have a "sponsor"—or *kafeel* (pl. kafala). The regulation stipulated that the sponsor had to be an employer, either a Qatari individual or company, and all legal rights afforded to the sponsored worker devolved from that tie. The foreigner's employment obligation to the sponsor was exclusive and binding. A worker could not change jobs without their sponsor's permission or quit their job until the end of the contract for any reason, including nonpayment of wages and abuse. A migrant's right to reside in Qatar was entirely at the pleasure of the sponsor, who could terminate and deport migrant employees without advance notice or cause. At the time that FIFA awarded Qatar the hosting privileges for the World Cup, the sponsor also controlled the ability of their foreign workers to leave the country; with few exceptions, foreigners required an exit visa, approved by their employer, in order to travel out of Qatar.

In most advocacy reports and press accounts of labor conditions in Qatar, the country's kafala system was described as only a somewhat more restrictive version of a cultural practice that was widespread in the Gulf, with Qatar's neighbors all also enforcing sponsorship systems to manage foreign labor. A smattering of scholarly and popular guesses about the origins of the kafala system alternatively characterized it as an indigenous form of labor regulation, a holdover from tribal social conventions for the treatment of foreigners, or an Islamic jurisprudential take on the obligations involved in wage-based employment relationships.[12] Regardless, the kafala system was implicitly represented as an endemic and timeless feature of Arab culture, peculiar and archaic, and reflective, at its worst, of the despotic and venal tendencies that had made Blatter's "lands of the Middle East and the Arabic world" at once so inscrutable and difficult to penetrate, yet so needful of civilizing intervention.[13]

This, however, was a mischaracterization of the kafala system—one that radically minimized its significance as an expression of global trends in the management of migrant labor.

Far from being a cultural aberration, the kafala system in Qatar as well as the Gulf more broadly was the product of more than a century of global economic exchange. The Gulf had been the site of modern global commodity production and extraction ever since the late 1880s, beginning with pearls and dates, followed by oil and gas exploitation after the Second World War, and in the twenty-first century, the production of platforms for global finance, culture, and transport. Vast numbers of workers had to be imported into the region to produce goods for global markets, and the kafala system that modern-day commentators maligned as tribal and backward was actually a composite of more recent international regulatory structures brought in to govern as well as control those workers. The regulations themselves reflected contemporary conventions of the treatment of labor, and were shaped by global debates on the rights of workers and definition of freedom. The Qatari kafala system, when that FIFA envelope was pried open in Zurich, was no different; it was produced by an uneasy interaction between existing regulation and international law, and contested and amended through global conversations about the rights of migrant workers.

Global debates about labor have explicitly wrestled with the definition of freedom, and how to distinguish and protect it from forms of unfreedom and bondage. In these conversations, past and present, and the regulations they produced, the idea of *skill* emerges as a central and definitional concept. Underpinning these attempts to delineate freedom has been the development of a set of understandings about skill—specifically, who is skilled and who is not, the agency required to acquire skill and exercise it, and the fullness of freedom associated with skill, as compared to the debased version of freedom associated with its lack. In many of these debates, skill was implicitly treated as having an ontological status associated with freedom rather than a reflection of work-related competence. In the Gulf in general and Qatar specifically, workers who were viewed as skilled were also seen as free, as people who acted agentically and volitionally, and their status as free actors was confirmed by the many regulatory layers that governed migration to the region. Migrants perceived as unskilled, however, were also viewed as having a propensity for bondage, lacking agency, and vulnerable to being bound in contractual arrangements that were unfree. For unskilled workers, the definition of freedom was narrowed from one that centered on the status of the worker as a contractually free person to one that focused instead on the conditions of work, and whether or not they were humane. Debates, local and global, about labor regulations that applied to workers who were considered unskilled dealt with how to shield them from bodily exploitation. Freedom for the unskilled, in law and advocacy, was less an expression of political autonomy than a bodily condition.

The kafala system in the Gulf and particularly Qatar, reformed, amended, and modernized, has always been a product of global economic exchange and debates about definitions of skill, agency, and freedom. The attention that the World Cup brought to the tiny desert kingdom turned Qatar into a place where regulatory structures for the global management and control of migrant workers were hashed out. International observers and advocates pushed for worker rights, and international organizations, from the ILO to FIFA, took on formal roles in amending Qatari legislation and advancing norms around the treatment of migrant workers.[14] As a result, Qatar become an arena where the relationship between migrant rights and skill was defined, and the definitions of freedom were stretched, contested, and honed. Represented as a strange and to some extent brutish kingdom, Qatar became the place where controversial questions about the political rights associated with skill, and whether rights should differ by skill level, could be asked and explored. Debates over the rights of migrant workers in Qatar became debates about the rights of migrant workers everywhere.

To understand what was old and new in these debates, we have to reach back to Qatar's participation in global commodity production over the past century, and examine the definitions of freedom and skill that have shaped labor regulations. These regulations and norms extend past the boundaries of modern-day Qatar to the Gulf more broadly and beyond. But since contemporary conversations about migrant rights and skill centered on Qatar, they pulled what was specific to Qatar into the current global debates. A review of the evolution of regulatory structures and norms during successive waves of commodity production in Qatar illuminates how contemporary debates reproduced as well as carried forward the political meanings these structures and norms encoded. This history helps us see when and why debates about the rights of migrant workers in Qatar affirmed, rejected, or amended the troubling idea that equates bodily welfare with freedom, and why, even after significant reform to Qatar's regulatory framework, they might continue to do so.[15]

Pearls and Slavery

"Pearls Growing Scarce: Rich Are Buying Them" announced a breathless 1906 headline on the front page of the *New York Times*. The article went on to recount that a certain Elbert Gary of the United States Steel Corporation had, on his return from Europe, reluctantly paid a duty on two loose pearls he was carrying in his pocket, valued at $53,000 (approximately $1.6 million in today's currency). The paper learned that he had also purchased three pearls from a specialty jeweler on Fifth Avenue for $110,000 (about $3 million today), and there was speculation that he was collecting gems for a necklace. In 1906, the acquisition of a handful of pearls was newsworthy enough to made the front page. It seemed that every commercial magnate, every scion of America's new class of multimillionaires, was vying to find pearls to buy to display their newly acquired wealth. "The most prominent jewelers are all making specialties of pearl collections . . . [yet these] are not displayed in showcases, but are kept in safes and only taken out and shown to visitors whose circumstances indicate a possible customer."[16] The wives and daughters of the new US elite, from the Vanderbilt, Rockefeller, and Whitney families, posed for portraits wearing long strands of pearls—necklaces that were four or five times as valuable by weight as those made of diamonds.[17] A symbol of luxury, pearls would quickly come to dominate women's fashion far beyond elite circles. *Harper's Bazaar* confirmed in 1909 that pearl jewelry had become "a necessary incident of the modern costume."[18] The Vanderbilt's jeweler, who had brokered the sale of a sixty-inch necklace of perfect sixteen-grain pearls for the family—at the time, the largest jewelry purchase in US history—announced "a new era—the day of the dearest of all gems, the pearl."[19]

Pearl production rose rapidly around the world. Pearl banks in Ceylon, Venezuela, and Australia were fished with unprecedented intensity. Thousands set up camp on the banks of the Mississippi River, wading in to collect freshwater pearls from mollusks buried in the mud. But the most costly and prized pearls were the soft cream-colored pearls, often with a pink hue, that came from the pearl fisheries along the Arabian coast and Red Sea. Individual specimens and strands of these "Oriental pearls," as they were called, were traded in exclusive auction houses in New York, London, and Paris for unprecedented sums in "spirited bidding" and "warm contest[s]."[20] Ludwig Neisen, a Broadway jeweler, was stunned by the demand: "Eastern potentates [were parting] with necklaces and strings which have been heirloom and treasured family possessions, sometimes for hundreds of years. . . . But the time will come when even the Indian Rajas and the Chinese Mandarins will have no more pearls to offer."[21]

At the height of the pearl boom, the entire breadth of the Persian Gulf coast was transformed by the pearling industry. Between 1886 and 1904, the value of pearls exported from the Gulf grew by 500 percent and would continue to rise over the next two decades.[22] At the peak of the market, some thirty-six hundred boats set sail from the Arabian side of the Gulf between April and September to harvest pearls from the seabed, and sixty-five thousand men worked to collect the natural gems. Wooden dhows, headed by a captain and manned by a crew of a few dozen divers, haulers, and apprentices, set out during the summer months to harvest pearls by diving down to the seafloor and prying off oysters one by one with a shucking knife.[23] By the early twentieth century, this massive flotilla accounted for 80 percent of the global production by value, generating more wealth from pearls than all other regions of the world combined.[24]

Qatar's shores offered the most productive pearling banks in the region, and even before the height of the pearl boom, its economy was organized around pearl production. As early as 1863, on the eve of the global pearl boom, Sheikh Muhammad bin Thani, ruler of Qatar, observed to European chronicler William Palgrave, "We are all, from the highest to the lowest, slaves of one master, the Pearl." By the turn of the century, almost a quarter of the region's pearling boats docked in Qatar's coastal towns of Doha and Wakra, and thirteen thousand men out of the twin towns' twenty thousand inhabitants worked in the industry, manning the country's nine hundred pearling vessels.[25]

Although Oriental pearls were fished off the seabed of the Arabian Sea, the production and trade of the gems was a global industry. Traders and middlemen in Bombay, Madras, and Baghdad financed Gulf pearling dhows and their crews, and prepared the gems in the clearinghouses to be sold onward to European merchants.[26] As demand for pearls soared in the 1900s, jewelers and commodity traders from London, Vienna, New York, and Paris elbowed their way into the trade, financing the harvest and distribution of pearls directly. The epicenter of the pearl market moved to Paris, where it remained until the eve of the Second World War.[27] Oriental pearls, spherical and opaline, made traders and financiers around the world fantastically rich. The most successful became multimillionaires, and in the case of the Rosenthal family—the family that would come to dominate the trade in Gulf pearls in the 1920s—billionaires in today's currency. Their fortunes paid for vanity projects such as new arcades on the Champs-Elysees and luxury buildings in Manhattan.

To meet the significant manpower requirements of pearl harvesting in an otherwise sparsely populated desert region, the industry imported vast numbers of enslaved persons from East Africa. The harvest of pearls came to depend on a system of bonded labor, either in the form of chattel slavery or hereditary debt bondage. The conditions under which men were brought in and used in this first wave of global commodity production laid the foundation for the labor arrangements in modern-day Qatar. The development of these early labor practices set the stage for kafala laws, and the ways in which bondage became imbricated with the recognition and use of worker skill.

The data on the number of enslaved persons shipped to the Gulf to meet the labor requirements of global commodity production for pearls and also dates in the first half of the nineteenth century are difficult to pin down. Estimates by historiographers suggest that the numbers of enslaved persons imported to the Gulf region rose from about fifteen thousand per year in 1800 to more than forty thousand by the mid-nineteenth century.[28] The East African slave trade was formally outlawed in 1873 when the British and sultan of Zanzibar signed a treaty prohibiting the transport of enslaved persons anywhere on the coast of East Africa. In 1879, the British commander in chief of the East Indies Station pronounced the slave trade to the Gulf extinct. Contemporary observers, however, reported a substantial revival of the trade in enslaved persons the 1880s, especially in the wake of a 1884 famine that devastated areas from Tanganyika to Kenya. The demand for labor in the Gulf led to the development of new transport routes that bypassed British controls.[29] Men, women, and children were seized, kidnapped, and shipped as slaves to the Gulf up until the eve of the Great Depression.[30]

Dispatches by Western observers suggest that many and possibly most of the divers on pearling dhows were enslaved men or freed men in debt bondage. John Gordon Lorimer, a British consular officer who produced a detailed survey of the Arabian Gulf, for example, reports in his account of pearling in his 1904 *Gazetteer* that the divers were "mostly poor Arabs and free Negroes or Negro slaves." His detailed descriptions of pearling centers in the Gulf add firmer contours to his sketch; in 1905, Lorimer notes that Doha had some twenty-five hundred slaves and a thousand "free Negroes" among its twelve hundred residents, and in neighboring Wakrah, a town of eight thousand, he counted some two thousand "slaves not living with their master" and a thousand "free Negros." Lorimer estimated that in Qatar as a whole, between one-fifth and one-fourth of the population was enslaved. Reports penned even as late as the mid-1920s confirm the industry's dependence on the labor of enslaved men. Charles Belgrave, British adviser to the rulers of Bahrain, estimated in 1929 that some twenty thousand of the sixty-four thousand men who fished pearls in the Gulf were enslaved persons of African origin. When the supply of enslaved persons from East Africa dried up during the European colonial control of sending areas, the pearling industry sourced slaves from Baluchistan—in particular, the coastal areas of present-day Pakistan.[31]

In the pearl industry, labor existed on a continuum—enslaved men, men in debt bondage, and freed men worked alongside one another on pearling dhows during the grueling months of the diving season. All were subject to similar levers of control. One lever was wage distribution. Wages to free divers were paid out as loans, generally at the beginning of the season, to be paid back when the share of the proceeds from the dhow's haul were partitioned out to them. Often, once they paid back their loans, they were in debt again to the boat captain. This industry-wide system of credit kept divers tethered to their captains for years on end, frequently with a debt that was no greater than the cost of several sacks of rice. Divers' debt obligations were considered hereditary, and both debt and its payment through labor were imposed on divers' sons. Slave owners rented their enslaved divers to dhow captains for the season, claimed their wages, and then sometimes leveraged the earnings they expected to collect at the end of the season as collateral, entering into debt relations of their own.[32] Divers, both bonded and enslaved, were traded by captains and slave owners to meet debt obligations they had incurred, or more speculatively, as debt securities that assigned monetary value to bondage relations.[33]

This web of debt relations muddied the distinction between divers who were enslaved and those who were bonded. Neither could refuse to dive. Indeed, as P. W. Harrison, a longtime missionary in the Gulf concluded in 1936, "The diver is known as a slave for the rest of his life. . . . As long as he is in debt, he cannot change his employer, no matter how badly he is treated, nor can he leave the town, except under bonds to return before the diving season begins, and he will never be able to get out of debt."[34] In fact, enslavers routinely added a layer of debt bondage onto their ownership claims as a surety on their property. They took out debts from diving captains on their slaves' behalf because the British would not manumit an enslaved person if there was any doubt that he was bound by relations of indenture.[35] Essentially, enslavers created debt bondage so that the workers they held in chattel slavery could never become free.

The pearl-harvesting industry was extremely labor intensive even by the standards of the day, but it also depended on a high level of relational and embodied skill. The harvest of pearls relied on the relationship between the diver and hauler, who worked together in pairs. The diver, stripped down to a loincloth, skin oiled against the saltwater, nostrils closed with horn pincers, fingers sheathed in leather fingerstalls to protect against abrasions, dove down to the seafloor, tied to his hauler by a coir rope wrapped around his waist. His descent was aided by a stone weight fitted to his foot with a loop of rope. On reaching the seafloor, the diver slipped his foot out of the loop, and the hauler immediately yanked the weight back up onto the dhow. The diver groped the seafloor with one hand and foot, using the second foot to propel himself along the bed, and the free hand to slice off open-mouthed oysters that snapped shut when the diver approached and place them in the basket hung around his neck. After forty to seventy-five seconds, the diver yanked on the rope around his waist to signal to the hauler to pull him up to the surface. The hauler had to act quickly and negotiate his diver's ascent against the tug of the water currents. This required an understanding of how the undertow pressure acted on the diver's body and how to negotiate those waves when hauling the diver up so as not to get pulled overboard into rough waters. Haulers were often experienced divers who had aged out of diving but continued to coach their partners in their dives. This process went on from early morning until sunset. Diving teams could make fifty plunges a day in good weather, but no more than ten on days when the currents were strong or the waters were infested with sharks, stingrays, or jellyfish.[36]

Skill, however, was difficult to quantify, and the system of slavery and debt bondage that was in place shaped how workers' skill was appraised and exploited. As Lorimer notes in 1915, the skill of divers factored into their price when they were bought and sold as slaves or indebted workers, but was attributed to the diver's physicality rather than his expertise. "The efficiency of a diver depends more on his skill and daring than on the strength of his constitution—the last being a point on which undue stress has sometimes been laid by writers upon pearling; and a slave diver who is not afraid to enter deep and muddy water containing weeds is ordinarily valued at considerably over R.S. 1000."[37] The divers and haulers, bonded and enslaved, were rarely rewarded, either in wages or working conditions, for their skill. Quite to the contrary, dhow captains and masters frequently used violence to drive their crews.

As manumission testimonies delivered to the British suggest, dhow captains relied heavily on corporal measures to push their crews. Enslaved divers were often beaten with sticks or placed in shackles. In an interpretation of a traditional curative procedure of scorching skin to purge the body of illness, many other enslaved workers were burned with hot irons on their faces and bodies to "cure" them of their unwillingness to dive. Hopper's study chronicles several manumission reports that comment on burns, mentioning, as one British naval commander did in 1921, "several burns with some hot implements which . . . his owner had given him because he had not (or would not) learn to dive."[38]

At a time when the Arabian Gulf was nicknamed a "British lake," it was the British who oversaw the use and treatment of the pearl industry's enslaved and bonded workforce. British antislavery efforts were reluctant at best; the British government recognized that the economies of the Gulf kingdoms that had signed protectorate agreements with the British Crown were entirely built on the use of enslaved and bonded labor. The British home government determined in a 1875 circular that if British ships provided refuge to runaway slaves, not only would "their masters . . . be entirely ruined" but British material interests would also be damaged "by the mistrust and hatred which would be occasioned."[39] The document laid out strict provisions for asylum: "The broad rule to be observed is that a fugitive slave should not be permanently received onboard any description of a ship under the British flag, unless his life would be endangered unless he were not allowed to come aboard." The British authorities confirmed this stance in later decades by enforcing an agreement, brokered with the sheikhs in the Gulf in 1897, that limited the ability of enslaved persons and indentured workers to cross jurisdictional lines, where they often petitioned for their freedom.[40] The compact provided for the mutual surrender of "fraudulent absconders, especially pearl divers and sailors," as Lorimer described it, with all related disputes to be adjudicated by the British.[41]

In a pattern that would continue through the present, the legitimacy of the enslaved or bonded worker's petition for freedom was measured in visible damage to the body. Today, labor conditions have been evaluated in relation to the condition of the worker's body, and are deemed satisfactory or unsatisfactory, depending on what is found there. In the nineteenth century, statements recorded to support manumission petitions focused on injuries caused by the runaway's master or captain—burns, scars from lashings and beatings, broken bones and teeth, or damaged eyes.[42] Yet injuries caused by years of diving, compelled by this violence, were not featured. The almost-ubiquitous damage to divers' eardrums, frequent blindness, and respiratory and skin ailments common among pearling crews were considered par for the course, and not "particularly injurious to the health" of divers.[43] Bondage and exploitation were seen as egregious only when they left marks on workers' bodies that could be traced back unequivocally to proscribed forms of violence.

Ultimately, even the intensified exploitation of bonded and enslaved workers could not produce enough pearls to satiate global demand. Entrepreneurs in pearling areas around the world explored methods to cultivate the gems by seeding oysters, and in 1908, the assays of a Japanese noodle shop owner named Kokichi Mikimoto bore fruit. Mikimoto filed for a patent on a method to produce perfectly round pearls by inserting a spherical piece of mother of pearl into pearling oysters.[44] Within a decade, millions of cultured Mikimoto pearls entered the market. Production from the Gulf remained steady in volume but slumped in value through the 1920s. In other circumstances, it's likely that the Gulf pearling industry would have endured a slow decline, but the onset of the Great Depression was a death knell for natural pearl production. The global trade in luxury items dried up overnight, and the Gulf pearl industry collapsed.

After the initial economic shock of 1929, the Gulf pearling industry limped along at a fraction of its previous production. Mid-1930s' pearl production barely reached mid-nineteenth-century production, when pearls were only produced for the regional market.[45] Qatar was hit hardest, and the conditions of residents, made worse by a punitive embargo from neighboring Bahrain, was so wretched that the pearling boats that had been the lifeblood of the area were broken up for firewood.[46] The collapse of the pearl industry led to a fall in prices for enslaved men. Qatari slave owners began funneling the enslaved persons they could not use for diving to Saudi Arabia, where antislavery legislation had been weakened. Qatar emerged as a source of enslaved persons and a regional entrepôt for the profitable trade, and it fostered the recrudescence of the trade in enslaved persons throughout the Gulf, which remained robust well into the 1940s.[47] By 1939, roughly 39 percent of Qatar's population was non-Arab, many likely enslaved persons. Their numbers were probably augmented by the growing number of enslaved persons imported from Persian Baluchistan, a route that circumvented the British and Portuguese patrol of the East African shoreline.[48]

Facing pressure from the League of Nations over the prevalence of bondage in what remained of Gulf pearling, the British administration passed a series of labor standards meant to regulate the industry in the 1930s.[49] Central among these were new provisions for a minimum wage for diving crews, a stipulation that debt incurred in the industry could not be extracted from a diver's offspring by bonding the son in place of the father, and the issuance of permission slips that allowed free divers to pass from one jurisdiction to another without risk of reenslavement. The new regulations were widely unpopular among merchants, financiers, and dhow captains, who routinely skirted them.[50] When riots broke out in pearling centers along the coast demanding that new standards be enforced, the British forsook the reforms that would have guaranteed members of diving crews some measure of political and economic freedom. They used military force to put down the protests, and force divers back onto pearling dhows and into relations of slavery and bondage.[51]

By the end of the 1930s, only a few hundred ships in the entire Gulf set off at the beginning of the season to fish for pearls.[52] Pearling in Qatar and the Gulf more broadly would never recover, but the labor force endured, along with the practices associated with slavery and bondage that were used to control it. When Qatar launched into its next wave of commodity production, the regulations that were applied to workers during the pearl boom—as well as the understandings of skill and freedom they reflected—were carried forward and modernized.

Oil, Bondage, and Skill

Rupert Hay, a British political resident in the Persian Gulf in the 1940s, opined in his reflections on his years of service in the region that "but for the large quantities of valuable oil beneath its barren surface, the Qatar peninsula would be nothing more than an ugly excrescence on the Arabian Coast."[53] Qatar, he observed, "was almost untouched by modern influences," with "practically no education and no direct contact with the world outside the Persian Gulf and Arabia. . . . The country had no attractions of any kind."[54] He described Doha, the nation's capital and home to half the country's twenty thousand residents, as "little more than a miserable fishing village straggling along the coast for several miles and more than half in ruins." The souk, he recalled, "consisted of mean fly-infested hovels," and Doha as a whole lacked even basic infrastructure, with residents forced to "fetch their water in skins and cans from two or three miles outside of town."[55]

Hay told a now-familiar story of how oil introduced Qatar to history and put its isolated tribes on a path to modernity. But Hay was also describing a moment of economic collapse precipitated by changes in global markets and the painful social unraveling that accompanied it. When the pearling industry cratered, Qatar saw its population plummet from around twenty-nine thousand in 1939 to twenty-five thousand in 1942 and possibly as low as sixteen thousand in 1949.[56] Doha lost its many resident non-Arabs; its Persian traders, Indian financiers, and other foreigners who had made up nearly a third of Doha's population decamped.[57] Only the British stayed to patrol the overland military supply routes they had charted over Qatar's territory and, more presciently, lay the groundwork for oil extraction. Oil would set the next wave of commodity production in motion, and Qatar's labor practices would once again be convulsed and transformed by global trade and investment.[58]

IMPERIAL OIL CONCESSION

The British had been aware of the oil reserves in the Arabian Peninsula since World War I and even began actively prospecting in the mid-1920s. Yet it was only when the Americans, having already developed oil fields in Saudi Arabia, expressed an interest in expanding into Qatar—perhaps even backing Saud's claims that large swaths of Qatar belonged to his kingdom—that the British began negotiating an oil concession with the House of Al-Thani in earnest.[59] In May 1935, after close to two years of tense back and forth between Sheikh Abdullah, ruler of Qatar, and the British, a political agreement granting the Anglo-Persian Oil Company (APOC) the exclusive right to exploit petroleum products in Qatar was finally concluded.[60] A hand-drawn map was appended to the contract to make it clear that the entire peninsula belonged to Qatar and the agreement thus gave APOC rights to extract oil anywhere on the territory. In return, Britain was "committed" to defending Qatar militarily against any encroachment, especially from its imposing neighbor, Saudi Arabia.[61]

The British sought political and jurisdictional control over oil development. They haggled with Sheikh Abdullah over rights to territorial ingress, the level of compensation for oil extraction, and the right to seize oil produced in Qatar in the event of a national emergency or war, "the existence of either of which His Majesty's government shall be the sole judge."[62] The Qatari ruler, whose fortunes had been so hollowed out by the crash of the pearl industry that he had been forced to mortgage his house, viewed the miserliness of the British as proof that they planned to use the financial devastation of the kingdom to advance the interests of their oil company at Qatar's expense.[63] "If the Anglo-Persian Oil Company do[es] not give me good terms . . . I will leave the oil in its place and give it to no one. I lived all this time without oil. I am now afraid of this company," protested the sheikh during negotiations with the British political resident.[64]

Tensions came to a head over the management of labor. For both parties, control over the labor supply was viewed as tantamount to control over the oil venture. Sheikh Abdullah insisted on primary authority over recruitment as a precondition to allowing APOC to begin its operations. He wrested a clause from the British that mandated preferential hiring for the subjects over which Qatar claimed legal jurisdiction. As recorded in the legal deliberations leading up to the signing of the concession agreement, these included "subjects of Koweit [*sic*], Bahrain, and the Trucial Coast," with some confusion remaining about whether "the subjects of Sultan of Muscat and Oman" were also subjects of Qatar. Article 17 of the concession agreement specified that "the laborers employed by the Company must be from among the Sheikh's own subjects or from amongst those approved by the Sheikh, excepting technical employees and the managers and clerks whom the Company may require and whom it cannot find in the country."[65] This was more than the standard national preference clause that the British included in their concession agreements; it gave the sheikh the discretionary power to determine which foreigners would receive preferential treatment in hiring.

The British, meanwhile, used hiring practices as a bargaining chip to lock down political control not just over oil development but also the political territory in which it occurred. The British government negotiators were not coy on this point. During the deliberations with Sheikh Abdullah, the British had intimated, not without menace, that if the Qataris concluded accords with petroleum interests from any other countries, the British might be forced to intervene militarily to guarantee the interests of British protected persons. ("This is a point that was emphasized more than once," remarked the political resident in his summary notes of the discussions.")[66] Draft versions of the concession agreement for Qatar reveal that the British negotiators pushed aggressively to widen the oil company's discretion in hiring to increase its political leverage, asserting its right to import laborers "if suitable laborers in the State of Qatar are insufficient in number."[67] The British government also cautioned the British oil company that the hiring of foreigners should be restricted to countries under British control, notably the Indian subcontinent, and that, in any case, the importation of labor would be subject to British government oversight through the direct approval of the political resident. "Greater caution is necessary in the case of [the admission of] non-British subjects," explained India Office official John Gilbert Laithwaite to the company, "because they might not understand so well as British subjects the desirability of following the advice of the political authorities."[68]

In the end, both parties used the convention of skill to resolve their political impasse over the labor supply. The British agreed that APOC would confine its recruitment to workers defined as skilled, while Qatar would provide unskilled laborers, which it would draw from among its subjects or those whom it had jurisdiction over. As a result, skill and its absence became conflated with nationality and race, with forms of bondage, unfreedom, and subjectivity. The political significance of skill had little connection to actual competence or mastery. It had even less to do with the ways that workers were actually used in the mining and export of oil.

THE GEOPOLITICS OF SKILL AND HIRING

APOC began operations as soon as the concession agreement was signed in 1935, and after a short hiatus during the Second World War, Petroleum Development Qatar (PDQ), the subsidiary established by APOC for oil production in Qatar, ramped up its operations. Its manpower needs were intense. Even before the company could begin exploiting the oil fields in the western desert area of Dukhan, it had to mobilize enough workers to lay in the massive infrastructure needed to transport the oil. It had to dredge a port in Umm Said, on the eastern coast of Qatar, the only harbor on the peninsula where the waters were deep enough to accommodate oil tankers, and lay down pipelines to transport oil across the country. With few passable roads and basic machinery—"Donkeys were used for road leveling work. . . . Lorries were no use for transporting the stones because they easily bogged down in the soft sand," recalled one Qatari worker—much of the construction, loading, and dredging work was manual. Within months, the company had hired a thousand men. By the following year, it had almost doubled the number of men hired locally and brought in another fifteen hundred from abroad.[69]

The practices that the oil company used to source labor sorted workers into two distinct categories. It marked them as either skilled or unskilled— with skilled workers being under the protection of the British Crown and unskilled being subjects of the ruler of Qatar. Skilled workers were treated as free and protected by a set of contractual and legal rights, and unskilled workers were treated as unfree, with the right only to be protected from serious bodily harm.

To recruit the local workers that the concession agreement had bound APOC to hire, the oil company relied on recruiting agents, from whom they purchased labor in bulk.[70] The agents collected a fee from the company that covered wages, which were meant to be paid to workers directly, along with an additional 20 percent or so layered on as commission. The main agents in Qatar, Salih al-Mana and Abdullah Darwish, were powerful courtiers and wartime black market traders whose control over labor provision as well as their influence with the sheikh fluctuated over time.[71] Of the two merchants, Salih was initially ascendant, parlaying his position as personal secretary to the sheikh into control over the labor supply. As the oil company's local representative, he also collected several salaries on the side. By the late 1940s, however, Darwish, whom the British political agent described as "a bearded, one-eyed man of between thirty and forty, clever, and with a really remarkable capacity for smooth lying," used his close personal friendship with the sheikh, cemented in their boyhood Koranic school, to move in on his rival's business.[72]

The agents used their personal ties to the sheikh as guarantors that the workers they had recruited were in fact subjects under the ruler's jurisdiction. In a region where the concept of nationality was still as fluid as the windswept borders that parsed out the desert kingdoms of the Gulf, the agents' designation of nationality was entirely transactional. The agents charged workers for this service; al-Mana, for example, reportedly charged local residents one rupee for the Qatari nationality chit that workers needed to access the oil fields, and charged workers from outside the peninsula between forty and fifty rupees to vouch that they were among the approved list of subjects.[73] The agents also charged the oil company for the provision of worker nationality documents, and the PDQ management complained bitterly to British foreign officers about the fees that the agents levied for this dispensation. "The Sheikh and his entourage regard the Company as a cow, to be milked as much and as often as possible," fumed E. V. Packer, a PDQ manager, to the British political resident in Bahrain in a 1941 missive. He further opined that the profit gleaned from the provision of local labor was the main reason the sheikh pressed the company to employ more Qatari subjects and dismiss foreigners.[74]

The recruitment process, then, became the arbiter of nationality, rather than nationality functioning as a prerequisite for recruitment. The oil company expressed alarm that the agents seemed to be stretching their interpretation of nationality a great deal, past the point, the company worried, where it could be judged as being in compliance with the concession agreement. In 1948, PDQ manager B. H. Lermitte sent a letter to the British political agent in Bahrain noting the high proportion of Gulf Arabs among the workers the recruiters sent them—recruits they had trouble distinguishing, the correspondence suggests, from Qatari workers.

> We wish to bring to your notice that the labor recruited in Doha nowadays includes a considerable proportion of non-Qatari subjects—Iranis, Baluchis, Omanis, Saudis etcetera. These laborers are all recruited by the representative to the government of Qatar and sent to the Dukhan camp. . . . In the majority of cases they are illiterate and possess no identity documents other than the green engagement chit issued by the representative. . . . We would be grateful for your advice as to whether the Sheikh of Qatar has jurisdiction over these persons and to what extent they are considered as Qatari subjects.[75]

The oil company's concerns about whether the agents' overly broad interpretation of the nationality clause in the concession agreement laid them open to regulatory sanction were borne out when British inspector Matthew Audsley, sent to verify the company's compliance with the concession agreement, issued a highly critical report in 1949. Among the infractions Audsley noted was his estimation that of the 2,712 workers registered as Qataris, only a little over half, 1,580 workers, were actually subjects of Qatar.[76]

Salih and Darwish's liberal dispensation of nationality chits muddied the distinction between workers who were officially subject to the ruler of Qatar's jurisdiction and those who were not. In similar ways, their recruitment practices blurred the distinction between wage labor and slavery. Workers who had been indentured in the pearl industry were hired out to the oil company in much the same way they had earlier been hired out to pearling dhows. The owner of the debt, often a dhow captain, appropriated the pay that the bonded workers earned with the oil company, supposedly applying the earnings against the bonded worker's debt. Slave owners also rented their enslaved persons to the oil company directly under the guise of wage employment. Using enslaved and bonded workers in this way was more lucrative for the slave owners and petty financiers than many of the other forms of economic activity to which enslaved and bonded workers were applied. Whereas a typical wage for a diver was around sixty rupees for a five-month season, for example, a local worker in the oil company would earn about double that amount, at twenty-five rupees a month.[77]

Opposition to manumission from local enslavers hardened, and as remarked by British political officers in the Trucial States, the wage premium for work in the oil industry may have helped reinvigorate the slave trade, which saw a resurgence in the late 1940s.[78] Consisting mostly of people kidnapped in Dubai or Sharjah, captives were transported to Buraimi, an important regional slave market, and purchased by Qatari and Saudi traders, who let them out to oil companies through recruiting agents.[79]

By sheltering the forms of enslavement and bondage that were widespread during the apogee of the pearling industry, the recruitment practices that the PDQ relied on merged wage labor with bondage. The oil company's use of bonded and enslaved labor destroyed any assumed equivalence between wage labor and freedom of contract, and the payment of wages actually reinforced the bondage of workers and enslaved men while strengthening the political backing for slavery in Qatar.

Historian and commentator Henry Longhurst, in his contemporary profile of British Petroleum, made plain that for the PDQ, these relationships of bondage were not just incidental to company labor practices but instead central to the way the company addressed labor control: "Climate and terrain are inhospitable and good labor hard to find. When prospecting operations were restarted, it was quickly apparent that their daily diet of fish and rice gave locally recruited workmen little stamina. . . . The most difficult employees were former slaves, who, after years of pampering by their masters, were inclined to be intolerant of the Company's hours and conditions of work."[80] As Longhurst's comments suggest, Salih and Darwish, in their role as intermediaries, provided the PDQ with plausible deniability about their use of slaves, but the British government was nevertheless well aware that the oil company masked its use of enslaved labor with wage payments. British diplomatic reports on the oil company's operations indicate that the PDQ employed enslaved persons from its very first year, and in 1949, at least 250 men out of the 2,220 Qataris on its roll were known to be enslaved, hired out to the company at the personal request of the enslaver, who often as not was a member of the royal family.[81] The British Political Office employee in Doha, M. B. Jacomb, bemoaned this practice as late as 1951: "I found that the possessed slaves working for the Company received their pay from the paymaster but almost at once had to hand over between 80 and 95 to an agent for their master. It was therefore obvious that the slaves were farmed out as a source of income for their masters." Jacomb was careful to clarify that "the Company do not of course do this by choice; the slave is to them one of many applying for work."[82] But credulity was strained every summer when management groused about the manpower shortage caused by slave owners who pulled enslaved men off the oil fields to staff the few remaining pearling dhows that went out in July and August.[83] The company was sensitive to the public relations problem that the PDQ's use of enslaved workers represented, and the British pressed the sheikh to outlaw slavery, but the most that the political resident was able to wrest from the ruler was a decree allowing the slaves to keep half their wages.[84]

The recruitment process, with its rigid channels of classification and systems of payment, also constructed particular meanings around the idea of skill. Local hires—who had been made local through the recruitment process and confined to situations of bondage through the wages they were paid—were contractually classified as unskilled manual labor. In practice, however, local workers brought skills to the oil enterprise that even the oil company acknowledged were critical to setting up oil rigs and building infrastructure. The PDQ and, soon after, Shell Corporation relied on the local knowledge of Qatari workers to complete their geologic survey of the peninsula. The PDQ's internal reports marveled at the abilities of their local guides: "He seems to have a mental map of the country and can find his way to any place, whether in a heat haze, fog, or even in total darkness," observed one PDQ geologist about his Qatari guide.[85] Shell likewise depended on the expertise of former pearl divers, their knowledge of the seafloor terrain and the currents that coursed over it, and their ability to maneuver underwater in order to set up its offshore rigs.[86] But the classification of these workers as unskilled, irrespective of their demonstrated expertise, suggests that the unskilled designation signified subjection to conditions of bondage and exploitation rather than accurately denoting a degree of ability.

The designation of local workers as unskilled, despite their obvious skill and value, was as much a product of the British imperial law that governed the movement of labor as it was of the hard divide between skilled and unskilled workers in the British-Qatari concession agreement. The British government preferred that the oil company recruit British citizens or citizens protected by the British Crown, and the most obvious source of those workers was India. At the time the oil concession agreement was concluded in 1935, the recruitment of Indian workers for work outside India was regulated by the provisions of the 1922 Indian Emigration Act, which was passed at the end of a grinding campaign against the exploitation of Indian indentured workers. The 1922 act was in part a public relations strategy to tamp down the upswell of resistance against British rule, which manifested in the mass civil disobedience that took place under the umbrella of the noncooperation movement of 1920–22.[87] The act ended the century-long system of labor indenture that had been rolled out in the British colonies when slavery was abolished throughout the empire in 1834.[88] It specifically prohibited the recruitment of bonded laborers and made illegal any scheme for the assisted migration of unskilled labor from India without a special act of exemption from the legislature—with one notable exception, made for labor migration to the hugely lucrative plantations of Ceylon, Burma, and the Federated Malay States.[89]

"Emigration, for the purpose of unskilled work, shall not be lawful," declared the act, but the definition of unskilled stipulated in it was peculiar and specific—a product of the imperial plantation economy that had relied on indentured labor. Unskilled work, according to the language of the act, was limited to "engaging in agriculture" (Government of India 1922, I-G). The definition of skilled work, in contrast, was much more expansive, and included such occupations as "working as an artisan; or working as a clerk or shop assistant; or working for the purposes of exhibition or entertainment; or service in any restaurant, tea-house, or other place of public resort; or domestic service; or any other occupation with the Governor General in Council may, by notification of the Gazette of India, declare to be skilled work" (Government of India 1922, I-F). The act not only continued a long tradition in the British Empire of controlling and restricting the movement of plantation labor but also explicitly confirmed the placement of the skill line, implicit in previous emigration controls, at the boundary between agricultural labor and work in industry or service.[90]

In addition to regulating which skill class of worker could emigrate, the act specified a set of rights and protections for skilled emigrants. Under the terms of the act, the Protector of Emigrants, an office in the government of India, oversaw the recruitment of Indian workers to the Gulf. The Protector of Emigrants required that all contracts be regulated by a foreign service agreement and filed with the office, and also mandated that recruitment occur through registered offices in India. The foreign service agreements laid out the protections that the employment contract would guarantee recruits. By law, the agreements were required to specify the minimum contract period under which workers could be recruited—typically ranging from one to three years—along with wage rates, terms of industrial accident compensation, and basic requirements for accommodation. Additionally, the agreements required that the employee's passage abroad, along with repatriation at the end of the contract, be paid by the employer.[91]

The effect of these regulatory protections was to equate the skill classification with access to a set of rights. For workers defined as skilled, the regulatory mechanisms set up by the act ensured freedom of contract, based on full information about the conditions of work to establish free and informed consent; it provided for the enforcement of the contract, and included safeguards against exploitation and abuse, such as redress for non- or partial payment of wages or involuntary overtime.[92] The time limits of the contracts allowed by the foreign service agreements guaranteed protection against indenture and bondage too, and safeguarded the freedom of emigrants legally classed as skilled.

The numbers of recruits from the Indian subcontinent who were imported by the PDQ as skilled labor, and used as builders, diggers, domestic staff, and clerks, expanded rapidly. In December 1947, the PDQ had 194 South Asian employees on its employment rolls. Within the year, that number grew to 552, and by 1950, their ranks had almost doubled again to 841, representing a third of the PDQ's total workforce.[93]

In practice, the skill distinction that shaped recruitment had little bearing on actual, practical skill. Workers brought in under these regulatory arrangements were assigned tasks that overlapped with those assigned to unskilled Qatari workers.[94] The PDQ's own hiring preferences suggested a slippage between the legal definition of skill used in recruitment and its operational skill needs. When the company first set up its operations in 1938, it petitioned the British government for permission to recruit Iraqi artisans, whom it viewed as more qualified and experienced than available Indian labor. The company sought in particular to hire Iraqi foremen who had worked on oil fields in Basra, and the company argued, not only had acquired technical expertise but also were suited by language, culture, and religion to control Arab workers. The British government, however, viewed this request as a political problem. In a series of agitated dispatches, a British political agent in Bahrain, Hugh Weightman, made clear that hiring non-British nationals was a political concern, and firmly communicated that technicians—as skilled workers—were to be recruited from among British nationals. "I am, as I hope you know, only too happy to do all I can to assist your company in regard to its operation in Qatar and elsewhere, but that happiness diminishes to a point of non-existence when I am invited to assist in facilitating the employment of foreigners," read one.[95]

SKILL, BONDAGE, AND BODILY WELFARE

British regulatory practices reinforced the equation the British drew between skills and rights. A skilled worker had legal access to a different set of rights than an unskilled worker—and a different conception of personhood. In 1949, and again in 1951, the British government dispatched Matthew Audsley, labor adviser to His Majesty's Embassy and British Middle East Office in Cairo, to the Gulf in order to report on operations in Dukhan and labor conditions in the oil concerns in which the British government had a political stake.

In his evaluation, Audsley drew on standards that the British government had initially defined to regulate indentured labor migration among its colonies. To mollify outrage at a system that its critics compared to slavery, the British government of India had created a highly detailed oversight regime designed to regulate the conditions for indentured workers, which it codified into law in 1864 (Government of India Act no. 13) and endeavored to enforce, with varying degrees of commitment, until the end of indenture in 1917.[96] The law specified matters such as the number of changes of clothes and blankets to be provided to workers, the minimum square footage to be allotted to each person aboard transport ships and in housing at plantation estates, the quantity and kind of food provided to workers, wages rates, hours of labor per week, and parameters for the health indicators for workers, including age, weight, and build.[97]

These regulations all focused on bodily well-being, and as historian Rachel Sturman argues in her analysis of the codes, their attention to the body of the indentured worker precipitated a fundamental change in the definition of freedom and humanity. "The focus of criticism shifted from the problem of the human status of the laborer, as in the antislavery movement, to the component parts that constituted humane or inhumane *conditions* of labor. The indenture system thus underwrote a silent transition from a vision of humanity imagined as a substantive status—in other words, the opposite of slavery—to a humanity that was achieved, or lost, in fragmentary, incremental measure of welfare."[98] Bodily welfare supplanted the notion of political personhood. Abandoned along the way was attention to the agency of the worker in entering the labor relation, and his freedom or lack thereof to abrogate the employment contract, should he so desire.

Audsley carried forward this regulatory attention to the bodies of workers when he evaluated the labor conditions of unskilled workers. In his report to the Commonwealth Relations Office, Audsley divided his evaluation into three discussions: the first considered the status of British and US staff (along with one Swiss employee), the second reviewed the conditions for Indian and Pakistani workers, and the third evaluated the welfare of the catchall designation for local hires as labor "other than Indians and Pakistanis."[99]

The differences between the sections of Audley's report reveal the subjectivity associated with each group of workers, and specifically, the extent to which that subjectivity was limited to bodily welfare. In his discussion of the British and US staff, Audsley attended to their pay, leave, and the hardship allowances they received, mentioning in particular the emotional cost borne by the 75 percent who were married and separated from wives, whose residence in the harsh conditions of oil fields was inappropriate. He also reflected on their motivations for joining the PDQ and their professional aspirations in the future. His evaluations of the conditions for Indian and Pakistani workers evinced a heavier focus on their physical well-being and included descriptions of their accommodations, noting that they were furnished, and "feeding and all other amenities are free." But he also mentioned approvingly that the company appointed "a liaison who deals with all matters affecting the well-being and general interests of the Indians and Pakistanis."[100]

His discussion of "local hires" stands in sharp contrast with its exclusive focus on the physical welfare of workers. He recorded their low daily wage rate, less than half of what the lowest-paid Indian or Pakistani received, but observes the "very high percentage of them who are completely unskilled." Audsley described their lodging—matted coir huts as opposed to the permanent structures provided to all other employees—and added that they are "fed free." He disparaged the physical bearing of "local" workers as "wiry" and "poor specimens by our standards," and remarked that the company lowered its cut-off weight from eight stone to seven. Audley assessed that the workers were "deriving physical betterment" from the living standards at the camp, which he judged to be much improved from the living conditions of their families, which some fraction of the men were allowed to visit in Doha on their rest days. In his evaluation, he also acknowledged that many workers were enslaved, but dismissed the company's involvement with slavery and bondage as a "complex problem" about which "it will be necessary to do something . . . later."[101] The welfare of "local hires"—defined as unskilled by the hiring regulations—was measured not in their freedom but rather in their working and living conditions.

Audsley's report captures the marked stratification of the oil company's employment practices. British and US managers and engineers occupied the top layer of the hierarchy. They were the foreign sahibs, for whom the privileges of decent housing, fruit and vegetables (any native worker caught consuming these could be fired), and the ability to negotiate their employment and careers directly with the oil company were reserved.

Indians, Pakistanis, and Portuguese Indians from Goa, retained under carefully regulated and monitored labor contracts as skilled workers, were slotted in the middle layer. They worked as clerks or company doctors tending to worker injuries, but also as cooks, drivers, household servants, and laborers and construction workers erecting rigs and building infrastructure.[102] Many worked alongside local hires "loading and unloading iron, cement, and big crates" at the harbor, as one veteran recalled. Workers with nationality chits— Qataris but also Arabs from Bahrain, Yemen, and Oman—were relegated to the bottom layer. Disparaged in company documents as "native coolies" and bought from recruiters in bulk, these so-called unskilled workers dug foundations for rigs, mixed cement with their feet, packed dynamite, and prospected for oil, both aboveground and on the seabed. As one Qatari worker recalled, they "worked day at night, without any overtime pay, expected to do any job— laboring, driving, it was all the same to the company."[103]

When Audsley returned to Qatar in 1951, his visit took place against a backdrop of official Qatari complaints about the treatment of Qatari workers and British government concerns at the PDQ's carelessness with the political sensitivities that were involved. For APOC, the PDQ's parent company, oil exploitation in Qatar was a small offshoot of its major operations, centered in Bahrain. The British tended to treat Qatar as a small concern and had no dedicated political officer stationed there, referring political issues to their office in Bahrain. Moreover, the British government's decision not to appoint a political officer to Qatar was a concession to the ruler, who according to British dispatches, was anxious that "such an agent would encourage slaves to seek manumission." Hay, the British political officer in Bahrain, assured him that "such an agent will not grant manumission to slaves existing at this time, except"—in a reprise of the standard that the British government adopted in determining whether to provide refuge to slaves in the pearling industry— "where definite cruelty of a master toward a slave seeking manumission has been proved."[104]

As a result of all this, APOC management tended to disregard many of the day-to-day labor relations issues in Qatar and subsumed concerns about worker welfare into its highly personalistic negotiations with the sheikh over concession payments. Hay, no friend to the worker, complained that the company's disregard of worker welfare was exacerbating political tensions, writing that the PDQ "appear to be generally inept in their dealings with local labor and the local government."[105]

But this neglect raised the political stakes around worker welfare, and turned a local dispute about working conditions into a regional matter that involved multiple governments and geopolitical interests. Sheikh Ali, ruler of Qatar, made a special visit to the PDQ operations that year to monitor the working conditions and living quarters for Qatari workers. Having returned from a trip to neighboring Saudi Arabia, where the sheikh's counterpart, Saud, had in 1946 insisted on parity of wages and accommodations between local and foreign workers, the Qatari ruler drew sharp comparisons in his formal complaints to the British government between the housing provided to local workers at the Saudi labor camp of ARAMCO and the dilapidated huts supplied to his subjects at the oil fields in Dukhan.

In his second 1951 report, Audsley again focused on the bodily welfare of workers. He noted that the mud or coir-matting shacks offered little protection against the crushing heat of the summer months, sandstorms that blew through the desert, and rats that multiplied in the encampment. Eight or more men were assigned to each small coir-matting hut. Meanwhile, Indian and Pakistani workers were housed in two-man rooms with solid walls or military-grade tents. The only local workers who were assigned bunks in concrete rooms were the small proportion classed as "artisans" and considered skilled. The PDQ's internal correspondence recorded that 100 percent of local artisans had walled shelter, while unskilled workers were housed in coir huts or tents.[106]

Audsley's second report also included a scathing critique of the PDQ's attitude toward the lodging problem and inadequacy of its plan to make improvements, and found the company's proposal for housing Qatari workers in small concrete blocks of eight rooms, with each room measuring twelve by sixteen feet and meant to sleep four men, with no outdoor sleeping space for the summer months, utterly inadequate.

> I recorded my extreme surprise when told that at Dukhan four men were to be accommodated in each room. . . . I drew attention to the space needed for four beds and the limited ventilation, and I expressed with some emphasis my opinion that it was disgraceful to compel four men to sleep and live in such a small space. . . . [I]n effect the company intend to allocate four Arabs to an area now providing sleeping space for only two Indians or Pakistanis.[107]

The company countered that providing permanent housing would result in a "considerable housing surplus" at the end of the development period. This argument foreshadowed the justifications provided by the Qatari government half a century later to explain its delayed construction of adequate housing facilities for workers. Nonetheless, the company implemented an improvement plan in 1953, somewhat ameliorated by Audsley's evaluation. Local hires, though, never saw the inside of the newly built concrete rooms. All new indoor sleeping spaces were allocated to foreign workers.[108]

The Qatari ruler, chafing at the politically problematic inequities justified through the skill classification system, pressed the PDQ through the British political officer to offer vocational training to Qatari workers. Oil companies throughout the region had created training programs to develop a local skill base that could support operations over the long term.[109] In Qatar, however, the PDQ was slow to act, and Audsley's assistant, F. C. Mason, in a 1952 official brief, described the training program it finally set up in response to British government pressure as mere "window-dressing," with a technical component that was "equivalent to a craft lesson in an English primary school."[110]

PROTESTS, POLITICAL CONTROL, AND THE KAFALA SYSTEM

The inequities in pay, working conditions, and lodging documented in Audsley's reports quickly became a source of political contention and unrest.[111] At the inauguration of the Umm Saïd Terminal in Dukhan in February 1950,

amid the fanfare of the first shipment of oil from its gates, al-Mana, labor sup-
plier, middleman, and dispenser of nationality chits for the PDQ, delivered
an impassioned speech criticizing the PDQ's housing and pay policies and
calling for better conditions for Qatari laborers. "They, being the sons of soil
under development, deserve, more than the others employed, the Company's
special consideration."[112] Within a month of al-Mana's speech, Qatar saw the
first labor strike of its modern history. Laborers in Dukhan and Umm Saïd
held a one-day work stoppage in response to the oil company's announcement
that it would replace a portion of its Arab workforce with Indians, along with
complaints about insufficient rations.

The strike was quickly resolved through a negotiation between the British
Political Office and ruler of Qatar (who had appealed personally to slaveown-
ers pleading with them to send the people they held as slaves back to work),
but it marked the beginning of a decade of labor unrest and political turbulence in Qatar. By the end of that decade, the protests, which cut deeply into
the Qatari share of oil revenues, would drive transformations in the regulatory
structure that governed labor.[113] They spurred the Qatari government to formally define who was Qatari and who was a foreigner, and pass new laws that
codified the rights of workers in each category. Most significant, the regulatory
changes that the protests drove would culminate in the development and codification of the kafala system that would shape the structure of the country's
labor force for the next fifty years.

In its regulatory reforms and the kafala system that those reforms would
produce, the government would carry forward many of the understandings
associated with skill, especially the distinction between the rights applied
to skilled and unskilled workers used in its recruitment and employment of
workers. But the regulations, passed in response to the labor protests that for
over a decade threatened the emir's hold on power, would shift the narrow
view of freedom, subjectivity, and bodily welfare used for local hires, who had
been characterized as unskilled workers, onto foreign workers, who had been
previously classed as skilled and thus afforded rights to full political personhood. By the end of this period of political unrest and regulatory codification,
foreign workers' rights had been stripped down to humane bodily treatment,
and the workers themselves came to be regarded as unskilled, irrespective
of their actual ability. The rights of local workers were enlarged to include
agency, aspiration, and freedom of contract, and locals were given the status
of skilled employees, even when they had little skill at all.

After the jolt of that first labor strike in Dukhan, frequent but short-lived
work stoppages over pay, working conditions, and accommodations followed,
causing production at the PDQ to sputter. In June 1951, the simmering labor
actions escalated into outright revolt on the oil fields and a general strike
that shut down the entire country. The protests were precipitated by a large
increase in the number of Dhofaris, workers from present-day Oman, that

al-Mana had recruited for the PDQ, providing them with nationality chits that allowed them to be hired as local subjects of the emir. The British had recruited Dhofaris as police, and used the Dhofari force to put down protests.[114] When Dhofaris were hired at the PDQ, workers saw it as a threat—the equivalent of incorporating security forces into their ranks. In response, nine hundred Qatari workers in Um Saïd struck, demanding the immediate deportation of the Dhofaris. Doha, by then a growing town of some twelve thousand residents, shut down in a general strike in support of the workers.[115] Merchants in the capital shuttered their stores, and Souk Wakif, the bustling commercial center of town that had operated continuously throughout the turbulence of the rise and then painful fall of the pearling industry, went dead.[116]

The strike was escalating into a national rebellion. To end it, the emir took an unprecedented step and deported the Dhofaris en masse. This action would be the first time that the emir would draw a line that excluded residents from the region from among subjects. It would be the beginning of the definition of who was Qatari and who was not.

The emir's concession to the protesters also marked the first time that the government of Qatar would deport workers from its territory, and the first time that the Qatari government would deny those defined as foreign the right to work and reside in Qatar.[117]

Still, strikes continue to flare: in 1951, over the working conditions for oil company drivers; in 1952, over pay and lodging, and the inequities in the treatment of and pay for local as well as foreign workers; and the following September, in a massive strike of two thousand workers over wages and the company's announced plan to charge local workers, but not foreign recruits, for their meals. Clashes erupted in Doha's marketplace, spreading through the city, and Ronald Cochrane's police force used British-issued rifles to put down the skirmishes.[118] In one way or another, these strikes all took aim at the regulatory structures that governed hiring and employment in the oil sector and Qatar. The persistent unrest, and the threat it represented both to the oil company's revenues and the emir's hold on power, compelled the emir and PDQ to renegotiate the terms under which local and foreign workers, skilled and unskilled, would be employed.

The most significant change that the protests caused was the manumission of enslaved persons in Qatar. During the roiling months of 1951, when the oil company and emir were negotiating the renewal of the oil concession, Sheikh Ali protested that he needed additional revenues to provide for his subjects and quiet the complaints of rival factions of the royal family, who felt that were not receiving the share of the benefits from the oil concession due to them. The Qatari elites provided political and material support to the protesting workers as a means to apply pressure on the sheikh for greater annuities. But they also backed the labor actions because an increase in wages for local workers meant an increase in the revenue that they could confiscate from the enslaved men they sent to work as laborers to the oil fields of Dhukkan and dredging flats near the port of Umm Saïd. The oil company, exasperated by the meddling of Qatari brokers and royal hangers-on like al-Mana, and chafing at the bad press it received from organizations such as the British Anti-Slavery Society, demanded that the sheikh provide a guarantee, as part of the concession renewal agreement, that no slaves were enlisted as company employees.[119]

The following April, Sheikh Ali finally conceded the issue and published a decree freeing all enslaved persons in the territory.[120] The decree compensated owners for manumitted slaves at a rate of fifteen hundred rupees for each person—an amount that made many enslavers wealthy and far outstripped the wages that they appropriated from the enslaved men they sent to work for the oil company. Six hundred and sixty enslaved persons were freed, and slavery was declared illegal in Qatar.[121]

The abolition of slavery did little, however, to improve day-to-day working conditions for local workers, even those recently manumitted, and did not rectify the discrepancy in pay and treatment between local and foreign workers. Wildcat strikes and equipment sabotage continued to roil the operations of the oil company and foreign construction firms set up to build the infrastructure for oil extraction.[122]

To narrow the gap between working conditions for local and foreign workers, international companies found a way to sidestep the British era regulations that mandated high wages and good working conditions for recruits from the Indian subcontinent. They used a loophole—one that was somewhat irregular and only marginally legal—to maneuver around formal recruitment channels. According to the regulatory framework governing emigration from India, local merchants and businesses already operating in Qatar could get leave from the political agent to bypass the Indian Emigration Act and recruit Indians without a formal foreign service agreement. For a "commission fee," they could obtain a no objection certificate (NOC), authorizing them to import one or more named migrants on the condition that they would act as the migrant's legal and financial sponsor. While most NOCs were obtained on the basis of the proposed expansion of local businesses, few of the immigrants recruited in this way ended up employed in the shops and restaurants that had petitioned for their entry to the Gulf. In practice, many immigrants paid their sponsor an agreed-on sum on arrival and subsequently applied for work with the oil company or in related businesses.

By the 1950s, the use of this loophole had become standard practice, and recruiting labor through NOCs and sponsorship had grown into the dominant pathway to hire foreign labor. India's independence in 1947 weakened the recruitment channel between the Gulf and subcontinent, but the war in Palestine in 1948–49 created a new pool of potential migrant labor. Workers from the Levant were brought to Qatar under the sponsorship system that grew out of NOCs.[123] Large companies, especially the construction companies that were building the infrastructure for oil exploitation, relied on this ad hoc sponsorship system to import foreign workers to meet labor needs that were quickly outstripping those of the oil industry.[124] This improvised sponsorship system would lay the groundwork for the modern kafala system, with its own NOC provisions, that the Qatari government would set up in the years to follow.

Still, workers continued to agitate throughout the 1950s, and with each strike, the difference in treatment between local and foreign workers became more of a lightning rod. The strikes escalated in intensity, and by 1955, the police force could no longer control agitation by Qatari workers. Qatari drivers in Dukhan and Umm Saïd walked off the job, and took the company cars. In Umm Saïd, the workers forced the oil company staff members to leave their offices and then cut off the utilities. The strike was only quelled when Sheikh Ali intervened, and pressed the oil company to address Qatari workers' grievances over housing as well as the quality of food and water. The following year, as Pan-Arabism captured the imagination of the region and anti-British sentiment sharpened after Gamal Nasser nationalized the Suez Canal in July 1956, the strikes seemed as if they might merge with larger popular and antimonarchical movements in the region. Palestinian and Egyptian workers, recruited as teachers, clerks, and government staff, swelled the local protest movement. They added their organizing efforts to the labor mobilization, forming social clubs and underground activist organizations that promoted the Pan-Arab and Nasserite leftist politics that connected political networks throughout the region.[125] In August, two thousand workers shut down operations in Dukhan and Umm Saïd, and marched on Doha waving Egyptian flags and shouting anti-British slogans. In October, workers attempted to bulldoze the oil pipelines that had been laid down.[126] The protests were eventually put down by the police and the emir's personal security service, and the police force was expanded. That same year, the government began inserting a ban on political activity into all labor contracts.

Tamping down the unrest became a matter of political survival for the rulers of Qatar. At the end of 1960, Sheikh Ali, politically weakened by the protests, stepped aside after an assassination attempt in Lebanon, reportedly ordered by a rival faction of the royal family. His son Ahmed bin Ali Al-Thani took the throne, with his cousin Khalifa bin Hamad Al-Thani taking the position of heir apparent. Both Ahmed and Khalifa expressed interest in changing the national composition of the population, and sought British support to recruit more "pacific" residents. During a consultation with the political resident, Sheikh Ahmed conveyed his concern about the large number of foreigners in Qatar, especially Palestinians, and told the British representative that he was keen to reduce the amount. His heir, Khalifa, was perhaps more pragmatic, and conferred with the political resident about how Arabs might be replaced by "quieter and more reliable people," namely Indians and Pakistanis.[127]

The first step in this process was to define who was Qatari. A law passed in 1961 assigned citizenship to anyone who had settled in Qatar before 1930.[128] Those who qualified as Qatari citizens received an array of subsidies and benefits. Qataris were guaranteed public sector employment, and members of the royal family were given lucrative administrative posts. The government also underwrote housing and land purchases through a major state housing program that became one of the main avenues for the state redistribution of oil revenues. A battery of laws was passed in the 1960s to give Qatari citizens significant commercial advantages. The new regulations required foreign firms to place orders through Qatari merchants, foreign real estate purchases were banned, and foreign firms wishing to do business in Qatar had to form a partnership with a Qatari company in which the local firm had to have at least 51 percent ownership. By the end of the decade, a thick line had been drawn across a population that had long been multinational and multiethnic, dividing foreigners from nationals, but also dividing the varied Arab subjects of the emir into those who were able to document that they had been in Qatar since 1930 and would be defined as Qatari, and those who would henceforth be defined as foreigners.

Those whom the law defined as foreigners were subject to an array of new restrictions. Qatar's first labor code, the Labor Act of 1962, specified that henceforth foreigners required a work permit issued by the government of Qatar to work in the country.[129] In a holdover from the original concession agreement, the act suggested preferential treatment for groups that had been included under the broad definition of the sheikh's subjects, specifying that employers could hire foreigners only if "no qualified nationals or Arabs are available." The 1963 Alien Act, which governed the entry and residence of foreigners, was enacted months after the Labor Act on the heels of a popular uprising during which oil workers shut down production for three weeks. The Alien Act radically tightened the control of foreign workers and required them to register with the Ministry of Interior. It also authorized the "deportation of any alien whose presence poses a threat to the security of the State, internal and external safety, economy, public health, morals, or becomes a burden on the State."[130]

The Alien Act specified that residence and work permits were coequal, and the right to reside in Qatar could not be separated from the right to work there. It layered restrictions onto the employment relationship that magnified the power that the employer had over the foreign worker. The Alien Act formalized the sponsorship relationship, which until the act's passage, had been an informal—though widespread—adaptation of Indian regulations on emigration. Sponsorship, in general practice and widely understood, was not explicitly defined in the act, yet the law pointed to the sponsor's responsibility for the foreigner's actions and underscored that the sponsor could revoke sponsorship "for any reason whatsoever."

The act also affirmed the sponsor's ownership of the worker's labor, specifying that a sponsor could send "his alien worker to another work owner" for up to six months (Article 19, section a). With its references to the "work owner" as a person who was distinct from the worker, the act gave the sponsor full property rights over the worker's labor for the duration of the sponsorship contract. And with this, the Alien Act turned a bureaucratic sponsorship tie into the modern-day kafala system, in which the foreign worker was bound to his sponsor.

Thus with the passage of the Alien Act, the Qatari government formally transposed the relations of bondage that had overlaid the employment of local hires—through enslavement, indenture, and the racketeering of Qatari labor brokers—onto workers defined as foreign recruits. The conditions of work and situations of bondage were once again equated with nationality, but this time it was foreign workers who were subjected to institutional mechanisms of control. Qatari workers were pulled into public sector work, into jobs that were higher status, with generous wages and subsidies. In the kafala system that the Alien Act formalized, only Qatari nationals could work without being bonded to their employers, in jobs where they could enact a broad expression of subjectivity, one where well-being was not just limited to freedom from bodily injury.

Bonding Workers for Economic Expansion

On September 1, 1971, Qatar declared its independence as a nation, ending British protection and with it British jurisdiction over residents not deemed subjects of the Emir.[131] Sheikh Khalifa, who seized power from his cousin Sheikh Ahmed when he was away on a hunting trip in Iran in the following year, nationalized Qatar's oil industry and plowed oil revenues into massive infrastructure investments. Between 1973 and 1981, Qatar's capital expenditures rose by close to 200 percent. Qatar under Sheikh Khalifa laid down new roads, new sewer lines and desalination plants, new communications lines, and new industrial and commercial buildings. The government invested in factories for industrial activities complementary to oil extraction, such as petrochemicals, chemical fertilizer, natural gas liquids, cement, and steel.[132]

The labor demands involved in these investments were significant. The number of foreign workers jumped by 50% between 1970 and 1975, growing from 40,000 to 61,000 workers. Over the next decade, as development plans picked up steam, the numbers grew exponentially. In 1986, the next year data were available, there were an estimated 180,000 foreigners working in Qatar, or a 300 percent increase over 1975. The proportion of workers in Qatar that were foreigners, already 83 percent in 1970, expanded to 89 percent in 1986.[133]

The country's economic growth hinged on ready access to foreign labor. The government doubled down on the regulatory framework it had developed in the 1960s to import and control migrant workers. Whenever geopolitical events or fluctuations in oil prices threatened its ability to source foreign labor, the government tightened the relations of bondage it had legislated in the Alien Act of 1962. In its response to financial and geopolitical crises that threatened Qatar's development ambitions, the government responded, time and again, by increasing the control that employers had over their workers, endowing them with the power to prohibit workers from leaving their jobs or even leaving the country. The hardening restrictions carried forward the notion that relations of bondage that did not violate bodily welfare and cause physical harm were acceptable, and even necessary, for economic development.

In 1984, after struggling for more than a decade with chronic labor shortage that hamstrung the country's economic expansion, the Qatari government revived controls that were reminiscent of the bondage ties that had been in wide use in the pearling industry in an attempt to hold onto the labor it had managed to recruit. Law No. 3, passed that year, reaffirmed that persons intent on entering and working in Qatar must have a sponsor.[134] But for the first time, the law also stipulated that expatriate laborers could not leave the country without their sponsors' permission. The justification for this new measure was rooted in past practice, specifically the use of debt to bond workers through indenture: the sponsor was legally made financially responsible for debts incurred by the sponsored worker, including in some cases the debts incurred to cover the cost of migrating to Qatar, and the foreign worker would remain under the sponsor's control until those debts were cleared. To travel out of Qatar, migrants needed an exit permit, signed by their sponsor in the presence of an official in the Emigration Department. This rule was firmly applied, with releases granted only in exceptional circumstances such as the sponsor dying while abroad without having named a representative or successor.[135] Remarkably, Qatar imposed these exit controls at a time when the Cold War was being litigated in part over the Eastern bloc's restrictions on the exit of its citizens, but the new exit visa system enabled local employers as well as the foreign investors—especially oil and gas companies—that entered Qatar to share in its expansion and retain their workers, even when their employees wanted to quit or change employers.[136]

When global oil prices plunged suddenly in 1986, losing half their value in the first few months of that year, Qatar relied on its newly draconian labor regulations to manage the unexpected yet acute economic downturn it faced as a result. Qatar's natural gas exports softened the drop in oil revenues somewhat, but the landing was still hard. The country lost 40 percent of its oil revenues between 1985 and 1986.[137] Amid stiff global competition, the country's steel and petrochemical investments floundered. With no clear indication that oil revenues would recover, infrastructure plans, including the development of the North Dome gas fields, were shelved. Qatar registered a 20 percent drop in national income.[138] The newly amended sponsorship system allowed employers to fire workers at will and send them back to their countries, and the available evidence suggests that they did—in large numbers.[139] Layoffs in the construction industry in particular, where investments were slashed by 40 percent, were substantial, and close to half the workforce was expelled.[140]

The next time Qatar amended its foreign worker labor laws, it was again responding to a crisis: the 1991 Gulf War. In the early hours of August 2, 1990, the Iraqi army invaded neighboring Kuwait. The occupation was brief; in January 1991, a US-led coalition subjected Iraq to the most intensive air bombardment in military history, and by April, Iraq had signed a cease-fire agreement and withdrawn from Kuwait.

Though quickly and definitely resolved, the war had massive implications for migrant workers in Kuwait and throughout the Gulf. By March 1991, an estimated two million workers had fled the region or been airlifted home by their countries of origin. A million more would follow in the summer and fall.[141] The World Bank estimated the cost of the conflict in lost remittances at $30 billion.[142] About a half-million of the displaced workers were Asian, but the large majority were migrants from neighboring Arab countries, primarily Egypt and Jordan. Most were fleeing conflict, but many were driven out as traitors by the countries that had once welcomed them. The Palestinian population in Kuwait decamped completely during the war, their presence made anathema in Kuwait when the leader of the Palestinian Liberation Organization, Yasser Arafat, pledged his support to Saddam Hussein.[143] Close to a million Yemeni workers left Saudi Arabia after Yemen refused to condemn the invasion of Kuwait.[144] Gulf countries that before the war had adopted an "Arabs first" policy turned instead to Asian workers and instituted greater controls, such as new identification cards, for those who were allowed in.[145]

During the conflict, Qatar's domestic intelligence services tightened their grip. The country experienced little internal protest against the war, but the government regarded its Arab population as a possible source of instability. A significant number of Palestinian residents, including prominent businessmen and civil servants, were expelled in 1991, and many Shia were placed under augmented surveillance as potential subversives.[146]

Arab workers had become less desirable in the region, and more Gulf countries turned to Asia for labor. Qatar struggled to source and retain Asian migrants as it was now competing with its Gulf neighbors. To make matters worse, thousands of Asian migrants sought to return home as the crisis continued. To retain their workers, employers invoked their right to withhold the exit visas that migrants needed to leave the territory.[147] This widespread reliance on exit visas to prevent migrants from fleeing a conflict that many worried would spread past Kuwait discouraged new migration.[148] So acute were the labor shortages that the natural gas exploitation in Qatar's North Field, launched with great fanfare by Sheikh Khalifa on the twentieth anniversary of Qatar's independence, suffered from significant operational delays due to a lack of manpower.[149]

In 1992, with oil well fires in Kuwait still polluting Doha's air, the government instituted a new law—Act No. 14—to bring the recruitment of foreign workers under direct government control. The law separated recruitment from sponsorship and stipulated that a sponsor recruiting workers or an agent acting on behalf of a sponsor had to obtain a license approved by the Ministry of Internal Affairs, the security arm of the state, authorizing them to import workers into Qatar. Employers were explicitly prohibited from importing workers outside this new system. The act also specified that labor recruiters were required to keep detailed records of their activities that would be subject to periodic inspection.

The management of Qatar's foreign labor force was explicitly framed as a national security matter. By determining which agents would be given recruitment licenses and monitoring contracts for third-party recruitment, the state was able to dictate the size of the labor force and intervene muscularly when the country faced potential labor shortages. It was able to monitor and control the makeup of its labor force, ensuring that no nationality became dominant and nationalities the Qatari state viewed as troublesome remained small. The state collected ever more granular information about migrant workers under this new system, but it also became more jealous of the data it tabulated. The government withdrew data on the nationality of migrants from the public domain. No numbers on the proportion of nonlocal Arabs in the migrant population are available from Qatar's statistical authorities for any time after 1992. Workers were doubly bound: first, to the state through its monitoring and control of recruitment, and then to their sponsors through employment.

SKILL AND THE ASIAN EXCEPTION

On the edges of this regulatory model, another pattern of labor importation emerged—one that was not based on the same ties of bondage and restriction. It operated alongside yet separately from the kafala system, in large part because it was premised on a view of worker skill and rights that could not be reconciled with the kafala system. Workers brought in through this alternate regulatory path were treated contractually as a skill resource that companies needed to cultivate rather than bond and constrain, and as a result, companies using this pathway sought to shelter their workforces from Qatari law.[150] By sidestepping the kafala system, they also highlighted how tightly bound up Qatari labor law was with understandings developed to control workers viewed as unskilled.

Throughout the 1970s and 1980s, East Asian companies were contracted to execute large projects in Qatar and the Gulf more broadly, primarily in construction, or set up and build turnkey factories in energy-intensive industries, like cement or steel. The cost and provision of labor was included in tender offers under a "collective contract." The majority of workers from East Asia, especially those from Korea, Taiwan, and the Philippines, traveled to Qatar in the 1980s as part of contractual packages negotiated with East Asian firms rather than as individual workers who were recruited and bound to a sponsor. Companies recruited workers for these turnkey projects from all over Asia. According to a 1986 study by Sooying Kim of Korean companies operating in the Gulf, a quarter of the workforce in Korean construction companies was sourced from other Asian countries, including India, Thailand, Bangladesh, Indonesia, and others.[151] But regardless of where the workers were from, they were shielded from the kafala system, treated as company assets rather than as workers subject to Qatari law.

While the value of these contracts was large—$40 billion for Korean companies alone in 1981—the proportion of foreign labor in the Gulf that they represented was small.[152] The tally broken down by Gulf country does not exist, but for the region as a whole, foreign labor brought in under these contracts in the 1980s represented about a tenth of all migrant workers. That percentage dropped in the late 1980s and early 1990s, as oil prices continued to slump and East Asian companies moved to other markets.

Still, the contracts were significant because their exception to the kafala model of labor management was based on the representation of workers as skilled, and the turnkey contracts that sheltered employees from kafala restrictions reflected understandings of worker rights and subjectivity associated with skilled workers. These companies explicitly used skill as the rationale to bundle their labor force into project execution agreements, and featured the comparatively higher skill level of their workforces in their project bids.[153] Jung Woo Development Co., the Korean firm that had built the Qatar Steel Plant, marketed itself as delivering "the supply of sophisticated technology and well-trained workmanship" in seeking contracts in Qatar.[154] Sheikh Jassim al Thani, minister of water and electricity, the ministry issuing large construction contracts, confirmed the value of Korean skill in statements during a visit to Korea in 1982: "Based on crude oil revenue, Qatar is undertaking massive development projects for its modernization. And the quick and efficient construction skills have helped us to speed up our modernization projects."[155] Skill assessments of East Asian firms operating in the Gulf suggest that the large majority of workers on the projects were classed as skilled or semiskilled.[156] In Kim's study of Korean companies, the management of those companies reported that only 14 percent of their workers were unskilled. The skill level of workers in Korea was reflective of a national government strategy built around clear incentives for workforce development and training that the Ministry of Labor extended to firms operating abroad.[157]

The bundled contracts negotiated by East Asian companies specified that workers' terms of employment were to be regulated by the laws of the executing company's home country; for example, Korean labor law covered workers employed in Korean companies. The regulations and guidelines referenced in the contracts were comprehensive; they addressed a wide array of workplace processes and rights, including health and safety, labor-management relations and grievance processes, job categories, working hours, risk pay, severance allowance, and goals for productivity improvement.[158] In the Qatari context, these regulations were remarkable for the kind of worker subjectivity they suggested; the regulatory frameworks addressed workers' contributions, aspirations, and voices at the companies that employed them.

While East Asian companies emphasized the skill of their workforce in their contractual negotiations, data published in the 1980s indicates that the labor force in Qatar as a whole was far from uniformly unskilled. Occupational estimates for the proportion of foreign workers that were unskilled toggles between 45 percent in 1975 and 38 percent for 1985.[159] But the regulatory frameworks that governed their employment tagged them with attributes associated with unskilled workers, irrespective of their actual skill level. The sponsorship system, along with regulations governing recruitment, bound even the most highly skilled worker to their employer and reduced the definition of subjective well-being to bodily welfare.

CONFIRMING BONDAGE

In the dawn hours of June 27, 1995, Sheikh Hamad bin Khalifa Al-Thani, the forty-five-year-old son of Sheikh Khalifa, deposed his father in what was becoming a family tradition for the management of succession. Sheikh Hamad then proceeded to push through changes to modernize the economy and broaden his political base. "We have simply got to reform ourselves," Sheikh Hamad told the *New Yorker* in 2000. "We're living in a modern age. . . . [C]hange, more change, is coming."[160] Hamad ramped up hydrocarbon production and infrastructure investment. He aggressively expanded natural gas extraction—a resource that had been neglected since the 1970s when it was thought be a useless by-product, flared off when recovering oil.[161] In partnership with oil giants like Exxon and Shell, Qatar invested heavily in processing technology to cool the gas into the LNG form, which it could then transport around the world in large thermos-like ships. Qatar also embarked on a bold project to turn natural gas into a clean-burning diesel fuel in a "Gas-to-Liquid" process.[162] Within a decade, Qatar's revenue from natural gas surpassed its oil revenue, and in 2012, the North Dome field was confirmed as the largest proven hydrocarbon reserve in the world. These new revenues were plowed into major investments in infrastructure. After a hiatus in construction during low oil prices, Qatar under Sheikh Hamad launched megaprojects like ports, highways, sports stadiums, and new urban developments on reclaimed land.

Hamad's modernization push, like his predecessor's before him, led, once again, to the exponential growth of expatriate labor in Qatar. The 1997 census counted roughly 385,000 expatriate residents.[163] By 2004, that number had doubled to 605,000, and by 2010, it would more than double once more and reach over 1,456,000.[164] Just as under Sheikh Khalifa, Qatar increased its control over foreign workers as in effort to ensure access to the labor force it needed for its economic expansion. Under Sheikh Hamad's rule, the government consolidated existing regulations and tightened the bondage ties of its kafala system. It modernized the two regulatory pillars on which its kafala system was based, expanding its labor code in 2004, and sharpening its regulation of the entry and residence of foreign workers in 2009.

Just like the previous cycle of reforms under Sheikh Hamid's father, the 2004 law treated the management of migrant labor as a matter of national economic security and brought foreign workers under more direct government control.[165] It instituted new reporting requirements for the employment of Qatari and foreign workers. Employers were required to supply full employment rolls to the ministry every six months, compiling names, genders, nationalities, job descriptions, remuneration, and all work permit details in their submissions. These provisos had the effect of funneling voluminous data about the labor market to the ministry. The reporting requirements were paired with new clauses in the laws that gave the government—now collecting data to survey the use of labor in great detail—full discretion over all employment decisions. The code stipulated that all new hires, whether Qatari or foreign, required the ministry's approval and permission for employment could be revoked at any time.

The new law also weakened or dismantled many of the protections that the 1962 labor law had instituted. The revised law removed any reference to a minimum wage, which the 1962 law had addressed in some detail. Similarly, the rights of workers to organize and bargain collectively, quite limited in the 1962 law but available to all workers, were confined in the 2004 law to Qatari workers only. The only form of worker organization that Qatari workers were allowed to participate in under the new code were "worker committees," and those were only permitted in establishments with more than a hundred Qatari employees and were to operate under the supervision of the relevant ministry (Article 118). For all intents and purposes, the law outlawed all forms of worker voice.

In lieu of these protections, the 2004 law created narrow grievance and arbitration procedures, housed in the Ministry of Civil Service and Housing Affairs, and later moved to the Ministry of Labor. The law stipulated that the ministry would adjudicate complaints from workers regarding the violations of the rights granted to them in the labor code. As extensively documented by Andrew Gardner, Silvia Pessoa, and Laura Harkness in a 2014 study, however, these procedures were in practice entirely inaccessible to foreign workers, even when their cases were presented and backed by their embassies.[166]Whereas the 2004 law increased the government's control of labor, the 2009 law strengthened the control that sponsors could exercise over their workers.[167]

Law No. 4 regarding Regulations of Expatriates Entry, Departure, Residence, and Sponsorship in the 2009 code not only reinforced the requirement that all foreigners in Qatar, with few exceptions—clearly identified in the law— were required to have a sponsor but also specified that the sponsor was the employer. The law confirmed the sponsor's authority over the foreign worker's right to enter and reside in Qatar as well as the foreigner's ability to leave the country, which required an exit visa signed by the sponsor. The law gave the sponsor full latitude to terminate the sponsorship agreement, which required the foreigner to leave Qatar, but did not recognize the worker's right to sever the sponsorship tie. The only recourse the law afforded to the worker, available only in instances of mistreatment or abuse, was to petition the Ministry of Interior to transfer the sponsorship tie or issue an exit visa.

The 2009 law also formalized the sponsor's property rights over their foreign employees' labor. The law confirmed the sponsor's legal right to lend their foreign employees to other employers for periods of up to six months or outside regular working hours. The law permitted the sponsorship tie to be transferred to another employer at the end of a contract, if and only if the sponsor assented and provided a NOC—an updated version of the "no objection certificate" that had been the early model for the sponsorship encoded in Qatar's kafala system. In the absence of a NOC, the law required the foreigner to leave the country immediately at the end of a contract, and banned them from returning to Qatar for two years, if the contract termination was amicable, or four, if the sponsor terminated the contract for cause. In this way, the sponsor's control of their foreign employees' ability to commodify their labor extended past the duration of the actual employment contract. The law specified the enforcement measures that the government could use to ensure compliance, outlining financial penalties and detention, and underscoring that the Ministry of Interior in any case retained the right to repatriate any foreigner deemed "a threat to [Qatar's] internal or external security and safety or . . . otherwise detrimental to the national economy, public health and public order."[168]

Between 2004 and 2009, when these crucial labor laws were written, Qatar's real GDP growth clocked in at an impressive 17 percent annually, outstripping China's by a wide margin, and the growth of its construction industry was outstanding, increasing at an average of 60 percent a year in 2006, 2007, and 2008.[169] Qatar relied on the restrictive regulatory framework as laid out in these two laws to control, retain, and govern the migrant workers it needed to staff its accelerated expansion. Together, the laws bonded workers to their sponsors, preventing them from quitting their jobs, seeking alternate employment, or leaving the country without their sponsor's permission. The laws also ripped out the floor on working conditions, removing any minimum wage protection or protection against being let out to other employers, confirming a ban on collective action, and narrowing avenues for redress. For all practical purposes, workers were at the mercy of their sponsor, to whom they were bonded by law.

This severe iteration of the kafala system was the regulatory framework that governed foreign workers in Qatar when the kingdom was awarded the World Cup hosting rights in 2010. With few exceptions, the laws covered all foreign workers, irrespective of industry, occupation, or skill level. The laws were the product of more than a century of global economic exchange. They reflected and recorded beliefs developed through those international engagements about the association between skill categories and political rights, and most pointedly, the political rights that unskilled workers were entitled to. In much the same way, the international advocacy efforts that the World Cup decision would set in motion also reflected beliefs about unskilled workers and the scope of their political rights. The global public conversation about the rights of migrant workers, sparked by the lurid press coverage of the conditions of migrant workers in Qatar, would itself reproduce definitions of rights that were developed to control workers classed as unskilled. It would reinforce a chain of meanings about workers and their rights that was built on a series of equivalences: the equivalence between bondage and being unskilled, followed by the equivalence of being unskilled and being limited to bodily existence, with subjectivity reduced from political freedom to bodily welfare. This chain of associations would ultimately inform what kind of regulatory impact global advocacy had in Qatar, and the ways in which those regulatory reforms would once again equate exploitation with the vulnerability of the unskilled.

Skill and Bondage before the First Ball Is Kicked

After Qatar won the World Cup hosting rights in 2010 and the first investigative reports by human rights organizations on working conditions in Qatar were released, the media headlines became unrelenting. The international press, from the BBC to CNN to the *New York Times*, called out "World Cup Slavery," decried "Death and Servitude in Qatar," ran exposés on Qatar's "squalid labor camps," and chronicled the rates of worker death and injury.[170] In response, Blatter, the president of FIFA, issued a statement about the working conditions and Qatar's intention to improve them: "I am convinced that Qatar is taking the situation very seriously. These very discussions about Qatar show just what an important role football can play in generating publicity, and thus, bring about change." His deputy, Theo Zwanziger, added that FIFA would work with the Qatari government to implement "concrete measures" for reform. "The international community must also accept its responsibility," he emphasized.[171]

To staunch the press coverage of labor violations in Qatar and protect the image of the World Cup—already sullied by accusations of corruption, including generous kickbacks, in the decision to award Qatar the World Cup hosting rights—the Qatari government took steps to improve conditions for workers in Qatar.[172] The reforms that Qatar instituted over the next several years— under Sheikh Tamim, Hamad's son and successor—would lead to the gradual dismantling of the worst aspects of the kafala system. Workers would be able to leave the country without their sponsor's permission and without an exit visa as well as change jobs after a specified contractual period, and would be granted minimum wages protections.

The reforms demonstrated just how enduring two key notions continued to be: that unskilled workers deserved fewer rights, and the rights that they did have were considered coequal with their bodily welfare. In their design and implementation, the reforms doubled down on the narrow conception of rights historically afforded to workers considered unskilled. The reforms focused on improving and protecting the bodily welfare of workers, and expanded past a concern with the bodies of workers only when the needs and rights of workers classed as skilled were taken up in the global discussion over labor rights in Qatar.

WORKER WELFARE ON THE BODY

In a first step toward reform, the Qatar Foundation, the quasi-governmental foundation responsible for the construction of the Education City district in Doha as well as an array of high-profile cultural buildings, and the Supreme Committee for Delivery and Legacy, the quasi-governmental organization responsible for building the World Cup facilities, issued new voluntary worker welfare codes in late 2013 and early 2014, respectively.[173] The handbooks they issued were loosely patterned on the codes of conduct used by international clothing and sporting goods companies like Nike and H&M to promote labor standards among the producers in their supply chains.[174] Like those international codes of conduct, the Qatar Foundation and Supreme Committee requested that the companies they contracted with pledge to comply with the standards detailed in their codes, and suggested that noncompliance could be grounds for the termination of a contract, although this proved to be a threat that was not acted on.

The documents purportedly covered all employees hired by the contractor, including managerial staff, but the standards they outlined focused on construction workers, implicitly unskilled, and laid out the "minimum mandatory requirements" for their physical welfare. The standards restricted their discussion of worker rights to contractors' legal obligation to abide by the labor code and pay their workers the wages due to them, and included no standards that addressed worker voice or grievance procedures. The standards did, however, deal with the bodily needs of workers in great detail, laying out minute specifications for their lodging and feeding. In their attention to the bodily treatment and condition of workers, the standards drew a straight line from the manumission reports produced by British gunships patrolling the Gulf at the end of the nineteenth century, with their emphasis on bodily proof of abuse, through Audsley's reports on the lodging and feeding of unskilled workers employed by the British oil concession, themselves patterned on earlier British government inspections of condition of indenture, through to present-day Qatar.

The "worker welfare" standards, as they were called in both documents, itemized the conditions required for the maintenance of a worker's body. They indicated the size and layout that living and sleeping areas for workers should display, specifying the area per person (6 meters squared) and maximum number of beds per room (four), but also the height of the beds off the floor (0.3 meters) and number of light fixtures per bed (one). The criteria for bathing and toilet rooms were also enumerated: the standards laid out the minimum ratio of urinals to toilets (two to one), number of washbasins and showers (one for every four people), height of the mirrors (eye level at the two-thirds' line of the mirror), and even in the Supreme Committee standards, water flow for toilet flushes (six liters). The standards for the dining area and kitchen were likewise laid out in detail, but the standards' emphasis on the bodies of workers was most evident in the specifications for the diet fed to them. The standards issued by the Supreme Committee indicated that the contractor should provide a rotating menu of three meals a day that supply sufficient calories and are appropriate to the ethnic mix of the workers. The Qatar Foundation standards took the specifications a step further and itemized a set of nutritional recommendations that the contractor was directed to follow in the provision of somewhere between three and four thousand calories a day. These included minutiae such as the cooking method (grilling or baking as opposed to frying), fat composition of the coconut milk used (low fat as opposed to cream), variety of rice (long grain), preparation of meat (removal of visible fat before cooking), and other directives.

In April 2014, DLA Piper, a British law firm, completed an audit commissioned by the Qatari government of the country's regulatory framework as it pertained to labor and specifically as it was applied to the migrant workers in the construction sector.[175] The report was meant to be confidential, but it was widely leaked and would eventually be cited in press and advocacy publications.

Like the Qatari worker welfare codes, the evaluation emphasized the bodily care of migrant workers, and encouraged the government to consider making the compliance with standards for accommodation as well as enhanced health and safety practices a prerequisite for any tender process. But the report also revived another trait long associated with unskilled workers: their vulnerability to employer malfeasance and the resulting need to create mechanisms to monitor employer behavior. With observations that could have been drawn from Audsley's account of the PDQ's employment practices in the 1940s and

1950s, the report called out employer misconduct, and suggested that the root of labor violations in Qatar was not the sponsorship system and its restrictions on worker freedoms but rather the inherent vulnerability of workers who were unskilled to the bad behavior of employers, who in their mistreatment of workers, were, in this narrative, clearly violating laws that were designed to protect the welfare of the unskilled. DLA Piper recommended increased inspections of worksites and housing facilities, along with the imposition of criminal sanctions for noncompliance with worker welfare codes. It also recommended two additional measures to protect workers from employer misconduct and increase transparency about employer behavior: the electronic payment of wages directly to worker bank accounts to allow the government to verify whether or not workers had been paid, and that the government shift the authority to grant an exit visa from the employer to the government so as to make it more difficult for employers to retain employees in Qatar against their will.

Perhaps because it was commissioned by the government and recommended reforms were already in place in neighboring Gulf countries, the report was influential. In August 2015, with the passage of Law No. 1 of that year, the Qatari government created a wage protection system, modeled on systems in the United Arab Emirates and Saudi Arabia, that required all firms to register by November of that year and pay their employees through electronic transfers to Qatari banks and in Qatari riyals.[176]

Later that year, in November 2015, with Qatar facing several formal complaints to international bodies, including a complaint to the ILO that Qatar's sponsorship system facilitated "forced labor," and a complaint from the Nepali government to FIFA regarding the fact that its nationals were refused exit to tend to their wounded and dead after the devastating Nepali earthquake of April 2015, the government passed a revised law on the entrance, exit, and residence of foreign workers. The new regulation, Law No. 21 of 2015, which went into effect late the following year, replaced the 2009 law, and though it largely replicated the previous version, it included two important reforms to the sponsorship system that were billed as interventions to eradicate employer malfeasance.[177]

The first reform created a mechanism for the government supervision of exit visas. The new law required that the Ministry of the Interior be informed of a migrant's desire to leave the country at least three days before the date of exit. It preserved the sponsor's authority to approve exit visas for their employees, but created a grievance mechanism for workers if their sponsor denied them the ability to leave and codified the Ministry of Interior's authority to override an employer's refusal to grant an exit visa. The second reform, announced but only implemented at the end of 2020 as part of an additional package of reforms, removed the requirement that workers secure their sponsor's approval to change employers at the end of their contract through the issue of a NOC. Previously, workers who couldn't secure a NOC had to leave Qatar immediately at the end of their contract and wait two years to return to work for another employer. Under the reformed law, workers would be permitted to change employers at the end of the contract contingent on approval from the Ministry of Labor and Social Affairs along with an undefined "competent authority." Workers on contracts who did not have defined time limits—so-called unlimited contracts—would still have to wait five years into their employment before they were eligible to appeal to their employers and the Ministry of Labor and Social Affairs to change jobs.

These reforms retained elements of bondage from the kafala system, but just as previous reforms had done, they brought the implementation of those controls under state supervision. The Ministry of Interior now supervised the allocation of exit visas and the changes in sponsorship that a change in employers required. Although the new law replaced the term "sponsor" with "recruiter," it not only preserved all the basic features of the sponsorship system but also enabled the government to manage and control Qatar's foreign labor force more directly.

Despite the fact that the reforms did not meaningfully change the sponsorship framework, they initially received global praise. The BBC announced a story on the changes with a headline that read "Qatar Abolishes Controversial 'Kafala' Labour System."[178] The ITUC, which had lobbied for the changes, called the reforms a "genuine breakthrough." Human rights organizations generally described the reforms as promising. The optimism about the reforms quickly dissipated, however, as investigations in Qatar showed that the conditions affecting the bodily welfare of workers had barely changed. In March 2016, Amnesty International released a report on labor violations in the building of the Khalifa stadium. The report cataloged instances of late or nonpayment of wages as well as the denial of exit visas, and also featured the "squalid" and "substandard" living conditions for workers that were "in clear breach of the [Supreme Committee] Worker Welfare Standards."[179] That same month, a delegation of ILO inspectors conducted a fact-finding trip in response to a formal complaint that was filed, and the delegation reported that the labor accommodations it visited did not "satisfy by far the minimum standards, with most accommodation housing ten to 12 workers per small room, unhygienic and poor kitchen and sanitary facilities."[180] International advocates also generally acknowledged that two newer labor accommodations, Labor City and Bawra al Baraha—large complexes built to lodge workers—complied with the higher humanitarian standards set out in the various worker welfare codes in use in Qatar, but evaluations noted the ways they were still inadequate, such as the lack of natural light.[181]

In these assessments, the focus was almost solely on the body. The impact of Qatar's sponsorship system and effectiveness of the reforms were considered only as they applied to workers who were viewed as unskilled, and as a consequence, labor rights were simply equated with bodily welfare. The reform's failure to address the rights that would allow workers to claim full subjectivity and freedom—the right to change employers at will, organize, and physical mobility—received less attention.

The fact that the bondage of the Qatari regulatory structure also applied to workers characterized as skilled received no attention at all in the global debates about labor reforms in Qatar. White-collar workers—executives, managers, engineers, professors, and doctors—were all employed under the same labor law as blue-collar construction workers and manual laborers. They were subject to the kafala system's constraints: they required a sponsor, who was their employer; they could not leave the country at will; and they could not quit or change jobs without approval. They also experienced a range of labor violations that the sponsorship system often produced, from the nonpayment of wages through outright bondage. And their subjugation to the sponsorship system was arguably more extended given that unlimited contracts—which under the reform, required a five-year commitment before the employee could petition for a change of employer—were almost exclusively used for white-collar workers.

REFORMS FOR THE UNSKILLED AND REFORMS FOR THE SKILLED

Under continued international pressure, especially the ongoing ILO monitoring of conditions in Qatar, the government continued to implement reforms. Over the next four years, the Qatari government would strip the kafala system of most of the elements that had reinforced migrants' bondage to their employers. The reforms left untouched the kafala system's core logic that migrants' political rights were contingent on their economic function in the country—a logic that the kafala system shared with most regulatory frameworks governing worker migration around the world. Still, the reforms were substantial, and the ILO assessed them as having "dismantle[d] the kafala system."[182]

The reforms affected the employment relations of workers defined as skilled and unskilled, and hewed closely to the definitions of freedom associated with each skill class. The regulatory changes designed to remove aspects of the kafala system that affected skilled workers came late and reluctantly, ratified only in 2020, after a long slog of incremental changes directed at the working conditions and bodily welfare of workers classed as unskilled. But because the final wave of reforms rolled back regulations that impinged on the subjectivity and expanded quality of freedom associated with skilled workers, they had the most radical effect on the kafala system, stripping it of all the aspects of bondage that still smacked of slavery even as they reaffirmed the tiered capacities for freedom attributed to the skilled and unskilled.

This last phase of regulatory overhaul began in November 2017, when the ILO closed the complaint against Qatar, citing progress on labor protections, and launched a three-year technical cooperation agreement to develop further reforms. Shortly thereafter, Qatar passed a temporary minimum wage law—at 750 riyal a month, or about US$200, less than the minimum mandated by the governments of sending countries like Nepal—and set up a fund to cover wages in documented cases of nonpayment. Issa Saad Al Jafali Al Nuaimi, the Qatari minister of labor and social affairs, said that the aim of the reforms was to "meet the necessary needs of the worker to live at an appropriate humanitarian level."[183] In September of the following year, the Qatari government passed Law No. 13 of 2018, abolishing the need for exit visas and allowing most categories of workers to leave the country at will.[184] When the law went into effect, the ILO tweeted, "Great news! As of today, exit visas no longer needed for the majority of workers in Qatar."[185] What the ILO did not mention in its statements about the reform was that the law permitted employers to require up to 5 percent of their staff to obtain preapproval before traveling. The employees subject to this restriction were those who were considered high value—in other words, those who were classified as highly skilled.

In a reversal that belied the association of bondage with unskilled workers, this Qatari law initially bound skilled workers more tightly to their employers. They were more likely to be contractually bound to their sponsors for longer stretches of time—a minimum of five years in many cases—and less likely to be able to exit the country at will. Even though both skilled and unskilled workers experienced many of the same kinds of labor violations, the bondage of these often highly paid workers was unlikely to be visible on their bodies. And bondage that did not leave marks on the body, even when it was codified in law, was not considered bondage at all. Bondage was understood by international actors like the ILO and even Qatari government to be a condition to which only unskilled workers could be subject, and from which only unskilled workers needed protection. The comments of Issa Saad Al Jafali Al Nuaimi, the minister of administrative development, labor, and social affairs, when the reform was announced implied as much: "The adoption of this law is another step in our continued drive to provide decent work for all migrant workers in Qatar and to ensure their protection."[186] This attention to physical well-being was substituted for attention to broader conceptions of subjectivity and the full ability to exercise freedom.

Although skilled workers were neglected in debates about labor rights in Qatar, they featured prominently for several years in Qatar's strategic planning for its economic development. As early as 2008, the government in its *Qatar National Vision 2030*, the overarching planning document that it issued that year, affirmed the country's ambition to become a "knowledge-based economy," and identified managing "the size and quality of the expatriate labor force" as critical to achieving that goal.[187] The *National Development Strategy* plans that followed—in 2011–16 and 2018–22—both outlined strategies that the government would take to recruit "highly skilled labor capable of competing in the global market."[188] The second development plan, published in the midst of the reforms to the kafala system that Qatar was making in response to international pressure, was emphatic in outlining this goal: "Target 1: Increase the proportion of highly skilled expatriate workers in the labor force to at least 20% by 2022." To reach that goal, the government contemplated several reforms to the labor law and sponsorship system in a bid to attract as well as retain skilled workers. As the plan notes,

> To achieve this outcome, the government will examine the development of a comprehensive recruitment policy and allow highly-skilled expatriate workers in the private sector, particularly in labor-intensive sectors such as construction, whose employment contracts have expired or who have been dismissed, to be moved to other sectors or re-employed after regularization in other suitable and vacant positions as an alternative to recruitment. Strategies should be developed to mitigate the risks of heavy dependence on unskilled expatriate labor.[189]

At the end of 2019, the government announced the planned extension of earlier reforms to the entirety of the labor market. Pending the emir's assent, envisioned for the following January, the exit visa would be abolished for all workers and the NOC requirements would finally be removed, enabling all workers to change jobs after a probationary period. The ILO praised Qatar for its pledge, and Sharan Burrow, ITUC general secretary, heralded the commitment as proof that "Qatar is changing. The new tranche of laws will bring an end to kafala and put in place a modern industrial relations system."

But for the Qatari government, and to some extent, even its international partners in this reformist push, the announced reforms were not about protecting worker rights, which it understood as being limited to the bodily welfare protection afforded to unskilled workers. Instead, these reforms were designed as measures to facilitate the recruitment and retention of skilled workers, and meet the target for the composition of its labor market laid out in the 2018–22 *National Development Strategy*. The minister of administrative development, labor, and social affairs, Yousuf Mohamed al-Othman Fakhroo, speaking on the sidelines of an event celebrating the ILO's centenary, specified that the regulatory reforms were a strategy to make Qatar "an attractive place for investors, for skilled workers."[190] The text of the new labor codes themselves also reflected this attention to the concerns of skilled workers and their employers. The law that ratified the removal of the NOC requirement (Law No. 18 of 2020) stipulated, for example, that workers whose employment made them "acquainted with employer's clients or business secrets" could be subject to a noncompete clause that prohibited them from securing employment with business competitors for up to a year.[191] The head of the ILO project office for Qatar, Houtan Homayounpour, similarly heralded the abrogation of the end of the NOC as a boon for skilled professionals: "The NOC was the last problematic part of the kafala system, this power imbalance that was created between an employee and the sponsor will no longer be there. . . . This will benefit workers, employer and the country. Employers will be able to look for workers that really match the job they have to offer and workers will be able to look for jobs that are more appropriate for them." Meanwhile, he praised the minimun wage reforms as a change that "really ensures a minimum standard of living and working for all workers."[192]

Thus even in its reforms, the Qatari government hewed closely to the difference in the definition of rights, well-being, and subjectivity ascribed to unskilled and skilled workers. The reforms and international interventions that shaped them carried forward as well as reaffirmed the two-tiered definition of freedom developed through global economic exchanges on the Qatari peninsula. Unskilled workers needed to be protected from bodily abuse and forms of bondage. Skilled workers, on the other hand, were valued for their agency and creativity, and the government sought to refine its regulatory frameworks so as to entice skilled workers to come to Qatar, and invest their energy and knowledge in the country's development. It was not that skilled workers were—or had even been—exempt from the subjugation and exploitation that the bondage ties of the kafala system produced. Rather, it was that exploitation was associated with unskilled workers, and so the legal remedies against exploitation were limited to the degraded definitions of freedom—freedom as bodily welfare—to which unskilled workers were supposed to be entitled.

Skill and Bondage, Again

From the day that Qatar won the hosting rights for the 2022 World Cup, the kingdom became a fulcrum in global debates about the rights of workers and migrants. But the debates were not new, and neither was Qatar's place in them. For over a century, Qatari regulations to import and govern vast numbers of foreign workers had been produced and honed through global exchanges, and the meanings encoded in those regulations reflected political trends in the management of labor and migration around the world. And although attention to skill and its political significance have sometimes been downplayed as technical matters, a review of the interplay between global trends and Qatari regulation shows that the political equivalence between skill and freedom, and lack of skill and bondage, has always been at the heart of these global debates.

That equivalence has only grown more significant. As debates over labor rights and working conditions in Qatar have shaped the parameters of the conversation around the world, the representational—and regulated—association of different skill levels with different forms of freedom and unfreedom has found resonance beyond its borders. As the political interest in reshaping migration policy around merit and skill level has grown, so has the conflation of bondage and lack of physical freedom with being unskilled. And as countries around the globe increasingly rely on carceral strategies to manage migration, the use of detention and control is made less controversial because migrants who are subject to them can be more readily dismissed as unskilled and disposable. As the World Cup approaches, the international community may congratulate itself on having ameliorated Qatar's laws. But it may be that Qatar, with its long history as an arena for global discussions on labor rights, has in fact only shored up global norms about migration and skill, and strengthened beliefs about who among us has the full capacity for freedom.

CHAPTER TWO

Production

HOW SKILL MAKES CITIES

IN THE BUILDUP TO THE WORLD CUP, Doha was already dazzling. A desert city perched on the Persian Gulf, Doha had a striking background for the rise of its metropolis. The skyscrapers along its shore turned the city skyline into a photogenic marvel of glass and steel arching into a hazy blue sky. At night, the buildings glittered like an ornate wall of light, mirrored in the still black waters of the bay—refracted streaks of colored light that bled into the sea. The city's futuristic structures, designed by world-renowned architects such as I. M. Pei, Jean Nouvel, and Zaha Hadid, were so cluttered against the shore that they seemed to jostle one another. The buildings were stunning and ambitious, such as the National Museum of Doha with its cascade of interlocking concrete disks, the kinetic twist of the Tornado building, the lonely geometric elegance of the Museum of Islamic Art, the soaring honeycomb of light and steel of Doha Tower, and many other examples of imagination rendered in concrete. To the north, Doha's coastline was framed by a curved archipelago of man-made islands called the Pearl, laid down on old pearling beds in a shape inspired by oyster reefs. The arabesque shores were lined with almost identical high-rises that laid their own lattice of light on the bay. Doha was a jewel box of light.

Twenty minutes' drive to the south, on the far edge of the city, was Doha's industrial district. This district, laid out on a utilitarian grid not much larger than Doha's international airport, was zoned for the garages, factories, and workshops that were excluded from the modern metropolis. With its squat concrete structures, banks of identical warehouses, and rows of parked, often damaged cement mixers and construction lorries, the district felt like a world apart. And for most residents of Doha, it was. The near edge of the district was marked by a string of car repair shops. Here, Doha residents dropped off their vehicles for tune-ups, negotiating the price for repairs in air-conditioned,

[76]

pink-granite-floored reception areas. But residents, especially foreigners, expressed a deep uneasiness about venturing past this littoral zone. Many believed that entering the district was illegal without a government pass, others expressed concern that an exploration of the quarter would attract unwanted government scrutiny, and still others felt that the area, devoid of streetlights or police, was dangerous and unpredictable.

While many city residents, mainly professional expats, viewed the industrial area as off-limits, the annex was home to hundreds of thousands of migrant men. The industrial area's cinder block buildings, wedged in between factories that produced construction materials, provided dormitory space for 350,000 workers in 2015. According to the census that year, 99.02 percent of the residents in the industrial area were male, all were employed, and close to two-thirds worked in construction or construction-related industries.[1] The district's thirty-square kilometers were the most densely populated stretch in Doha, on par with downtown Delhi.

The first time I visited the industrial area, I was struck by how flat and desolate it seemed. My driver refused to cut through the district on our way to a meeting point at the area's southern edges, and so he drove me and my research assistant along the district's periphery. As we drove, the gray monotony of warehouse after warehouse, the repetition of panels of sheet metal and concrete, made me deeply sad. My driver dropped us off at an auto repair shop belonging to a Qatari patrician, senior official at one of the many ministries, and manager of his family's construction business. There I met Amer, the official's Palestinian mechanic and assistant, who had been assigned as my guide and minder. Amer had been charged by his boss to take me to see labor accommodations. He had gone to school in Doha with his boss and considered him his dearest childhood friend. This dear childhood friend was likely also his sponsor and controlled his ability to reside in Qatar. "My driver," as the official called Amer, "will take you to see the good, the bad, and the very bad." I later learned that Amer had taken many international consultants on the same tour. We had all seen the same two examples of the "good"—one of them still under construction.

The district at midday was an industrial moonscape. The thump of the wind pulsing against the buildings and parked lorries could be heard through the closed car windows. Clouds of cement dust smudged out the black asphalt of the roads, turning the entire space into an unsettled expanse of plaster-gray dunes. The roads were potholed, cratered by the tractor trailers, cranes, and cement mixers that barreled out to construction sites from the lots where they were stored. We drove past workshops of industrial tile cutters, generator factories, metal smelters, and belching manufacturers of cement blocks, all located haphazardly in the district's grid of unmarked blocks.

Low-slung dormitories for workers were interspersed among the factories. Billboards advertising rooms for rent, washed out and peeling, cauterized by

Qatar's harsh sun, were hung on the exterior of the buildings and the walls enclosing the worker compounds. The signs specified whether the facilities came equipped with water and electricity, and whether twenty-four-hour per day security services were included in the rent. Huge tanker trunks that provided potable water and sewage to the barracks were parked outside the buildings. Several of the tankers had rusted out, and large slicks of foul-smelling sewage spread from under their wheels into the worker compounds. Tata passenger buses, ubiquitous in Doha, were also parked outside the compounds, ready to transport workers on off-cycle shifts to construction sites in the city. A few of the labor camps had courtyards or basketball courts, but these were piled high with discarded rebar, broken toilets, and other refuse from neighboring factories. Larger enclosures doubled as lots for forklifts, small earth-movers, and cement mixers.

The streets were empty. The lone barbershop I saw that day and scattered corner stores were shuttered, closed for business while workers were at their construction sites. I stepped out of the car to take photographs, and a single man walked by. He had wrapped his face in stained calico cloth to protect against the thick dust and intermittent plumes of black smoke that rose from mounds of garbage being burned.

The worker dormitories were also largely empty. The few workers we met at the different barracks had worked the night shift. In the midafternoon, they were just waking up. At one labor camp, a few men squatted at outdoor pipes to wash their bodies and dishes. At another, men walked along the outdoor hallway, past piles of trash, to the communal bathroom wearing towels around their waists.

Hand-laundered uniforms hung from wires strung in outdoor hallways and inner courtyards to dry. In one labor camp, where I stopped to read the flyers stuck to the wall with blue electric tape warning that gambling was prohibited and would be severely punished, I looked up and saw a thicket of blue, green, and yellow overalls, hung from wires that had been pulled across an inner staircase. Their color was remarkable in that colorless place. Flip-flops were piled high in front of the doors to sleeping rooms; their owners were currently at their jobsites, wearing work boots.

At almost all the labor camps we visited, doors were labeled with the nationality of the residents: "Punjabi" or "Bengali," or the more generic "Indian," were stenciled across the front. On one door where "Nepali" had been painted, someone had added a preamble of "we welcome you to" in marker. In most of the worker accommodations we saw that day, men slept six to eight—and sometimes even twelve—to a room on stacked bunk beds. The men personalized their bunks with makeshift curtains made of towels and pillow covers, and some placed their prayer mats on their mattresses. Storage bins made of repurposed plastic soda bottles, cut in half and affixed with wire, held toiletries. On the walls as well as the lockers provided in most camps, residents had pasted cutouts of Bollywood movie stars, the Nepali flag, and photos of their wives, mothers, and children. In the hallways outside, security cameras hung precariously on slack wires.

Amer, as tour guide of "the good, the bad, and the very bad," offered up the men's bedrooms and bathrooms without compunction. He neither knocked nor announced our presence in any way, and the men, some of them woken from sleep by our entrance, said nothing. This kind of incursion seemed to be a regular occurrence—so ordinary that not even the presence of women, exceedingly rare in this male district, highlighted the violation of privacy. When we refused to enter rooms unless the doors were already open and we got explicit consent, Amer at first seemed nonplussed: these were not bedrooms; these were labor camps—storage facilities for labor. But as the afternoon wore on, he grew increasingly anxious at our conversations with workers, and we decided to leave.

Later, when I went to the labor camps on my own, unminded, invited by the workers affiliated with my field sites, the men sometimes described the camps as a "jail" or "prison," but always as "temporary" spaces. Even so, they tried to make the spaces their own. They painted the walls of their rooms in bright colors. They added bunks to some rooms in order to empty out another so that they could use it as an air-conditioned common room where they could watch movies on the TV they had pooled funds to buy. In one camp, the workers cleared the courtyard of old rebar and plywood to make a pitch for volleyball, and a place to sit outside and play cards. One worker had even planted green pepper plants in Nestlé powdered milk cans. When I returned a month later, the company had dumped a load of construction refuse onto the pitch.

Amer drove us back to his mechanic shop just as workers began to return to the district at the end of the workday. The streets had started to fill up with buses as the changeover between the day and night shift began. The mad rush would have begun at the worksites, where exhausted men ran from construction sites to idling buses, hoping to board the first bus to leave and avoid the full crush of rush hour traffic, when the trip to the industrial area, along highways packed with back-to-back buses and lorries, could take over an hour. At labor camps throughout the industrial area, buses would soon disgorge many tens of thousands of men. At the dormitories, the workers would quickly strip out of their work clothes and jostle in the kitchen to prepare their dinner, and in many cases, their breakfast and lunch for the following day as well. They would wash enough to sleep comfortably, and by nightfall, the industrial area would be quiet again.

And dark, because the district had few streetlights. No cafés, no gathering places, no mosques with lighted minarets. The district was a storage area for labor.

Segregation by Skill

The industrial district was not originally designed for worker housing. During the 1980s and 1990s, migrant laborers were housed in the older segments of the city, in downtown Doha, which had been abandoned by Qatari residents and expatriates when they moved to new land grant developments in the suburban areas. By the 2000s, however, the value of downtown real estate had soared, and several new large-scale urban redevelopments were planned for the city center, most notably the Souk Wakif and Msheirib projects. Employers relocated their workers to buildings that had been hastily erected on empty plots in the industrial area, and soon the district was a hub for worker housing.[2] The population of the industrial area grew exponentially, from a little over 20,000 in 1997 to 62,000 in 2004. By 2010, it had skyrocketed to 260,000, and by 2015, it had swelled another hundred thousand, topping 365,000 men—a population equivalent to more than half of the 587,000 residents in downtown Doha.[3]

In 2005, in the midst of this industrial district population explosion, the Qatari government formalized the segregation of worker housing to areas outside the city limits of Doha. The government addressed worker accommodation in this first 2005 decree, specifying that employers were required to lodge their workers in accommodations that were "located outside of residential areas."[4] Five years later, the government issued a stronger prohibition against worker housing in Doha, designating most of the city as reserved for families, and specifying that no owner or property manager should "rent or allocate property or parts of property of whatever nature to be a residence for workers groups within family residential areas."[5] It underscored the new zoning rules with clear penalties for the violation of the decree, including seizure of property, detention, and a sizable fine.

Initially, there was confusion over who qualified as a worker. All migrants in Qatar, from the construction laborer to the managerial executive, worked under the same regulatory structure. All were bound to their employer through the sponsorship system, which prohibited employees from terminating their contracts at will and leaving the country without their employer's assent. The authorities responded to this confusion by clarifying that the new regulations applied only to bachelors.

"Bachelor" was a term in wide use in the Gulf, and its meaning was only tangentially related to its formal definition of an unmarried person. In Gulf vernacular, the term referred to foreigners who had not been granted the right to bring their families with them when they migrated, irrespective of their actual family status. Bachelors could be married men or women who had been made "single" by a visa status that did not recognize those family ties. But the term, whether used in Dubai, Barhain, or Kuwait, was laden with all sorts of class, gender, and racial connotations.[6] In Qatar as in much of the Gulf, residency permission for spouses and children was granted only to professional workers, based on the argument that only their salaries were high enough to support dependents. As a result, the status of "family" denoted an elite income and class bracket, whereas bachelor was associated with a subordinate class position. While bachelor was sometimes applied to professional women in cities through the Gulf, the term in Qatar referred exclusively to men. It was a term that suggested, none too gently, the moral and sexual danger that the largely South Asian and African men were depicted as representing to Qatari society. "These bachelor workers are threatening the privacy and comfort of families, spreading like a deadly epidemic that eats through our social fabric," editorialized one columnist widely syndicated in the government-vetted local Arabic press.[7]

It turned out that "bachelor" was not a clear enough designation for the government's housing restrictions. After several incidents where doctors and lawyers, working in Qatar without their families, discovered that their utilities had been cut off and found notes posted to their doors informing them that they were being evicted, the Ministry of Municipality and Urban Planning further specified that the so-called bachelor ban applied only to male construction workers. White-collar workers, along with the grocery store clerks and the restaurant staff who served them, would be exempt, regardless of marital status or presence of family in Qatar.[8] The government did not initially specify that women would be exempt, regardless of their occupation, because it would have been unthinkable to require them to be housed in the all-male industrial area. Women were "families" by default. The ministry published an array of color-coded interactive maps of all the municipalities in Qatar that clearly indicated which areas were reserved for families and stepped up enforcement of the law. On the maps that covered the Doha metropolitan area, which included the municipality of Doha but also portions of several neighboring municipalities, the industrial area stood out as a gray rectangle in an expanse of family friendly yellow.[9] But the confusion about who was a family and who was a bachelor remained, and in 2019, the ministry issued a further clarification of this spatial segregation. It confirmed that women, regardless of marital status, were to be defined as a matter of zoning law as families. The bachelor areas were renamed "worker areas," and the ministry issued maps for every municipality in the country, with the category of "workers" referring to "blue-collar" workers engaged in occupations viewed as having a strong manual component. It backed this new, clearer designation with steeper penalties for violations.

In issuing its clarification, the government made it explicit that Doha was to be segregated by skill category. The designation of areas of the city as family or bachelor zones was merely the instrumental language of a policy designed to divide Doha by skill and occupation.[10] Of course, the division of the city by skill category had little relation to the actual technical competence of the people banished from the yellow-coded family zones. Expert machinists, laborers, and even clerical staff were all housed in the industrial area, tagged through their location with the interchangeable labels of blue-collar, worker, and bachelor. Instead, the policy confirmed the function of skill as a social status. The categories of blue-collar and white-collar workers were expanded far beyond workplace function, and even beyond a more straightforward economic sense of class, to include national origin, race, language, and gender. The slippage between the labels of "blue-collar," "worker," and "bachelor" only reinforced the racialized and sexualized connotations that government actions affixed to the category of skill.

Both the policy of segregation by skill and the social significance of skill categories in Qatar were amplified by private, ad hoc, and informal practices of exclusion. Urban spaces nominally open to the public, like malls, museums, and parks, published times when they would be reserved for families. Most of these spaces banned bachelors on Fridays, the only day that most workers had off. On other days, the security personnel of many shopping centers and cultural spaces actively, and oftentimes muscularly, discouraged anyone whom they judged to be a worker from entering public premises. Police removed bachelors from public parks. These enforcement practices marked any dark-skinned foreign man on the streets of Doha as a potential threat to public safety and morality. External signs of wealth and professional status— clothing, grooming, and accessories—offered some protection from policing, but otherwise, any dark-skinned man not working on a construction site and not wearing the construction overalls that indicated he was fulfilling a legitimate purpose was trespassing, and thus subject to security measures.[11]

Modernist Planning and Designing Skill Categories

More than the skyscrapers lining the coast, more the human-made islands arching out across the bay, more than the futuristic stadiums for the World Cup, more than any built structure in the country, the industrial area embodied Qatar's development model. The city's urban form and spatial design were used as a vehicle to create a specific vision of society and direct residents to comply with that social order. Qatar—and the metropolis of Doha in particular—embraced a program of high modernist development.

Modernism is less a specific aesthetic than a method. It is based on the inversion of the widely assumed approach to development in which development starts from the existing society and acts as a practice that works to enrich, uplift, and even transform it. In the conventional take, urban development reflects the needs of the city's residents, and builds the city to carry out the aspirations that current inhabitants have for their homes, communities, and shared spaces. The modernist approach, by contrast, starts with an idealized future, and imposes it on residents, whether or not it is the future they imagined for themselves, whether or not it is the future they want. Modernist development overwrites existing social structures and spatial patterns, erasing histories and enforcing compliance to the new vision where necessary.[12] In this method, people do not make the city. The modernist city—avant-garde, disruptive, and futuristic—makes persons.

The design of the modernist future is done by experts, an elite group of architects, engineers, scientists, and other visionaries whose rarified abilities endow them with the responsibility—in a form of noblesse oblige—for the projects of nation building and social transformation. Modernist utopian plans, designed to bring order and rationality to social structures and cityscapes, drag the backward, unschooled, disorderly populations on whom they are imposed into a regimented and idealized future.

The modernist method also espouses a highly stratified view of skill, and in some ways, its hubris stems from the view that it is possible to separate labor from skill. It is not a coincidence that modernist planning became faddish around the turn of the twentieth century, around the time when Frederick Taylor and Henry Ford received great acclaim for organizing factories based on the belief that workers' effort could be broken down into precise, repetitive, and isolatable actions, all of them automatic and unthinking, that managers could allocate and direct. Their claim that workers' labor could be split apart into raw energy, motion, and physics, on the one hand, and conceptual design and imagination, on the other, spurred the reinvention of production and the proliferation of mass production lines. Workers became labor, divested of skill and decomposed into discrete mechanical movements, and skill became the property of managers, who orchestrated their workers' physical movements through the marvels of scientific engineering.[13]

In practice, however, neither modernist factories nor modernist cities could function without the agentic contribution of workers and residents. The mass production methods relied on dense social systems to operate. Automated and standardized assembly lines, seemingly engineered in their entirety by managers at their desks, drew on rich and layered relationships between workers, through which they trained and mentored one another, developed ties of solidarity for collaboration and problem solving, and experimented with innovative solutions to the problems that top-down directives produced or did not perceive. Modernist urban experiments, with their dogmatically clean lines and rational order, depended on a messy web of social interactions to make them livable. The imaginative actions of residents, and their constant reinterpretation and reinvention of modernist spaces, housing complexes, and boulevards, turned radically austere urban tracts into vital, complex, and usefully untidy cities.

The belief that concept and execution—or more broadly, skill and labor—can be split apart continues to motivate both modernist planning and modernist approaches to production. Because this divide is ideological, and not reflective of the lived existence of cities or everyday work of production, modernist approaches have to produce it politically. Workers have to be represented as unskilled or de-skilled, their contributions devalued and debased, even as production systems rely on their capacity and creativity. Urban residents have to be recast as having lived chaotic and disorderly existences until their social identities were elevated and ordered by the design of urban spaces, even while their quotidian and disobedient refashioning of those urban spaces is what allows them to be functional.

In Qatar, the modernist insistence on the divide between design and implementation, and split between skill and labor, was the organizing principle of its national development plan. Through its regulatory system, the country implemented a political divide between migrants classed as skilled professionals and those classed as unskilled workers, and through its urban planning strategy, the country reinforced this political distinction and made it spatial. Qatar sought to build Doha to create the city-state it wanted to become: a hub for global elites, and a center for cosmopolitan cultural experiences along with luxury consumption and leisure. There was no place in this modernist imaginary for workers, the blue-collar bachelors who were banished and confined to zones, like the industrial area, that were left off the modernist plan, set aside for machines and raw materials. With its modernist planning approach, the government drew a boundary between elites and workers, and partitioned, with police backing, its built environment into spaces for design and spaces for implementation—into spaces it reserved for skill and spaces where it stored labor.

Ironically, if predictably, the modernist divide of Qatar's city spaces into those reserved for the elites and those abandoned to blue-collar bachelors only increased the country's reliance on the skills of those it classed as unskilled. Qatar's modernist approach to planning, with its ostentatious emphasis on engineered luxury and order, created chaos for the industry that that was building it. Production of the city's gleaming skyscrapers, human-made archipelagoes, and futurist stadiums was as erratic and disordered as the plans were utopian, glossy, and elitist. The construction industry faced rises and falls in demand that were exceptionally volatile—far more unpredictable than any changes in demand caused by fluctuations in the oil and gas revenues that financed the city's development. Doha and its opulent satellites grew not in response to the needs of its residents but rather in fulfillment of the modernist dreams that the emir and his government had for what the city should become. It grew in gushing multibillion-dollar spurts, massive vanity project by massive vanity project, with whole sectors of the city added on to manifest the latest modernist ambition. And when those dreams burned themselves out and were abandoned, construction came to an abrupt halt. The industry idled, sometimes for years, falling into a deep slump until modernist plans were once again issued by the government. As a result, the story of the construction

industry in Qatar was one of high peaks and deep troughs—and for companies, of feast and famine—with the highs following right on the heels of the
lows, until everything came crashing down all over again.

This extreme and completely unpredictable volatility molded the construction industry in fundamental ways. It shaped the organization of production
in construction firms; it influenced the interplay between the processes of
design and construction; it shaped procurement strategies and subcontracting relationships; it ordered the sequence of construction processes; and it
informed decisions about the use of technology. Unsurprisingly, the volatility
of construction bore down most heavily on the workers who were excluded
from the city they were building. The worker experience of modernist planning in Qatar included wage theft, forced overtime, unsafe conditions, and
degrading living arrangements.

Most saliently, given the country's political partition by skill, the wild
swings in the industry magnified the importance of workers' construction
skill. To cope with the volatility of a planning process dictated capriciously by
the emir's latest modernist vision, firms substituted labor for capital, swapping
in workers for machinery wherever they could. Unlike machinery, which by
design was restricted to specialized functions, workers could become anything
that a firm needed, whenever it needed it. (As one manager on a construction
site in Doha explained, a crane can only lift but not dig; a worker, however,
can do both, and much more.) But in order to get the job done, companies
required workers who had skill that was deep and specialized, craft-like in
its feel, yet also versatile and multifaceted. Firms dedicated significant organizational processes to developing this kind of skill in their workforce and
structured their production processes to double as training systems. Firms
competed based on their ability to reinvent themselves to meet any planning
whim, but their success in this regard depended on their workers' agentic
engagement in learning processes on-site.

The way that firms used their workforce and appropriated their workers'
skill reflected the very same practices of exclusion that shaped the city they were
building. Firms adopted an approach to developing the skill base they required
that reproduced the same modernist ethos that divided Doha into a sector for
skilled elites and an industrial zone for unskilled workers. Construction firms
in Doha relied on worker skill to build the technically complex and aesthetically
avant-garde buildings that anchored Qatar's modernist imaginaries, but they
nevertheless defined skill as distinct from labor. They characterized technical
competence as a resource that management produced, engineered, and owned.
The role of workers in developing skill, sustaining the social practices of learning, and adapting technical competence to the specific production requirements
of advanced construction was as excluded from industry representations of skill
as the workers were from the cities they were building.

Building Imaginaries

In the press coverage of Qatar's construction boom, the stadiums that the country was building to host the 2022 World Cup games received outsized attention. The renderings of the stadiums, fantastical images of architectural innovation in brilliant colors, became avatars of Qatar's transformation.[14] The promised stadiums announced that Qatar, with its gleaming cities, was taking its place as a country that was helping to define the future of global urbanity. As a result, the stadiums' construction became a flash point for both the enthusiasm and controversy elicited by Qatar's selection as host of the global games.

But the stadiums represented only a tiny sliver of the total construction that took place in Qatar in the decade after the games were awarded in 2010. In fact, the eight soccer stadiums, down from the twelve that were initially slated, represent only about US$4 billion in construction spending, out of a projected total of US$200 billion, with some estimates of the total government spending reaching as high as US$280 billion.[15] Two hundred billion US dollars was a significant outlay even in a country with the highest income per capita in the world. With a population of only 2.5 million, Qatar's expenditures amounted to about US$80,000 per resident, although given that most non-citizen residents had permission to remain in Qatar only temporarily, a more meaningful reflection of the level of government investment was a tally of the expenditures per citizen. Over the 2010s, this amount edged past US$650,000 for each of its 250,000 citizens.[16]

Most of the construction in the kingdom was dictated by a master plan. *Qatar National Vision 2030*, the strategic framework adopted in 2008, provided the framework for the country's urban development program.[17] The projects that the government pushed through were massive and ambitious. They fundamentally transformed the city of Doha, pushing its skyline upward and its expanse dramatically outward.[18] Doha more than tripled its footprint over the 2010s, much of it on land coaxed from the sea.[19] The Hamad International airport alone, opened in 2014, added thirty kilometers to the city, more than half of it backfilled and reclaimed from the bay. Its construction cost US$17 billion, one of the most expensive airports per square foot ever built, even before the government broke ground on a second terminal.[20] It was designed to claim the title of world's most luxurious airport. The Pearl luxury residential development, a US$15 billion project, added another four-square kilometers to the city's footprint and thirty-two kilometers of coastline. To the north of historical Doha, Qatar sovereign wealth fund poured US$50 billion into building Lusail City, a planned luxury satellite city for 450,000 residents, covering thirty-eight-square kilometers, including four man-made islands. Barwa City to the south of Doha, covering four kilometers, envisioned as a somewhat less exclusive development than Lusail, still totaled an estimated US$8 billion in investment. Thematic developments also featured among the megaprojects. Eight billion dollars went toward Education City, a cluster of campuses and cultural buildings; another US$2.5 billion was invested in Energy City, an integrated business hub for the hydrocarbon sandwiched between Doha and Lusail; and the sovereign wealth fund paid US$5.5 billion to redevelop the old city of Doha, renaming the urban center the Mshereib Downtown Doha project and billing it as the world's first sustainable downtown regeneration project.[21]

Equally ambitious were the infrastructure projects that the government built in the ground beneath its shiny surface developments. Qatar began boring for its Integrated Rail Project in 2013, and with a budget of US$35 billion, it was the world's largest civil engineering effort. The government also launched the Local Roads and Drainage Program, plowing US$15 billion into the arteries that would connect its newly constructed urban centers. To Doha's south, the government invested US$7.5 billion in the New Doha Port, the world's largest greenfield port project, which covered an area of close to thirty-square kilometers, and included a base for the Qatar Emiri Naval Forces and Qatar Economic Zone, an export processes and manufacturing area.[22]

The government bankrolled this national construction effort with oil and gas revenues. To ensure the continuity and expansion of those resources, the government also directed some US$50 billion to build capital improvements in its hydrocarbon sector. Qatar in the 2010s was the world's largest producer and exporter of LNG, but with Australia and the United States nipping at its heels, it upgraded its infrastructure to protect its market share. The government began construction on six additional underground wells, along with the associated bridges, pipes, and subsea manifolds, to draw up more natural gas from its north gas field, located some eighty kilometers off Qatar's shores and thought to hold the third-largest reserve of natural gas in the world.[23] These capital investments boosted its capacity to liquefy natural gas and increase its exports by 43 percent.[24] Qatar also invested in facilities for crude oil production, petrochemical processing plants, and shipbuilding installations for natural gas transport.[25]

For a time, the megaprojects that Qatar's oil revenue funded turned the entire eastern edge of the peninsula into an enormous construction site. The ground was torn open—a giant earthen wound. The skyline was darkened with the clutter of scaffolding and arms of construction cranes. Lorries, cement trucks, and earthmovers barreled down newly drawn roads. Dust dulled the horizon, and the air smelled like wet concrete. The entire country was being reinvented and re-created.

Modernism without Bounds and Cities without People

The megaprojects remaking Qatar were deeply modernist in both their method and aesthetic.[26] In many respects, they were the twenty-first-century expression of twentieth-century modernist urban planning, except that Qatar's

modernism in the desert took modernist principles and visions of what could
be accomplished through urban design to an extreme. For twentieth-century
modernists, urban planning was a tool to rid the city of "rot" ("*la pourriture*"
as modernist Le Corbusier termed the spaces of urban poor) and remake it,
in Le Corbusier's words, into "the great city [that] commands everything:
peace, war, work."[27] In Qatar's twenty-first-century version, the ambition was
greater. The city was used to create the future, define citizenship and belonging, and manifest power through wealth. (It is worth noting that this was a
vision shared by many of Qatar's neighbors in the GCC, with the Emirates,
Saudi Arabia, and others aggressively using urban planning to coax the future
into existence through concrete and glass.)[28]

At the core of that earlier modernist movement was the belief that society could be transformed and propelled into an imagined future through the
design of urban space. The city was not just the outcome of development; it
could be turned into a catalyst for social change. Its physical form was meant
to push inhabitants to enact patterns of behavior and social order that reflected
the planner's imagination of what modernity should look like. The city was
reinvented as a vehicle to drive inhabitants into the future. Its old identity—a
place where people lived out their lives, laid out their own futures, and defined
their own forms of sociability—was annihilated. For modernist planners from
Le Corbusier, with his highly ordered and Taylorist visions of Paris, which he
described as a "machine for living in" to Oscar Niemeyer and Lúcio Costa, who
drew up the plan for Brasília, a futuristic national capital for Brazil built on
empty scrubland where the residents were segregated by bureaucratic function,
to Soviet brutalists who sought to stamp out private property and class division
through superblocks, urban form was the means to engineer futuristic utopias
into existence.[29] The highways, superblocks, and neat rows of high-rises were
designed to exclude forms of sociability at odds with the image of the city as a
rational and ordered enactment of the future.[30] Urban plans actively designed
against pedestrians, informal markets, self-built housing settlements, and
open-use plazas. Le Corbusier, in his deeply influential "principles of urbanism," famously called for "the death of the street."[31]

Because city dwellers, with their layered subjectivities and untidy lives,
might object to the death of their streets, these modernist ambitions depended
on a particular conception of government as fundamentally authoritarian.[32]
Modernism not only prioritized the implementation of the plan above all else
but also viewed government authority to implement the plan, and override
existing laws, political structures, and public objection, if necessary, as an
essential precondition to modernity. As James Holston observes in his account
of the design of Brasília, "The only kind of agency modernism considered in
the making of history is the intervention of the prince (state head) and the
genius (architect-planner)."[33] The prince and architect needed one another
to force the development plan on an unwilling populace. Le Corbusier put it

more succinctly: "The Plan: Dictator."[34] The kind of social transformation that high modernist planning envisioned required massive state intervention and centralized coordination.[35] It also required that the government exercise the authority to make the plan as inevitable and incontestable as the future that it supposedly embodied. Once the urban plan had been defined, explained Le Corbusier, "authority must now step in, patriarchal authority, the authority of a father concerned for his children. . . . [W]e must build a place where mankind will be reborn."[36] The optimal future, mapped out by the visionary planner, required the resources and power of the state to become manifest— and compel residents that might be resistant, or reluctant, to being displaced to adopt modes of sociability dictated by the plan while relinquishing modes of being that had been central to their lives.

The plan in which Qatar laid out its desired future, *Qatar National Vision 2030*, was a somewhat generic and superficial document published in 2008 by the Qatar's General Secretariat for Development Planning. The document sketched out a vision of society organized around "a knowledge-based economy characterized by innovation; entrepreneurship; [and] excellence in education." The specifics would emerge in the planning and marketing documents produced for the megaprojects implemented under the auspices of the *Qatar National Vision 2030*.[37] Taken together, they laid out a proposal for a society organized around two economic nodes in which increased production and specialization in the oil and gas industry would support the development of residential and service hubs for the global elite.

This vision evinced an aesthetic that foregrounded leisure, luxury, and consumption. Qatar's many developments strategically tethered themselves to this vision, pitching their projects as fulfilling the country's modernist aspirations. The mission statement for the Lusail development, one of the largest of the 2010s' megaprojects, provides just one example among many; it described the satellite city as core to the *Qatar National Vision 2030* and billed it as "a futuristic project, which will create a modern and ambitious society. The smart, peaceful and inspirational environment combines artistic elements of architecture with various practical and versatile services in order to satisfy all the needs of its residents and visitors."[38] In Lusail, this aesthetic was expressed in much the same way as it was in Qatar's other megaprojects: through planned luxury residences and commercial spaces; in its elite, often-gated cultural and sporting centers; and in the embrace of architectural styles that were anything but utilitarian, and instead ostentatiously extravagant and expensive in their design.[39] Even the physical environment was molded to fit this luxury aesthetic; coastlines of islands dredged from the sea were engineered as interwoven geometric curves, in lines contrived as organic, but designed to provide for large numbers of waterfront vistas.

The governance structure in Qatar was well suited to the modernist project of creating society by building a city. The country was governed quite literally by a prince with authoritarian power, who could hire genius architect-planners from abroad in the form of international urban planning firms. The sovereign in Qatar had more resources and power to order the development of the city and structure society than even the most ardent twentieth-century modernist could have imagined. The government had vast hydrocarbon revenues at its disposal to direct to urban development; approximately 90 percent of the government revenues were derived from oil and gas, and over the course of the 2010s, it pulled between US$40 and US$90 billion per year in fiscal revenue directly from hydrocarbon exports, depending on the global price for oil, and more from investment funds where it placed those revenues.[40] Decisions about urban development were dictated by the sheikh along with a tight circle of relatives and associates at the helm of the Qatar Investment Authority, the country's sovereign wealth fund, and Qatar Foundation, which laid out the cultural vision for the country.

Not only did the ruler of Qatar have absolute political latitude to impose an urban vision on the country and ample financial resources to do so, but the ruler did not have to contend with an existing population reluctant to having its lived context utterly transformed. Urbanists George Katodrytis and Kevin Mitchell have described urban development in the Persian Gulf as a process of "drawing on sand."[41] Nowhere was the characterization more apt than in Qatar. While other countries in the Gulf had cities with larger and more established populations, with urban fabrics that reflected the rootedness of local and immigrant communities alike, Qatar's cities on the eve of its construction boom were small, with residents counted in the tens of thousands. Doha's skyline, so vaunted in the media spreads in the buildup to the World Cup, was low and dun colored well into the 2000s, broken only by the squat pyramid of the Sheraton Hotel that dominated the coastline.

With a citizenry that made up less than a fifth of the country's population, and the remainder of the population made up of foreigners who were transient and recent arrivals, Qatar could design cities without concern for its residents. Qatar was free to plan without people. It could implement its master plans and build its megaprojects, and import the global elite who would live in luxury installations and lifestyle developments once construction was complete. In this sense, Qatar had a degree of freedom that the modernists of the twentieth century could have only dreamed of: rather than use the city to transform society, Qatar could build the city to enact the future it imagined and then import the society that best fit that vision. Residents, well-heeled wealthy professionals, would be brought in to provide atmospherics for a society already laid out in urban form.

One practical result of this version of modernism was that the construction industry that would build this vision was also wholly dependent on the sovereign and his monies. It feasted and starved based on his whims (as implemented by the government). The private sector did not provide a project stream based on the needs of urban residents—independent from government contracts—that the industry could use as a hedge against changes in government planning. While precise data on the share of private sector investment in the Qatari construction industry in the 2010s is not available, in part because the distinction between private and public investment in Qatar is often blurry, estimates suggest that it was negligible, less than 15 percent at most, and far outweighed by government investment in urban and infrastructure mega-projects. This is because the residents that would live in the city still being imagined did not yet reside in Qatar and perhaps never would.[42] (In existing luxury developments, to say nothing of those that would come online in the late 2010s, occupancy remained worrying low—five-star ghost towns that the government struggled to fill.)[43]

But even before this latest wave of construction, Qatar's urban development had been obeisant to the sovereign's desires. Modernism—as a method—was an established practice in the country; post-independence Qatar, from 1971 on, was willed into existence through the sovereign's urban planning imagination. In 1974, after the Organization of Petroleum Exporting Countries' oil embargo caused petroleum prices to spike, Sheikh Khalifa, flush with petrodollars, began a massive urban development initiative explicitly designed as a nation-building project.[44] A phalanx of international planning firms developed the country's first master plan. The planning document produced by William L. Pereira Associates, one of the lead firms in the group, indicated that "the whole urban growth structure of Doha must be reoriented" and "a new growth pattern, reinforced by a planned transportation infrastructure, must be developed in a lineal pattern," which it characterized as rational and modern, suited to automobiles, in contrast to the traditional radial pattern that it argued had to be abandoned.[45]

As a first step in the ambitious reimagination of Doha, the bay was dredged and filled in.[46] An army of lorries, seconded from the oil industry, transported and dumped quarried stone into the marshy, malodorous bay. A deepwater area was dredged to allow the approach of ships to the recently inaugurated port, and the waste was used to fill in the area that would become the New District of Doha, called Dhafna or "the buried" by locals, and later renamed the West Bay. For seven years, the dredging and infilling of the bay noisily churned the coast that had defined Doha and its livelihood for centuries, and the aggressive installation of basic infrastructure in the dried-out shallows turned the area into a massive construction site.[47] In less than a decade, the project increased Doha's footprint by a third. It more than doubled the length of the urban shoreline and turned its ragged edge into a crescent moon, sleek in its geometric precision.[48] Alongside this unprecedented civil engineering project, the new plan called for capital investment in ministry buildings, port facilities, an airport, a hospital, and a luxury residential and diplomatic neighborhood on land reclaimed from the bay in the new West Bay section. The traditional core of the city, around the old souk (Souq Waqif), was demolished and slated for redevelopment.[49]

In the early 1980s, oil revenues fell, plummeting to a trough in 1986 from which they would take almost two decades to recover. Qatar's revenues crashed, and its income per capita dropped by more than half. A period of painful belt-tightening followed. Still, the emir and his council, the Emiri Diwan, remained stubbornly committed to the new urban plan. The state continued to bankroll construction in the West Bay, sometimes paying contractors in oil barter deals instead of cash, even as it shelved many urban development projects that were arguably more vital to people who lived in the city. The *Financial Times* reported at the time that "the Emir has a habit of 'losing his check book' if too many payments fall due."[50] The bulldozed area of the old city remained vacant for a decade, with empty stretches of detritus, while infrastructure projects for residents who had been forced to relocate to the outer edges of the city were put on hold.[51]

The emir's commitment to the urban development plan, even in the face of a budgetary crisis, softened the blow for the construction industry, but it generated political backlash that was fierce. The Qatari government tamped out resident complaints and sporadic protests with muscular security measures—the political memory of the unrest that had threatened the ruler's hold on power only a short decade earlier still fresh.[52] Nevertheless, it would be more two decades before a new emir, Sheikh Hamad, would contemplate an urban development program, beginning gingerly in the early 2000s with a series of projects related to the Asian Games, which Qatar hosted in 2006. In the twenty-year lapse between modernist imaginings, however, the construction industry capacity collapsed utterly. International planning and construction firms decamped, many tens of thousands of workers were sent home, and whatever construction activity was left built small and low-budget residential and commercial projects for the local market. When Qatar won the 2022 World Cup hosting rights and returned to large-scale and transformational modernist urban planning, the construction industry itself had to be entirely reconstructed.

Pop-Up Construction Industry and the Risks of Modernism

Qatar's $200 billion investment in the 2010s detonated its construction industry. Year after year, its industry grew by more than 20 percent in real value, pushing past a 28 percent growth rate at its peak in 2016.[53] In less than a decade, the value of the industry more than tripled in size, mushrooming from US$7 billion in value produced in 2010 to US$25 billion in 2018.[54] Qatar's construction market was growing faster than anywhere else in the Middle East.

Construction companies from around the globe rushed to take part in the bonanza. With their entrance into the market, a construction industry equal

to the government's mammoth development plans appeared seemingly overnight. International firms provided almost all of Qatar's construction capacity.
In 2018, for example, the value of major contracts awarded to international
firms totaled an estimated US$115 billion compared to a mere US$13 billion
awarded to Qatari firms. The companies that flooded into the Qatari market
were from around the world; the lead firms on contracts valued at more than
a billion were from China, the United States, Malaysia, Greece, Turkey, South
Korea, Australia, the United Arab Emirates, India, France, Germany, Italy,
Saudi Arabia, Austria, and Spain. While domestic firms were able to establish
a small presence in the industry, the workforce for this construction boom was
almost wholly international; out of 805,810 people employed in the construction industry in 2017, for example, only 1,314 were Qatari.[55] In any given year
in the 2010s, Qataris represented no more than a fraction of a single percent of
those working in construction. To build out its modernist vision as a city-state
for the global elite, Qatar relied on a construction industry that was entirely
imported from abroad.

Companies came because there was money to be made. How much money
was a matter of luck, connections, and hustle. The contracts were mammoth, and according to the managers I surveyed, the profit margins that they
could expect, on paper, to collect were double what they could earn in other
international markets: 10 to 25 percent as opposed to the more standard 5 to
10 percent on the contract. In practice, however, the industry volatility produced by modernist planning tossed and battered companies operating in
Qatar. While some companies made out like bandits, most found that their
profits had been pummeled down to a few percentage points by the time they
completed their work, if they were fortunate. Some left having operated at a
loss or unable to wrest payment for work completed. Profits were as volatile as
the industry, and those companies that did well were lucky, to be sure, but they
were also good at developing strategies to ride the turbulence.

Each firm operating in Qatar imported its production capacity. For each
contract, lead firms had to assemble their means of production. They pulled
together construction capacity through subcontracts to smaller and specialized international firms. Materials were procured and imported into Qatar
on a project-by-project basis. Specialized machines were shipped in. Workers
were recruited from abroad and employed on short-term contracts that typically lasted for no more than the duration of the project, and often for less. In
this sense, construction in Qatar was a pop-up industry. Firms brought construction capacity together—sourced from abroad—on a contract-by-contract
basis. At the completion of construction, the assembled capacity dispersed,
dissolving as rapidly as it was created. At times, firms could reassemble the
materials, machines, and workers they brought together to complete another
project, but more frequently than not, they had to ship out the resources they
had gathered, send workers home, and dissolve the contracting chains they

had so painstakingly strung together. With virtually no construction demand independent of government contracts—either directly through the Public Works Authority, widely known by its Arabic name, Ashghal, or indirectly through projects funded by Qatar Petroleum or the Qatar Investment Authority (the kingdom's sovereign wealth fund)—there was no other business that would allow companies to idle in place until they could secure another project.

The industry's dependence on government contracts already made demand unpredictable and volatile, but the regulatory structure the government used to manage the construction projects was what really magnified the chaos that construction firms faced. Qatar's modernist visions came from the emir and royal family, but the details were hashed out and implemented by Ashghal and other ministries, which contracted out to architectural and construction companies. These government agencies also devised the regulatory framework for the projects they had commissioned. This meant that the government was both the client for construction projects and its regulator. And as regulator, the government shaped firms' ability to complete the work for which they were contractually responsible. In an interview with the regional press, the manager of the Qatar branch of Faithful+Gould, an international construction management company, conveyed the political challenges of a system where client and regulator were the same entity: "A company must 'prove itself' first before gaining the confidence of local business and this is magnified when the 'local business' is government, the entity that holds the purse strings to all the mega-projects transforming Qatar."[56]

The distinction between rules that the government enforced as regulator and the contractual demands that it made as the client was hazy at best. Ashghal was constantly revising its regulations and building codes, revamping contractual requirements, rewriting construction standards, and reclassifying which technologies and machineries were approved for use. ("Not this crane, but that one; not this earthmover, but that one; cement from this company but not that one; workers fron Bangladesh but not India," lamented an executive manager at one of the largest firms in Doha. "That's today—tomorrow, who knows? You have to trust in God, and get a good [well-connected] sheikh to negotiate for you.") The rationale for this regulatory changeability was inscrutable to firms in the industry, but they often caused delays, cost overruns, and bottlenecks of all kinds—all of which the government, as client now, could use to deny payment for services rendered and work completed.[57] This created a loop of power that heightened the industry's dependence on the Qatari government. Construction companies viewed government—to them, unpredictable, unaccountable, and self-interested—as judge, jury, and executioner, and when surveyed as part of a 2015 study, identified the conflation of the contracting and regulatory functions as the most critical risk they faced.[58]

On the surface, the contracting structure for Qatari projects was no different than for any large project anywhere in the world. Lead companies relied on long and intricate subcontracting chains of companies, with most operating on the project site, to carry out the construction project. But in Qatar, the links in these subcontracting chains were strained by regulatory pressures, and they made firms uniquely vulnerable to abrupt changes in demand and regulatory approach.

All foreign companies were required by law—specifically Law No. 13 of 2000 Regulation of the Investment of Non-Qatari Capital in Economic Activity—to form partnerships with Qatari counterparts.[59] The vehicles for these legally mandated partnerships were usually joint ventures. In order to operate in Qatar, international construction firms generally created spin-off companies that were majority owned by their Qatari partner, which was usually a well-connected member of the royal family or one of the country's wealthy merchant clans. The Qatari partner had to own at least 51 percent of the joint venture.[60]

While the ownership structure favored the Qatari partner, the costs and risks involved in construction tended to land on the foreign partner.[61] As a general rule, large project contracts, especially where the government was the client, operated under a "joint and several" liability rule. Under this regulatory provision, either party in the joint venture could be held solely responsible for any contractual obligations or injuries caused by the other partner in the venture. Additionally, the Qatari law governing project bids—Law No. 26 of 2005 on Organizing Tenders and Auctions—required that companies submit tender bonds with their bids, making them liable to complete the project under the terms dictated at the time of the initial bidding process.[62] Moreover, clients, especially on government projects, required a supplementary performance bond specifying timelines and quality standards. What these contractual stipulations meant in practice was that the international partner in the joint ventures shouldered most of the risk involved in the projects while being required to share the profits with their Qatari partner, usually split along the same 49–51 percent as the ownership of the joint venture. Where the government was the client, it often intervened to ensure that risk was allocated in this fashion—even insisting on additional guarantees from construction firms (such as collateral warranties).[63]

To cope with the high level of risk transferred onto them, lead companies relied on a contracting structure that allowed them to pass some of the risk down the contracting chain. They used contracts that were "back-to-back" with the main agreement, with "pay-when-paid" clauses. Under these terms, subcontractors had to agree to receive payment for work completed only when the main contractor had been paid, even if payment issues stemmed from performance shortfalls by other firms in the subcontracting chain.[64] Subcontractors pushed back-to-back contracts onto the smaller firms they had, in turn, subcontracted as a way to palm off the risk they were forced to take on by the lead firm. Risk and cost were driven down to the weakest link in the subcontracting chain, to the smallest and least capitalized firms on the project. In an interview published in a trade magazine in 2016, striking for its outspokenness in an industry where managers tended to be restrained in their critiques, the director of a construction firm operating in Qatar spoke to the power dynamics involved in this contracting structure: "They then come to the contractors and say these are the terms, there is no room for negotiation, this is how it is, take it or leave it. . . . [W]e have no diversified market around the world to redeploy to. The big multinationals are well financed. . . . SMEs [small and medium-size enterprises] on the other hand deal in millions not billions; if we have a problem with millions it can make or break a company, whereas the multinationals can afford to write off the odd billion."[65]

Nonpayment and late payment for work completed were endemic in the Qatari construction industry, with government contracts displaying a chronically poor track record for payment. Industry observers and lead firms noted in the trade press and at trade conferences that the delays were not a matter of mere weeks or months but rather years. Every single firm, executive, and construction manager I interviewed flagged delayed payment as a major factor harming their operations. A large survey study conducted by business analysts Abdulaziz Jarkas and Jamal Younes evaluating operations in the Qatar construction industry confirms these observations. The study, published in 2014, found that 85 percent of the firms surveyed indicated that "delay in payment process by the employer" was a significant pressure negatively impacting construction.[66] Nonpayment to a firm at the top of the subcontracting chain had devastating consequences all the way down. As one international consultant for the industry observed, "Cash flow is the lifeblood of construction. If [the] main contractors get paid late (or not at all . . .) they cannot pay their subcontractors, who in turn cannot pay suppliers, who simply 'turn off the taps' and then clients and their project managers surprisingly wonder why projects are not meeting schedule and why there are no materials on site."[67]

Delayed payment and nonpayment were as much a product of political decision-making as they were the result of bureaucratic bottlenecks in processing invoices. In true modernist fashion, the government shifted its budget around when it revised its planning goals, sometimes in response to revenue pressures, but just as often due to shifting design ambitions. When the global oil price plunged in 2015, dropping from US$100 a barrel in September 2014 to US$36 a barrel in January 2016 before it began to inch upward again, the government reordered its urban development priorities. It mothballed vanity projects, shelving several stadiums, the Doha Grand Park, modeled after New York's Central Park, and the Sharq Crossing, a series of interlocking bridges over the bay, among others. But it also slashed funding for services for current residents, putting the construction of health clinics, schools, and public parks on hold, cutting spending for these projects by two-thirds. It siphoned off funds from those social service needs and redirected them toward projects deemed core to the World Cup endeavor and essential for turning Qatar into a global and elite service hub.[68]

The same political calculations created significant and unpredictable time pressures on construction processes. Projects considered politically important—sports stadiums that signaled readiness to host the 2022 World Cup, transport infrastructure, and entire sectors of new luxury cities—were regularly "fast-tracked." The project timelines were compressed beyond what the industry calls the "crash point"—the point at which the increase in effort and cost to complete a project rises exponentially.[69] Projects generally hit their crash point when they double the speed at which they build—so a project with a two-year optimum project timeline generally has a crash point of one year. Up until that point, the investment required to complete the project will increase proportionally to the acceleration. After that point, any changes made to the project will make the cost skyrocket, if it even remains feasible.[70] Construction firms in Qatar complained that they were working beyond their crash points and could not absorb the cost.

Many high-profile projects in Qatar were fast-tracked right from the get-go, with compressed timelines specified in the contracts. Others, however, were fast-tracked during the construction process, generally in response to changes in government planning priorities. And still others were fast-tracked implicitly, when companies had to speed up their work to make up for delays earlier in the building process. Some of these delays were due to changes to the design of the structures being built, as they were being built. Because building designs were based on modernist imaginaries, and disconnected from the needs of any people who might use or live in the buildings, design parameters on the buildings in construction were dictated entirely by the government client. And government clients changed their orders a lot and unpredictably. Contractors and construction managers complained in interviews with me that changes to the design often reflected no more than the whimsy of the specific royal in charge of the project. As one executive at an international construction management company put it, "I found it impossible to work here until I realized that everything is backward. Instead of design and build, in this country you design around what is already built. You design around what some sheikh ordered the contractor to do. Without looking at the plans. Just because he felt like it. You end up designing and redrawing plans to make 'facts on the ground' cohere into a design that makes sense." The changes added construction work and cost onto timelines and budgets that were already exceptionally tight, and more important, that the builders had to meet contractually if they wanted to get paid.[71]

The risks related to money and time played out when firms sourced the inputs they needed for construction. Firms in Qatar had to import the bulk of the raw materials and machinery required for their projects. Their ability to do so was pincered between skyrocketing local demand and inadequate infrastructure—specifically the absence of sufficient deepwater port facilities to import the supplies. The new Hamad port only opened in 2017, but wasn't slated to be fully operational until 2020. Indeed, Jarkas and Younes found that the "unavailability or shortage of material" was the top reason that firms cited for construction delays. These constraints were reflected in the costs of core construction inputs; in 2018, for example, the prices for basic construction materials in Qatar—cement, concrete, timber, and steel—were 20 to 50 percent higher than in neighboring countries of the GCC.[72] And firms were lucky to get them at all, even at those prices.[73] Every year between 2011 and 2015, the shortfall of cement rivaled the amount imported, and in 2016, the shortfall was triple the amount that Qatar was able to import.[74]

Here too the government shaped these risks and decided what access firms would have to which materials. In 2006, the government established the Qatar Primary Materials Company (QPMC) to create strategic stockpiles of aggregate and sand materials for the government. But in 2015, the QPMC specified that these materials would be procured and disbursed by agreement with selected contractors, most of which were building projects that were a priority for the Qatari government. After Saudi Arabia imposed an embargo on Qatar in 2017, subsequently closing most overland routes into the Qatari peninsula, the QPMC played a pivotal role in securing construction materials, sourcing and stockpiling cement from Iran, and allocating them to preferred projects.[75] The government also structured firms' ability to import construction machinery. It regulated which firms could import equipment and for what purposes, and a complex permitting process that wound through several ministries was required for construction technology that was new to the Qatari market.[76]

The government also regulated labor. The ability of firms to bring in the labor force they needed was disrupted by a web of regulations that restricted and defined the labor force that companies could use. This happened first in the tendering process, when the government as client reviewed the labor bill included in bids, evaluating both the number and compensation of workers. As one contractor I spoke with explained, "When you are designing a bid, you have to know that the labor costs are being analyzed. Do I have a better chance of winning this bid if under the same budget I bring in two hundred workers from Tunisia or a thousand from India, even if the two hundred Tunisians can do double the work?" The government then shifted roles and stepped in as a regulator to review requests to import labor. Firms had to apply to the government for visa approval for the workers they sought to recruit. The Ministry of Labor and Social Development, backed by the Ministry of Interior, vetted applications by the number of workers, country of origin, and wage rate for a given skill class, and determined which workers firms could import, and when they could bring them into the country.

For companies caught on the wrong side of these risks, the legal system offered little protection. Contractual disputes, particularly over the nonpayment of fees, were common in Qatar.[77] Industry ratings for construction risk over the 2010s assessed Qatar as the highest-risk country for construction contracts in the GCC by a significant margin.[78] When large international contractors that were the lead firms on projects sought legal remedy, they found themselves impaled on the horns of a conflict of interest: the same government that commissioned the project that the claimant argued they had not been paid for was also responsible for assessing the validity of the claim.[79] Moreover, contractual disputes could jeopardize access to future contracts in what was projected to be, at least for the near term, a lucrative market. As one legal counsel advising construction companies in Qatar explained, "The difficulty is that, the majority of projects in the sector are government-led and there remains a fear, within international companies at least, that they can only consider taking legal action against a government body if they accept that they are never going to work in Qatar again."[80]

Firms took whatever payments they could get. Several managers disclosed that they used informal strategies to secure a reliable stream of contracts in the midst of this acute market volatility. These included kickback schemes, where the subcontractor agreed to pay some percentage of the value of the contract—typically around 10 percent—back to the main contractor or the specific personnel at the main contractor tasked with allocating contracts. Given the unpredictability of Qatar's construction market, these kickback schemes look less like bribery and more like a way of creating incentives for lead companies to pay their contractors.

Labor for Modernism

During my fieldwork, I conducted several roundtables with managers at some of the largest construction contractors, consultants, and design firms operating in the country. Each with a dozen or so managers in attendance at them, I asked about the risks they faced operating in Qatar and specific challenges created by the volatility in industry. At the first of these roundtables, these questions were met with an uncomfortable silence. The managers shifted in their seats, a couple looked down at their phones, and one tipped his empty teacup and ran it around the edge of the saucer. After an interminable minute, one of the participants, a manager at a large construction firm, tore through the silence with his response:

> "Look, in this part of the world, you cannot plan for the future. It's either feast or famine. And this applies not just to the market. It has to do with the ways the contracts are awarded here, because price and quality are not all there is to it. You have one company who comes in from nowhere and for two years goes *whoosh* with ten thousand projects—let's not mention names—then *bam!* they get nothing. And then some

other company sweeps in with political connections and gets all the projects. And in the meantime, you are struggling with government procedures to get paid, to release payment for work you completed months ago."

"Sometimes there are delays, sure, but that happens everywhere," interjected another participant.

"No, no, let's be frank, it's a war of attrition trying to get the client, what we are really speaking of is the government, to get it to honor its obligations," responded the manager.

"Come on . . . at the end of the day, you get your money," retorted his interlocutor.

"They are doing this research because they want to know the facts, so we have to give them the facts!" exclaimed the manager.

"The delay is procedural, nothing else. These are complex contracts with very detailed verification procedures. You maybe have to take a cut, 10 percent . . . ," responded his interlocutor as they began to speak over one another.

"We are talking about millions . . . hundreds of millions! It is always the contractor who gets squeezed," emphasized the manager, his voice rising.

"You are talking about hypotheticals. This does not happen here. The government is a reliable partner," boomed a third participant.

"Please, *ya doctora*, can you turn off the recording?" asked a fourth person who had been listening to the discussion with increasing anxiety.

[*Recording off.*]

In the reflections that followed, in this roundtable as well as subsequent ones, the participants said that project management was tantamount to managing chaos. They described the ways in which the volatility in the industry shaped their production processes on-site. They mentioned the shocks of time and money upending their production schedules and straining their ability to assemble the inputs they required for construction in critical ways. They described production sites with thousands of men and millions of dollars in play idling because the materials or machinery they required were held up by regulatory reviews or bottlenecks at Qatar's ports. They described visa approvals for hundreds of workers being completed months after the trade-specific tasks for which the workers had been recruited were complete, such as hundreds of scaffolders arriving when scaffolding had already been taken down, welders after the skeletons of buildings were erected, or machinists arriving once the excavation work was done and foundations already laid. They described the building designs and timelines for construction that were completely revamped midstream, with projects being redesignated as fast-track halfway through or delays early in the project forcing the contractors to accelerate production dramatically in later stages. These shocks played havoc with their budgets and contracting structures, and reverberated from the lead firm all the way down the long and intricate subcontracting chains on Qatar's megaprojects, and subcontractors that were unable to complete their work as a result had to be swapped out at the last minute.

But all the contractors I spoke with noted that the most consequential impacts of Qatar's volatile construction industry were those that affected the sequencing of production tasks. The tasks on any construction project anywhere, large or small, are interdependent and sequential: a house cannot be built before its foundation is laid; a roof cannot be built before there are walls for it to brace on; and walls cannot be painted and plastered before they stand. The construction plans for Qatar's megaprojects also reflected a sequential logic, with tasks arranged to layer on one another. At its most basic, the logic required that foundational work be completed first, followed next by a middle stage for wet work (tasks involving concrete) and the erection of the building skeleton, and then by finishing, a final stage that included everything from electric work to tiling and painting. The importance of capital investments and size of the labor force on a given project followed a parallel life cycle, with the use of capital and labor following each other like two parabolic curves: the initial phase of construction typically involved a large and rapidly increasing reliance on heavy machinery and few workers; the wet work and building structure phase required continued but declining use of machinery and a large labor force; and in the final finishing stage, capital use was minimal and declining, and the use of labor, initially large, descended gradually as the project neared completion.

The time and money shocks to construction in Qatar shattered this sequential logic and forced contractors to finish tasks out of order. Contractors, under significant time pressure, had to complete tasks at the moment that the material, equipment, and labor for that task were available and could be assembled. They could not afford to hold off until the appropriate phase of the project life cycle. What this meant in practice was that wet work was done before foundations were finalized, and finishes were done before building skeletons were complete. One, perhaps apocryphal example that several contractors recounted had to do with the construction of Sidra hospital in Doha. The client requested that conifer trees several stories high be imported from Scandinavia for the healing garden in the hospital's central courtyard, at a price tag of over $1 million each. The trees arrived and were planted before the hospital's air-conditioning system was installed, and soon the conifers, suffocated by heat and construction dust, died. I was able to observe many other instances of disordered sequencing on the sites that I visited, some distressing and dangerous, such as heavy machinery driving over and crushing fine marble tiles that had been laid out on the floor the week before, scaffolding being erected around a building for roof glasswork while cranes lifted and swung large glass panes over the workers, and indoor plaster being applied while the steel frame for the ceiling was being welded, releasing waves of sparks and dust on the workers and wet walls below. "Definitely when we have a crushed schedule, it affects safety, and it affects quality," conceded one contractor. "The way we rush, the way we go out of sequence, we use all methods. The client wants the project. There is a lot of pressure, and the compromises start. You have to overlap more, and this is where we have the problems and the damages to the material, and if I am honest, to the safety of workers as well."

Labor as a Shock Absorber for Modernist Chaos

When I surveyed contractors on how they coped with industry volatility, the answer was that labor was an antidote to chaos. They used their workforces as a source of flexibility and responsiveness and designed their production systems to allow them to lean on their workforces more heavily when they were faced with unexpected production challenges—accelerated timelines, unforeseen and unforeseeable material or equipment shortfalls, or sudden cash crunches. Contractors substituted labor for capital and used workers instead of the machinery and equipment in wide use on comparable projects around the world.

The sheer density of men was the most remarkable feature of Qatar's megaprojects construction sites. The workforces on the project sites I studied were large, numbering from many hundreds to many thousands. The sites felt as crowded as any busy city street; men worked elbow to elbow, workers massed at the entrance in passageways turned into bottlenecks on the site, and workers labored so closely together that they had to negotiate their movements with men working above and below them on structures that were being erected. Men clustered in groups wove in and out of active construction operations; crowds moved around active cranes and blazing welding torches, while steel beams and large segments of cladding were suspended in the air, cement pumps churning and nozzles targeted, earthmovers drilling and grinding. The techniques on-site for building structures that were state of the art in their design were strikingly labor intensive and clearly reflected a managerial choice to substitute labor for capital. I observed large scrums of men digging with shovels alongside idling hydraulic excavators. I saw rows of workers manually assembling steel cages for building columns, using pliers and a twist of the wrist to tie thousands of thin wires, one by one, to hold rebar grids in place. I witnessed waves of workers retreating on their knees as they sanded vast stadium floors by hand, and many other instances of workers manually completing tasks that are typically mechanized, and have been for decades.

The data on Qatar's construction industry preference for labor over capital is circumstantial, but even so, it bears out my observations. The number of workers used on Qatari construction sites was far higher than in other economies in the world. A back-of-the-envelope comparison of industry size divided by the number of workers employed tells us this: that in 2017, the labor ratio in Qatar was five times higher than in Germany, three times higher than in the

United States, one and a half times higher than in Singapore, and even higher than in neighboring Saudi Arabia, though only marginally.

At a basic level, firms used labor as a buffer against the financial shocks that they faced. They did this by not paying wages, either on time or at all. When faced with nonpayment from their client or fluctuating materials prices, firms pulled from their wage bills to cover other operating costs. As noted previously, the nonpayment or late payment of wages was endemic in the Qatari construction industry. As documented in numerous reports by international human rights organizations and press accounts over the 2010s, construction companies routinely failed to pay their workers, delaying payment for months or even years at a time. Managers, engineers, and supervisory staff, as they divulged in interviews with me, also experienced delays in wage payments that were frequent and extended. "You learn to live with it. The cure for fate is patience," reflected one manager when describing months-long delays in receiving his salary.

The regulatory structure governing the employment of migrant workers— the kafala system—allowed firms to use this strategy for much of the 2010s' construction boom. During that heady decade, the kafala system, which bound foreign workers to their employers, prohibited them from quitting their jobs for any reason, including the nonpayment of wages, even when over an extended period. Moreover, workers required an exit visa issued by the Qatari government to leave the country—a stipulation that effectively trapped them in Qatar and their employment relationship, regardless of whether or not they were being paid for their work. In 2017, the Qatari government reformed the kafala system to allow most workers to leave without an exit permit and quit their jobs after one year. Yet these reforms did little to alter the structural factors that enabled employers to commit routine wage theft. Workers were often too indebted to leave their jobs given that most had taken out large loans to secure their visas to Qatar, too tied to their employer, which in most cases provided workers with their housing and meals, and too restricted in their ability to move throughout the city, confined as they were to bachelor areas, to quit their jobs and seek other opportunities. Unpaid workers had little recourse: they were banned by law from striking, and if they used the cumbersome and inaccessible complaint and arbitration system at the Ministry of Labor and Social Protection, they were required to continue working while their case was being reviewed. In late 2015, the government took steps to curtail this practice and set up a wage protection system that required firms to pay their worker electronically into accounts that were subject to government review. This intervention, however, did little to lessen wage theft; the requirement was poorly enforced, and companies quickly discovered ways to sidestep it, including compelling workers to agree to contracts with lower wages. Many companies, as reported to me by both managers and workers, also prevented workers from accessing their wages, generally by holding their bank cards, in order to maintain high current balances in their accounts.

For companies with variable and unreliable cash flows, the factors that compelled employees to work regardless of whether they had been paid made them an attractive alternative to machinery. Capital equipment had a rigid cost structure; it required a significant investment to purchase and import, and if production hiccups occurred, such as the unavailability of construction materials or delays in the preparatory tasks required before the equipment could be used, the machinery sat idle, depreciating rapidly in the humid Qatar air, with the investment unable to be recouped. A day when a hydraulic excavator sat unused, rusting away, was a day the capital investment was lost. But a day when a worker wasn't digging was a day he could be ordered to do another task. Labor required little up-front investment, with the costs paid out over time, and in Qatar, it could be put to work even if it wasn't paid. Furthermore, wage payments could be diverted to pay for materials, ensuring that progress on-site was not held up by a lack of cement, steel bars, or Italian marble.

Managers I spoke with were frank in their description of how widespread the nonpayment of wages was as a strategy to manage volatile cash flows, but they also were clear in their assessment of this tactic as suboptimal. Their concern was that the productivity of workers declined markedly when they were not paid, and continued to decline precipitously the longer wages were withheld. Likewise, they observed that the nonpayment of wages had an impact on production quality. As one manager put it, "The treatment of workers translate[s] directly into quality of work. You see this in construction errors and the need for rework. And rework slows down progress. When you are redoing the work, it takes time, but you will also see damage to work that is already completed." Some contractors described discouraging their subcontractors from leaning too heavily on a strategy of nonpayment because it was counterproductive (not because of its impact on workers per se), and some mentioned intervening directly with subcontractors to ensure that wages were paid. "I give you the example of a current project where we have a major subcontractor, who has a major part of the project," volunteered a manager at one of the largest firms in Qatar.

> Whatever we paid him, he took the money for materials for our project or even some other project. And so we told him, give us your payroll and we will pay your workers on your behalf directly. To make sure that the money reached the labor for *our* project because it was affecting his ability to deliver, and we were on a crushed schedule, and we suspected that he was using payroll to pay for materials on another project. . . . Our cash flow was not good. If it were good, he would not suffer. So we went the extra step with him and opened up LCs [a form of incorporation that limits liability] on his behalf so he could get material and also pay his workers.

More significant to contractors than the financial flexibility that they extracted from their workforces was the functional flexibility that workers could provide. Workers could be made to perform a wide array of tasks. Whereas a hydraulic excavator could only excavate, a power sander could only sand, and a crane could only lift, a worker could fulfill any one of those functions. They could do so either directly, such as by sanding on their hands and knees, or indirectly, such as by assembling steel cages that would be filled with concrete to make columns and walls so that those components did not have to be lifted by a crane. Contractors valued this functional flexibility as a crucial asset in managing unpredictable production schedules. As one contractor observed, "With a crushed schedule, when you are doing things out of sequence, you want to direct workers wherever you need them."

The reliance on workers over machinery also allowed firms to overlap tasks more easily. Coordinating the use of heavy machinery for different tasks areas was often impossible. It was frequently not feasible to use equipment in close proximity; for example, a crane could not easily be operated over an excavator. But crews of people could be spatially overlapped. A steel-fixing or scaffolding crew could be dispatched to construct a roof while another crew could be ordered to sand or complete a basement floor below them. Likewise, the production capacity of a crew performing a given function could be expanded rapidly by simply adding more men to complete tasks that external factors had suddenly made pressing. Men could be added to crews to install materials that had finally become available, or so that design changes could be executed quickly and wouldn't hold up production, or they could be added in numbers and shifts to meet accelerated production schedules.

Firms leaned so heavily on their workforces to cope with industry chaos that when they needed more workers for a given task than they could pull from existing crews, they turned to external manpower agencies to source them. Manpower agencies were companies that recruited and sponsored migrant workers as a standing workforce that they rented out to construction firms on a time-limited basis. They paid the workers some fraction of the jacked-up fee that they charged construction companies. These manpower agencies, widely regarded as shady—"they are selling bodies, really, but you have no choice [but] to take what they give you"—and well connected—"they are all owned by locals with connections, you know, sheikhs with good names"—were viewed as central players in the construction industry. They were lifesavers that rescued companies desperate for manpower to meet accelerated deadlines.

Training for Modernism and Modernist Training

"A big challenge that contractors face in Qatar is that they don't know what kind of workforce they will able to bring in," began a manager at a large construction management firm as he reflected on the industry's use of labor to deal with industry volatility.

There may be government restrictions that affect the quality of the workers that [a contractor] is able to bring in. There may be valid reasons [for these restrictions], but contractors on a monthly basis—no, really, it's on a daily basis—have to worry, if I take this project, a rail project for example, I may not be able to build the workforce that is qualified to build that station. I may not get the workforce when I need it. But contractors here have to learn to overcome this challenge. So what will happen? He will train them.

For workers to become anything companies needed—for them to replace equipment, to be scaffolders one day and steel fixers the next, to sand floors while avoiding the rain of sparks from the steel frame being welded above them—they needed skill. And companies had to train them. Firms developed rapid training systems to teach unskilled workers or workers unskilled in trades other than their own the basic competence that would allow firms to assign them to different task functions. Since Qatari regulations generally obligated workers to leave at the end of the project they were hired for, however, companies were careful to train their workers only up to the minimum level they required for tasks on a specific project and no further. As one contractor explained, "Since you can't retain the labor force, you train them for what you need on the project, and that's it, knowing that at the end, you will send them home. The whole workforce goes, you go from five thousand men to zero, just like that, and then with a new project, you have to start from zero again with a new group of workers. It is like training a new army with new recruits who have never had boots on their feet every few years. Can you imagine that? This is a huge project." Another added that overtraining was tantamount to lost investment: "Your company suffers because you invest so much in training good skilled workers, people who are made accustomed to the country, the conditions, the technical know-how, and then the project is completed and you cannot maintain your workforce. Your investment is on a plane back to Nepal, Bangladesh, wherever."

Some firms, particularly large ones on megaprojects, set up pop-up training centers on-site to support intensive skill development in task areas where they had needed to direct workers. At one of the roundtables I held, contractors described the temporary training schools they set up on their project sites:

> On one of our sites in oil and gas, we needed three or four thousand welders in a very short time period—four months. To find that many welders at the skill level we required was impossible. We tried to get them from all different sources: Bangladesh, Thailand, India, China, Indonesia, any country that could send them, but it was not enough. So what to do? We opened welding schools at the project sites, and there were massive numbers that went through the training. We brought them from outside, but we also pulled them from inside and trained

carpenters, MEP [mechanical, electric, and plumbing], all kinds [of tradesmen already on the project]. . . . It's not a school that will give a credited certificate that you can use in Qatar or that he can take to his country. It's training for us, and we make it so that it fits our specific project needs, narrow to our building specs.

Other contractors emphasized the fact that training centers lasted only for the duration of a project and were dismantled at its close:

We were having around a twenty, twenty-five thousand workforce. So it made sense to arrange a training facility, starting with steel fixers, carpenters, different trades, whatever we needed at that time. Training is on demand, in a way that is beneficial for that project, and only short term. Because at the end of the project, you lose your workers and you lose your cash flow. I cannot sustain them paying wages, and I cannot move them to another project, because all of a sudden, there is no other project. I can't even keep the trainers I used in the school.

Because of the demand volatility they faced, many firms preferred to fold training into the construction work already taking place on-site. They did not do this by focusing on on-the-job learning or developing robust apprenticeship networks. Instead, they concentrated on simplifying and narrowing the tasks they assigned to workers, and shifting to production procedures that required more rudimentary skill sets, which were generally more labor intensive, and less dependent either on the specialized skills needed to operate machinery or the precision handling needed to install prefabricated components. They also established clear and simple sequential steps for the completion of different tasks, dividing complex and interdependent processes into discrete physical movements that they felt could be learned by rote. "Our quality system became based on having well-organized systemic procedures that have to be strictly followed," explained one contractor. "It's not up to the worker or the supervisor. It is the procedure that defines what to do and how to do it. For the worker, he has to go step-by-step, one by one, not jumping steps however he feels. This increased the level of the company in terms of knowledge, in terms of qualification, and it allows us as a company to get more and higher value jobs."

In this way, companies in Qatar used a modernist take on skill that defined it as an asset held by managers and engineers. Guided by modernist assumptions about the distinction between skill and labor, they used their expertise to turn their engineering, construction, and design knowledge into simplified, repetitive, and isolatable motions that workers could do automatically and unthinkingly. Companies sought to train workers to repeat these well-defined physical movements so that they might become the cranes, earthmovers, and industrial polishers that they were replacing.

Construction companies viewed the strength of their training systems as their main competitive edge in the Qatari market. It was the organizational feature that allowed them to cope with the unpredictability they faced, but it also established their companies as durable and profitable firms, or even preferred contractors for clients. "Your training systems don't appear in the bid. There is no separate budget item called training. But it shows in your production results. You can increase your productivity by 300 percent if you have good training systems, and this record for productivity and on-time delivery is what the clients sees." The construction consultants that evaluated bids on their client's behalf concurred that the strength of upskilling strategies informed their assessment of the proposals submitted. As one contractor explained,

> One of the most important things that we look at is their track record of having a skilled workforce. Can they get their workforce to the level where they can actually execute the project, meet the technical challenges, and can they reach the productivity levels we need in a couple of months, not six months or a year? When I am assessing contractors, I am not looking at the laborers and whether they can give me a certification for their skills as steel fixers or whatever. The skill of the contractor in building training systems plays the largest role here. This is one of the reasons we don't have an open bid. It is very high risk for us. We need to be able to check past practice with training before we allow firms to compete.

The view that strong skill-building systems were a competitive advantage was so significant that firms protected their training systems as proprietary information. "Skill is looked at as a trade secret," griped a manager for a large contractor. "You cannot get a release to work [for] any other company because they are afraid that you will take [the company's] training systems with you." Firms jealously guarded the organizational know-how behind the design of their training systems, but they also sought to maintain sole control over the skill they had developed in their workforces. Most contractors I interviewed were dismayed by the Qatari government's moves to loosen the constraints through which the kafala system bound workers to their employers. They were opposed to regulatory changes that would, in 2017, allow workers to change employers after a probationary year. "You get a worker fresh, you train him from zero, this is your investment, and then your investment will walk out the door. Some other company will take from what you put into training him," remarked one manager in a roundtable discussion of the regulatory reforms, at the time still vague proposals. Another manager added his reflection on the proposed reforms:

> Yes, when I get [the worker], he can only produce 20 percent. I keep him because 20 percent is better than 0 [percent] and I invest so that

I get him to 80 [percent]. Now, another company will take him, and get the 60 percent for free. So I will have a choice: I invest 60 percent, or I pay him a little more, maybe better accommodations, and I take the 60 percent that some other company invested. This will be the war between the companies. Nobody will invest; everybody will get their money and get out.

In late 2017, when Qatar changed its laws to allow some workers to change firms without their employer's assent, firms did not take their money and leave, and in any case, the workers who had legal permission to move were largely unable to exercise their new rights and change companies, bound as they were by debt and other constraints. The approach to training that firms in Qatar developed—rapid, hierarchical, and controlling—remained a core feature of their production processes.

This is because, on some level, the training strategy was more than a tactical response to the shocks and volatility that the government's approach unleashed on the construction industry. It was deeply bound up with Qatar's modernist approach to urban development. Like the modernist cities dreamed up by modernist architects, the training systems and task specifications were designed to create men. Planners like Le Corbusier or Niemeyer used the layout of city blocks to stratify relationships among social classes, and the design and placement of buildings to shape the social activity of residents, and even define their subjectivities. In the same way, Qatari construction companies used their training systems to reinforce hierarchies on-site and transform workers into the instruments of management. "We enforce our procedures strictly," noted one contractor. "You don't want carpenters or steel fixers trying things out, or thinking they can figure things out on their own. Without obedience, construction becomes very expensive."

Since political economist Harry Braverman undertook his Marxist analysis of production and sparked interest in de-skilling—or separating workers from their skill—a rich literature has emerged examining the training structures that businesses establish to develop and manage their workforces.[81] Many of these have added nuanced to Braverman's claim that employers dumb down work tasks by decomposing them. They have shown that company training systems rely on workers to set the social systems required to support training structures, and have suggested that these strategies counteract some of the ways that employers try to claim ownership over worker skill.[82] This was true on construction sites in Qatar as well, as the next chapter will show in greater detail, but training systems there were also designed not just—or even primarily—to develop workforces but rather to erase workers' contribution to training. They were structured to prevent workers from claiming any role in their own learning and block them from expressing ownership over their own skill.

Urban development in Qatar—in true modernist fashion—defined persons through the design of urban spaces, but equally through the process of building the buildings that made the modernist city. It turned some into residents, classed as global elites, members of families, and skilled persons. It turned others into machines, stripping them of the right to the skill they had developed, their families and social connection, and their humanity. It banished the bachelor workers from the gleaming city they had built, modernist structure by modernist structure, and denied the skill that workers had to develop and use to turn Qatar's modernist imaginary into tracts of concrete and glass.

Labor City and the Construction of Skill-Based Exclusion

In reflecting on wage theft, one manager explained, "You have to remember that in these conditions, no one is talking about money. If [the worker] is out there working ten or twelve hours, he is not caring about what he is getting or not getting. He will try to do the work and get through the day safely. Then he is running like crazy at 5 p.m. to catch the bus. You are asking political questions. He has not come to Qatar to do politics. He has come to work."

For workers, the question of whether or not they were paid was political, but it was a politics of basic livelihood and survival. It was a politics that grew out of the way their skill and labor were treated in Qatar. As the country's modernist urban development accelerated into the 2010s, the politics that reduced workers to bodies only hardened. As the construction industry relied more heavily on worker skill to cope with the volatility that the modernist approach created, the tendency to deny worker contribution to construction and represent them as unskilled, with no rights to the knowledge-based city they were building, also grew.

In keeping with modernist practice, these representations took shape in new and increasingly draconian physical structures meant to exclude workers from the urban spaces they were making. In response to international outrage over the living conditions that construction workers endured, the Qatari government built Labor City. Inaugurated on November 1, 2015, the development was a large and prison-like labor camp, slated to hold seventy thousand workers, located on the edge of the industrial area.[83] The barracks, identical and modernist in their design, were built to strict specifications, with rules about the square foot allocation per male resident, size of the bunks, and basic ventilation requirements.[84] The new Labor City complex also included a cricket pitch, recreation facilities, and a gym, "fitting the tastes and cultures of its inhabitants," according to the government's promotional material.[85] But apart from the media tour offered at the inauguration, the complex was closed to the public, surrounded by high walls and security at each of its nine gates.

The human rights monitors, journalists, and researchers who had from time to time been able to access labor camps in the industrial area were barred from entering, and no one could smuggle out workers' views on having been housed there. CCTV cameras were ubiquitous, mounted on walls throughout the new dorms as well as on the complex's perimeter. Additionally, some of the companies building dorms in the compound were introducing technology that would track the movement of residents in real time through GPS locators on their cell phones, or the Wi-Fi-enabled smart tags that they would carry with them to access kitchen facilities or receive meals. The tracking data, collected by AirPatrol platform, would provide "real time locationing and asset management," and have "a direct impact on improving the experience of expatriate workers in Qatar," according to Sysorex, the California-based firm delivering the service.[86] The new platforms augmented technology already distributed to employers for the purpose of monitoring the movements of their workers, including a downloadable app issued by the Ministry of Interior allowing employers to report missing—"absconded" in the terms used by the ministry—workers for immediate search and detention.

Through the use of urban planning and physical design, the government sought to mold the political subjectivity—the personhood—of the migrant workers it used to build the country. Segregated from the city and its public spaces, their movement monitored and controlled, their tastes and leisure defined, unskilled bachelors were confined to an existence dictated entirely by their function for production. The high-walled structures of Labor City were designed to prevent them from becoming more than labor—from exercising forms of agency and personhood through which they could express their needs, preferences, and solidarities. Labor City was used to turn migrant men into labor inputs—to transform them through the alchemy of modernist planning into labor that could substitute for capital, turn the production systems that built the camp into vast and flexible machines, not concern itself with the politics of being paid.

With its sparkling city center and gray carceral workers barracks, Qatar reminds us that both the design of spaces and the design of production are built around definitions of skill. Our cities, factories, and visions of the future all reflect social understandings of skill—its content, quality, and most important, who has it and who doesn't. These definitions of skill are political, with little relation to the actual competence that people display, but they are the foundation for a politics of exclusion. In Qatar, that exclusion has been overtly and emphatically spatial, with a clear physical border delineating the skilled from the unskilled. In other places, that exclusion is more layered. But everywhere it is based on the claim that skill can be lifted out of the people who enact it—a move that reduces them to laboring bodies. This is a political fiction, demonstrably, because the production of our skill-stratified visions—the actual work of making our urban and economic imaginaries real—depends on the skill of those who have been defined as unskilled. Yet it is a belief that justifies theft—the theft of skillful practice and effort, and its appropriation by our designers, innovators, and financiers. More significant, it justifies erasure— not only of skill, but also of the political existence of those represented as unskilled. In Qatar, the evidence of that erasure was in the bodily removal of workers from the places they built. The industrial area, with its grim tracts, challenges us to look for similar evidence of the way that skill politics shape all of our cities, spaces, and systems of production.

CHAPTER THREE

Skill

HOW SKILL IS EMBODIED AND WHAT IT MEANS FOR THE CONTROL OF BODIES

EDUCATION CITY, a sprawling fourteen-kilometer-square university campus, was a jumble of iconic buildings, each one vying for attention. But at the far northeastern edge of the complex, pressed up against a busy highway, one building stood out. This building, the home of the Qatar Faculty of Islamic Studies (QFIS), contained both a faculty and mosque. From the air, it looked like a gleaming piece of three-dimensional Islamic calligraphy. From the ground, it resembled an overturned shell, its curves hinting at the spiral inside that connects classrooms and contemplative spaces to the cavernous mosque at the structure's heart. At the foot of the building's curve, two minarets rose up like inverted sunbeams that streaked upward in ninety-meter diagonals toward the sky. These minarets were the final élan of the spiral unfurling toward the heavens. Some compared the building to a white dove landing with its wings still stretched behind it. Others thought that the minarets reminded them of a jet, idling in preparation for takeoff.[1]

The design of the building was meant to capture the relationship between knowledge and faith, deeply rooted in Islamic practice. Architects from the Spanish Mangera Yvars office sought to embody the interplay between the two in the building's structure, organizing its flow around the interplay of matter and light.[2] The mosque space was illuminated with hundreds of tiny light fixtures and openings in the ceiling that sparkled with the brilliance of stars on clear desert nights. The prayer room had no processional entrance—an allusion to the many pathways to the light of faith. At one end, an ablution stair acted as a light well and waterfall; the elegant curve of the stairs was wrapped in a thin metal mesh that directed a cascade of water flowing from the top of the structure, through the building, into the four gardens of paradise on the ground level. Verses from the Koran poured across the building's walls, from

the interior mihrab out to the spiraling corridors, along the upswept para-
pets that lined the courtyard, and up the side of the minarets. The calligraphy,
embossed on the ceramic walls and cladding, reflected different periods of
the art form, and in some places included contemporary graffiti. The project
was recognized at the World Architecture Festival in 2015, commended as "a
cultural breakthrough where client and architect have produced a remarkable
building," and praised for its organic feel.[3]

The building, so weightless and fluid in its design, was cumbersome to
build. The structure, with its broad sweeps, was put together like a three-
dimensional jigsaw puzzle, fitted with joints that allowed different areas of the
building to move in response to high desert winds. To offset the give of these
joints and support the gravity-defying curves of the roof, the building was held
up by a cross section of beams shot through with dense networks of steel cable
tendons. The dome of the mosque ceiling relied on a crosshatch of vertical and
inclined steel columns along with a network of arched beams bolted in place
to create the curve of the heavens. The mosque floor, suspended at its edge,
was braced in part by five sculptural columns, each representing one of the
five pillars of Islam, and each constructed with a custom-bent rebar cage. The
entire building was covered in cladding, with some panels of aluminum and
glass, and others made of cast gypsum, all of them specially designed for the
project. All the panels were installed by hand in keeping with intricate facade
design and the flow of the verses captured by the calligraphy. In the main
courtyard, where calligraphy was laser cut in stainless steel affixed to the inner
walls, patterned glass screens were installed to defuse the sunlight and ensure
that the verses cast no shadow that a believer might inadvertently walk on.[4]

The most technically daring component of the project was the minarets.
Made of steel, but designed to look like light, the minarets, which towered
some eighty meters above the ground, tapered as they rose, from about two
meters at their base to twenty-five centimeters at their tip. They did not rise
straight into the air but instead were cantilevered at an incline of twenty-
five degrees. Hydraulic devices that would allow the beams to sway with the
intense pressures of desert wind sheers were installed in the base. The minarets themselves were made up of dozens of steel plates, each ten meters long
and twenty tons in weight, and many engraved with calligraphy that grew
bolder as it stretched to the sky. The plates were bolted in place, with the joints
fixed at slight and precise angles to create a gentle camber that would reduce
pressure on the minaret structure.[5]

To erect the minarets, the contractors had to build one of the largest and
most elaborate scaffolding structures ever attempted. The freestanding scaffold rose up some eighty-five meters, or twenty-six stories high, with only its
wide base and tight joints supporting its weight and intense wind pressures.
The scaffold cocooned the minarets as they rose up from the ground, ten-
meter steel girder by ten-meter steel girder, and provided a platform where

workers could stand as they joined the metal pieces together, affixed the cladding, and applied glaze to the building's skin.[6]

Hundreds of workers hauled the pieces required to build the scaffold up dozens of stories, manually carrying them up temporary stairs and ladders, and passing them up man to man along the outside of the structure. They pulled up four- and 6-meter-long scaffolding pipes, which weighed four kilograms per meter. They lugged thick wooden scaffolding planks; they hoisted metal joints, swivels, gravelocks, and clamps; and they carried up their tools, spanners, and wrenches tucked into the bulky harness vests they wore, their movements constrained by the heavy clamps and nylon rope they used to tie themselves to the structure, for safety, as they climbed up the provisional frame.

Each scaffolder handled one ton of material every day. The steel and wood components moved through the hands of more than of thirty men every eight hours. During the life of the scaffold, which was built, dismantled, and rebuilt several times over the course of the construction process, each piece of material was handled several hundred times. In the heat and din of the construction site, the pipes, planks, joints, and spanners were all manipulated wordlessly. The men relied on hand gestures and manual signals, like a twist to the pipe to convey the soundness of their grip to those passing the material or a tug to signal the direction in which they were moving the material. Workers fit tens of thousands of joints and locks, and as they tightened the bolts, took care to secure pipes, planks, and ladders at sharp right angles. The structural integrity of the scaffold, and its ability to hold their weight without collapsing beneath them or being knocked over by a gust of wind, depended on their precision. The workers read and interpreted blueprints that evolved as the building did. The more experienced scaffolders evaluated the orders they received, deciding which areas to hollow out and dismantle in order to keep the structure from buckling. As the men hauled, measured, and joined, workers from other trades hustled right below them on recently completed scaffolding, welding and fixing the minarets from the platforms of the industrial honeycomb.

The men who built these scaffolds called themselves "the people who hang from the sky." And indeed they did. To build these self-standing structures, scaffolders hung from pipes crossed in an inverted T shape, made of a vertical pipe hanging down and a horizontal pipe fasted to its base. These metal crosses were clamped to the edge of scaffolding built several stories high. Scaffolders balanced on the lower horizontal pipe, only a few inches in diameter, on the balls of their work-boot-clad feet. Perched tens of stories up in the air, with nothing below them, they fastened together ten kilogram pipes to build the temporary exoskeleton.

During the entire project, there was not one fall. Not a single scaffolder sustained a serious injury, nor was anyone gravely hurt by falling equipment, which when dropped from stories up in the air, had the collision force of a weapon.

This was no small achievement. The skill required to build the towering scaffold, and do so without serious injury or mistake, was substantial. The skills had to be developed on-site because the scaffolding structure was unlike any other anywhere in the world. It was record breaking and vertiginous, and customized in response to the challenges that the minarets and organic shapes of the QFIS project represented. To build it, new construction techniques had to be developed on-site, and the men working on the structure had to learn abilities beyond any standard roster of scaffolding skills.

In this sense, the scaffold was unimaginable to the men who built it. In part, this was because only a few of the hundreds of workers who constructed it had ever worked on a scaffold of that size. Only those transferred from the massive oil and gas construction projects in the north of the country had experience with scaffolding on that scale. Most of the men on the scaffolding detail had arrived in Qatar only months before from small towns and rural areas in Asia and Africa. The mammoth construction sites they worked in Qatar diminished any previous construction experience they might have had.

Managers on-site expressed frustration at having to train workers who could not envision what they were building—"you are asking them to build a tower, and they only know huts"—and grumbled that they were forced to contend with "poor-quality workers" who were "backward" and "lacking wisdom." But managers and engineers were also amazed at the scaffold they had managed to build. "It's a new wonder of the world," said one. The scaffold was a feat of structural daring, and before it was built, it had been in some sense unimaginable to everyone.

LEARNING AND HEART

How migrant workers learned to build structures like this unimaginable scaffold is the story I tell here. At the heart of it is a jarring paradox: the learning that was so critical to project completion was unsupported and often actively undermined on-site. The source of this paradox was the managerial definition of skill in Qatar's construction industry. Skill was measured not in competence or dexterity but rather obedience. In an inversion of the more common use of the term, which includes some component of self-direction, skill in Qatar was equated with adherence to the detailed and exactingly sequenced procedures that management defined for different construction processes. Under the rubric of this definition of skill, training was less a process of developing competence than it was a matter of enforcing compliance with the regimented method defined for each construction task. Reframed in this way, training became a means for controlling workers and, more specifically, their bodies.

For companies in Qatar's construction industry, workers were a production component, sourced like any other raw material from outside Qatar, purchased and imported in bulk, by the hundreds, from around the world.

They viewed their challenge as transforming the brute labor power they had sourced, as undifferentiated as orders of steel or cement, into a workforce that could execute the specific construction tasks demanded by the project at any given moment in the construction cycle. As they raced to build one iconic structure after another, they used disciplinary training systems to turn manpower, which they calculated by the hour and budgeted with an almost performative precision for each of the detailed steps stipulated for various tasks, into a machine that could complete the construction processes required to turn the ambitions rendered in engineering drawings into buildings that no longer had to be imagined.

Workers were keenly aware that the depth of their skill was not perceived by management and their learning was discounted. They complained bitterly about the fact that their wages did not rise in keeping with their ability. But they were even more troubled by what they described as a managerial carelessness with their bodies. They described managerial disregard for their physical safety and personal welfare. They spoke about the humiliation they felt when they understood how cheaply their bodies and lives were assessed by the companies that employed them.

Some months into the QFIS project, when the scaffold was largely dismantled and only a few stories of latticework remained at the base of the minarets, I interviewed workers who had been transferred from the QFIS site to a new stadium project on the outskirts of Doha. The stadium was designed as a conch that captured natural elements of Qatar's seafront, reflecting water, sand, and pearls on its surface. Its dome was broad and low, with structurally complex waves creating the illusion of movement and lightness. The men I spoke with had been working since dawn on the internal scaffold. The structure they were erecting, some seventeen stories high, was like an industrial frame for the dome that would be built on top of it: an eggshell of cladding applied on the surface of a temporary skeleton of scaffolding and held in place with a conical steel core. The scaffold was built from the outside in: the edges were erected first, holding up the perimeter of the building. Scaffolders built toward the center, using hanging scaffolds that reached for the empty middle like stiff tentacles.

A team of three workers, Ahilan and Modi from Nepal, and Prince from Ghana, climbed down from the scaffold during their midmorning break to talk with me. I interviewed them in the back section of a trailer just off the main construction platform, and while we spoke, secretaries and workers from the scaffolding detail dropped in to pick up work orders, file paperwork, or send in reports of material or equipment problems via walkie-talkies to the site's central office.

"Yes, we are the men who are hanging from the sky," said Prince, the scaffolder from a small town on the outskirts of Accra, when I asked him about the moniker. He spoke with me in English. "That's our job. We have to do it because it is our destiny, whether we like it or not. But I like it," he added with bravado.

> This project is high pressure, fast track. It's very tough, but we are going to make it. Because it's our destiny. Three years ago, I never would have thought we could build something like this. And six years ago, when I first came [to Qatar], I had never climbed anywhere higher than the roof of my house. But that is why it is our destiny. And after this, we can work anywhere in scaffolding. We are already spending 90 percent of our time hanging from the sky. We are the number one team. All the teams wish they could learn from us.

He laughed and slapped his Nepali teammate on the back.

The translator I brought to help with the interviews, Muzi, a construction worker from Bihar who had become fluent in English, translated Prince's comments into Hindi for his coworkers. Ahilan and Modi did not speak English, and Prince did not speak Hindi. Ahilan and Prince had worked together for six years, and Modi had joined them a year before I met the team, but apart from a few words of the pidgin of English and Hindi construction terms that was the lingua franca on project sites in Qatar, they had no common language between them.

When the laughter died down, Prince explained his choice to migrate to Qatar.

> I migrated for a better salary than I got in Ghana. But when I came, I found that it was different than what the agent told me. The money is too low, but I have no prospects in Ghana. So I decided that I would try to manage here for sometime. . . . Our work is our life. We cannot move anywhere in this country. If you go anywhere, they stop you and ask you where you are going. The slave trade is over, but it feels like slavery is back. They force us to do what we don't want to do, but we don't have a choice. We are not treated like men, and if I am not treated like a man, how can I smile?

As Prince spoke about the treatment that he experienced in Qatar, his voice began to rise. He was too agitated for Muzi to keep up with his translation into Hindi.

> I am a man, but if you work with somebody and that person loses his life. . . . They compensate you ten thousand riyals [about US$3,000] and then they send the person back to his family to bury him. So you ask yourself, how much are you worth, out there, hanging from the sky, risking your neck. Ten thousand riyals. Yes, in this rich country. How is ten thousand riyals going to help my family, my children? I am a man. It is very difficult, because this guy, Abdulai . . .

All of a sudden, Prince stopped talking. His body seemed to crumple in his chair, and he began to sob into his chest. Ahilan put his arm around Prince's shoulders and pulled him close. Modi put his hand on Prince's knee. A foreman who had been filing paperwork in the background stopped and wrapped his arms around his own chest, swaying slightly as if he were holding himself against the sorrow in the room. Modi asked the foreman to please make a tea with three sugars.

Ahilan lifted his face up from Prince's shoulder and turned to Muzi: "This man [Abdulai] was from Ghana too, and his mother called and said that she had no money for a burial plot." Modi put the mug of tea in Prince's hands, cupping his own around them to steady Prince's grip. Ahilan wiped Prince's cheek with his hand and then explained to me, through Muzi, whose face became serious as he translated, carefully and deliberately now to make sure that I understood, "All of us must live with the understanding that this is a dangerous job. Once you see it, you know it can happen. You have to take care of yourself and your brothers. Because it is better than being dead. We all want to go back to our families."

"Yes, he is right," added Muzi, taking a break from translating to chime in. "We all know this. It hurts your heart."

Clearly, these workers understood the risk that they took each day on the job and pain they felt at their company's response to a death. They understood the value that they brought to the project through their scaffolding skill while understanding that they were mere bodies to the company, which would only take financial responsibility for shipping their corpses back to their countries. But the exchange also captured the deep nonverbal understanding that the teammates shared. Ahilan and Modi knew, without being able to access Prince's words, the death he was speaking of. They understood the contours of his heartache too and knew how to comfort him.

The sensitivity of this physical communication—the ability of workers like Prince, Ahilan, and Modi to share nuanced experiences as well as emotional detail through their bodies and gestures—was what enabled minarets to rise up like suspended beams of light. This physical and empathetic exchange was the language that workers on Qatar's construction sites used to communicate. It was the language that Ahilan, Modi, and Prince used to coordinate their movements for hauling up heavy scaffolding pipes, and harmonize their actions so that each pipe was held at the correct angle when it was clamped into place. This embodied exchange was also the language through which they learned from one another. Ahilan and Prince taught Modi the craft of scaffolding, in all its complexity, through gesture and touch. They modeled scaffolding tasks for him, slowing down and exaggerating their movements to make the steps involved in specific scaffolding tasks visible and accessible to Modi. These demonstrations were also acts of generosity and friendship that strengthened the practices of mutual care in the team. Learning on Qatari construction sites was interactive and empathetic, and took place among many teams of workers made up of men from around the world who often shared no single spoken language.

The physicality of skill and the interactive, interpersonal learning taking place on Qatari construction sites are a striking illustration of theories of embodied cognition that have begun to revolutionize the way we conceive of knowledge. Francisco Varela, Eleanor Rosch, and Evan Thompson summarize this perspective along with its radical departure from the representation of knowledge as a stand-alone resource in the following way: "By using the term *embodied* we mean to highlight two points: first that cognition depends upon the kinds of experience that come from having a body with various sensorimotor capacities, and second, that these individual sensorimotor capacities are themselves embedded in a more encompassing biological, psychological and cultural context."[7] There has been an outpouring of works on the different manifestations of knowledge and learning as embodied, with attention paid to everything from the neurons involved in physical synchronicity and mimicry, to the effects of emotion on learning and memory. Far less developed in these explorations are the political and institutional forces that shape the way that embodied cognition is expressed, acquired, and shared.

The stark realities of the Qatari construction process offer vivid insight into how embodied cognition and learning are affected by structural power dynamics. The Qatari process reveals the way that power plays out through the definition of competence. Specifically, it shows how a definition of competence—or cognition—that limits itself to observable skillful behavior, and dismisses the affective, interpersonal, and experiential parts of knowledge, can easily become a vehicle for control or even subjugation. The rich array of practices that phenomenologists call the "lifeworld"—the expression of human connection, social beliefs, self-understanding, forms of creativity, and subjective avenues for the interpretation of the material world—are not merely the backdrop for skillful action.[8] They are what skillful action is made of. When the experiential aspects of skill are excluded, it is not just that the definition of skill is flattened, reduced to mechanical action. It is that the experiential dimensions held in skillful action are erased. When definitions of skill are stripped of the creative, agentic, relational lifeworlds that the term holds, skillful actors are also stripped of the full array of their humanity. Pared-down definitions of skill can pave the way for skillful actors to be treated as bodies that are executing skilled behavior instead of people who are skilled.

On Qatari construction sites, workers experienced a power structure rooted in a stripped-down, strictly behavioral definition of skill. Skill was measured in the satisfactory completion of the highly specified and mechanical steps that management identified as necessary for the completion of construction tasks. Workers were treated as instruments, reduced to bodies that were subject to management control. This definition allowed management to claim ownership over worker skill, capturing it by controlling workers' labor while simultaneously denying or undermining the rights of the worker to own their own skill.

To be sure, the effect of this stripped-down definition of skill as a means for worker control was magnified by the institutional context in which it played out. The sponsorship—or kafala—system increased workers' dependence on their employer's view of skill. It did this by limiting workers' access to other spaces where their skill might be evaluated and valued, most notably by dramatically restricting their access to the labor market. Until 2017, workers by law could not change or quit jobs for the duration of their contract, as described in the previous chapter on regulation. In 2017, modest reforms enabled them to change jobs after a year on their contract, although various barriers continued to make changing employment difficult. On-site, the kafala system ensured compliance with the managerial definition of skill: because workers had no right to residence in Qatar separate from their work contract, those who did not follow the highly regimented procedures through which skill was defined on-site or expressed skill in ways that management viewed as insubordinate could be summarily deported. Short of deportation, management could implement many other disciplinary measures, including suspended pay and forced overtime, against which the labor law in Qatar afforded little or no protection.

Taken together, the definition of skill management used and the kafala system that backed it up allowed employers to treat workers' bodies and skill separately. Workers were reduced to their bare physicality. It was the managers who claimed ownership of skill. Managers viewed workers' skill as mechanical and rudimentary, separate from the embodied imagination, sensitivity, and thoughtfulness that was so critical to their ability to learn, and their competence. Defined in this way, worker skill became a disembodied resource that managers could control. Managers controlled skill by relying on the ability to control workers' bodies that the kafala system afforded them, treating workers as inputs to a production system. But this also affected the workers' expression of their embodied knowledge. It disrupted the unfolding of learning processes in ways that were often blunt, sometimes complex, and even surprising. More important, this control of workers' bodies enabled the erasure of workers' contribution to the architectural marvels they built. Their creativity, generosity in teaching and learning, and sensitivity all got worn down by the bonds of the kafala system, and the idea of skill it was used to defend. There is a reason that this approach to skill, as Muzi put it, hurt the heart.

Embodied Cognition, Learning, and Power

Construction is widely characterized as a low-skill occupation—a port of entry for unskilled migrants into the labor markets of a given receiving country. Certainly, the migrants who travel to Qatar to work in construction have generally been represented as unskilled. Press accounts, accompanied by photos of nameless men in their anonymizing blue overalls, underscored human rights reports that borrowed the same tropes, emphasizing workers' lack of skills as a correlate to their political vulnerability. Meanwhile, industry analyses and government reports bemoaned the low skill level of workers as a factor that hamstrung productivity.[9] To be sure, data on the levels of the formal education of migrant workers in the Qatar construction industry lent some backing to this representation of the men who worked on the sites. In 2015, for example, almost half of the workforce in construction (352,679 out of 785,075) had no more than a primary education, and three-quarters (600,403) had not finished secondary school. (It is worth noting that the government of Qatar, in its assessment of the country's labor force, equated skill level with occupation; those workers in "elementary occupations"—mostly concentrated in construction and household employment—were counted as unskilled in the labor force survey, whereas workers in "craft and related trades occupations" and "plant and machine operators and assemblers" were counted as semiskilled. In 2015, the government reported that 14 percent of the construction labor force was considered unskilled, and another 74 percent was semiskilled.)[10]

Even a cursory look at buildings in Qatar, however, reveals that construction practices required skills that were complex and sophisticated. The designs of Qatar's buildings, elaborate and daring in their conception, required the manipulation of materials that pushed the boundaries of what concrete and sinews of steel could achieve. Their execution required construction firms to routinely come up with pathbreaking solutions. Moreover, the design details demanded a level of attention to craft and artistry no longer seen in most modern buildings. Because the buildings were all bespoke, the technological solutions and craft expertise required had to be developed anew for each building project.

The process of translation from architectural rendering to actual building proceeded through many layers of iteration. For each building, architectural drawings were turned into construction documents and mapped into 3D construction process software, and the workflow was meticulously laid out; each construction phase was itemized and sequenced, and the labor hours and expertise required for each phase were specified as well as tracked.[11] But ultimately the plans were all theory. Their execution depended on the men who carried out the thousands of tasks they specified and the skill they brought to their jobs. The drawings became buildings thanks to the abilities of those who secured the scaffolding joints, affixed the cladding, and hoisted steel girders into the air and turned them into cantilevered columns of light.

The chasm between the educational level of workers and the skill required to build the structures seems unbridgeable—until the quality of that skill is more closely examined. On-site, the skill that workers used was embodied and tacit. It was expressed not in language or abstract drawings, although those were useful tools, but rather through bodies, made visible in the physical material that they skillfully manipulated. It manifested itself through action, enacted in response to the specific requirements of a construction task, as it emerged on a given project at a given moment in time. Workers could talk about the feeling of competence, and they did at length, with pride and eloquence. But the skill itself had to be felt, and it resided in their bodies. Their competence resided in the ability to interpret bodily sensations and respond to those sensations skillfully so that they could manipulate materials and change their physical environment.

This kind of embodied skill is often associated with occupations such as construction that have some manual component, and implicit in this attribution is the sense that the kind of embodied knowledge involved in manual labor represents lower-level cognitive tasks. Arguably, this characterization of embodied skill is based on the fact that these skills may not require a full cycle of schooling in formal educational institutions. It is also based, though, on a deeply entrenched but increasingly outdated view of cognition.

For a long while, cognition was understood as an abstract computational process in which the mind worked and action followed. People used information to deduce mental models of the world and then acted based on those representations. According this theory, perceptions of the world outside the self were brought into these mental models as information. In this input-output take on cognition, perceptions fed information into the system, and actions were a function of what that information meant when filtered through the model. Higher-order cognitive processes could be captured and shared by describing these cognitive models, with the caveat that some were more articulate in expressing these models than others.[12] And in this view, which dominated cognitive science and early robotics for much of the twentieth century, formal educational systems transmitted these higher-level models so that it was reasonable to assume that jobs that did not require advanced schooling must be devoid of these higher-level cognitive processes.

Recent findings in neurobiology and cognitive science, however, suggest that absolutely all cognition is embodied.[13] They show that not only is there no distinction between cognitive processes that have traditionally been classified as lower or higher level but there is also no meaningful difference between being in the world as a body and thinking.[14] Evoking a mathematical formula in the mind seems to require many of the same physical processes as walking across a room. The Cartesian and computational approach to knowledge—"I think, therefore I am"—has been debunked by one that defines cognition as a biological engagement with the world—"I am, therefore I think."

This research has defined cognition as the process through which we generate meaning about the world through our bodies. Knowledge is not an end, or a stable and identifiable resource. It's an ongoing trajectory, a contextual process that changes minute to minute. It is insight developed in real time through bodily interactions with the physical environment, through the ongoing and immediate sensorimotor processing of feedback.[15] Cognition is something that occurs while we are in action, and we act and adjust in the world based on that cognition.[16] "I move, therefore I think."[17]

In fact, since cognition relies on engagements with the world, some have argued that it is more accurate to think of cognition as a loose system that involves the body, behavior, and the environment. The dense interplay between sense reactions to the physical world and bodily adjustments to those sense perceptions begins to erase the line between the internal and external.[18] In other words, not only is cognition situated in real-world environments but the environment is in fact part of the cognitive system too.[19] And crucially, the environment includes other beings that are also involved in sense making, and are acting and changing the world through their actions.[20] So our own cognition and the action it informs are based not only on our own embodied engagement in the world but on the embodied engagement of others as well.[21]

For social scientists who look at knowledge, a central concern has been how we relate to the embodied engagement of others—how we relate to others in our environment.[22] In a complement to cognitive science, which has sought to map out the biological processes by which we make sense of the world, social scientists have considered knowledge as a social process and concentrated on the social exchanges through which knowledge is made.[23] They have broadened the inquiry past a focus on "how do we know"—the way we exercise cognition to navigate and engage with a specific environment at a given point in time—to questions of "how do we come to know" and "how do we understand what we know"—which takes in processes across space and time as well as through other people.

Like their peers in cognitive science, social scientists have found that the way we come to know, and the way we understand what we know, grows out of the relationship between body and matter. Different people experience matter in different ways, and social scientists have explored what that diversity of experience means for learning. "What one has learned appears in the way the world shows up; it is not represented in the mind and added on to the present experience," explains philosopher Hubert Dreyfus in his description of embodied learning.[24]

This means that the world not only appears differently but actually *is* different to people with different degrees of skill, with different depths of experience. Skill resides neither in the actor nor the physical world. It exists in a fine-grained, sensorimotor perception of the environment. The environment that presents itself to the master is more variegated than the one that presents itself to the novice.[25] A master and novice standing side by side are in different worlds. For the novice, the world appears in black and white, whereas to the master, it is filled with riotous color. The novice hears a note played; the master hears the notes rise and fall, with their sigh, warble, and feeling. The novice lifts their arm; the master feels the air push back against their arm as they move it. Because the solicitations of that environment to the master are more nuanced than they are to the beginner, the master's response is more finely discriminating and subtle—and more effective. Learning, it follows, is simply the process of developing a more sensitive relationship between body and matter. It grows out of a history of relationships between a person and their environment, and the repeated experience of those interactions as positive or negative, as moving closer to some goal or further away.[26] Teaching is the process of guiding a student to experiences that will provide them with a more subtle understanding of their world.

These teaching and learning interactions, maintain their observers, happen through the direct engagement with the physicality of others. It's always body to body. (This is true even when learning appears autodidactic: learners draw on interpersonal interactions as they exist in the form of social norms and institutions, symbolic referents, or memory.) At a gross level, this happens when we mirror the movements of others, when a student, for example, copies the motions of their teacher.[27] On a more nuanced level, it occurs when we interpret the sensory reactions of others and engage with those reactions in a way that allows us to refine our own sensory experiences.[28] The student tries to understand what it feels like to be the teacher and discover the same feeling in their body, and in the process, as their perceptions become more refined, they discover an environment that is more chromatic and offers greater options for action.

Anthropologists Greg Downey and Trevor Marchand have observed that this type of physical empathy emerges especially when teacher and student often participate in the same flow of action.[29] When the teacher interrupts a student's movement and then guides the student in the completion of that movement, this reveals to the student the many possibilities that a given environment can solicit. Through these body-to-body interactions, a student may discover the possibilities for movement—affordances—that a body allows. As the body changes with practice—as a finer ear is developed, musculature becomes stronger, or kinesthetic perceptions of space and whether a floor is level, for example, become more refined—those options for movement may change as well.[30]

The composite picture of skill that emerges from these studies on cognition is a highly nuanced and almost lyrical one. Skill is an embodied ability to respond to the physical world in an going way. It is a living process and not a static resource. It grows out of the relationship between body and matter, and is nurtured by the relationships between people in their bodies.[31]

These studies paint a picture that may be too rosy. The shadows are left out. How these qualities are affected by power dynamics in the environments where people move and act is less finely sketched out.

To be sure, social scientists have conceded that learning exchanges, like all social processes, are shot through with power dynamics. Anthropologist

Jean Lave and educator Etienne Wenger famously coined the phrase "legitimate peripheral participation" to convey the power relations involved in learning. In any social group with a specific practice at its heart—a community
of practice—social power is acquired through mastery. New learners, still
developing their competence, are relatively disempowered in apprenticeship
structures. Their very ability to participate in learning practices depends on
the assent of the master at the center of the learning system, and anyone who
joins these learning practices agrees to replicate the values around what constitutes knowledge and expertise. While the master may bear down heavily on
the apprentice, the power dynamic within the learning relationship is usually
viewed as useful, even benevolent.[32]

Power dynamics outside learning relationships are viewed with more skepticism. Scholars have long called out the social inequalities that shape how
we value knowledge. Skills associated with a specific gender are frequently
cited as illustrations.[33] Women who acquire "male" skills or men who invest in
learning "female" crafts might find that their social standing is undercut rather
than enhanced through mastery.[34] Others have pointed to strategies designed
to control what is learned and how skill is used.[35] Organization studies scholars in particular have detailed management practices designed to "harvest"
and "channel" knowledge produced by employees to support the productivity
goals of a given company.[36]

But curiously, when observers of embodied learning focus on power, the
embodied quality of learning is somehow sidestepped. The insights about the
ways that knowing in the world is the same as being in the world are somewhere left behind. Analyses of the impact of power dynamics on learning
leave out the iterative relationship between bodies and knowledge that is central to the theories on embodied learning; they forget to pay attention to the
ways that embodied persons move through the world and in relation to one
another; and they neglect the effect of power plays on the bodies of learners
and the ways that they can damage the knowledge that learners can embody.

Instead, in these analyses, the knowledge that is evaluated, captured, and
controlled is once again represented as a fully formed resource, independent of and separate from the bodies that enact it.[37] When scholars note that
managerial routines and dictates are used to harness knowledge, observe that
mastery is invoked to privilege some social identities over others, and document that organizational power and resources means that some skill is valued
more highly that others, we do not learn how these power expressions shape
the ways that embodied persons engage with matter, one another, or their
environment.[38]

And because the knowledge that is wrangled over is separated out from
the people who enact it, the learning process too seems somehow cocooned
from these power stratagems. Actors try to control the output of that learning exchange, but they don't disrupt the learning within the cocoon in any

fundamental way. So while these dynamics are not entirely ignored, the effect of power on the embodied quality of learning exchange is ultimately not examined. Moreover, the societal power dynamics that are not directly concerned with the control of knowledge have little bearing in these accounts on how learning unfolds. They are left out of the social analyses of the management of skill and expertise.

In Qatar, the kafala system, the main institutional framework that governed employment, centered on the control of bodies, and as a system of bonded labor, it shaped the ways that workers held knowledge in their bodies and shared their knowledge with others. Embodied cognition and learning were deeply affected by the power relations encoded in the sponsorship system, and carried forward into the production spaces of construction sites. The exercise of power over embodied knowledge happened on the bodies of workers engaged in knowing. These power dynamics shaped the relationships that workers experienced between body and matter, and disrupted the body-to-body learning exchanges that were so critical to the development of embodied knowledge on-site. These disruptions undermined workers' ability to teach and learn and threatened their on-site physical safety.

Body to Matter

The first time I went to the stadium site where I met Prince, Modi, and Ahilan, my research assistant and I drove up to the construction site at dawn. The site was located on the desert outskirts of Doha, and as the sun rose behind the skeletal structure, the orange rays of the new day poured through openings in the silhouette of steel. At a distance, the structure already looked majestic.

In the parking lot, the intense activity required to build the stadium became clear. A long line of white buses with company logos disgorged men who streamed toward the construction site, many carrying their lunch pails, while a crowd of men, tired and eager to return to their labor camp after working the night shift, amassed in a growing scrum waiting to board the buses.

At the edge of the site closest to the highway, the managers' air-conditioned trailers were arranged in two neat parallel lines. Beyond them, the site exploded into a jumble of cranes, material sheds, cement mixers, and trucks. In and around the structure itself, the site thundered with activity. The grind of construction equipment whined against the heat even in the early morning; the deafening clanging of steel against steel was broken up only by the sound of industrial whistles when steel or cladding was being transported on cables overhead; spark clouds burst out from behind the fire mats that were hung to keep the wooden scaffolding platforms from going up in flames.

At any given time of day, there were close to eight thousand men working on a site no bigger than a couple of soccer pitches. The density of men on-site would have been shocking if it wasn't like every other site I had visited in Doha. Men amassed at different corners of the construction site, pressed together as they waited their turn to access the corridors, marked out with tape ribbons on sticks, between task areas. Men worked cheek by jowl.

The men on-site were from all over world: supervisors along with health and safety coordinators from Britain and South Africa, engineers from Lebanon and Palestine, and workers from a wide swath of countries in Asia as well as East and Central Africa. One cladding supervisor told me that he had at one point decided to tally the languages spoken on-site. "We counted twenty-two languages—and not just the usual ones. Minor languages from the Filipino islands, parts of India, African languages." The diversity of this workforce was a uniquely Qatari creation; the entire staff on the site, from worker to manager down to a man, was a migrant, brought into the country to build the physical and cultural infrastructure Qatar dreamed of. The only time a Qatari national was seen on-site was when the representative of the stadium's Qatari client arrived to survey the construction progress. Reportedly he visited the site infrequently, "less than a handful of times," but each time he reiterated that the compressed schedule for the project was nonnegotiable, and if the deadline for the project was not met, the entire managerial staff on the project would be immediately deported along with their families.

The timeline for construction had been shortened by half, from the three years estimated by the stadium designers down to a year and a half, and the time pressure was causing mistakes. The day before my first visit, a gravelock coupler, used to clamp together scaffolding tubes, had been dropped from ten stories up in the air. No one had been hurt, but the incident was judged to be serious enough to warrant a stand-down—a review of practice—at the start of the next day's shift.

So it was that shortly after sunrise, several hundred scaffolders, most of them with their faces already wrapped in calico against the sun's blistering rays, gathered in front of a scaffolding platform erect at the edge of the construction site. The scaffolding supervisor for the stadium project stood on the improvised podium, flanked by the chief foremen and a member of the health and safety crew. Yelling into a bullhorn, the Englishman, Matty, exhorted the workers, "As you all know, right, gentlemen, a few concerns on the site so it's time to stop and think about what we are doing again. . . . We're now working at the very high heights. Time to step it up, men. We can't afford for anybody to fall or any dropped objects." The supervisor paused every so often so that the health and safety officer could bellow his translation into Hindi through a bullhorn of his own.

"Do not store loose materials on the scaffold, on the steel way, or on the concrete. You take material up and you use it immediately. You are responsible for the area you are working in. You are to maintain good housekeeping at all times. Lads, make sure it's done properly. Anybody who fails to follow these rules will be removed from the project immediately, I guarantee you."

The supervisor brought the ten-minute stand-down to a close with an almost martial call and answer: "I say safety, you say first. Safety!" "First!" yelled the men in unison as they pumped their fists into the air.

"Safety!"

"First!" they replied, fists thrown up again into the air.

"Safety!"

"First!" roared the men in a response that rose up like a wall of sound blocking out the din behind it.

"Right, lads, go about your business." The men picked up their water canteens and dispersed, quickly and quietly.

At the stand-down, the scaffolders had been ordered to work safely. They were told that any failure in adhering to the standard protocol would get them kicked off the site and possibly expelled from the country. But they were given no additional instructions about how to avoid the kinds of mistakes that led to injury and no guidance on how to comply with the safety standards for handing off material.

Later that day, I asked the scaffolding team I was shadowing about this. We were at the base of the scaffold near the equipment stores as we waited for one of the supervisory engineers to radio permission for me to climb up the structure. "How do you learn how to not drop equipment? What makes practice safe?" I asked the team. In response, Santosh, the team's Nepali foreman, picked up a scaffolding pipe from the neat stack behind him, and extended one end of the pipe toward me and waved it. "Take it," he said. I wrapped both my hands around the end. Santosh twisted the pipe clockwise a full semicircle and back, twice. "Do you feel that? This is how I tell you that I have the pipe." He twisted the pipe twice again as if to make sure that I had understood the signal. "It's very loud up there. This way, you can use your hands to listen. Now you," he ordered. I did my best imitation of his double twist, and as soon as I was done, he let his end of the pipe go. The pipe was much heavier that it had felt when Santosh was holding up his end, and my grip was not tight enough to restrain its torque. Santosh had anticipated this and kept one hand just below the pipe when he released it. As he caught and steadied the pipe, he admonished me, "You must never twist until you are sure that you are holding it well."

Santosh's demonstration was an introduction to the way that he taught the workers in his charge. By manipulating the scaffolding pipe, he elicited sensorimotor perceptions in his student—me, in this instance—and offered interpretations of those sensations that his student could adopt. He began the process of refining the environment that his student experienced. He started the process of transforming the relationship between body and matter that his student perceived. He also offered a critical beginning lesson into the ways that scaffolders communicated through their engagement with the material— their particular kind of Morse code, tapped on pipes and clamps, through twists and other gestures executed pipe after pipe, hauled up story after story, to the tune of one ton of material each day. Over the course of my fieldwork, it became clear to me how basic this initial lesson was. Scaffolders reported that they could feel through the quality of the twist of a pipe whether their team-mate at the other end was tired, a little off-balance, or working on a platform that was not level. One scaffolder told me that he could feel if his teammate's gloves were too loose; the twist, he explained, felt muffled.

Training in other trades followed a similar methodology. More experienced workers taught newer arrivals how to engage with the material specific to their trade. They taught them how to interpret the sensations in their body elicited by their interaction with that material and then act based on their interpretations. Steel fixers, masons, welders, cladding fabricators, and tiling crews all shared with me that they learned their trade, and taught others, through guided interaction with the materials that they used. And workers clearly identified the embodied, enacted character of this learning process in their conversations with me. Sameer, for example, who was new to the cladding fabricators crew, had arrived from Nepal only six months prior with no experience in construction. He described his experience with embodied teaching in his interview with me. "When I first arrived, I had some fear in my mind. How will I do this work? But afterward, some Nepali people arrived, and they showed me how to do the work." He pantomimed the training interactions that he had with his coworkers as he spoke, building an imaginary cladding panel on the table in front of him, gesturing as if he were moving and installing the aluminum plates that make up a panel: "Like this, they said, take this, then this one, and see how this one is flat, and then see this, and cut like this, and put your hand here, don't let the edge feel rough, and put this like this."

Although Sameer acted out his learning through gesture, the men on his team shared a language, and thus could provide verbal descriptions to clarify the sensations that Sameer felt in his hands and body as he cut and placed the aluminum sheets that went into cladding panels. Sandeep, a steel fixer from Nepal, was on a team that had absorbed workers from Ethiopia, and as the team's chargehand, he was responsible for training them. I asked him how he taught the new workers when he could not speak their language. He looked nonplussed at my question, and without speaking, took his right hand with his left and moved it in the gesture of tying a steel knot. He taught his new workers by moving their hands, guiding them physically through the movement of twisting steel wire around rebar. He then looked down at his boots, sighed deeply, and put his head in his hands and rubbed his head. "I should have been a driver," he said. "I should have moved to Katmandu and been a chauffer. It would have been less of a headache and the money would have been almost the same. Here I have to do two jobs. Mine and the job of the guy next to me while he is learning. Everything, I have to show him."

"YOU MUST TEACH HIM WITH LOVE"

One of the reasons that Sandeep may have found teaching so tiring is that it was based on much more than blunt mimicry and physical transfer. Getting new arrivals to copy them was not enough. They had to show their students how to respond to material in ways that were contextual, informed by the contingencies of the construction process—the bend in the rebar to be tied, different slant of aluminum in a cladding piece for the side of the building compared to the roof, and height of a scaffolding platform. And they had to show workers how to sort out which changes in the construction process were salient and which were just part of the chaos on-site. Experienced workers were aware of the subtlety involved in this and kinds of attunement to novices that this required. "If someone doesn't understand, you must teach him with love," said one Nepali steel fixer when I asked him what was most important for on-site training. I was surprised. I had been expecting an answer that had to do with management attitudes or time allocation for training. Vihaan, another experienced steel fixer from India and working on the far side of the stadium for a different contractor, likewise answered about skill by reflecting on the quality of attention required for teaching: "You have to study the mind of different people. Every person has a different mind. I spend the first few days of every contract of a new person trying to understand their minds," he observed. "I will teach them: one time, two times, three times, ten times. But if these ten times finish, and I see that he is not learning, then I know that he is not good. His mind is not for learning. But the most important thing is to give and take respect because people all have different minds, and they are from different regions and countries also." In many cases, this discovery of a worker's mind happened without the benefit of a shared spoken language. "Some are from India, Nepal, Sri Lanka, Bangladesh, but each speaks a few words in Hindi. Little, little, but it is enough."

These pedagogical exchanges were often ad hoc and situational. Workers learned from each other as they confronted new tasks and building approaches. But sometimes these pedagogical relationships were more enduring. When new workers arrived, they were generally assigned as helpers to veterans on the project. This happened irrespective of the new workers' trade-related experience. Like the QFIS project, each project required specialized skills, frequently created and mastered for the express purpose of the particular project in question, so that even workers who had previous experience in the Gulf needed to be taught the techniques created for the unique challenges of the building design. And workers were usually hired on helper visas even if they had previous construction experience. It was left to veteran workers to assess the expertise of the new workers. "If someone already knows how to do the work, you find out quickly. You want him to carry his load, not sit around or sleep," explained one steel fixer.

But the true novices stayed on as helpers for months before they were allowed to work independently in the trade they were hired for. They carried material, shuttling the steel rods, tiles, plaster, or pipes that were specific to their trade; they lugged tools and learned to pass the correct ones to the worker they were assigned to; and they cleaned up, sweeping metal pilings and wiping down plaster after the job was done. "He can't tell you anything about the job, what he knows, what is difficult, what is easy, because he is a helper. He just follows orders. If someone says, get a spoon, he gets a spoon, and then six months, seven months, he will be able to talk about his work," explained Manish, a senior tile layer and foreman from Uttar Pradesh working on the stadium site. It was grunt work to be sure, but it was also an apprenticeship. Over the course of those six or seven months, helpers watched and learned, and the veteran workers paid attention to their progress, allowing them to try out a technique with their guidance and supervision when they felt they were ready. "When I see that the helper is ready, I let him put down a tile, but I am looking over his shoulder the whole time. I don't want problems because of his work," clarified Manish. "How do you know if a worker is ready?" "I look to see if he sees the lines on the tiles," Manish replied. He waited to see if his helper noticed the marbling on a tile and placed it next to others that were laid down in a way that knitted a coherent pattern of the lines across the floor.

Manish's helper, Niral from southern Nepal, sat in on the interview. Barely eighteen, he was the youngest of four siblings and had come to Qatar to earn money to pay back debts left behind by his father when he died in a bid to keep the local moneylender from seizing the family land. Niral looked dejected after telling us the story of what brought him to Qatar. "My happy day will be the day I leave from here," he said. Manish reached over and patted his hand. As the conversation moved on to questions of skill building and trade techniques, and Manish's twenty years of experience working in the Gulf and the pride he felt at putting his two daughters through college, he kept his hand on Niral's, and patted it again reassuringly every so often. At the end of the interview, when we began packing up our notebooks, Niral turned to Muzi, our translator, and said, "This man is like my uncle. I love him. On the days that the headache comes, and I want to go home, he helps me." Muzi translated, and Manish added, "Next time he will not come as a helper. The money will be better and it will be easier."

The affection between Manish and Niral reflected the empathetic quality of the interactions that supported embodied learning on-site. As workers who took on the role of teachers observed their students and noticed when they were ready to try out new tasks, and as new arrivals watched their experienced peers closely, they developed an affinity for one another that deepened beyond a utilitarian exchange of information. As scholars of embodied cognition might describe it, they participated together in the same flow of action and interpreted each others' sensory reactions. And as mentors guided novices to develop a new embodied understanding of how the body can engage with matter, they also developed an embodied understanding and empathy for each other. Or as one cladding foreman put it, "The most important thing is friendliness. If you shout and scream at people, they stop learning. If I do this [they think], I will get screamed at, if I do that, I will get screamed at. No, no, you must be alongside them." Saleem, a foreman for the glaziers on-site, said with forbearance, "Mistakes will come."

Not all relationships were as intimate and caring as the one between Manish and Niral, and not all experienced workers were as thoughtful as Vihaan. There were certainly tensions between workers. Fights occasionally flared at the worksite or in the labor camp, and a couple of workers told me about a brawl at a labor camp where workers had smuggled in pipes to settle a score about the use of tools on-site. Nevertheless, in my interviews with workers and on-site interactions with them, it was common for them to refer to each other in filial terms. They called each other "brother" and "uncle," and their view of each other as kin stretched across differences of national origin, language, or from time to time, even religion.

Many workers drew an explicit line between this feeling of kinship and the process of skill building on-site. Tran, a Vietnamese welder, said, "Because we are away from our families, we become like a family. We work together, we live together. We rely on each other. The old teach the new, and they become your elders." When Prince reflected on how he trained the men on his crew to keep from making the kinds of mistakes cautioned against at the stand-down, he also spoke of how enduring their friendships became. "Some of my men, even when they go back to their country, Nepal, India, they call me, and I ask them, Why are you calling me? and they say I miss you so much. And I feel very happy for that. They call me from Saudi Arabia, Malaysia, from their countries, from other places. It makes me happy to hear their voices. I ask them about their families. It makes me so happy, truly." Learning occurred through relationship, and many of those relationships became so meaningful that they endured even when the day-to-day worksite exchanges had ended.

Body to Body

In many ways, the learning exchanges on the sites I visited resonated with the most laudatory descriptions of apprenticeship in the social sciences and embodied cognition research. Workers taught one another how to use their bodies to manipulate materials and tools—to refine their sensorimotor perceptions (the feel of the material against and with their bodies), and move the rebar, scaffolding pipe, and mortar spatula with agility and even grace. They taught each other how to interpret the physical world around them and distinguish which actions were required in any given situation, at any given moment in time, as the chaotic, massive, and noisy site rose up around them,

changing shape every day. This initiation happened without structured, pedagogical activity that was separated out from the flow of activity. It happened
without what Lave calls "didactic structuring"; none of the workers on-site
were there as trainees, and few of them had received any formal instruction on
the skills they needed, either on the site or off.[39] Instead, learning was structured through social relationships. Knowledge was shared along the dense ties
of friendship and empathy that crisscrossed the scaffolds and cages of rebar.
As the workers grew more attuned to one another, the process of teaching and
learning wove ties that felt like family. In this changing and unique social as
well as physical world, learning, teaching, knowing, and acting all manifested
as relationships among people.

Studies on embodied cognition and apprenticeship tend to focus on skills
that are blatantly embodied—craft-like expertise where mastery is visible both
in the body of the practitioner and on the material that the master engages
with. The cellist, woodworker, beekeeper, and bread baker take center stage.[40]
They analyze skills where the body engages with matter. Certainly that kind
of expertise was essential on construction sites in Qatar. But equally important, and arguably even more central to workers' safety and effectiveness, was
the skill required to interpret and anticipate the movements of the bodies all
around them. This was a kind of body-to-body expertise—the ability to discern
how the cognition of the workers all around them unfolded in their bodies
through their movements and actions.

The steel fixers at the stadium offered one of the most vivid expressions of
this body-to-body expertise that I came across in Qatar. They were building
a steel cage to reinforce one of the building's bearing columns. The workers
affixed horizontal steel ribs to the vertical rows of steel rods that shot up from
the cement floor. They placed the ribs at ten centimeter intervals and tied
them in place with steel wire that they twisted into specialized knots called
saddle ties. The cage floated about a dozen meters off a floor that was already
some ten stories high, but it was no more than four meters across. The men
worked eight abreast, with layers of men below working on scaffolding platforms stacked three high. The men worked in such close physical proximity
that their upper arms touched. The steel fixers had to develop a kind of synchronicity in their movements so that they didn't jab each other with their
elbows as they twisted the wire. They had to develop a clear sense of when
or how their neighbor might move. On the ground level, this was perhaps
a matter of courtesy and productivity, but on the upper levels, where men
reached out over the scaffold to yank the steel ribs up and around the rods,
a stray movement could knock a man off the platform and cause a serious
fall some several stories down. Steel fixing required a body-to-matter physical
attunement to the steel rods, wires, and pliers that the workers used, but it
also depended on the body-to-body physical awareness of how other workers
embodied and enacted their skill.

Scaffolders executed similar body-to-body expertise. To support the construction of the stadium's dome, the scaffold was built from the sides of the stadium inward. The structure they were erecting was hollow, almost like an internal membrane, for the eggshell stadium roof, and the workers were closing the gap at the building's center, at the dome's highest point. At the lip of the scaffold, which was twenty stories high at the center of the hollow, they stepped out on a sort of perch, a solid plank the width and length of a ladder, that had been fixed to one side of the scaffolding platform that served as a base for their work. From there, they hung in the air on inverted T shapes of scaffolding pipe and began to build toward the center of the stadium. The men worked four or six to a scaffolding platform. On the platform, the workers had to be aware of how their teammates moved or might move, but they also had to be attentive to the ways that those movements would be amplified by the material they handled. A scaffolder on the stadium site had to not only attend to a teammate's grasp of the aluminum pipe, and the speed at which he moved to haul it up and lay it down, but he also had to anticipate the kind of torque that the movement would create in the platform, and place his body in a way that would allow him to absorb and withstand the force without losing his balance. A scaffolder perched on pipes attached to the edge of the platform had to compensate with his body for the way that his teammates' heavy footfalls and movements on the platform would travel down the hanging pipes, causing them to swing and sway. He had to be aware of how his own safety harness, weighing some twenty pounds, would shape his movement, yet he also had to be aware of how his coworkers' harnesses shaped their movements along with the ways that their ability to adjust their bodies was restricted by the lanyards they attached to the scaffold to help protect them in case of falls.

"The people on the ground, they watch us, and they say the scaffolders are brave because you have to be brave," boasted Farooq, a Pakistani scaffolder I interviewed. His crewmate, Usman, also from Pakistan, laughed heartily but then cautioned, "A lion's heart is not enough." He added, "Your crew member is like your brother. If I have a good crew member, I will survive. I will come back at night. And one day I will go home to my family. Good communication is very important, and patience." On teams where there was no common language, this communication and attention to the movement of other members of the team was as much through gesture and observation as it was through language. And as Usman went on to clarify, these were qualities that were learned on-site: "We work next to each other all day long, we live together, so we must also learn to talk to each other, no matter if we only have a little language." The scaffolders I met spoke eloquently and passionately about the quality of mind that this heightened body-to-body awareness and interpersonal coordination required, emphasizing the total focus that was needed.

"When you start your work, you have to think constantly about your work," explained Ahilan in my interview with him, Prince, and Modi. "Don't think about your family or every other thing. You have to focus on your work. When you finish your work, then you can think about those things." The distractions were many: a difficult conversation with family, worry over money problems, anger at a fight in the labor camp, or simply poor sleep or the heat. But it all had to be put away on the scaffold. As a scaffolder on a different project summed it up, "The fastest way to die is to bring your phone. One text and your mind will be gone the whole day."

Workers needed to be mindful of their own focus, but they also had to be attentive to their colleague's quality of attention. "If one is not OK, none of us can be up [on the scaffold] safely," explained Modi. A core element of their body-to-body skill was to read the emotions of others and notice when their focus began to break. To illustrate this for me, Prince recounted an experience that he'd had up on the scaffold.

> One time someone was upset, you could see it in his face, it became closed and his mind was not up [on the platform] with us. His wife was going to divorce him. I told the supervisor and I took him down to the down floor, and I sat with him. And I said no need to be upset. I told him about my life, my marriage, my difficult times, and I told him that life is ups and downs. And when he was better he could go up, but not before, because without communication it is impossible to work. No need to be upset. You stay with him until he is ready to go up.

Emotional sensitivity was as indispensable a part of their skill as the ability to pass up a pipe.

Fear stalked the scaffolders and could overtake even the most experienced workers without warning in the middle of a job. "Like an electric current running down your legs," said one worker. "You feel your stomach folding over," said another. Workers talked about the importance of attending to the fear in their own bodies, but also about the importance of observing the flickers of fear in their coworkers. Prince explained that, "sometimes someone will panic, someone who works with you every day. When this happens, you have a duty to stop him, and do his work for him. Whatever it is. This is your duty to your brother. Do you understand me? Whatever scaffold it is, I will do it for you. If someone is not brave, even just that day, you have to block him and not let him up." Ahilan confessed that this could happen to even the most seasoned worker. Indeed, it had happened to him: "One time we were working at twenty-two-meter heights. And we had a new foreman. We had to build a hanging scaffold and the foreman told us to do it quickly. And that day I was scared. And my brother [Prince], he told me, don't do it. Sit down, don't do it. I will do it for you." Ahilan and Prince were unequivocal; their survival depended on attentiveness and empathy, theirs and the coworkers'.

Body-to-body cognition was essential for crews that worked together, and empathetic embodied attention to others was a norm of practice within the trades. But the construction processes on-site required workers to extend this attunement to men from other trades working near them. Scaffolders, for example, had to be aware of the welders who soldered the stadium's steel skeleton on platforms below them; masons had to be aware of the tile layer putting down marble squares on the floor alongside the buckets where they were sloshing plaster to apply to the wall. On fast-track projects like the stadium, where the sequencing of tasks was compressed along with the time-line, this body-to-body cognition was even more necessary. The image that comes to mind is a neat timeline, with clear phases laid out one after the other, crushed and folded over like the metal of a car in bad crash. Tasks were overlaid onto one another in ways that would have been unthinkable on an ordinary project. Scaffolders built the hanging structures that would support the dome as installers worked below them to put in the seats for an audience, and as a result, they labored under the pressure of knowing that any fallen object, even as small as a screw or spanner, could injure or kill someone below. Tile layers had to anticipate and plan for the work of the electricians putting in the building's wiring. The electricians drove mechanical lifts on the newly marbled floor, and even though the tile layers put down protective cardboard, some portion of the tiles would be damaged; one engineer explained that "we calculate a 20 percent loss." The tile layers set up obstacles on the floor with stacks of material to force the electricians to drive their lift on a defined set of pathways. "They don't think of us. They drive anywhere, and then we have to start again," remarked a tiling foreman. Workers found this kind cross-trade attention to be particularly challenging because it required an attunement to repertoires of movement that were different than those in their own trade. And yet body-to-body cognition was what allowed for the coordination among the hundreds of task areas that went into building the stadium. The embodied empathy among workers across teams and trades was the mortar that held the project together. It was what made the project possible at all.

Management and Manpower

Workers' reflections on the process of skill development on-site suggests that the frenzied construction at the stadium site was at its essence a vast social system for the development and sharing of embodied knowledge. Workers became deeply attuned to one another—to the way they used their bodies and minds—as they taught one another how to perceive of and interpret the physical world around them, and how to manipulate material with their bodies to produce outcomes that collectively would give rise to a stadium. They also taught each other how to become attuned to those working with and around them. In essence, construction in Qatar functioned as a massive, multinational, multilayered, and multitrade apprenticeship.

And yet when I asked Michel, from Lebanon and one of the managing directors for the stadium site, about worker skill, he dismissed the question out of hand, maintaining that "when it comes to laborers, what matters is the quantity not the quality." His concern was how to obtain and allocate the number of manhours required to complete each task at each phase of production. "I have to plan for the fact that I am going to get a 20 or 30 percent return on the manhours I budget. In other countries, you might get 90 or 100 percent productivity, but here there are no norms about skill. We collect labor from all parts of the world and we do not have control over the quality of worker we get. The government decides who we get, how many we get, and when we get them." Michel flipped through the production histograms in front of him, printed out on large plotting paper that draped over the side of his desk, and pointed to the gap between the company's projection and the actual progress on-site. "We have an overuse of manhours for every single one of these tasks and a delay with completion. The question is how to meet our deadline with this shortfall. Maybe we should have budgeted for more manhours, but it would have been impossible to get the client's approval for the budget." A worker brought in coffees for us, and as Michel rolled up the paper sheets and moved them to the side of his desk, he added, "But here at [company name], we make miracles. At the very last minute, even after you have lost all hope, it comes together."

Later, one of the lead engineers on the project told me that Michel would absent himself from the project for weeks at a time, unable to face the distance between the compressed timeline that the company had promised the client and the actual progress on-site. "We would see him drive by the project, several times a day sometimes, but he wouldn't come in," confided Marwan, from Palestine. All the managers on-site were under pressure that grew more intense with each passing month. They heard from the general contractor that both their jobs and the survival of the company were on the line. The successful completion of the stadium project would mean priority access to some of the $200 billion in construction slated in preparation for the World Cup. Meanwhile, their Qatari client, through an abrasive representative, issued ever more strident warnings about deportation of the entire managerial staff and their families. "He arrived in *shibshib* [sandals] and refused to wear a hard hat when he toured the site," gossiped Marwan about the client representative. "And still, he says he is an expert in construction! He asks for impossible things. He wants the roof closed by next week, and he says that if it is not finished, he will submit paperwork to have us all sent home." Even managing directors like Michel, who had lived prosperously in Qatar with his wife and children for over a decade, were employed under the kafala system. They worked at the pleasure of their sponsor and could be expelled from the country without cause at any moment.

The miracle that Michel was hoping for was dependent on the intricate, interactive, and affective training networks that workers had developed on-site—yet for Michel and the rest of the managerial staff, the workers were understood and counted as manhours. These manhours, units of undifferentiated labor power, were bought in bulk, and came into Qatar as packages of men who were recruited abroad by the tens and hundreds. From the managerial perspective, the men were a production input, budgeted for and sourced like any other raw material used on the site—except, Marwan explained, labor was less reliable than material goods were. "When you buy cement, you get cement. Maybe you have some issues with quality, but basically, it's cement. Workers are different. You think you are bringing a hundred carpenters from Thailand, and instead you get a hundred masons or ditch diggers. And that's if you are lucky. Last week, one of my supervisors came to me very upset. He told me, 'Did you bring me these guys straight from the paddy fields? It will be months before they are useful.'"

To speed up work on the project, the company added shifts and men. On average, four hundred men were added to the workforce every fortnight. The challenge faced by supervisors for the different task areas was how to integrate the new arrivals. Cognizant that the skill base of the new workers was uneven, supervisors strategized about how to support enough skill development so that the new workers would contribute to construction, or at the very least, wouldn't impede progress. Supervisors for cladding fabrication—the assembly of the specialized external panels for the stadium—spoke with me about the kind of crucible this was for them. "There are five hundred people here in our company, and there are two hundred people working inside the assembly shed. You can't keep track of every guy. Ten, fifteen, twenty guys might be missing, and you wouldn't notice. How can you tell who knows how to do what?" explained Rajit, a cladding supervisor from India. His colleague, Jason, a supervisor from South Africa, explained that they handled this by "mixing the old workers with the new ones." He continued: "I have fifty guys under me, and we have four or five guys working at each table. I recently got a batch of thirty. I put three old ones together with a couple of new ones. And then after a couple or three weeks, I get another group of thirty, and so I start again, three old ones with two new ones." And then he added, "Next week, I am getting a shipment of 150 Thai workers. I haven't yet figured out how I will handle it. I am glad for the workers, but it sort of mucks up my system."

Some version of Jason's strategy—mixing the old with the new—was adopted by virtually all the supervisors on-site. It was widespread because the view of skill on which it rested was common among managers, engineers, and supervisors. The skill attributed to workers was a degraded version of craft. Supervisors like Jason defined it as physical imitation, without an understanding of the broader reasons or the consequences of the actions that workers mimicked. Skill was described as the product of a "monkey see, monkey do" reproduction of bodily movements—a process that not only bypassed worker creativity, initiative, and comprehension but also, as Jason explained, made those qualities irrelevant.

> You need to get workers to wear their hard hats, so some of the foremen will tell them that a roof will fall on their heads. Obviously that's not true, but it doesn't matter because what you need to do is to make sure that they wear the hard hats. And they won't understand about all the different risks on-site. You can explain, and the guy will still have no idea what you are talking about. The point is that the guy should wear the hard hat. He doesn't need to understand why.

Moreover, worker skill was defined as a standard repertoire of physical movements that workers would learn by rote. That repertoire was understood as a catalog of automatic, almost robotic actions that could be pulled out of both context and specific bodies. To the managers, it was the same set of movements regardless of the day, panel being assembled, or stature and agility of the person doing the assembling. They viewed skill like a set of directions that could be passed from worker to worker, like a baton, as new workers arrived. It was physical but not embodied.

This definition of skill was enacted through the practices of supervisors and engineers on-site, but it was augmented through the reliance on manpower agencies to cover labor shortages on the project. As described in the previous chapter, manpower agencies in Qatar were shadowy outfits that rented out workers to construction projects on a short-term basis. Unlike construction companies that had to apply for worker visas based on specific jobs, these agencies secured floating visas, unattached to any particular project, and it was not an accident that the agencies were reputed to be owned by Qataris who were well connected to the royal family. These agencies had little public presence—and in my experience, a categorical aversion to being interviewed. But once a project started, managers reported that they received relentless marketing pitches from them. "I have no idea how all the manpower companies got my number, but I get calls day and night offering me labor. It's crazy," said Marwan. And although companies relied on their services, managers complained that the agencies focused, as they put it, "on quantity not on quality."

They reported, for example, that manpower companies would agree to send workers in a given trade and then send workers from another—if the workers had any experience at all. "You'll ask for welders, and they will send you workers who have never seen a blowtorch, so you have to send them back. And the next day, you ask for carpenters, and they will send you the exact same guys you sent back. So what are they, welders, carpenters, or just laborers?" complained one engineer I spoke with. Another compared manpower agencies to drug dealers: "You never know what you are going to get, but you know you still need it." And still another manager, after he received a team of workers in flip-flops for the second time and had to supply them with footwear before he could put them to work, shared his suspicions with me that the agency was running a side racket selling used boots.

While these managers couched their complaints in terms of quality, their concerns were at base about unpredictability and not skill. Companies regularly pulled workers they employed from other areas of their own projects and even other sites to cover a labor shortage. "When we are in a bind, we get anyone we can," explained Jason, "rope artists, silicon applicators, welders, helpers from any trade, whoever we can find." When their own labor supply was reorganized, at least supervisors knew the workers were "new" and did not have the skill set they needed. Not so with manpower agencies. The unpredictability of this labor stream meant that site supervisors often had to reorganize production on the spot with no warning.

While the managers that used manpower agencies complained that the agencies misrepresented the skill of the workers they offered, both parties shared the same basic view of skill. For both contractors and manpower agencies, skill was external to particular workers; it was a portable and standardized repertoire of physical movements that any worker could just pick up. For the workers loaned out by manpower agencies, their employer's view of skill was clear, and as Tho from Vietnam confided, "demeaning." He told me, "There is no day when I am proud of what I do. The manpower company assigns us to jobs that have nothing to do with our skill. One day it's steel fixing, the other day it's fabrication. They are just looking for bodies. One man is like another."

Because manpower agencies—and to some extent, the companies that used their services—considered one body to be like another, they practiced a form of wage arbitrage. Once workers hired out to a company had received on-site training, the manpower agency would market those men, although still under contract, as experienced workers in a given trade and hire them out to a different company at a higher rate. "As soon as they get a better rate, and I mean that second, they pull their men," explained Rajit. "We worked with this manpower agency, and the workers were with us for a month, but then all hundred workers—out of two hundred total—were pulled within one hour. It took us almost twenty days to build the labor force back up." Contractual questions aside, the practice of moving workers from one site to another without regard for context or task was rooted in the reductive definition of skill that manpower agencies as well as company management adopted. Because skill was viewed as a standardized toolbox of movements that was specific to the worksite and not the workers, and was considered proprietary to management, moving workers was considered equivalent, on some level, to moving loads of cement from one site to another. Cement was a raw material, and would be shaped, based on engineering specifications, into columns, foundations, walls, or minarets. Workers likewise would be shaped by management and based on production requirements, and made into masons, carpenters, or steel fixers.

QUALITY AND CONTROL

As described in chapter 2, construction projects in Qatar were executed by consortia of construction companies, organized in long and frequently tangled subcontracting chains. One of the most effective vehicles for managing those relationships was the quality assurance and quality control process—referred to by the industry shorthand of QAQC. Firms monitored, intensively, the quality of their subcontractors' work product, and the quality assessments informed issues ranging from payment to timelines to coordination on-site—even occasionally determining the outcome of contractual disputes. These QAQC mechanisms ran down subcontracting chains in cascades. The QAQC processes imposed at the top flowed all the way down to specialized subcontractors, which controlled the quality of the smaller firms they hired to augment their production capacity. QAQC reviews were applied to all aspects of the construction process from design and engineering, to procurement and technology selection, to the evaluation of completed components on-site. But perhaps most significant, the QAQC processes doubled as a mechanism through which supervisors could enforce their definition of skill and discipline their workers.

The evidence of QAQC processes were everywhere on construction sites in Qatar. Construction components—welded joints, tiled floors, wall frames, and cladding seams—were spray painted with quality evaluations: "no good welding," "bad" or "no," an "x" across the seam, or sometimes simply just a mark in white or orange paint. QAQC specialists circulated through the site daily, sometimes with plans and a clipboard in hand, often with a can of spray paint in their belt, checking the quality of their subcontractor's work. Firms also had their own internal quality control processes. Supervisors and engineers did QAQC checks, daily and sometimes hourly, on their own work products, evaluating quality by construction elements—checking welding seams in one area of the structure, for example—or construction crew—evaluating the seams welded by one particular segment of their workforce.

"Our QAQC team is always in play," noted Rajit, the cladding supervisor. "Our QAQC checks are how we catch the mistakes, and catch them early. The inspections are ongoing so that [the mistakes] never affect the whole run. Hour by hour, each and every panel." As Rajit explained, and supervisors in other trades confirmed, a failure to pass a quality control check triggered a process of rework. The component would have to be redone until the quality specifications were met. It was not unusual for components to have to be redone two, three, or even four times. Supervisors charged with completing the internal QAQC checks for their firm evaluated the work product, but they also frequently evaluated whether workers had followed firm-specified procedures in completing those products.

To be sure, these QAQC checks were critical in catching mistakes and supporting workers in developing the skills they needed to complete construction tasks correctly and well. But supervisors also drew on this process of rework to compel workers to follow the regimented steps that the company laid out for the completion of specific tasks. "You tell them what to do, step by step, number one, this, number two, this, number three, this, and so on. And you get them to do it over and over until they get it. When they get the steps, in the right order, then you get the quality," noted Rajit. Supervisors across trades used this top-down training approach and QAQC rework to enforce the rote completion of specific processes, and discourage the development of skillful competence—including problem-solving abilities—outside company-defined procedural guardrails. Srinivasan, a supervisor to a mason crew on the same site, offered a similar perspective on the function of rework as both a training strategy and mechanism to enforce compliance with company-defined processes.

> To meet QAQC standards, you must open the laborer's brain. If you give them daily chores and just tell them what to do, carry this, move that, they will be like wearing blinkers. They will not look anywhere else and they will be like an animal. But if you tell them, do this to get this result, and even better if you show him, you will see good output. But then you have to make sure that they follow what you tell them. You need a hierarchy system, otherwise it is better to put blinkers on your workers. For quality, you need to follow the rules.

Supervisors had various means at their disposal to enforce compliance with their step-by-step instructions on how to execute different tasks, and they used them. They drew on workplace disciplinary strategies as well as disciplinary mechanisms that stemmed directly from the kafala system. These included docked pay, mandatory—and frequently uncompensated—overtime for rework, and in cases of repeated insubordination, deportation. While the threat of these punitive actions turned training into a disciplinary process, supervisors expressed reluctance to lean too heavily on them because of the detrimental effects they had on morale and productivity. Instead, supervisors fobbed off workers who did not meet QAQC standards and did not follow the specified steps for task completion, assigning them to other crews where they were someone else's problem, generally demoting them to laborer and helper positions in the process. This reallocation of workers only augmented the churn of workers on-site, already intense and unpredictable because of project demands coupled with the unreliability of manpower agencies.

But the tumult that management's manpower strategies and disciplinary actions injected into work crews fundamentally disrupted the ways that workers developed and shared their embodied competence. It undermined the development of skill that as the workers themselves explained, was far more nuanced, sensitive, and relational than anything that could be spelled out in a standardized step-by-step set of instructions. The ways that managers and supervisors inserted themselves in the learning process tore at the empathetic relationships through which skill on-site was actually cultivated and undermined the embodied attunement that workers developed to others working with and alongside them.

RUPTURES AND CONNECTION

To preserve and develop their skill, workers were constantly compensating for the relational instability that managerial practices created. They found themselves perpetually building and rebuilding the kind of empathetic relationships needed for teaching, even as the relationships that had already been forged were ruptured by their supervisors. The mentorship relationships between "old" and "new" workers were disrupted as new workers became old ones overnight, responsible for new workers of their own. More experienced workers found their workload and hours increased dramatically; they found themselves teaching not just their helper but also their helper's helper. When large numbers of new workers were brought on, it was not uncommon for their shifts to stretch to fifteen hours. With at least an hour back and forth to the labor camp, they were left with only a few hours to prepare food for the next day, bathe, and rest.

Management practices disrupted the broader social norms that supported embodied learning on-site too. Management's brusque shuffling of men affected the empathetic character of interpersonal relationships and didn't allow for the relationship to deepen and acquire the feel of kinship. When large numbers of new workers were added—a doubling of the workforce, for example—the negotiations involved in assimilating new workers erupted into conflicts around national origin, language, or religion. Most of the workers I spoke with tended to emphasize the camaraderie on-site and were more reticent about conflict among nationalities, and although they did from time to time recount specific fights, they flagged the specific grievance that sparked the conflict. Foremen, on the other hand, stressed national difference and uninformed prejudice as the source of tension. "We will get a new batch of workers, and they will come and say they can't work with Filipino foreman. The Chinese people, the Thai people, they are very clicky. Difficult to integrate," reflected Jason. Manu, another foreman in his company, added, "Some people think they are better than others. Creating a mixed national group is not easy at the beginning."

The quality of construction also suffered. At the height of construction at the stadium site, legions of new workers were brought on-site every fifteen days, and other workers transferred in from other crews because of their failure to meet quality standards. Workers had little time to learn from one another. There was no time to cultivate the embodied, interpersonal aware-ness needed to manipulate materials and adapt to changes on the construction site. Construction became coarser and less tailored to the specifications of the stadium. This was an outcome that even supervisors acknowledged. As Rajit put it, "Quality wants less people." Management's singular focus on manhours and its reductive approach to skill undercut the processes through which workers developed what I have called here a body-to-matter awareness—impairing their ability to teach one another how to weld, bend a steel rod, and clamp a gravelock around a scaffolding pipe.

This approach also undermined the embodied awareness that workers had of others working around them. The constant churn of new workers meant that many had not yet developed the situational body-to-body attentiveness that allowed workers to work safely in close physical proximity. It meant an added strain for experienced workers on-site; because they could not assume that new arrivals—often the latest group of manpower workers—had learned how to pay attention to the workers around them, especially those in other trades working near them, they had to be extra vigilant. For workers in trades that were especially hazardous—scaffolders, rope artists, and the crew that craned large cladding panels onto the stadium roof—the lack of body-to-body awareness was a constant source of anxiety. During the time that I was on-site, the scaffolding foremen complained repeatedly to the health and safety officers about stray foot traffic underneath active scaffolds. When tradesmen worked below them, scaffolders would take additional steps to prevent falling objects. Unplanned and unannounced incursions into the workspace below them made it impossible to take preventive measures and dramatically raised the risks shouldered by the men hanging from the sky.

Skill, Violence, and Power

One afternoon while I was interviewing the director of health and safety on-site, one of his staff came into his office to report a foot traffic violation under an active scaffold. The director was white Afrikaans and his officer was from Nigeria. After the safety officer finished describing the incident, the director turned to me and said, "You know what I tell him? If he walked onto my farm in South Africa, a Black man walking onto my land like this, I would shoot him dead, without thinking twice." He cocked his hand into the shape of a pistol, pointed at his safety officer who stood in front of his desk, jerked it back as if from the recoil of a bullet, and laughed. This was not the first time I had witnessed this kind of bullying on-site, nor was it the first time that the threat had been delivered in such blatantly racist terms.

There was a pattern to the bullying: it flared up when workers referenced their own embodied knowledge and used that competence to push back

against some managerial or supervisory practice. Santosh, a scaffolding foreman, was told to speed up his team's output, extending their shift into the
night if necessary. When he objected, saying that his team was already working as fast as they could and that working any faster would mean injury, he
was threatened with deportation. Saleh, his Syrian supervisor, assured him
that he could put him on a plane before the end of the day's shift. Subash, a
steel fixer from Nepal with a dislocated shoulder and busted eye socket from a
fall into an on-site foundation hole, said that he knew he should not have been
walking in that area without a protective tie, but when he hesitated and told
his supervisor that the platform did not feel secure, his supervisor had become
upset and threatened to dock his pay. "If it were my little brother, I would tell
him, say no. Even if he sends you back home, you will return as a whole person," he said when he reflected on the fall.

These kinds of threats only underscored the view that skill was a disembodied resource, separate from the men who enacted it. The intimidation was
a way of reinforcing the notion that skill was the purview and property of
management, and workers did not have the right to express it in unsanctioned
ways. Or as Michel put it, "We do not look at the labor but at the supervision.
We think *for* the labor." This approach to skill made the labor practices that
management adopted grueling for workers. The hard work and long shifts
took a toll on the men, but their job was made much more challenging because
the relationships that supported learning and competence were broken up,
over and over again.

In practice, the notion—the fallacy—that skill resided in supervision was
dangerous. Ultimately, workers would be held responsible for any mistake or
other shortfall in skill. In the dawn stand-down that I observed, when Matty
reiterated the importance of safety at the stadium site, he made this clear to
his scaffolders. If they did not have—and did not develop among their peers—
the competence to scaffold safely, then they were the ones who would be sent
home, not the engineers or supervisors, who provided little support for the
development of embodied relational skill that they needed to be safe. In fact,
management and supervisors often pressured scaffolders to act in contraven-
tion of what they knew. The workers were tallied as manhours and treated as
brute power. And yet the project relied on scaffolders like Prince, Modi, and
Ahilan developing the communication and trust to step down off the scaffolding platform and onto a pipe hanging in midair, with a hundred meters of
emptiness under them, to build a scaffold unlike any other before.

The law provided no viable pathway to challenge employer practices.
The kafala system gave employers contractual purchase over their workers'
bodies. Migrants could not walk off the job, even if they wanted to, and for
some portion of their contract, they were legally bound to the employer that
had recruited them. Workers had seen colleagues who had disobeyed orders

summarily deported, with little explanation or notice; many had the direct experience of having their pay docked or being subjected to forced overtime as retaliation for refusing to complete tasks a certain way.

Employers' contractual power was significant, but skill was the language through which it was expressed. Armed with a definition of skill as an abstract resource, transferrable and separate from physicality, management enforced a view of skill on the worksite that stripped workers of the deep competence that construction depended on. Men stripped of skill became manpower; bodies without skill became raw material. They became expendable, interchangeable, and subject to physical violence—if not direct, then intimated.

The impact of this view of skill, when abstracted in this way and used as a language of power, may have been heightened in Qatar because of the kafala system, but the experience of workers on construction sites there reveals what is at stake in academic and managerial definitions of skill. Although skill, learning, and embodied cognition are frequently represented as neutral technical matters, the way that the concepts play out is often highly political, attaching themselves to political rationales that differ by context. Scholars have begun to speculate about the ways that the rhetoric around cognition and knowledge have been used to justify the weakening of labor protections, with rationales for lower wages and working conditions pegged to arguments about the diminishing value of certain kinds of human capital.[41] The competing definitions of skill on Qatari construction sites give us access to a more granular understanding of how conceptions of skill can become structures of power. It shows how the representational disembodiment of skill is an expression of power with important consequences: the separation of people from their embodied cognition can be a precursor to the separation of people from their right to full personhood.

Holding fast to definitions of skill as being outside the body is not a mere misconception. It is a kind of violence. Denying the embodied cognition and creativity of persons is tantamount to denying them both their agency and human sentience. This denial is different than a Marxist understanding of alienation, where workers lose access to their creativity—as expressed in the labor—and the full expression of their agency as a consequence. Defining skill as strictly behavioral not only enables the denial and erasure of their contribution to the production process, in the fullness of its creativity, discernment, and agility, but also enables the denial and erasure of their humanity.

Scholarship on embodied cognition has begun to consider the interplay between cognition and power, yet much of the research still overlooks the most pernicious expression of power in relation to skill. At issue is not the power over knowledge that has been created but rather power over the people who know and learn. And power over knowledge is not deployed solely over a set of abstract ideas. It is exercised over the bodies that enact cognition. When knowledge is targeted, then the embodied actors expressing and developing that knowledge are always also in the crosshairs.

My interview with Prince, Ahilan, and Modi stretched well into late morning, and Matty came into the trailer to remind his team of the time. The men teased him and said that the interview had gone for so long because they were telling me all of Matty's jokes. Everyone laughed good-naturedly, and the tension dissipated. And then when the room settled, Matty added, gaze fixed on Prince, "Did you tell them the one about how to kill an African?"

CHAPTER FOUR

Protest

HOW SKILLFUL PRACTICE BECOMES RESISTANCE

THE BANGING SHOOK the trailer that housed the management office. Twenty Ethiopian workers had gathered outside in the late afternoon. They pounded the trailer's aluminum siding, demanding that the supervisors meet with them. They were yelling angrily and urgently and calling for the site manager, a Thai foreman turned supervisor named Phichit, to come out. Phichit, graying, slightly stooped, and soft spoken, had a reputation among the workers for being unfair and even tyrannical. They reported that he was quick to dock their wages for the slightest infraction, such as for things as trivial and demeaning as stopping to take an unscheduled bathroom break or protesting damage to work boots retrieved from the nightshift workers they were forced to share them with. Some workers had been docked just for meeting Phichit's gaze when he berated them.

It had already been a tense day at the site. I had been interviewing workers since early morning, talking with them in an enclosed area in a back corner of the managers' trailer. Several workers made of point of bypassing the side entrance that offered direct access to the makeshift meeting room and instead used the front entrance so that they could circle past the managers' workspace. As they walked past their managers' desks, they complained loudly about unpaid wages and forced overtime, ostensibly to me and my translator as we waited down the hall, but their grievances were clearly directed at their bosses. One worker, a Nepali man who had worked on construction sites throughout the Gulf for a decade, stopped at his supervisor's desk, locked eyes with him, and deliberately knocked over a pencil holder as he held his gaze. Flustered, the supervisor wordlessly gathered the spilled pencils. The worker glared down at his boss who had knelt before him to pick up the pencils that had rolled onto the floor.

The workers on-site had not been paid for more than two months. Their employer, N&W Builders, had been contracted to do the cement wet work for a high-rise that was going up in Lusail, the new modernist city for a half-million residents being built to the north of Doha. Halfway through the project, there was a dispute, and the contractor suspended disbursement to N&W Builders. The company had not received the payments stipulated in its contract for close to five months.

The quarrel between the Lusail contractor and N&W Builders was typical of disputes in Qatar's construction industry: it had started with some petty regulatory matter but had hardened into a financial standoff. N&W Builders, a cement and masonry company, was awarded the project to complete the floors and walls for the Lusail high-rise because of its pitch to use a "table form" technology to layer the floors. A decades-old technology routinely adopted in global markets, table forms would have enabled the company to pour cement floors and fill in the supporting walls without having to build a new wood frame for each layer. The managing engineer on the project, Khan, explained to me that the table forms would have allowed the company to build the floors twice as fast and at half the price as its competitors could since its competitors largely relied on an older manual approach. But the municipal government had held up the authorization that the company needed to import the table forms. The Egyptian engineer at the government office informed Khan that the table forms were not on an official list of preapproved construction inputs, and the company would have to have its Qatari sponsor apply for a new import license from the Ministry of Economy and Commerce. N&W Builders was forced to fall back on a manual strategy, and as a result, it fell short of the target that it had agreed on with the main contractor, which used the delay to justify withholding payment entirely.

Initially, the company spent down its cash reserves to pay its workers, hoping that the bureaucratic holdup would be resolved in short order. After a couple of months, however, it determined that it could no longer continue. Employees were told that they would receive their wages as soon as the company received payment for work, which they were assured repeatedly, payday after payday, was imminent. The salaries of managers and engineers were also withheld, but this was of little comfort to the workers and did not make managers' assertion that they would be paid "next week" any more believable.

Workers, unable to send money home, had begun receiving desperate calls from family members about school payments and medical bills, and even more ominously, visits from the local moneylender and threats to repossess the family land. And workers were starting to run low on food because in addition to their wages, the company held back their monthly food allowance of 200 Qatari riyals, roughly $50. The money, which workers pooled to buy ten kilogram bags of rice, lentils, and pickled vegetables in bulk along with the occasional chicken, did not go far in the big-box stores where they shopped, but without these monthly stipends, they were unable to buy groceries. The few corner stores in the industrial district where they lived sold food in smaller quantities, but their shelves were stocked mostly with overpriced ramen noodles, Nestlé cookies, and coffee creamer. Workers had begun rationing their food stocks.

Workers going hungry because they had not been paid was not an uncommon occurrence in Qatar. Reports by international human rights organizations and even the local press cataloged some of the more extreme instances where workers suffered hunger. In one notorious case, Amnesty International documented the nonpayment of wages by a company building Al-Bidda Tower, a prominent high-rise in downtown Doha, recognized by the Aga Khan Trust for Architecture for its innovative and daring design. After withholding wages for close to a year, the company stopped paying workers their food allowance. Within the month, the situation became desperate. Workers supplemented food donations from nearby residents with cash loans from underground moneylenders at usury rates.[1] Many similar cases were chronicled, and news outlets reported that local restaurants and residents were collecting food for unpaid workers who were stranded in their camps.[2] No matter how hungry and cash poor they were, workers were prohibited by the terms of their contracts from seeking other employment. (As detailed in chapter 1, these restrictions were softened starting in 2017, but even with the reforms, the vast majority of workers remained unable to change jobs.) They were bound to their employer by the kafala system, which made it illegal for workers to withhold their labor even when their wages were not paid. Under Qatari law, workers facing these types of labor violations could take their grievances to the government, but they were banned from organizing, striking, or withholding labor in any way.

The workers at the N&W Builders site finally had enough of management's empty promises. About two weeks before the protest took place, a third of them resolved to strike. "We decided all together we would not work unless we got paid," recounted one of the workers. Some 250 men—all residents at one of the three labor camps that the company used for the Lusail project—refused to board the buses that would take them from the labor camp to the site.

Initially, all the men who had decided to stay back in their camp were Thai. The company had sorted its workers by nationality, housing workers from the same country and language group in the same camp. The Thai management at N&W Builders lodged its compatriots in the only camp with an outdoor courtyard, where in the evenings, workers gathered at the picnic tables and determined that they had to take action. Reflecting on their decision, one of the workers explained that although they were concerned about management retaliation, they felt that the national identity they shared with management would make the company more receptive to their demands. "We knew that the managers would understand why we were not working. We speak the same language. We have the same moral education. If a Thai worker sees that someone is carrying something heavy, he will go and help. We wanted the managers to see that we needed their help, that this burden was too heavy for us to carry."

Without the strikers, the site operated at half capacity. Faced with a labor shortage on-site, the company reached out to a manpower company and used cash reserves that it refrained from using to pay its standing employees to hire thirty Vietnamese form builders and a small team of North Koreans to do the manual framework for the building. Aside from these hires, the only other remaining workers were a couple hundred Nepali steel fixers along with a few crews of Tamil and Ethiopian workers. Thai and Sri Lankan supervisors oversaw their half-hearted work. As one Nepali worker put it, "My body is here, but my spirit cannot work. The company broke our trust." On that late April day, the heat had already pushed past 100°F, and by midafternoon, many men put down their tools and went to sit in the shade cast by the cement floor curing above them.

As the strike wore on, some twenty Ethiopian workers decided to join the work stoppage. The company had lodged its Ethiopian employees in a separate block of rooms at one end of the Thai camp. After observing that their Thai coworkers experienced no disciplinary consequences for staying in the camp, the Ethiopian workers decided to join the Thai strikers after close to eight weeks of working without pay. For two days, they too refused to board the company bus.

Three of the Ethiopian strikers decided to use the time away from work to visit the public park along the shoreline in Al Khor, a city near their labor camp. The park offered one of the only strips of green vegetation around, and the rumor in the camp was that pickup soccer games were sometimes played on the pitch there. According to several of the strikers, the three men found a spot under a tree and laid down there to rest. After about ten minutes of reclining on the grass, a Qatari man and his wife pulled into the parking lot at the edge of the green. The Qatari man rolled down the window of his SUV and began yelling at the men that the park was reserved for families and started honking his horn aggressively. The Ethiopians decided to ignore him, and the honking stopped. But a short while later, the Ethiopians were approached by police. One of the men, terrified, got up and ran. The police detained the remaining two and charged them with stealing the Qatari woman's cell phone out of her car, even though the couple had not stepped out of their SUV. Within a few hours, an Ethiopian worker at the camp received a phone call from one of the detained migrants explaining that he and his coworker were at the airport in the process of being deported back to Ethiopia.

Their compatriots commandeered the company bus parked outside their labor camp and drove to the site to seek out management. They pounded on the trailer, where I had been conducting interviews, desperate to get management to help their detained coworkers. Phichit, backed by two other managers, one who spoke frantically into his cell phone, came out onto the steps of the trailer entrance. Phichit assured the workers that the company had not been informed about the deportation and said repeatedly that the company would do everything possible to get to the bottom of the situation. The company would stop the deportation, Phichit promised. The gathering began to dissipate, and by sunset, the Ethiopian workers had gotten back on the bus to return to the camp.

Phichit's assurances notwithstanding, the two detained workers were deported. Within days, the company had arranged to have all its Ethiopian workers sent back to their country, irrespective of whether they had participated in the strike or not. The Ethiopian workers were yanked out of their bunks before dawn, taken directly to the airport, handed their passports, and put on a plane. None of the Thai workers were deported.

"WE COULD NOT CONTROL THEM"

The day before the Ethiopians were deported, Phichit sat down to talk with me about the company's training practices. At the time of the interview, I was unaware of the Ethiopian workers' immanent removal, as were all but the company's top management, yet Phichit, who had been organizing the deportation, shared reflections that were telling. "When the Ethiopians came here, we realized that they are too much of a problem. Because they have difficult ideas and they are very impulsive. It was an experiment, but we could not control them."

The arrests also broadened the scope of concern for N&W Builders. Because the two Ethiopians who had been detained were arrested in a public park, at some distance from their labor camp, they revealed to the Qatari government that N&W Builders did not have full control of its labor force. Their contact with the police had brought the protest to the attention of the authorities as well as the company's Qatari co-owner and sponsor. In the Qatari construction industry, everyone was a migrant. Managers and supervisors were employed under the same kafala system as their workers. They resided in the country at the pleasure of their sponsors. A demonstrated failure to maintain industrial discipline might trigger a decision by the company's sponsor, embarrassed before the government by his charge's inability to bridle the company's workforce, to deport management as summarily as management had deported the Ethiopian workers. If the managers suffered no immediate consequences, the company's business might be impacted, with its ability to secure future contract undercut by the stigma of labor strife.

So the company shunted the responsibility for the labor discontent onto the backs of its Ethiopian workers. To its managers, the deportation of all the Ethiopian workers seemed a small price to pay to restore the company reputation and protect its managers from expulsion. Legitimate protests against the extended nonpayment of wages were transformed into a character flaw associated with a particular nationality. "We have tried with Ethiopians for three months now, and we are unhappy with this experiment," explained Phichit, with no acknowledgment that the men he referred to had not been paid for two out of three months. "It is clear," he added, "that we should get Nepali workers instead. We have some visas that we can still fill for Ethiopians, but we have decided to stop with them." For the workers who had not been deported, the message was explicit: labor disputes should remain a private matter between a company and its workers, and workers that refused to go to the worksite were to remain sequestered at the company's labor camp. Any contact with the authorities, however unsolicited—any action that made the protest public—would result in immediate deportation.

A week after the Ethiopians were deported, N&W Builders received official permission to import a more basic version of the table form technology it had planned to use, and the lead firm released an advance payment to the company to restart work on-site. The company used the cash to dispense two weeks of back pay to the workers, along with a vague promise that the rest of the money owed would be forthcoming. I visited the labor camp where the company housed its Thai employees the morning after workers received their pay. I was met by Phichit and another manager, who had decided to supervise the visit. "For your safety," insisted Phichit.

The workers had celebrated their wages the night before with bootlegged alcohol and a chicken feast. In anticipation of our visit and possibly on Phichit's orders, the camp was hosed down, and puddles of dirty water, covered with a film of bleach and chicken fat, had pooled in the courtyard where we sat at picnic tables with some three dozen workers.

All of a sudden, a heavyset man in a tank top and cutoffs burst into the courtyard. Still drunk, he shouted a loud greeting to Phichit, and then bent over the cooler with the sodas we had brought and began tossing the cans to his coworkers. Phichit looked on, his face set. The worker started to compliment Phichit and the company extravagantly and sarcastically, and said how pleased it made all of them, as Thai workers, to be working for such a respectable Thai company. A few snickers at the edges of the tense silence escalated into a roar of generalized laughter. Some of the workers explained the hilarity to my translator. The night before, when the jokester had passed out on his bunk, his coworkers had tied his arms and legs to the bed frame. They were worried that he would speak out about working conditions and the back pay still owed. The escapee clearly had a lot of sway in the camp. In fact, for a time, the company had assigned him the role of "camp boss," a thug appointed and paid by the company to keep workers at the camp in line. But when the cash dried up, the company stopped paying his stipend, and soon the company's disciplinarian turned into a labor organizer. As camp boss, he had bullied the Ethiopians into letting him keep their electronic bank cards—"for safekeeping." These cards were linked to accounts where the company was required by law to deposit the workers' wages (a measure to prevent the nonpayment of wages). During the strike, he pressed—perhaps even strong-armed—the same workers he had previously bullied to stay behind with the Thai workers at the camp until the company decided to pay them all.

The Thai workers in the camp had been shaken by the sudden deportation of their Ethiopian housemates, and now that they had received some portion of their wages, they were eager to put the strike behind them and rebuild the privileged rapport, based on shared nationality, that they felt they shared with their supervisors and employer. Phichit's comments to me made it clear that their anxiety at the strike was prescient: "If the workers stay with us for a long time, more than two years, they become very lazy. They get to know the system, and they will start to create conflict. All they care about [is] money, but of course, we have to control labor costs. Even the Thai people—they start to link with others and make big problems. [That's why] we don't keep them more than two years—sometimes less if we need."

When their labor action expanded past their national compatriots to a broader group of peers, the Thai workers escalated their work stoppage from an intraethnic spat to a protest based on their position as workers. The nascent solidarity that they had begun to build with their Ethiopian coworkers, a coalition based on class and their function in the production system, was a bridge too far for their employer, and had it not been for the resolution of the bureaucratic logjam that was holding up the company's progress and income, and the urgent need for labor that came with it, it is not inconceivable that the company would have decided that many of its Thai workers had run out their time as compliant workers.

Repertoires of Control

In Qatar, strikes and others forms of collective action by foreign workers were illegal, but wildcat strikes like the one I observed at N&W Builders were common. Every single construction site I visited had at one point or another experienced some sort of worker action. These protests rarely made it into the local press, although the international press occasionally reported on strikes that were unusually large or explosive. But wildcat strikes were so ubiquitous that managing them came to be regarded as a core responsibility of the health and safety staff that companies retained. "A fit of pique" is how Aidan, the South African health and safety director at a midsize firm I visited, dismissed the wildcat strike that had hobbled progress at the site he supervised.

The Pakistanis decided on Saturday morning, after too much gambling and drinking on Friday [the rest day], that they didn't feel like working. Four days later and they are still hung over. Next time, it'll be the

Filipinos. . . . We all get paid late, and we all have to learn how to deal with it. I can tell you there are days when I don't feel like getting up to go to work either. You give them a few days to get their heads back on straight and then it's back to work.

Brett, British ex-military and health and safety director at a lead firm, shared similar sentiments in a separate interview, and added that the protests that lasted for "a few days or a week" were just men "blowing off steam." He described containing the strikes as a form of expertise central to his job: "You develop a feel for when to let people stay back [at the work camp], and when to draw the line and make them get on the bus. You have to keep things tight. It has a way of spreading; today it's the Indians and tomorrow [you'll] have the Nepalis want[ing] to stay back too. You can't let things get out of hand."

As Aidan's and Brett's reflections suggest, the strikes that health and safety managers corralled and controlled were less carefully planned actions than they were spontaneous refusals to work by men who were exhausted by excessive overtime and anxious for their back pay. For all their desperation, the protests had little or no effect. Management treated them as a routine part of production—a mundane disciplinary matter. The labor actions seemed to have no influence on working conditions, the disbursal of wages, or the length of the workday. Companies paid wages when they were solvent; they decided working hours based on production imperatives; and they determined which work stoppages they would tolerate and for how long, and more important, which ones they would cut short through deportation.

The parameters of protests were entirely defined by management. As was the case at N&W Builders, managers across the companies I studied tolerated some forms of protest even as they ruthlessly repressed other expressions of discontent, often stemming from the same grievance. They deported some workers, but allowed others to stay on, even when all the workers had participated in the same protest. Some protests they countenanced for a while—and then suddenly, they would decide to scuff them out.

The labor law in Qatar equipped employers with the legal authority to deal with labor protests any way they saw fit. As previously noted, under the kafala sponsorship system, collective action, protest, or bargaining of any sort was outlawed. Instead, the labor law laid out an arbitration process through the Ministry of Labor for disputes over wages and working conditions. But as analysts of this avenue have observed, the process was purely symbolic, inaccessible to workers and ineffective in providing redress.[3] In addition to restrictions specified in labor law, zoning regulations layered on measures of employer control on worker action by confining workers to spaces controlled by their employers. As described in chapter 2, workers were banned from most areas of the city, and their physical mobility within the country was restricted to the project site where they worked and labor camps where they slept—both spaces surveilled and policed by their employers.

Against this institutional backdrop, the question that arose for me was why employers and sponsors, armed with overwhelming institutional power, had allowed worker protests, and especially forms of protest as overt and confrontational as wildcat strikes, to take place at all. Why did managers terminate some protest actions through the mass deportation of workers and allow others to simmer? What informed which protests they chose to tolerate, and which to suppress?

After comparing wildcat protests at different sites—protests I had observed directly as well as those reported to me by management and workers—I noticed that company approaches to managing the labor unrest all followed the same pattern: protests were restricted to a single nationality at a time, migrants in a work stoppage were expected to remain in their labor camps, and the number of strikers had to remain low enough so that the strike would not meaningfully affect productivity on-site. Crucially, labor protests were only tolerated when they happened at the labor camp. Any resistance on the project site, including acts as individual and reactive as a worker throwing down his tools, a worker yelling at a supervisor, or even just turning his back to a supervisor in the midst of a dressing down, was harshly punished and frequently resulted in immediate deportation. "You have eight thousand men here. A worker who does not follow orders—it's like a spark. Impossible to control the fire [once it starts]," reflected Brett. "You've got to tamp it down right away."

Sociologists of social movement have a way of describing protests that all follow the same basic template, as they did in Qatar. They call the patterns that protest follow "repertoires of contention." Sociologist Charles Tilly, who coined the term, observed that protests tended to follow certain patterns at certain historical epochs, and defined repertoires as "a limited set of routines that are learned, shared, and acted out through a relatively deliberate process of choice."[4] Under the best of circumstances, repertoires—"social relations, meanings, and actions [that] cluster together in recurrent patterns"—act as a kind of normative lexicon through which different interests in society can articulate their needs, make claims, and express grievances.[5] This protest vocabulary allows a movement to make demands on an authority—a government or employer—and have that authority recognize the protesters' actions as the articulation of a demand.[6] Protest marches are often invoked as a classic example of a form of mobilization that is a well-used and well-understood tool in the repertoire that social movements routinely use to make their claims.[7] In a march, masses of people walk together toward some physical center of power—a city square, government office, or firm's headquarters. They carry displays—banners, signs, or other symbols—that communicate their demands. After the protest, they disperse peacefully.

Repertoires of contention are patterned on institutions in a society and reflect the broader social definitions of justice and understandings of the responsibilities that different groups have toward one another at any given moment.[8] For example, political scientist Sidney Tarrow has shown that labor strikes over wages in postwar Italy initially emphasized notions of fair pay for work, but picket lines were displaced in the late 1960s by factory occupations, when the workers' movement turned instead to debates around who should own the means of production.[9] Likewise, labor protests have swelled past strikes at places of employment to include boycotts of goods or other broader forms of protest when the organizers determined that the conditions they were challenging were imposed not by any specific employer or actor but rather were produced by an entire industry, overarching governance structures, or unfair laws.[10]

Although they are an extension of the organization of a given society, and in particular its organization of production, conventions for protest are not set in stone.[11] They are negotiated among different interest groups in society. They appear as stable and intelligible because they are recurrent; they are restatements of social norms of fairness and justice, and protests target the institutions meant to defend those norms over and over again.[12] Protests adhere to set patterns and cohere into a repertoire because actors on opposing sides of some social conflict tacitly agree to stick to a set of practices to make their claims and direct their demands to a clear set of institutions.[13]

Because repertoires channel social conflict in this way, they also define the limits of political expression, even when the political expression swells to include many millions of people. They hem protests into a set of mundane gestures—the same protest marches with the same signs held high, the same strikes and picket lines, the same speeches amplified by the same megaphones—sometimes sapping them of their disruptive potential. State actors frequently enforce repertoires through the use of violence; people who deviate from repertoires—who step off the designated protest route—may be shoved back in at gunpoint. As philosopher Judith Butler notes, "All public assembly is haunted by the police and the prison." The protesters that arrive at the public square, she adds, "are defined in part by the population that could not possibly arrive there; either they are detained at the border, or have no freedom of movement and assembly, or are detained and imprisoned."[14] But even at gunpoint, as Butler observes, protesters agree to be herded into the public square only so long as the dissent they are able to express there is still likely to have some significance and sway. Repertoires that no longer provide a meaningful avenue for redress are bowled over by revolution—"moments of madness," as political scientist Aristide Zolberg calls these revolutionary floods, when "all is possible" and "politics bursts its bounds to invade all of life."[15]

Protest is generally used as a vehicle to press for change. But the norms of protest in Qatar only produced stasis; they allowed workers no venue to express grievances or negotiate for different interests in any meaningful way. The conventions around which protest expressions were permissible, and for whom, and which actions were emphatically not, were defined entirely by management and ruthlessly enforced. Workers that stepped beyond the limits of the established repertoire were speedily removed from the territory, and any protests other than those tacitly sanctioned by management were made unfathomable. The protests fell into set patterns, and the ever-present threat of deportation turned repertoires of protests into repertoires of control.

The suppression of protest, even a violent crackdown on dissent, can set a process of social negotiation in motion. In the wreckage of torched buildings and violated norms, against the ache of broken bones and bruised bodies, in the silence after the desperate keen of funerals, a space can open up for the interrogation of social practices through which societies enact standards of justice and fairness. The social compacts that give governance structures their legitimacy are reexamined and challenged: the government's claims that it acts as a protector are rebuffed, and the practices it asserts are necessary to safeguard the public are called into question. To be sure, the contestation that the brutal suppression of protests can spark does not always produce political aperture. Police repression and the detention of protesters can spark the public to push for the establishment of new legal frameworks for police accountability, but just as often it can embolden the police in their use of violence and cause the public to retreat from the streets. The reaction to protest may not produce outcomes that people marched for. It may not foster social justice, create more scope for freedom, or lead to improved conditions and the redistribution of resources, but the presence of protest, and shock of its suppression, does create movement in patterns of social and political interaction.

In Qatar, even this route to change was cut off. Protests that did not adhere to the rules set by management were simply disappeared. Armed with the weapon of deportation, management unilaterally and without deliberation decided which kinds of protests could occur. For a gun to have any disciplinary power, it must be confronted with a body. In Qatar, bodies were deported rather than threatened, detained, or wounded. Migrants who engaged in protests that management didn't sanction were sent away and erased— not harmed as a public display of repression, but silenced, their discontent removed from the territory as if it were an impossibility.

A more accurate description of the protests allowed in Qatar is that they were repeated performative exchanges between managers and workers, stage-managed by employers or their representatives. Managers at Qatari companies used the emergence of discontent as an opportunity to strengthen industrial discipline on their sites. The wildcat strikes and work stoppages became dramatic enactments of labor conflict. They were facsimiles of protests: actions that seemed like rebellion, but were instead sanctioned actions— boundaried and routinized by management. The strikes did act as forms of claims making, but only insofar as they signaled compliance with managerial norms about what claims workers were allowed to make. Protest actions existed because—and only because—they were allowed to exist.

The protests that were allowed to exist were those that reenacted the strategies that management used to split workers from their skill and redefine them as a labor input for the production process. More specifically, the protests that were tolerated were those that reinforced the appraisal of workers' bodies prevalent on Qatari construction sites. Workers, politically represented as unskilled, were depicted as raw material, devoid of any legitimate social existence independent of their function as labor. Whatever skill workers had was attributed to their bodies; ability was defined as an outgrowth of inate physical features, like stature or musculature, rather than the expression of the skillful practice that workers had developed and refined through their agentic effort, imagination, and connection. With their skill downplayed or denied, workers were not viewed as laboring with their bodies, embodied as they worked. They became, in the Qatari context, bodies for labor.

Managers on Qatari construction sites sorted, assigned, and used workers on-site based on the ways they interpreted their bodies. They relied on a set of racialized beliefs to assess workers' aptitude for particular tasks. The racialized typologies varied across construction sites; different companies appraised workers for the same nationality or racial group differently. But these racialized rankings were all based on the belief that the abilities associated with racial and national categories were unchanging; abilities were as fixed and inherent as a worker's height or skin color. There was no room in this racial hierarchy for learning.

The protests that employers tolerated were those that tacitly affirmed the definition of workers as bodies for labor that management could sort and deploy based on the physical characteristics attributed to them. Labor actions that were limited to workers from a single nationality were countenanced because they did not challenge the way that national and ethnic groups were separated, categorized, and ranked in the assignment of work on construction sites. Protests that were small and confined to labor camps were brooked for a time as one element of a broader strategy to maintain control over workers. Meanwhile, protests through which workers challenged elements of the kafala system or rejected their treatment primarily as bodies were uncompromisingly put out. Protests in which workers questioned the basic justness of employment contracts, transgressed restrictions on their movement and stepped out of the confines of the labor camp, or expressed solidarity that cut across the national and racial distinctions imposed by management—protests in which workers affirmed their identities as persons who were workers as opposed to bodies used for labor—all these protests did not exist, could not exist, because the protesters were summarily deported.

Even as management was forcefully curating the wildcat protests that flared up throughout the industry, workers at a few sites were quietly developing different practices of resistance that stepped out of the narrow band of actions sanctioned by Qatari repertoires of control. These unsanctioned acts of resistance leveraged something particular: the power of skill. Workers drew on their own construction skill to enact ways of being on-site that challenged their treatment as bodies for labor. They used the performance of competence and overt displays of learning to assert themselves as agentic actors whose active participation in the production process affirmed their full personhood.

The way that migrants used their skill to contest their treatment suggests a kind of praxis—an application of skill that rose to the level of political action because of the reflective, deliberate, and transformative ways it was used. In accounts of the ways that workers have drawn on skill to resist exploitation in employment and improve their working conditions, skill is defined as a resource that workers can use for a strategic purpose. Skill is defined as competence, local knowledge, or specific expertise that workers own and can use as leverage in negotiations with their employers. The use of skill as resistance that I observed in Qatar, by contrast, was not limited to the use of skill—as stand-alone and identifiable competence—as a bargaining chip. Rather, workers invested in the ongoing engagement with skillful practice as a way to push back against managerial control. They used skill to assert their imaginative capacity, their right to desire, and the vibrancy of the social connections they established with one another. They laid claim to their full political personhood through the everyday exercise of skill.

This political role of skillful practice is arguably part and parcel of applications of skill that appear more clearly strategic, as observed in other employment contexts. But in Qatar, skill praxis was the only avenue for meaningful resistance, and so it emerges in heightened relief in that setting. To understand why the skillful praxis of migrant workers in Qatar was so transgressive and powerful, we need to begin by examining the practices through which workers were turned into bodies for labor.

BODIES FOR LABOR

The equation of workers with their bodies—their treatment as bodies for labor—organized managerial practice at construction firms throughout the country, and the application of this principle at N&W Builders was emblematic of its use at companies throughout Qatar. The company employed migrant workers from several different countries at its Lusail site, and company managers made decisions about whom to hire as well as how to deploy workers based on racial and ethnic assumptions about their bodies. They viewed the workers as having intrinsic traits that were unchanging and unchangeable, produced in their countries of origin, and could be read off the bodies of the workers they hired. "Six hundred men, Indian, Nepali, Vietnamese, Ethiopian, Thai. It's not easy to control them," reflected Prasert, a Thai engineer and supervisor with N&W Builders, in response to my question about manpower allocation. "It is very difficult to control the quality of the workers. They come from all over the world and they have very different minds. And you cannot change their minds." The confrontation with the Ethiopian strikers at the manager's trailer had occurred just the evening before and was still on his mind. He used the Ethiopian workers to illustrate his point. "Like the Ethiopians, they don't want to learn. They want to do it like in their own country because in their country they have no future, so they see no point in learning. And when they learn a little bit, they say, I need more money or they won't work. And they make problems with the other workers."

Phichit, the Thai managing supervisor on the project, concurred with his colleague and bemoaned the raw deal he felt the company had gotten with Ethiopian workers. His consternation was rooted in the company's racialized and racist beliefs about the physicality of Ethiopians, and the characteristics of African bodies. "They cost us 400 more riyal than the Nepali workers—1,000 per month compared to 750 for the Nepalis. We got them thinking they are strong. You know, Black people, they are strong. Big guys. And they are from a hot country, and they have Black skin so they don't burn, and they can handle the heat. Like the Egyptians. We thought, these guys can even carry steel rebar without any gloves. They will be good for us."

The notion that certain bodies are more suited to certain kinds of work has long been used to justify certain types of labor arrangements, such as well-worn tropes about women's small hands and nimble fingers making them more suited to garment production and electronics assembly, or racialized Brown or Black bodies being suited to the backbreaking "stoop labor" of agricultural work. These narratives have provided cover for larger social or economic dynamics; women were hired to sew garments because they garnered lower wages, and the workers assigned stoop labor were used because they could be hired under employment arrangements that made it almost impossible to resist exploitative labor practices. Even against this backdrop, the racial estimation of workers' bodies structured the organization of work on Qatari construction sites in ways that I found both shockingly blatant and intricate. When staffing decisions were made, workers' competence, experience, or skill were secondary considerations; the interpretations of their bodies were primary.

The views held by management at N&W Builders about African bodies, for example, had direct implications for the tasks allocated to Ethiopian workers and conditions under which they were required to perform them. When N&W Builders was forced to abandon the table form technology for building floors, it turned to a manual technique of pouring the cement walls and floors around rebar cages. The cages were built using rebar of various shapes and widths.

When the rebar was delivered, the bars were mixed together and dumped in a large pile to the side of the building. Over the length of hot afternoons, the unshaded mound of metal, as tall and wide as three cement lorries parked side by side, absorbed and concentrated the sun's heat. A heap of metal that size in direct sunlight can reach temperatures several times higher than the surrounding air temperatures. Depending on other climatic factors such as the wind speed and cloud cover, a mound of steel absorbing the sun on a 90°F day could conceivably reach temperatures up to 250°F.

Ethiopian workers were tasked with sorting the rebar manually, piece by piece, and outfitted only with thin fabric gloves for the job because their palms were viewed as being resistant to the heat. Rajan, a junior engineer from Sri Lanka, stood on top of the pile in his ironed shirt, holding a clipboard against the sun, and barked at the workers. "This is how I spend my whole day," griped Rajan to me later in the air-conditioned management trailer. "Pick up this one and move it to that pile. Now pick up that one and move it to that pile. The Ethiopians do not understand these differences. They cannot tell which piece is short, [and] which piece is long. Every single piece, you have to tell them what to do." This kind of intensive supervision, in the direct sun, was not typically assigned to engineers, and when I inquired about this, Phichit explained, "If no one is watching, they will stop." Quite possibly, I thought, because the metal was too hot to handle. The palms of many of the Ethiopian workers at the site, assigned to tasks like carrying hot metal, were peeling—a burn symptom—with the skin curling off in layers.

Because workers from different countries were treated as distinct inputs—each providing a unique brand of labor—the managerial task of organizing production on-site was as much about assembling different varieties of labor to create an output as it was about constructing a building. Phichit praised the North Korean workers for their speed, even though he did have complaints about their exactitude. "They come from a rough country, but with strong leaders. They know how to obey. You can put them to do a job, and they will finish." Rajan grumbled to the side, "They are sloppy." Phichit caught Rajan's comment and conceded that sometimes their work was less than perfect. Rajan also confided that management viewed North Koreans as threatening. "The Korean people, they are dangerous. You cannot get close to them. They will kill you." But this perception of North Korean workers meant that they received minimal supervision, and were given little to no guidance on how to make their work more exact. They were also assigned to jobs where they would have no interaction with other workers on-site. Their work at N&W Builders was roughshod because their supervisors made it so.

The Vietnamese were unpredictable, Phichit continued, in his exposition of the taxonomy used to rank workers, but if they had a strong foreman, their work was good and quick, and they were stronger than their size suggested. "They are fierce and committed warriors, and on the site too," said Phichit.

Nigerians were the optimal health and safety workers, because according to Phichit, they were "big, and Black, and strong, and the men are scared of their big voices." And Indians were fair in quality, but a headache, Phichit remarked, to have around when one relied on large numbers of Nepali workers. The Indian and Nepali workers often shared proficiency in Hindi, and they discovered soon enough that the Indian workers were paid some two hundred more riyals a month than their Nepali peers, even though they did the same job, frequently working side by side on the same steel-fixing teams. The pay rates of Qatari firms were set at the time of recruitment and were benchmarked against wages in the country of origin. This meant that it was common on Qatari worksites for workers from different nationalities completing the exact same job to be paid different wages. "This," explained Phichit, "awakens the hidden envy in the Nepali heart. Soon, he'll come, 'I ache here, I ache there, I cannot work,' and then you are forced to threaten them with sending them home. Truly, my job is difficult here. The men are not easy to control." The notion that the Nepalis and Indians should be paid the same wage for the same work was as nonsensical to Phichit as the suggestion that wood and steel be sold at the same price since they both held up walls. For Phichit and N&W Builders, Nepali and Indian labor were not interchangeable; they were two entirely different commodities.

RACIAL TAXONOMIES AND SKILL

When the managers at N&W Builders spoke about worker skill, they defined it not as an ability but rather as a fixed trait—a physical affordance rather than an aquired competence—that differed by nationality, as unchanging and unchangeable as they viewed migrants' bodies to be. Workers were slotted into the hierarchies embedded in the organization of production based on their nationality rather than their experience or demonstrated aptitude. Phichit's ranking of workers was unambiguous:

> I would have to say that no worker compares to the Thai worker. They are skilled and they know how to control their mind, and their culture is good. You tell them to do a job, and they will follow through. I am from Thailand, but I am not saying this because they are my countrymen, but because it is the truth. I know people from other countries, I have been doing this work for ten years now. I know which nationalities have skill, which ones can learn, and which one you have to control.

He also described physical vulnerabilities that the Thai management attributed to Thai workers. "In our country, in Asia, people are not good in the heat because in Thailand we have no humidity," he affirmed, contravening the reality of Thailand's often humid climate. "Some Thai people could become sick and collapse so we have to stop them from working in the outdoors when it is very hot." Management used this idea to rationalize its desire to shield its Thai compatriots from the most difficult working conditions.

Phichet ranked Nepali workers just below Thai workers. He prized Nepali workers for their obedience and docility, despite his reservations about their innate ability. "Nepali workers don't know how to do construction. They come from a poor country. But the good thing about Nepal is that their culture is good. They know right and wrong in their mind, and they bring values from their local area. When we tell them something, they believe us and they follow us. They follow orders and they respect their superiors." His view of Nepalis— their qualities and limitations—informed the function he assigned to them on-site. "When the Thai workers complain to me about the heavy work, I tell them, that's why we brought you Nepalis. Train them, and they can be good helpers to you. You won't have to carry the heavy stuff by yourself and you will see that they don't complain." Management's classification of Nepali workers as subordinate and racially inferior to their Thai coworkers was reflected in the pay scales on-site. Thai workers were classed as chargehands or foremen and paid an average of thirteen hundred Qatari riyals as opposed to the six hundred Qatari riyal that the company paid its Nepali recruits.

Management's ranking of Thai and Nepali workers would play out in the strike, ultimately undercutting the bargaining power that Thai workers sought to leverage through the strikes. The racial hierarchy created by management structured the interactions between the two nationality groups and shaped the kinds of solidarity that workers were able to construct. Before the strike, Thai and Nepali employees spent their days working elbow to elbow, and the labor camp for Nepali workers was located across the street from the Thai camp. But the Thai workers adopted the disdainful attitude that management displayed toward their Nepali colleagues. The Nepali workers reported that their Thai neighbors regularly broke into their camp to rough them up and raid their food stocks. During the strike, not a single Thai worker walked over to the Nepali labor camp to encourage their coworkers to join them.

Ironically, the habit adopted by many Thai workers of shunting work onto their Nepali teammates softened the impact of their strike. Because building the rebar cages manually, which the company was forced to do when its table form technology was rejected, was monotonous and physically taxing, Thai workers on construction teams had pushed their share of the work onto their Nepali helpers. After close to two months, the Nepali workers had mastered the task, and the speed of cage assembly improved steadily over the company's initial performance. By the time the Thai workers decided to go on strike, Thai workers had become largely superfluous to the construction of cages, and the withdrawal of their labor was reduced to an irritant that didn't meaningfully affect productivity.

Job assignments meant that over time, these beliefs about racial taxon-omy were reified in ways that were difficult to disrupt. Phichit's views about the innateness of worker capacity, for example, informed how he organized production, and the subsequent organization of production reified his problematic beliefs. The allocation of tasks produced the kinds of skill differences that Phichit and others used to justify their racialized taxonomy of workers. Specifically, the opportunities afforded to workers for skill development were shaped by perceptions of worker bodies, and as a result, so were the skills they were able to acquire. Because the management at N&W Builders considered Nepalis to be docile and weak, they structured teams so that Nepalis were always in a subordinate position to Thai workers, who relied on them as helpers, using them to carry equipment and clean. Nepali workers' access to more complex tasks, where they could practice more sophisticated techniques, was blocked. Supervisors at N&W Builders then used the fact that Nepalis on their site were not skilled—in the construction of floor and column frames, for instance—to affirm their belief that Nepalis were dim-witted people and slow to learn, even if their compliancy was valued.

This kind of racialized classification of workers and the racialized assignments to different work tasks that went with it were prevalent on all the sites that I visited in Qatar. To be sure, some managers were subtler in their exposition than others, but the practice of assigning capacities and limitations to workers based on their nationality was widespread. The attributes ascribed to workers varied somewhat across companies. Some, like the managers at N&W Builders, viewed Nepalis as weak and docile, and thus the perfect helpers. At other sites, Nepalis were seen as brawny and unafraid of heights; the image of Nepali Sherpas who scaled the Himalayas was held up as proof of this quality—a myth that managers expounded even when the Nepali workers they recruited were from the flat agricultural lands on Nepal's southern border with no direct experience with the mountains.

By controlling access to learning, managers corroborated the taxonomies they used to staff projects, and turned their bias into technical judgments about their workers' human capital and aptitude. On some sites, Egyptian workers were viewed as strong but mentally slow, and so were assigned tasks that required physical strength but not much dexterity, whereas on other sites—where Egyptians were also hired as engineers or clerks—Egyptian workers were prized for their sharp intellects, and quickly promoted to positions such as chargehand or foreman, where they could learn to interpret construction drawings. Filipino workers were viewed as meticulous problem solvers on some sites, assigned to health and safety staff, quality control teams, or quasi-supervisory positions in many companies. Other employers perceived them as troublemakers who were more likely to challenge management practices and hence put on teams where their contact with workers from other nationalities was more constrained. On sites where Nepalis were praised for supposed comfort and their agility climbing mountain ranges, managers placed Nepalis workers on scaffolding teams under the tutelage of experienced scaffolders.

On the job, they apprenticed to the specific technical skills required to build complex structures while hanging several stories aboveground. They became competent scaffolders because they received the training they needed, and not, as management would have it, because of some innate feature of their racialized bodies.

Labor actions that stayed within the bounds of this system of classification were treated as an unavoidable nuisance, as expected and routine as the occasional botched delivery of materials or delayed disbursement of funds. The protests expressed discontent, but they did not threaten the social system that produced their grievances. In contrast, the protests that called into question the racialized sorting of workers, and challenged its legitimacy and usefulness in assigning work tasks, were alarming to management. Many workers found such actions thrilling and empowering. During the tense days of the work stoppage at N&W Builders, the Nepali workers whom I had interviewed messaged me cell phone videos of wildcat protests at other worksites. A favorite clip captured workers yanking the condescension hoses out of the air conditioners attached to management trailers, disabling the units. Management, including at N&W Builders, viewed such actions as violently threatening and acted swiftly against any protest expressions that stepped out of the established repertoire. Even the video that was sent to me multiple times ended abruptly with the final seconds showing the police entering the worksite and beating a worker at the edge of the frame.

The protest at N&W Builders was a case study in the kinds of repertoires of contention that were allowed on Qatari construction sites. When the strike initially adhered to the racial and national divisions that management used to allocate manpower, the supervisory crew had a lackadaisical response. But when the Thai strikers pulled Ethiopian workers into their protest, the work stoppage that management had considered a passing display of impatience over unpaid wages blew up into an existential affront to the organization of work on-site and the company's version of the racialized taxonomy on which it depended. By deporting the Ethiopians, whose inclusion turned the strike into a broad challenge to the system of worker commodification in Qatar, the company not only extinguished the strike but, more importantly, expunged interethnic protest actions from the repertoire of contention available to the workers who remained.

Skill and Protest

Even as N&W Builders was deporting its Ethiopian staff wholesale, workers at a stadium site across town were developing strategies of resistance that sidestepped the repertoires of contest and control altogether. Rather than challenging exploitative practices directly, pushing back against the nonpayment of wages or forced overtime, they drew on their construction skill to challenge workplace practice from within, quietly and steadily creating alternatives to the taxonomies that management used to control workers and suppress protest. They forged ties across nationality and ethnic groups, deliberately drawing on the language of their craft to find common ground across the differences in pay, status, and stereotypes that management sought to reinforce. They reached up into the managerial ranks to build common cause with supervisors who shared their investment in the practices of learning and in many cases had been construction workers in their own countries before taking positions as management in Qatar. They used their skilled practice to begin to articulate politics based on their shared position as workers—politics premised on an understanding of themselves as a class (as a class for itself, in Marxist terminology) with interests and aspirations based on their position as workers in a particular system of production. They emphasized that they were lending the labor in their bodies, as they expressed it in skillful and masterful ways, to the project of turning Qatar into a dazzling mock-up of modernity, and rejected the notion, codified in the kafala system and underscored by management practices, that they were mere bodies for labor.

One scaffolding foreman on the stadium site put it to me this way: "We know how to do our work. The company can bring the bus to the camp [to take us to the site], but they cannot make us act against our heart." Soon, events at the stadium site would make it clear how profound a challenge to management practices such a sentiment could be.

One late April afternoon, Robbie, the scaffolding manager for all ABC Builders' operations in Qatar, took me up to the concentric circle of scaffolding that would support the workers who stand on the platforms as they built the stadium roof from inside. The scaffolding looked like a honeycombed shell of metal and wood around a central hollow. Scaffolders worked in teams of four or five on the platform. Below them, men hung from poles affixed onto each of the scaffolding frames, and although they wore safety harnesses, they dangled unsupported over the cavernous fall beneath them. The scaffolders wore jumpsuits of blue or yellow depending on their employer. As I climbed up the highest portions of the structure, on the staggered ladder that linked one level to another, I looked up to see the men make interlocking crescents of blue and yellow against the gray scaffolding boards, with the yellow streaks concentrated to the east, and the blue to the west. The teams didn't mix, and at the yellow end of the structure, workers had laid down enough scaffolding planks to block out the sunlight.

After a couple of hours of interviewing scaffolders and observing them at work, Robbie and I headed back down. It was near the end of the day shift, and teams of men started climbing down behind us. The men in yellow came down first, the network of ladders being closest to their end of the structure. They worked for ABC Builders. In the zone at the entrance to the scaffold, a clear dusty space the size of a small parking lot, the men came up, greeted Robbie, and reported how many scaffolding segments they had erected. "Six, boss, six today." Many stood around, enjoying a social moment on the solid ground, where they could unbuckle their safety harnesses and relax.

As teams of men in blue jumpers started exiting the scaffold, the ABC Builders scaffolders began taunting them good-naturedly. "Here," yelled one scaffolder, as he pointed to his chest, "see the number one team!" "We saw you sleeping," said another, to the uproarious laughter of his comrades. "Tomorrow, watch and learn from the masters!" ribbed another.

Robbie explained that the ABC Builders scaffolders and the scaffolders in blue, employees of Castle Contractors, had a friendly rivalry going, and at the end of the day, the scaffolders who had completed the most frames stood at the entrance of the scaffold and heckled the other crews. "But the Castle boys, poor things, they always come out the losers. Our boys are chuffed today; they get to give them a hard time in front of company," he said as he winked at me. "Castle [Contractors] doesn't give them proper training," he added. "Their productivity is about two-thirds of ours. They've had to bring more men to the site to keep up with their contract."

When I returned to the construction site a week later, the mood was less congenial. Robbie explained that nerves were frayed because a labor conflict had flared over the past several days. Some weeks earlier, the Qatari client for the stadium had moved up the deadline for completion by two and a half months, the first, and most disruptive, of the speedups that the client would demand. The managers pushed the speedup down to the trade teams on the project, and the engineers overseeing the scaffolding crews ordered a double shift work cycle, with a morning shift running from 6 a.m. to 5 p.m. followed by an evening shift from 4 p.m. to midnight. Additional crews were going to be brought onto the project, but scaffolding crews would also be expected to work extended overtime as well as double shifts when needed—meaning men were often being asked to work 6 a.m. to midnight, or sixteen hours in a row. Management had pledged to create a sleeping shed so that the men who worked a double shift could sleep a few hours before their next turn. Sanjay, the senior scaffolding supervisor, pulled Robbie aside and told him that one of the engineers had called him down off the structure. The engineer had spoken to him roughly and threatened that if the ABC Builders scaffolders didn't make the production target, he would see to it not only that Sanjay was deported but also that a different scaffolding supervisor was deported each day until they did.

The ABC Builders scaffolders were outraged by the pressure from management. Chargehands and foremen hinted to the engineers on behalf of the group that if the new work schedule were implemented, the scaffolders—all of them—would refuse to board the bus from their labor camps to the worksite. Any work stoppage that they would have launched would have been the kind censured in Qatar; the strike would have spanned national and ethnic distinctions, uniting workers from India, Nepal, Pakistan, Ghana, and Nigeria against management. It would have forcefully foregrounded their identities as scaffolders. As a result, if the scaffolders had gone on strike, especially with the Qatari client overseeing the project so closely, ABC Builders would have almost certainly determined that it had to deport the strikers en masse.

During the course of that tense week, scaffolding foremen, elevated by their crews to the role of spokesmen, push backed against the proposed work plan. The foremen tried to reason with the engineers doing quality control rounds of the building and explained the difficulty of working in the dark: without adequate daylight, workers could not effectively secure the joints on the scaffolding frame; the risk of dropping scaffolding components rose dramatically in the dark, as did the possibility of tripping on tools or a loose plank. Management countered that the company would provide high-powered lamps for illumination. Several of the foremen had worked emergency night shifts in the past and referenced their experience to explain that the lamps' high beams cast sharp and confusing shadows as they filtered through the scaffolding lattice. The optical illusions forced them to work at a more deliberate pace, making it unlikely that they could meet the production goals that management had planned to set for those shifts. Tired men also made for slow and hazardous work. Crews that worked double shifts or did not get enough rest would likely have material hand offs that were less precise. They would drop ties and spanners, which would break bones and crack skulls when they fell on the men below. Some men would undoubtedly lose their balance trying to grab onto a plank or tube and would fall to the ground, resulting in an injury or death, the foremen reminded the engineers, that would force the company to halt production for several days or weeks until it completed the incident review required by its insurers.

Faced with arguments about safety and productivity, ABC Builders management relented. While the company backed away from its order that its own employees work double shifts, however, it did not retract its demand that Castle Contractors meet the higher production targets for the fast-track project. As a result, the contractor initially kept to the plan of instituting night shifts. Yet soon the Castle Contractors' workers heard from their colleagues at ABC Builders that they had refused the extended shifts and been able to persuade their employer to back down. Castle Contractors scaffolders decided to follow their coworkers' lead and said that they would strike if they were forced to work double shifts. They invoked the decision of management at ABC Builders—made based on its scaffolders' input—that the safety risks were not worth the production gains: if it was not safe for scaffolders in yellow to work at heights in the dark, why would it be for scaffolders in blue?

SKILL PRAXIS

Alongside visible but ineffectual wildcat strikes and dogged work stoppages at worksites throughout Qatar, stage-managed and corralled by management, the kind of skill-based resistance that I observed at ABC Builders levied an understated yet powerful challenge to the widespread treatment of migrant workers as bodies for labor. To be sure, this skill-based resistance did not shield workers from many of the structural forms of exploitation that were endemic to industry, such as the nonpayment of wages. But it did allow workers to push back against the racialized taxonomy that management used to structure production. It enabled workers to form cross-national ties of solidarity that they used to create space for agentic action, claim some autonomy, and resist managerial control. In drawing on skill as a resource for resistance, they leaned in particular on their engagement with the practice of skill—or skill praxis.

Praxis is a form of practice that marries action and reflection; it denotes a process of both interpreting and considering action in the moment—as it is being carried out. This reflection is what makes praxis purposeful, turning otherwise routine activity into creative actions that can transform the social worlds in which they unfold. Praxis is the action that becomes political because of the way it enacts the human agency of the actor, and how it carries the power of freewill and choice.[16] In its Marxist formulation, praxis represents a process in which representational knowledge is drawn into the action itself, erasing any distinction between theory and action, so that any action holds the potential to change, in one fell swoop, both the material world in which it takes places and the social understandings through which people interpret as well as engage with that world. Educator and political theorist Paolo Freire articulated this perspective in his treatise on learning as a political act: "It is as transforming and creative beings that humans, in their permanent relation with reality, produce not only material goods—tangible objects—but also social institutions, ideas, and concepts."[17] In praxis, learning, transformation, and creativity are ongoing projects.

At construction sites throughout Qatar, skill-based praxis offered workers a method to affirm their humanity. Through their reflection on skill, they created a social system that affirmed their capacity to learn. They used their everyday construction practices—their skilled manipulation of building materials, collaborative engagement with teammates, and coordination with other building crews—to embody identities as agentic actors.

Political theorists who have championed praxis as a vehicle for social transformation have identified two elements that turn what might otherwise be an unexceptional version of "awareness while doing" into a radical, if unassuming, political method. First, they stress that praxis is collective.[18] Second, this collaboration creates the possibility for organized action that is entirely new and unexpected.[19] Both of these features were foundational to the skill praxis that I observed on Qatari worksites; they enabled workers to escape the constraints of the protest repertoires that were used to discipline other forms of labor actions and refashion their skillful practice at work into a kind of resistance against the exploitative working conditions they often faced.

SOCIAL PRESENCE

Political theorist Hannah Arendt, who described praxis as the highest form of political action, highlighted this aspect of praxis, calling it "a mode of human togetherness."[20] She argued that its revolutionary potential stems from the way it opens up possibilities for connecting with others, and in turn, possibilities for the creation of a new social world. Migrant workers on the sites that I visited used the interpersonal interaction and joint sense making that are part and parcel of skill development to build intentional ties of solidarity. They drew on routine training exchanges, and the interpersonal and physical attunement on which they depended, to forge social bonds based on allegiance to a trade and reverence for technical competence. As crews made up of workers from Nepal, India, Ghana, and Pakistan sorted through the methodological and physical challenges of erecting massive, complex scaffolds, they came to see one another as part of the same community, with identities rooted in their trade and, as many scaffolders told me, the bravery required for working several stories in the air. Prince from Ghana explained how that common experience helped them bridge divisions:

> Sometimes there is racism between people. And sometimes we fight in the housing accommodation. So you go outside for a few minutes to cool down, or someone will pull you apart, and then you will find us laughing together again. When you work with people, you see that they are good. Even from different countries. You understand: he is my brother. We are far from our families, but we are together in that feeling. We are a family here too.

Because their coalitions were rooted in technical mastery, they were able to extend their bonds of skill affinity far up into firm hierarchies to include supervisors and managers. Through these vertical alliances, they found advocates who made their skill and contribution to the construction process visible.

At the stadium site, the scaffolders worked in concert with the rope artists and cladders who installed the panels that would make up the stadium's eggshell exterior. The scaffolders built the platforms on which cladding teams perched as they maneuvered the panels through the air. During one of my visits to the stadium site, I shadowed the cladding manager and his team. Our scrum stopped to observe a team of workers that was lifting cladding panels up onto the massive vaulted steel frame. The panels were curved triangles of aluminum and tempered glass, four meters across on each side and weighing close to half a metric ton each. Workers were using a pulley system, with ropes lashed around the massive triangle and then threaded through a crane head, to raise the panels one by one, high enough to place them on the stadium's outer skin some fifteen stories above the scaffolding platform where we stood. As the panel dangled above us, another team on a scaffolding platform astride the stadium skeleton of reinforced steel tubing grabbed hold of the ropes that had been attached to the triangle's corners and used them to maneuver each of the triangles into their socket in the steel web.

"In my opinion, the workers who do this job must be very strong," opined Samir, a junior engineer from Jordan, as we watched the team. "Well, when you find any strong workers, you let me know," snapped Dean, the Irish managing supervisor at Aluminum Cladding Solutions, one of the companies that provided and installed the cladding panels for stadium's exterior. "This is a scrawny bunch. Look at them! All of them small and thin, malnourished-looking every one. . . . Strength has got nothing to do with it."

Dean went on to detail the technical skill involved in hoisting up the panels and slotting them into the domed frame. He explained how workers had to be attentive to wind sheer and adjust the tension of the ropes accordingly. As the crane pulled up the panel, the workers on the ground had to use the ropes at the corners to position the triangle, and guide it up so that it wouldn't swing back and slam against the building or the men working in the scaffold frame stacked around its edge. He noted that the team that stood atop the steel frame receiving the panels had it even harder than the team on the ground; after directing the crane with hand gestures and loud whistles, they had to grab onto the dangling ropes and move the panel into place by using the angle of their bodies. On the platform, there was little room to step back or forward, and the men had to pull the panel by leaning out or in while their feet were fixed—but they had to do so in concert to create the degrees of freedom necessary to guide the panel against the wind-force and into its slot. Dean spoke of the coordination among the workers as they pulled the ropes and talked about how their movements had to take into account the movements of the scaffolding teams nearby, calling the synchronization required as they stepped backward and forward a high-risk dance. "They have to communicate. They trust one another."

Dean's explanation of the skill required for this task was in response to my question, but he delivered it as a sharp retort to one of the two junior engineers who accompanied us, who (I later learned) had suggested that the company should swap out its current employees for new recruits, presumably with bodies coded as strong, at a fraction of the wage the company was paying its cladding installers.

Dean's observations carried weight because of his status as a senior manager, but while his job title may have set him apart from his crew, his opinions reflected his participation in a broader set of practices that workers had authored. Through interactions based on skill, workers were able to forge social connections that reached up into the ranks of management and created lines of solidarity where the allegiance was to craft rather than status. As Dean himself reported, he found it easy to join the flow of these practices. He had worked as a welder and glazier in the United Kingdom for over two decades before he migrated to the Gulf and took up managerial positions at a series of firms, culminating in his position at Aluminum Cladding Solutions. In my observation of Qatari construction sites, Dean's experience was not unique—many of the managers for different trades were white Europeans or Australians who had been skilled journeymen before they moved—but it was still uncommon. Most managers and supervising engineers had never done the manual tasks of construction work. Dean's prior work experience meant that he understood the cognitive and physical challenges involved in mastering a trade skill; he sympathized with the fatigue that workers felt after hours of detailed and high-risk work in the heat, and connected with the sense of accomplishment that workers felt when they completed a difficult task like hoisting and installing a cladding panel in the face of winds and desert dust. Drawing on his experience as well as his observation of workers on-site, he defended the worker competence as stemming not from the brute strength of individual bodies, interchangeable if they were of the same "national brand," as Samir would have it, but rather from the social connections that supported learning.

SOCIAL WORLDS

The second element that turned praxis into resistance was an outgrowth of the first: through the web of social relationships they formed, migrants used praxis to turn production sites into social worlds of their own making. Migrants appropriated the stadium site, a fast-track project where management pushed for speed through grinding overwork into a world where they could express their values, aspirations, and social ties. The landscape of the construction site—the towering, layered scaffolds, massive cranes swinging in the desert wind, maze of pathways between management trailers, equipment sheds, and welding stations, and shaded canteen areas where men crowded at the entryway when the lunch was called—became a space where they could explore their identities as men who developed skills that in many cases were completely unknown to them before they arrived in Qatar. They became learners who redefined themselves in the process of learning and joined a community organized around an ethos that equated expertise with valor.

Jean Lave, in her decades-long study of apprenticeship, rebuts the notion that learning is a process of skill absorption, where individuals acquire skill that is "out there."[21] She posits instead that learning is nothing more and nothing less than the participation in a social world—one in which the knowledge that the learner seeks to acquire has some social meaning, some social value, often associated with social status and power. That social world is not static but instead, like all social contexts, shaped by those who participate in it. As the learner participates in the social world, the learner's practices change the social world they seek inhabit as well as the meaning and makeup of the knowledge the learner sought to master.[22]

If one takes seriously the proposition that knowledge is not some stand-alone resource but rather an expression of collective doing in a social world, as Lave encourages us to do, then the praxis of skill is at once the praxis of both becoming a social person and engaging with the power relations that structure that world. The scaffolders at ABC Builders appropriated the grueling tempo of work on the stadium and recast it as a competition with their peers at Castle Contractors. The scaffolders in blue and those in yellow were publicly recognized for high levels of performance. Through their good-natured teasing, scaffolders celebrated the status of the workers on the teams that had completed the most frames as master tradesmen and affirmed the social value of the skill and learning in the community of scaffolders who descended the ladders and congregated in the dusty entryway. And that skill, praised and protected through the practices of the social world migrants had created, became a bulwark against management attempts to denigrate it. While management focused on extracting more labor from its workers, units defined as bodies for labor, workers challenged this notion, arguing that productivity was achieved only through their expertise and volition.

Praxis, in this definition, is no less than the practice of becoming. Freire describes praxis as "affirm[ing] men and women as beings in the process of becoming—as unfinished, uncompleted beings in and with a likewise unfinished reality"—a reality built by the men and women who are engaged with praxis.[23] Applied to the context of construction sites in Qatar, praxis was a process of personal becoming for the workers: they stepped out of management's characterization of them as nationally and racially differentiated bodies, and into a process of defining what it meant, as an identity and experience, to be at once a worker involved in building a skyscraper or stadium and a participant in the social world that arose in and around the scaffolding lattice and steel skeletons on-site. Praxis was likewise the process of knowledge's becoming: workers developed the competence they needed to complete construction tasks on-site but also created de novo the knowledge—embodied, enacted, and specific—required to build the challenging and untried structures, dreamed up by star architects in offices far removed from the radiant heat of steel rebar and lashing dust storms.

Arendt identifies this capacity for innovation as the singular feature that makes praxis revolutionary. She calls this capacity "natality" and defines it as the faculty to have a new beginning, to support the birth of new expression—something that "cannot be expected from whatever may have happened before." This newness—this natality—is deeply political in her view: "The new always happens against the overwhelming odds of . . . probability, which for all practical, everyday purposes amounts to certainty; the new therefore always appears in the guise of a miracle. The fact that man is capable of actions means that the unexpected can be expected of him, and that he is able to perform what is infinitely improbable."[24] Viewed through the lens of natality, the new knowledge, expressions of competence, and ties of solidarity that workers created through skill praxis were not just "startlingly unexpected" against the backdrop of the Qatari system of labor use and control but also fundamentally transformative of labor processes on-site.

Resistance that invoked skill as a counterargument to managerial dictates, like the scaffolders' stance against obligatory night shifts, represented a moment of political natality, a moment of political being. Workers discovered the possibility of pushing back. In their assertion of expertise, they claimed a new source of power, and by forging ties across nationalities, rank, and companies, they revealed to management their ability to amplify that power.

In the social connections that workers forged on Qatari construction sites, they found resources to challenge managerial practices that divided them against one another and sorted them into racialized categories, reducing them to bodies for labor. Against managerial practices that ranked their bodies and pitted them against one another, they built ties of solidarity, friendship, and even kinship that cut across difference. They created social worlds based on skill. The ethos of the rich community they cultivated in the shadow of scaffolding structure and under cladding panels was collaborative and creative, rooted in shared practices of teaching and learning. Workers' skill praxis was folded into the flow of construction and was much quieter than the protests so muscularly curated by management, to be sure, but it represented a challenge far more consequential to the system than any wildcat strike could ever mount.

SHELTERING PRAXIS

Praxis is a form of resistance folded into skill. Because skill is a resource that companies need for production, workers there were able to draw on company resources to contest company practices. They were able to appropriate the space, processes, and organizational support that companies allocated to skill development and use them as fuel for resistance. At ABC Builders, the scaffolders used company-mandated vocational training to deepen their skill praxis, shielding still-nascent expressions of social connection and social identity from company intervention or retaliation until they were strong enough to become resources for resistance.

The ABC Builders training center was established the early 2000s in response to client concerns about the structural integrity of ABC Builders' scaffolds. After a legal battle over poor scaffolding (one structure crashed down, and several others, in the wake of the collapse, had to be dismantled because they were found to be unsound) and a couple of failed bids for projects, the company set up the center to improve scaffolding quality and repair the damage done to the firm's reputation. Over time, however, the training center grew into something far more significant than a space for the acquisition of technical skill. Workers turned it into the fulcrum of the social world that they inhabited. It became something of a cultural hub that influenced how skill was perceived and valued among other trades at the company as well as scaffolders at other companies.

When ABC Builders was confronted with the quality issues of its scaffolding in the mid-2000s, it had contemplated hiving off that capacity and subcontracting it out instead, but Robbie, the company's managing director for scaffolding, had proposed setting up a training center. Robbie was himself an experienced scaffolder and craftsman; after getting his start on construction projects in and around Liverpool, he went on to build scaffolding structures on complex oil and gas projects in the British North Sea, Malaysia, and Nigeria. When I asked him about the pedagogical strategy he used to develop the training, he explained that he drew on his own felt experience of scaffolding.

> I make a point of renewing my CISCR [Construction Industry Scaffolders Records Scheme—the UK national scaffolding certification body] card whenever I am back home, but you know, a lot of the guys who come in for the test, they'd sooner use a pencil than a spanner. Building a scaffold is not theory. You feel scaffolding in your bones, and you have to keep doing it to keep that feel. You have to feel the relationship between the small—whether a joint is tight—and the large—the whole structure. You can feel it, level and solid. You have to know how to carry yourself up there and you have to be damn sure that your mates know how to carry themselves too. That's how you know the scaffold you built will hold you and your mates. That's the most important thing.

In designing the center and its curriculum, Robbie drew on his own felt experience of scaffolding practice and attunement to the social connection that scaffolding required.

Robbie set up the center on a hectare of land in the desert leased by ABC Builders about an hour outside the city at the far end of a dirt road. A ring of storage sheds, full of scaffolding material some eight or ten units deep, formed the perimeter of the center and marked it as a world apart. In the clearing at the center of this ring was a staging area about the size of a soccer pitch where workers built scaffolds in multiple configurations. On one side of the pitch, classroom and office trailers were parked in an open rectangle so that a small courtyard opened between them. This space had been turned into a garden, with shaded areas, park benches, and potted flowers on one end, and a plot for vegetables on the other. Asif, a junior engineer from Pakistan, had even jerry-rigged a fountain out of scaffolding components, which gurgled under a trellis tangled with vines. "To remind us that gardens wait for us in paradise," he told me.

The formal training provided at the center was short term, with training modules running either six or twelve days. The workers who took the course arrived at the training center with some scaffolding experience. Although there were no set criteria for being enrolled in the training, Asif explained that they preferred that students had completed at least one scaffolding project before attending. "It takes some time to understand that there are many ways of scaffolding—there are so many types, formwork, hanging scaffold, tank inside, tank outside—to be familiar with all the parts. . . . Here we learn how to work easier and find a way to progress forward even if there are obstacles."

The training itself followed a set pattern. A couple of hours every morning were devoted to lectures on specific scaffolding elements; PowerPoint presentations covered everything from the different types of couplers, to the angle at which scaffolding tubes should be fitted to support different scaffolding structures, to the correct posture one should use when moving heavy loads. For the rest of the day, scaffolders were given practical assignments to develop a felt sense of the theory they had learned in the morning.

It became clear over the course of several extended visits to the center that training was not providing scaffolders with new technical skills so much as it was teaching them a language to talk about their skill. At the most basic level, the training was teaching workers the English terms for the components they used and techniques they were engaged in. English was the lingua franca on large construction sites in Qatar, but most workers spoke it poorly, if at all. Much of the morning lectures was devoted to rote memorization of the names of things. At various points during the lecture, which was simultaneously translated by teachers who spoke both English and the language of the trainees (generally Hindi), the instructor would stop, pull out something from the jumble of equipment he kept at the front of the hall or point to something on his PowerPoint drawing, and yell out, "What's this called?" A few tentative voices would respond: "gravlok tie" or "ledger bracing." The instructor would yell out again, "What's this called?" and few more voices would join the response. The call and response continued and reached a crescendo in a rhythmic chant: "gravlok tie! gravlok tie! gravlok tie!" Through this ritualized chanting, workers memorized the terms for the materials they used in their trade and developed together a shared language for their work. More important, however, the call-and-response sessions were moments of social bonding, and even communion, that allowed workers to develop a shared cultural identity and sense of belonging.

The training concluded with a written multiple-choice test—in English—to ensure that workers had acquired enough of a familiarity with the trade language to articulate the logic behind various scaffolding processes. Some questions focused on technical skill—"What is the safe working load of a swivel coupler, which complies with BS-EN 12811?"—but many other questions asked about strategies for negotiating organizational dynamics at the worksite—"If a scaffold is not complete, what action should you take?" with answers such as "Put danger signs on the scaffold," "Tell all operatives not to use the scaffold," and "Tell the site manager or site supervisor" listed among the options.

Asif described the development of language as a crucial source of power at the worksite. Knowing the logic behind different scaffolding steps and having the language to explain them empowered workers to defend their building practices against supervisory pressure. Asif reflected on his own experience to illustrate this aspect of the training. Before graduating to the role of trainer, Asif had been a trainee at the center. Asif remembered the significance of the training in shaping his working conditions:

> What I learned in this training is how to work safely, even when the supervisor says hurry, hurry. Before, we would build one lift, and put [in] two or three boards, and start on the next one. There were gaps and people could fall, but we could finish quickly. But after the training, we now make a full platform of boards and we put a handrail, and only [then] do we start the second and third lift. If the boss says hurry, we say no. We must be safe, and we know how to build so that we are safe.

Asif thought that it was important for workers to return to the center for training several times, ideally once a year, not to reinforce skillful practice, but to fortify workers in their ability to use their skill to protect themselves.

The social connections that workers developed during their training periods were a critical resource to this end. Workers drew on the friendships they formed at the center as a source of solidarity and support on the worksite. Every time I returned to the center, I was struck by the level of conviviality and frequency of laughter, which seemed in such sharp contrast to the grim determination required to get through the day that I observed on the jobsite. During breaks, men relaxed, drank sweet tea, and socialized in the garden, quite possibly the only green space they had access to in Qatar. The rapport between the trainers and trainees seemed easy, softened with mutual teasing.

Many of the social interactions that took place at the training center became touchstones for the scaffolders when they were back on the construction site—resources they drew on to contest exploitative practices. To take one example, the morning lectures at the training center took place in one of the air-conditioned trailers. When the lights went down for the PowerPoint presentation, it was not uncommon for some of the men to begin to doze. Robbie would jokingly order the men who had been nodding off to come to the front of the class and do a set of push-ups—to general hilarity in the room. This had become something of a trademark shtick, and the trainees ribbed one another about whether or not they had been called out to do sleepy push-ups. On construction sites, I observed former trainees using a reference to push-ups to remind tired or sleepy colleagues to renew their focus on their work, which at the heights that the scaffolders were working was critical to all for their safety. "Hey, hey! You need to do some push-ups!" was a call we often heard. On a day when Robbie went to the ABC Builders stadium site, a scaffolding foreman approached him as he was giving me a tour of a scaffolding section and used the reference to push-ups to invoke a sense of solidarity that could reach up into the company hierarchy and perhaps provide redress against the work speedup. "Boss, there are too many push-ups. Please tell them that we need to slow down."

The training center nurtured this ethos of solidarity, rooting it in trade identity and price. Robbie repeatedly stressed that the workers were scaffolders first and their allegiance to the trade should supersede national division, or ethnic or religious resentments. Some of the strategies he used to drive home this point were humorous; Robbie screened blooper videos of scaffolders having mishaps. A fan favorite was a video of a heavyset scaffolder trying to climb up a scaffolding tube while his crew cheered him on and joked about his belly as he managed to get not more than a foot off the floor. Though lighthearted, the video carried a subversive political message in the Qatari context: the men depicted were British and white, and yet the trainees were relating to them through their experience and identities as scaffolders in ways that would have been proscribed in the racially stratified jobsite where they worked. Robbie also made frequent references to the UK certification system for scaffolding, and pinpointed for the workers where in that framework the skills they were learning were measured and valued. The ethos emphasized at the training center was that workers were not bodies for labor, measured and classified according to racial or national characteristics. Instead, they were men who chose to become scaffolders and join a community—a noble gild—that stretched far past the narrow confines of a single construction project, and where respect was earned through competence and generosity with knowledge.

The training center placed cultural value on skill. That meant that the possibility for creativity—natality—which can make reflective practice so transformative, was also prized. The practice exercises at the center brought together technical capacity and social connection, and this blend allowed for the critical investigation of scaffolding practice. As groups of trainees built the same scaffolding formations over and over again, areas of difficulty in the construction process became clear. Robbie and his team of instructors turned to those challenging stretches of practice every time they emerged and worked with the trainees to explore what might make the process easier. This repeated on-the-spot problem solving allowed the instructors to work with multiple teams of workers to try out different solutions, and this continuous experimentation generated new approaches and components. "We've come up with five patents," said Robbie, "and we're working on a few more. The latest is a safety collision cage for cherry pickers. They're manlifts, technically called mobile elevated work platforms. . . . We have the prototype and we're testing it now. We are always sorting things out here."

Scaffolders brought this ethos of innovative problem solving back to their worksites. At the ABC Builders stadium site, for instance, workers suggested scaffolding strategies and work-arounds to the scaffolding designers and supervisors with whom they had forged allegiances. A few weeks after the scaffolders at ABC Builders had threatened to strike rather than work mandatory night shifts, I toured the roof structure with Robbie. An ABC Builders supervisory manager for welding and coordinating engineer joined the tour too. The carapace of steel beams was painted with white protective coating to prevent rusting, except for a concentric pattern of half-meter patches that had been left unpainted. As Nader, the welding engineer, explained, the untreated areas were where the temporary brackets to support the cladding application had been placed. The beams already showed chafing where the bracket had been welded on and then removed. "All will be painted white by the time we finish," he said. "How you going to repair that? You'll need wings. You'll need to be drinking a lot of Red Bull," countered Robbie. "Helicopter or by rope access," responded Nader. "Look, my guys, they can do it when they dismantle [the scaffold]. They'll build out hanging scaffolds as they go down," answered Robbie. Saleh, the managing engineer, told Nader in Arabic, which Robbie did not speak. "Actually this is a problem. We need to solve it. See if you can work with the scaffolders." Robbie later told me that the solution he suggested had been proposed by the scaffolding supervisor, who had worked it out in collaboration with several of the scaffolding foremen who had noticed the problem, and been skeptical that the rope artists would be able to do the repair safely or effectively.

Through this kind of unbidden and worker-driven problem solving, workers drew on the skill praxis nurtured at the training center to challenge—or even defy—the power structures on-site. By offering solutions, they contested the managerial view that reduced them to labor inputs. They asserted their expertise, capacity for creativity, and the potential for collective action.

They also turned ABC Builders into a leader in the field of scaffolding construction and design and positioned the company to win large and high-profile projects in Qatar and throughout the GCC. Much like Dean at Aluminum Cladding Solutions, Robbie, as a member of the company's top management team in Qatar, played a critical role in making the scaffolders' contribution to company outcomes visible. His scaffolding management team produced PowerPoints at the end of each project detailing the accomplishments of the scaffolding crews as well as compiling the highlights of various projects. Robbie screened the PowerPoints in top management meetings, meetings with current and prospective clients, and also occasionally, for management teams on specific projects such as the stadium site when the scaffolding supervisors felt that the support they were receiving was inadequate.

The slideshows featured stunning photographs of the scaffolding structures that workers had built, highlighting their massiveness and improbable design. But they also gave prominence to the effort and skill of scaffolding crews in a manner that ran counter to the prevailing narrative about workers on Qatari constructions sites being nothing more than interchangeable bodies for labor, with fixed attributes, that could be sorted into racial categories. The presentations described the impressive scaffolding structures as accomplish-ments not of design but rather cumulative scaffolding practice and translated the magnitude of these achievements into terms that people with little expo-sure to the trade could understand. "As can be seen from this map," read the caption superimposed on a map of Asia in one presentation, and cut across by an arrow marked as 4,387 miles long, "if all the scaffolding on the site was laid end to end we would have enough scaffolding to make it all the way [from Doha, Qatar] to Incheon, South Korea, which is the head offices of the ship-yards that are building the LNG fleet for Qatar Gas." The slideshow listed the amount of tonnage that each man handled per day, but also stressed the team-work and shared competence required for any individual worker to complete his work. Alongside photos of teams working on scaffolds, the captions read, "Teamwork: What we do—every man on the crew handled exactly the same [tonnage]," and "This fantastic achievement is a result of near perfect team work and effort."

Protest and Praxis

With its celebration of skill praxis, the social world captured in this presen-tation as well as other ones like it did not sit easily within the norms about labor at ABC Builders. The company operated in a regulatory and norma-tive setting where workers were turned into bodies for labor. Workers at ABC Builders were treated as labor inputs, ranked and sorted according to racial-ized interpretations of physical attributes, in much the same way that workers were ranked and sorted on other sites. But through their skill praxis, nur-tured at the training center and protected through alliances with advocates in management, scaffolders found ways to enact a social world where they could take pride in their own learning and expertise, value their own and their colleagues' imagination and effort, and draw on their skill and the relation-ships they forged through skillful practice to protect themselves. And their skill praxis ultimately began to transform managerial practice from within: not only did the management at ABC Builders pull back from its demands for more speed—based on the skill-based arguments that workers made—but it also started to view expertise in scaffolding as a company asset. The company continued to invest in scaffolding development, funding the training center along with expanding its role as a hub for scaffolding research and innovation. In the process, the company was supplying material support to the place that provided scaffolders' skill praxis with an anchor and refuge, thereby strength-ening workers' ability to appropriate the construction site and transform it into a space for their social world to unfold.

To be sure, worker resistance through skill praxis was not unalloyed. Their claims to competence faced skepticism and hostility from many managers, their wages were not commensurate with their skill contribution, and many of the benefits of their learning and creativity flowed to management. But workers were nevertheless able to carve out a space for autonomy, connection, and creativity within the constraints imposed by the skill politics in Qatar, and the management practices that grew out of it. By exploring and cultivating resistance through a shared language of skill—keeping in mind that worker skill was a resource that employers needed badly to construct the buildings they envisioned—they discovered a narrow sliver between brutalization and deportation and widened it enough to allow for fellowship, expression, and the imagination of the unexpected as well as surprising. Through their investigation of skill as a resource for resistance, workers were able to sidestep the constraints of the repertoire of contest, which employers enforced so heavy-handedly that they turned it into a repertoire of control. By not clashing with employers at the boundaries of allowable protest, they denied employers an opportunity to reinforce racialized bodies-for-labor norms that had been incorporated into the employer-policed protest repertoire. Instead, out of the thousands of hand offs of scaffolding materials, innumerable interactions of teaching and learning, and embodied collaboration on which their work and welfare depended, they created an alternative social world where they were not bodies but men.

CHAPTER FIVE

Body

HOW DEFINITIONS OF SKILL CAUSE INJURY

ON SEPTEMBER 27, 2013, under the headline "Revealed: Qatar's World Cup 'Slaves,'" the *Guardian* reported that dozens of Nepali workers had died in Qatar over the summer.[1] According to documents collected from the Nepalese embassy in Doha, the workers were dying at a rate of nearly one per day. The story featured an embassy table that kept a running tab of worker deaths, and this document, annotated by hand in blue ballpoint pen to add the names of those who had perished after it was printed—almost as if the official record could not keep up with the onslaught of death—confirmed that half of the forty-four men who had died between June 4 and August 8 had suffered a heart attack, heart failure, or workplace accident.

The news report was accompanied by a video that juxtaposed Qatar's gleaming skyline and massive construction projects with footage of a family in rural Nepal receiving the body of their son. In the video, the body is delivered to the family at night, and the men in the village unload a simple red coffin from the white van that shuttled it home. A small label with the person's name had been stuck to its front, distinguishing this coffin from the identical boxes that had arrived with it at the airport. Women line the path, keeling, holding onto one another to steady themselves against their grief. Their faces, wet with tears, are lit by the beam of flashlights that the men use to illuminate their footfalls in the dark.

The footage transitions to the preparation for the cremation ceremony the next day, and we learn that the shrouded body belonged to Ganesh Bishwa-karma, a young man who had traveled to Qatar for work just six weeks prior. He died at the age of sixteen of cardiac arrest. His relative holds up a passport photo, and we see the face, boyish and startled in anticipation of the voyage. When the camera pans back to the village, we see his grandmother kneel down to kiss and caress this same face one final time before he is covered with flower petals in preparation for cremation. Her sons hold her up and coax her away from the body, pulling the shroud back over Ganesh's face. A daughter leans forward and gently wipes tears from the grandmother's cheek with her hand. As the video cuts to footage of the men from the village carrying Ganesh's body across fields to a river and then building a funeral pyre at the riverbank, we learn that the family took out loans to pay exorbitant recruitment fees for Ganesh. The young man's death had plunged the family even deeper into poverty. "The lender won't spare me," says Ganesh's father, as we watch the pyre burn.

This story, underscored by the poignant documentary video, drew intense interest to the steady flow of reports on the working conditions for migrants issued by human rights and international labor organizations that had been sounding the alarm since Qatar had won the bid to host the 2022 World Cup. In June 2012, Human Rights Watch reported that the Nepali embassy counted 191 Nepali deaths in Qatar in 2010, with 19 dead due to worksite accidents. An additional 103 workers died from cardiac arrest, even though the workers did not "fall into the typical age group at risk of cardiac failure."[2] The report also noted that it could not confirm the number of deaths with official tallies because the Qatari government did not publish data on worker injuries or fatalities. The Ministry of Labor had even countered the publicized information, claiming that only 6 Nepali workers had died over the previous three years, all from falls. Amnesty International issued a report of its own in 2013, citing information from the Nepalese embassy that indicated that 174 of its nationals had died in 2012—102 from cardiac arrest, and 3 from workplace falls.[3] The ITUC, after its own review, warned that 4,000 workers risked losing their lives due to workplace fatalities in Qatar before a single ball was kicked at the World Cup games.[4]

Within days of the *Guardian*'s publication of its "World Cup 'Slaves'" story, Nepal's ambassador to Qatar was recalled. Her previous statements, including comments calling Qatar an "open jail" for Nepali workers, had taken on a heightened valence.[5] In her absence, the legal adviser at the Nepali embassy held a joint press conference with the chair of Qatar's National Human Rights Committee. Both governments refuted the information presented by the *Guardian* as "false" and "exaggerated."[6] The riposte marked the beginning of an extended international debate about working conditions and work-related fatalities in Qatar. The opinion pages of papers around the world published pieces excoriating Qatar and the World Cup promoters for the intensive exploitation of workers, and several international campaigns were launched to press FIFA, the organizing body for the World Cup, to retract its award to Qatar and move the games to a different location. FIFA sponsors were called out. Modified versions of their logos—"antilogos" designed to highlight the sponsor's complicity with abusive labor practices—ricocheted around the internet: McDonald's iconic golden arches were redrawn as whips, Coca-Cola's arabesques were reinterpreted as arms handcuffed together, the Adidas stripes were reimagined as gravestones, and Visa's letters were portrayed as being carried by prone and subjugated naked bodies.[7] Soon, companies in FIFA's "2022 sponsorship portfolio" began issuing statements about their commitment to human rights and fair labor practices.[8]

After the *Guardian* story, the controversy about labor conditions in Qatar remained pitched and wide-ranging, but the crux of the debate shifted perceptibly toward a focus on worker deaths. The international conversation about working conditions in Qatar devolved into a debate about how many workers had died as a result of their employment in the Gulf country's construction industry. International observers and human rights organizations collected death certificates and ledgers from local embassies, along with, in some cases, records from the main Qatari hospital, Hamad General Hospital, to pull together a number that could offer an estimate of the death rate that could be compared to those in other countries. The Qatari government hired DLA Piper, an international auditor, to produce a confidential evaluation of working conditions in construction. Its report was widely leaked. The consultant was able to compile records for 2012 for deaths of Nepali, Indian, and Bangladeshi workers, with partial data for Filipino and Sri Lankan workers. Their composite indicated that in 2012, at least 39 workers had died from falls or other workplace accidents, another 139 from unclear causes, and 304 from sudden cardiac arrest.[9]

The concern was with the number of fatalities, but also, crucially, whether or not that number fell within international parameters for expected injury on construction projects of comparable size and complexity. The number compiled by DLA Piper and other international observers put the rate of fatal injury in the Qatari construction somewhere between five and twenty times the rate of fatal injury in the US construction industry, and between twenty and a hundred times the rate of fatal injury related to construction in the United Kingdom.[10] The Qatari government countered that the fatality rate in Qatar for 2014 was only three times the rate in the United Kingdom, and improbably, less than half the rate in the United States. With death evaluated through this actuarial lens, the main question was whether worker fatalities were due to employer negligence and exploitative labor conditions, or merely due to the inherent risks of production. The issue in the debate over worker fatalities in Qatar was not whether workers were returning home in coffins but instead whether or not their employers had created the conditions that had put them there. Stated differently, the controversy over labor conditions in Qatar came to pivot on whether worker deaths were accidents or injuries.

The line between accident and injury—between bad luck and criminality—was drawn with the body, and specifically the dead bodies of migrants. The focus on the dead excluded living workers from the conversations about injury in Qatar. This was because the dead are voiceless; they cannot offer an interpretation of the reasons for their own fatality. Their bodies can only offer evidentiary material to be interpreted by others. The marks on the body are read by others, the living, who based on their analysis of the wounds on the body, determine whether the body's death was caused by the conditions it faced or its own vulnerability. To be sure, workplace fatalities foregrounded the extremes of exploitation of many construction sites, and showed that workers were not infinitely exploitable. Their bodies—in death—set limits on the employment conditions they could withstand.

In the global tallying of coffins, the testimony of those still alive about how their bodies were being damaged was counted out. Living workers could have spoken about the dynamics that produced injury and even death on construction sites: the work speedups and casual bullying of supervisors, design errors or planning mistakes, failures of materials and machines, or exposure to extreme environmental conditions. They could have indicated whether wounds and death were accidents or injuries, but they could have also pointed out that wounds and deaths were often only separated by a matter of degree.

With their emphasis on the dead and their inattention to the living, global debates about worker fatalities in Qatar reproduced the divide between skill and the body that was so central to the representation of migrant workers as unskilled. Workers were included in the conversation only through their bodies—inert, mute, and implicitly unskilled—whereas those who did the work of sorting injuries from accidents shaped the conversation about injury by invoking their expertise. Those skilled professionals—the statisticians, auditors, and legal advocates—invoked their authority not only to interpret wounds but also to define what counted as a wound to begin with. The bodies of the unskilled did not speak for themselves; the damage they sustained only became visible and politically manifest when the skilled—the expert professional—chose to recognize the wound as an injury and interpret its cause.

Lost in the silencing of living workers were injuries that were not legible to skilled experts as marks on the body or death. Painful, often debilitating damage to the body that was not visible and incontrovertible to those outside the wounded body did not make it into global debates about the bodily welfare of workers. This was especially true of injuries that harmed workers' embodied capacities for cognition, connection, and action, seriously and sometimes permanently, but did not register as broken bones or dead bodies. These wounds were ignored largely because workers, tagged as unskilled, were not viewed as having the expertise to interpret their own suffering.

The most serious of these invisible injuries were those that grew out of the extreme temperatures that migrants in Qatar were compelled to work in. Workers on Qatari construction sites did heavy physical labor in heat conditions that frequently threatened lives even for bodies at rest. Workers described the heat as a kind of torment. In interviews with me, workers ranked extreme temperatures as the most difficult and harmful pressure they faced by far. "I had never imagined a climate like this," said one worker from

Nepal. "Until you feel it, you cannot believe it." "The heat is like a wall," said another from Kenya. "It melts the air, and you feel you are drowning. You cannot breathe," added his compatriot. "It is like the sky is pressing down on your body," described another worker. They reported that heat wrecked their bodies; they found themselves vomiting, suffering from headaches and muscle cramps, experiencing sudden shortness of breath, or feeling exhaustion so intense that it felt like crushing physical pain, rendering them unable to eat, wash, or undress at the end of the day. Rashes spread across their bodies, and shivers racked them. These were all symptoms of heat stress injury, frequently indicators of organ damage.

With temperatures that pushed past 110°F for weeks in the summer months, heat forged all aspects of work and working conditions on-site. It concentrated the power dynamics and exploitative practices. It heightened the effects of the kafala system, whose institutional constraints blunted the ability of workers to resist their conditions of employment or leave their employment altogether. But even more dangerously, heat dissolved the skill that workers needed to protect themselves against injury. Through its effect on the body, heat disrupted the embodied cognition that workers relied on to move through the construction site and complete their work safely. Heat disoriented and confused; it dulled perceptions and slowed reaction times. Internal physical distress made skillful attention to practice and the hazards involved in construction impossible to sustain. Heat assaulted the biological processes required for cognition and damaged especially the cognitive abilities that workers needed to connect and work with others on-site.

In its assault on embodied skill, heat amplified the skill politics that structured work in Qatar's construction industry. Because heat injured workers' cognition and damaged their bodies in ways that made it difficult for them to access their skill, it seemed to reify the political disaggregation of labor from skill and confirm the representation of workers as unskilled laboring bodies, without skill of their own, only good for following the orders of others. Heat, in compromising the embodied cognition that is the basis for all skillful practice, turned workers' own bodies against them in ways that mimicked the skill politics that were arrayed against them.

The representation of skill as an abstract resource that could be pulled out of the life of the body only magnified heat's involvement in skill politics. It made it possible to represent skill as inured to heat's effects—how could heat, after all, melt something that was conceptual and immaterial?—but it also made it possible to represent workers as culpable for any injury they suffered. The location of skill outside the body, in other words, made it possible to portray embodied workers as responsible for *succumbing* to heat. If workers did not draw on skill that was undamaged by heat and could not be damaged by it—skill packaged in the form of managerial directives and standardized safety training—then they were choosing to surrender their bodies to it, choosing to sacrifice their hearts, kidneys, and lives to the heat bearing down on them. And if it wasn't a matter of choice, then workers' failure to apply the safety procedures necessarily reflected their lack of capacity; their injury was proof of their inability to learn and their want of the agentic creativity that learning required. The view of skill as an abstract resource made it possible to paint workers as responsible not only for their own deaths when they died on-site, like Ganesh, but also when they died years later in their countries of origin from injuries caused by the way that heat, magnified by managerial practices at the worksite, damaged their kidneys, hearts, and immune systems.

Qatar allows us to see the intersection of heat, skill, and definitions of occupational injury because of the influence of the politics of skill on work there, and because Qatar today is already one of the hottest places on the planet. The average temperatures on the small peninsula have already risen more than 2°C over preindustrial levels and are accelerating rapidly—faster than the global average.[11] Qatar's high levels of humidity—close to 70 percent relative humidity in the summertime months and increasing every year—accentuate the felt experience of heat and its danger to the body.[12] With its extreme and fast-changing climate conditions, Qatar provides us a window onto the future of occupational health and safety in a warming world.[13]

In many areas of the world, this future is not far behind. Climate change has also already manifested in temperature rises that are dangerous and even life-threatening. Since global temperatures are projected to rise even further in the years to come, the threat that heat represents to occupational safety will only become more pressing and deadly, pushing past the threshold of human adaptability.[14] Studies on the effects that heat will have on work have already begun to note the impact of elevated temperatures on productivity.[15] These studies have estimated the number of work hours lost to heat through nonwork or lower productivity—by some calculations, as much as 15 to 20 percent in hot regions—and detrimental consequences for national and family income.[16] But the way that heat affects working conditions has not yet received comparable attention, even though the physiological damage to the body from heat is well documented and well understood. The ways that heat can magnify managerial control and exploitative practices at the worksite has received even less attention. This is because of the way that occupational injury is defined, and in particular, the distinctions made between accident and injury, cause and effect. As global temperatures rise, heat as a hazard will require us to develop new ways to think about injury, skill, and power at work. Qatar gives us a place to start.

Prying Open the Grammar of Injury

In the *Guardian*'s video, Ganesh's father expresses inconsolable bewilderment at his son's death. "I am in a lot of pain," he says. "My son was strong and healthy. He didn't even have a cough. He was such a good son, and I sent him abroad. He died unexpectedly. Was it the climate? Or was it something else? These questions are weighing on my heart. I think about them night and day."[17] The questions that Ganesh's father asked about his son's death were excluded from the global debate over working conditions and fatalities in Qatar. In both legal and colloquial usage, an injury is an act committed against the rights and body of another person, whereas an accident is an incident without fault. Accidents just happen. Injuries, on the other hand, are acts of harm that violate a person's bodily integrity. The distinction hinges not on the wound or fatality itself but instead on whether or not an author of the injury—a perpetrator—can be formally and often legally established.[18] Without a perpetrator, the reasons for death were merely unfortunate. Questions about the cause of death were the railings of a brokenhearted father against fate and nature.

The exclusion of questions like those asked by Ganesh's father point to a limitation with the way that injury is defined, and the politics of that definition in assessing injury caused by heat. From a legal perspective, the notion of injury depends on a particular grammar of wounding: it requires damage to the body, a weapon through which that damage was caused, and an actor or perpetrator who wielded that weapon. Without the clear interpellation of these three components, a wound does not rise to the level of injury.[19] The grammar of injury always starts with damage to the body, but for the damage to anchor the construction of injury, it must be visible and legible to observers outside the injured body. Moreover, it must be discrete enough from the ordinary life of the body that it can be entered into actuarial discussions through which the damage is assessed. The damage may be judged to be a product of natural processes or expected risk, or instead, determined to be the result of negligence or willful harm. Once the bodily damage clears the bar of statistical probability, then the effect is linked to its cause, which is inferred from the wound on the body. The knife wound points to the blade; the mesothelioma-ravaged lung points to asbestos fibers; the rash of childhood cancers in a community indicates chemical poison in the well water. The cause—the knife, asbestos, or chemical substance—can then implicate the actor that wielded it.

During this process of evaluation, the injury is turned into an artifact.[20] The harm is lifted out the flow of experience and turned into the static objectification of suffering. The body of the injured becomes secondary, and the voice of the injured is likewise silenced, even when the injured person remains alive. The body that was injured is reduced to a passive or even inert imprint of the injury. The injury, fixed in time, is discussed in the past tense—in legal terms, the action of injury is always complete. The knife has already cut the flesh, the asbestos has already set off the cancer in the lung, the children in the community are already ill, and the worker in Qatar has already fallen from the scaffold. The cause has already made contact with the body, and the injury stands as visible, observable proof.[21] Because the past cannot be undone, the only remedies for injury are restitution for the injured and protection against injury for those as yet uninjured, either through the removal of the cause or the constraint or regulation of the perpetrator.

Ganesh's body, however, arrived without an imprint of injury that could be traced to a singular cause or implicate a perpetrator. With no clearly identifiable and discrete wound, no weapon could be identified, and no wrongdoer blamed. Heat dissolved the grammar of injury.

Many families that did not receive coffins received wounded sons, but it was unclear whether the damage to their sons' or husbands' bodies met the standards of injury. In villages all along the border, locals reported that young men who returned from work in Qatar and other countries in the Gulf were having heart attacks in their twenties and thirties. Others developed chronic and serious kidney disease. In 2014, I visited the Dhanusa district in eastern Terai, where medical personnel and service providers relayed to me that they had observed a worrying spike in kidney disease and cardiac issues among young men, and begun to forge institutional partnerships with dialysis centers in Kathmandu to respond to the rise. Reports in the local Nepali press featured stories of young men, former migrants to the Gulf, languishing in the nephritic wings of hospitals in Kathmandu, and a smattering of articles in medical journals observed an increase of kidney disease in Nepal generally.[22]

One widely cited analysis of the fatalities of Nepali migrants, based on 2009–17 mortality data compiled by the Foreign Employment Promotion Board in Nepal, and supported by interviews with workers who had worked in Qatar and returned to Nepal, suggested how dangerous the heat was to workers. Though impossible to prove conclusively, the available rate of deaths of young Nepali men (aged twenty-five to thirty-five) from "cardiovascular causes" in Qatar seemed higher than global rates for this age group. Approximately 15 percent of deaths among young men around the world are due to cardiovascular disease, but in Qatar, the rate for Nepali men was 22 percent in the winter, and far higher in the summer months at 58 percent. These rates pointed to heat exposure as the cause of fatal cardiovascular distress; the authors argued that at least 200 of the 571 men who died in Qatar between 2009 and 2017 had likely died of heat injury.[23]

Even with the dead as evidence, however, the damage was confusing. Heat damage could not be unequivocally read off the wounds: hearts and kidneys could have failed for congenital reasons; diseases could have been produced by multiple causes, many of which, like certain pesticides, are present in the Nepali environment; and the time between the wounding and visible emergence of a wound—sometimes months, and sometimes years—made it all but impossible to pinpoint a causality that could link heat to physical damage. Without a univocal wound, a clear cause, to say nothing of a perpetrator (who, after all, can be responsible for the weather?), heat damage dissolved in the face of the established grammar of injury.

Ganesh's father was unconcerned with injury, however. He was troubled by the process of injuring. He asked about the process through which his son—who had left him healthy and strong—was returned to him six weeks later in a coffin. He was interrogating the conditions that produced his son's death. The shift encapsulated in his question from a singular focus on the injury to a broader inquiry into the process of injuring creates an opening to explore how wounding happens. It moves the lens from the wound itself, and onto both the practices of wounding and experiences of being wounded. With this change in emphasis, the debate breaks away from a simple yes-or-no debate over whether an injury has occurred and tackles instead how certain interactions produce wounding. The analysis shifts from a retrospective one, in which past harm is evaluated and explained, to a real-time exploration of the process of wounding as it takes place. With the widening of the temporal lens, the completed injury becomes just one source of information about how harm was sustained. The interpretation of injury expands to include the felt sense of being harmed in the moment, and an analysis of how moment-to-moment encounters with physical vulnerability inform behavior and belief. Paying attention to the process of injuring creates room for the injured to describe the complex tangle of practices, power relations, and bodily reactions that cohere to produce a wound. It opens up the space for a story of injuring in which the causes are multiple, the wounds layered and changing, and the perpetrators (with shifting alliances of their own) are unclear.

Attention to the process of injuring also unmasks the methods through which the wounded are made culpable for their own wounding. This displacement of responsibility for injuring onto the injured is a core but overlooked or even disregarded feature of injury. The practices of harming create their own alibi, and indeed, the denial of injuring is central to the purpose of injury. The injured are represented as participating in their own wounding, having betrayed and turned against their own bodies. In blaming the victim, those who injure assert the sole right to interpret injury. It is the strongest expression of the power over another that is enacted through injuring.

The standard grammar of injury, with its demand for a wound, weapon, and perpetrator, fails in capturing heat injury. But it is not just that heat injury can be more clearly perceived and understood when we look at the process of injuring. It is that heat injury can *only* be identified and apprehended in this way. Only by examining how the practices on Qatari construction sites interact with the region's temperatures do the ways in which workers suffered exposure to extreme heat stress become apparent. When we consider injuring instead of injury, the way that heat wounded by magnifying and expanding the power dynamics in the Qatari construction industry becomes visible. We are able to see how heat turned those power relations—and their skill politics specifically—into the bodily suffering that workers experienced and eventually carried home as bodily wounds.

Heat

The heat in Qatar was extreme, intensified by the high levels of humidity in the Persian Gulf. Summertime temperatures rose from an average 100°F at the start of the season in early May, through an average of 107°F in July and August, with temperatures rarely regularly breaching 120°F at the summer's peak, before they finally dipped below 100°F again at the beginning of October.[24] At those temperatures, the chassis of cars radiated enough heat to fry eggs, and the door handles were hot enough to brand skin on contact. Car tires deflated, and their batteries died. Cell phones short-circuited and failed, and the edges of their plastic cases turned soft. Asphalt began to buckle and melt, and walking across the pavement, even in the shade, without adequate footwear could cause second-degree burns in less than thirty seconds.

The heat in Qatar warped materials and destroyed machines. It also injured human bodies. It harmed not as a blow from some external weapon but rather as an ongoing entanglement with the body's cognitive capacity. It warped neural networks, destroying their ability to keep the body's core temperature below the threshold at which the body starts to shut down and die. It pushed the nervous system into a frenzy that caused the body to generate heat internally, magnifying the effect of external temperatures. It turned the body against itself, drawing the body's own cognitive functions into an accelerating cycle of bodily warming so that soon the body's organs could no longer withstand the heat and began to shut down.

Heat injury unfolded as a process, and interpolated multiple layers and protagonists as it progressed. The injury inflicted through this process was not precipitated by heat alone, though. Instead, heat's damage to the body was a product of the tension between the complex actions of heat on the body, on the one hand, and the managerial response to heat as an occupational hazard, on the other. These two dynamics sheared against one another in the context of Qatar's skill politics. Understanding how the process of heat injuring was refracted through skill politics first requires a review of exactly how heat interpolates the body's own processes as it harms and specifically the ways in which it enlists embodied cognition. It then needs an account of how heat came to be defined as an occupational hazard that was external to production in the first place.

THE BODY IN HEAT

Heat is treacherous. It attacks the body from without, as extreme temperatures in the environment suffocate, burn, and send the body into crisis. But it also attacks the body from within. As the body revs up in order to metabolize external heat, it generates heat of its own, which the body must then also struggle to survive. In this double gesture of wounding, assaulting the body from the outside even as it enlists it to burn it up from the inside, heat targets cognition. Heat injury begins and ends with an attack on the person's ability to make sense of the world and adjust to the environment it perceives.

A body first senses the pressure of heat through its central nervous system. The anterior hypothalamus, an almond sliver–sized area of the brain located where the brain narrows into the spine, receives information from the body about changes in temperature. The skin, muscles, stomach, central nervous tissues, and blood that flows through those organs all telegraph bulletins to the brain about warming conditions. When the environment heats up past the narrow band of temperatures where the body is not stressed, the hypothalamus triggers the physiological responses that the human body has developed to survive heat. In response to the brain's directives, the body sweats and the skin dilates to dissipate heat in the body, but the core temperature of the body is raised too, as in a fever, to lessen the difference between the external and internal temperatures.

The body relies on its neurocognitive capacity to cope with the heat that it produces internally. The greatest source of that heat is muscle. At rest, muscles generate about a quarter of a body's heat, but that proportion shoots up the minute a person starts moving. This heat can continue to build and compound even if the person maintains a steady level of activity. The heat produced by the muscles stokes the body's core temperature, which sets in motion thermoregulatory responses. The body redirects blood to the skin to dissipate heat. This sets up competition between the muscles and skin for the oxygen that blood transports. Muscles invariably lose out in this struggle, and are forced into anaerobic functioning. Lactic acid accumulates in the muscles, causing fatigue, burning sensations, and soreness. Because the body's oxygen is shuttled to the skin, there's little left over to metabolize the lactic acid in the muscles, which accumulates painfully. The oxygen debt that this produces must be paid for the body to recover, and in hot environments, the rest period required to settle this liability, and eliminate both the lactic acid and heat from the body, can take twenty-four hours or more.[25] If the body does not rest and lactic acid is not neutralized, muscles become leaden, disconcertingly unresponsive to the brain's orders.

How well the body is able to respond to heat also depends on whether the body's neurocognitive capacities can direct a person to keep their body hydrated. This is a constant challenge because sweating is one of the body's main strategies to deal with heat. The hotter a body gets, the more it sweats. For every liter of sweat that evaporates off the skin, the body releases about twenty-five hundred kilojoules of heat—an energetic amount equal to a television running for ten hours straight. Healthy bodies faced with heat conditions can sweat out two liters of sweat a day at rest, and workers engaged in moderate physical activity routinely perspire out between six and eight liters—the equivalent of the energy required to run an air conditioner during the workday. Depending on a person's stature, six to eight liters of sweat can represent several percentage points of their bodily fluids. A loss of liquid above this amount can quickly become hazardous; sweating out more than 8 percent of one's body fluids or any amount above twelve liters can be fatal.[26] How well this system functions to expel heat from the body depends on the environmental conditions it encounters. Sweat is only effective if the air it touches allows for evaporation. In humid climates, sweat does not evaporate, and the body's frantic release of fluids happens completely in vain.

At a certain point, even in dry conditions, the body cannot keep up, and it is not able to generate a thirst impulse strong enough to incite its owner to drink the quantities of water necessary to replace the fluids that have been sweated out. Dehydrated muscles are harder to move, and the increased effort generates more heat, raising the core body temperature further and causing even more sweating.[27] In this vicious cycle, muscles require even more oxygen and blood to function, and the heart is taxed. Meanwhile, the body desperately shuttles blood from its overheated core to the skin, where it can release heat into the environment. Dehydration robs the blood of fluid, concentrating it and turning it sludgy, and so the body needs to use more of the blood that remains to move heat from its core to its skin, thereby leaving even less for the acid-soaked muscles. The heart has to work harder to push the increasingly viscous blood out to the body's edge.[28] Its beat accelerates, and the heart starts to clamor for more oxygen to continue pumping.[29]

In these conditions of scarcity, the body's priority becomes keeping the body's core temperature within survivable limits. It begins to ration blood flow to any organ not directly involved in dissipating heat. It constricts the veins that carry blood to the internal organs, especially the digestive system and kidneys.[30] The brain is sacrificed. As oxygen flow to the brain is restricted, the person facing environmental and internal heat conditions begins to experience difficulty with even very basic psychomotor tasks, psychological reasoning, and vigilance.[31] With even a modest rise in core temperature, a person can start to experience disorganized central nervous system activity, which manifests in poor motor functioning, blurred vision, confusion, volatile irritability, and personality changes.[32] As dehydration increases, the body's own emergency responses turn the body into a furnace, generating heat that it desperately tries to expel through sweating, and cognition is impacted even further. As fluids in the body decrease, the space between the cells shrinks, the volume of plasma drops, and the cells themselves begin to shrivel.[33] The output of the heart falls, regardless of how hard it pumps, and the supply of oxygen to the rest of the body plummets. The fluid-starved kidneys stop producing urine, and the waste matter normally processed and expelled is retained in the body. As the kidneys suspend their functions, the concentration of toxins in the blood spikes, and in another pernicious feedback loop, this impairs cognitive performance even further as the brain is slowly poisoned by its own blood.[34]

If these feedback loops continue to spin, the body sustains injury—sometimes temporary, and sometimes irreversible—and if these cycles of damage continue uninterrupted, they end with death.

The first signs that heat has started to damage the body and harm its neurocognition are disconcertingly ambiguous: a vague malaise, often identified as heat exhaustion only in retrospect. Headaches, nausea, and dizziness are common expressions of heat stress. These symptoms occur in clusters or alone and are frequently magnified by a sense of light-headedness, possibly leading to fainting, especially if the person makes a sudden move to stand up. A person may feel irritable, confused, and even trapped. Thoughts may become turgid and more difficult to form. The body may feel heavy and weak, indifferent to the will of the person trying to move it. Muscles may cramp, and the person may experience spasms in the abdomen, arms, and legs that range from a mild tightness to a violent, sudden retraction.[35] Sweating can be profuse, and a heat rash may spread across the skin as clusters of red pimples or small blisters that bloom in waves on the neck, chest, or groin.

These symptoms, which may appear aleatory, indistinct, and ordinary, nevertheless indicate that the neurocognitive ability that the body relies on to cool itself has been significantly compromised. As it strains to move the thickened blood throughout the body, bloods pools in the lower parts of the body, placing additional strain on the heart. The sweat gland ducts, overworked, begin to swell and close.[36]

At this point, heat injury can quickly escalate into a fatal heatstroke. A worker who complains of light-headedness or a bothersome headache may be dead a few hours later. As the thermoregulatory function of the body breaks down, the skin becomes hot and often, but not always, dry as the body suspends perspiration. When the neurocognitive system, simmered by the heightened core body temperature, starts to collapse, a person's fuzzy confusion can quickly tip into a loss of consciousness or seizures. As the muscles operate under increased stress, they are pushed beyond their capacity. The muscle fibers die and break down into acute rhabdomyolysis.[37] As the contents of necrotic tissue are released into the bloodstream, the toxins overwhelm the kidneys, and the kidneys, already under duress, begin to shut down. The blood vessels also begin to break down; even the membranes of cells start to disintegrate.[38] Under these conditions, the blood can no longer clot, stressing every organ, especially the heart and liver. In a last-ditch effort for survival, the body launches a massive inflammatory response to try to strip away the damaged tissues, and as the hurricane of sepsis tears through the body, the destruction caused by the body's own cytokines outstrips the heat injury to the organs.[39]

Heat's final assault on the body incinerates cognition utterly. With insufficient blood making it to the heart, where it can be reoxygenated, the brain is suffocated, and then as the core body temperature rises, cooked. Cells throughout the brain begin to die, but they die fastest in the cerebellum, the gateway to the brain that contains nearly half the brain's neurons, and is responsible for interpreting and responding to sensory input, including heat.[40] Under the best of conditions, including the administration of prompt and appropriate medical care, the survival rate for heatstroke is no more than 50 percent.[41] And even if a person recovers from heatstroke, the damage to the brain, heart, kidneys, and others organs is lasting.[42]

HEAT AS EXTERNAL PATHOGEN

The dangers that heat represents to the body have been well understood since the 1950s, and the impact of heat on bodily system—especially cognition—has been robustly documented in study after study since the 1970s. In response, international regulatory organizations have sought to set protective parameters around working in high temperatures. They have established indexes to predict the physiological strain of different levels of physical activity in hot conditions. The most widely adopted metric for forecasting stress on the body due to heat is the wet bulb globe temperature (WBGT) index.[43] Developed by the US Marines in the 1950s after an alarming number of soldiers collapsed during their training drills in humid South Carolina, the WBGT index was created to capture a composite picture of the environment factors that cause heat injury. The US military combined the temperature measured by a normal thermometer with readings from two additional thermometers modified to measure compounding environment conditions.[44] One thermometer was wrapped in a wet cotton cloth so that it would mimic the cooling effect of the evaporation of sweat as it dried out, and another was inserted into a large black globe, about the size of a bowling ball, to estimate the effect of solar radiation on the body. These thermometers gave the index its name. An algorithm translated these readings into a single number, expressed as a temperature in Celsius or Fahrenheit. The levels were then mapped onto stages of physical distress experienced by the human body—or the bodies, in this case, of the soldiers performing callisthenic drills. The resulting matrix laid out activity levels that could be considered safe in an array of environmental conditions, specifying the minutes per hour that a healthy person could perform physical tasks, the rest periods required, and the amount of water that had to be consumed to preserve protective hydration.[45]

According to the standards set by the US Marines, and then adopted globally and refined by regulatory agencies from the International Standards Organization to the ILO, a WBGT reading at 32.5°C or 90.5°F is the red line for heat injury—beyond which physical labor of any kind becomes dangerous.[46] Workers already used to the heat should work only a few minutes at a time, rationing their movements carefully, and remain at complete rest when not moving. They should drink at least four cups of water an hour—the maximum amount a body can absorb. Given the intensity of heat, however, national and international regulatory bodies around the world recommend that work at those temperatures not be performed at all because of the high risk of heat illness and fatal heatstroke.

During July afternoons in Qatar, the temperature dances on the 32.5°C or 90.5°F WBGT threshold, often reaching it early in the day, and the environment becomes treacherous. In the last ten years, temperatures in Qatar have been on a clear upward trajectory, and the WBGT readings have frequently pushed past 33°C or 91.5°F, with readings reported as high as 35°C or 95°F—a WBGT level at which the body's cooling response is defeated, and heat can become fatal even for bodies at rest.[47]

For some occupational health specialists, temperatures like those observed in Qatar indicate that the WBGT heat safety matrices that have been widely adopted overstate the dangers of heat to the human body. These observational studies have pointed to rates of observable heat injury—injuries that are immediately visible—on worksites in the GCC, Thailand, and India that are lower than what existing activity matrices based on the WBGT would predict.[48] Other studies have made the opposite claim, arguing that if anything, the WBGT discounts the heat load that bodies have to contend with because it does not take into account the heat produced by the body itself.[49] Nor does the effect of clothing, especially bulky nonbreathable safety apparel, factor in when considering the body's ability to dissipate heat.[50]

The controversies around the WBGT point to a far more fundamental problem with the way that heat safety is addressed. The WBGT model along with virtually all heat safety protections are based on a particular view of the human body and heat. The body is defined as distinct from the environment it operates in, and heat is cast as a pathogen that enters the body as a foreign agent to disrupt and harm its natural functioning. In a take that is at odds with the science on heat injury, the body's role as protagonist that accelerates heat injury is omitted completely in these protective standards.

The WBGT focuses on heat in the environment, external to the body, and the matrices that predict the heat's physical effect assume that the heat is acting on a body at rest. The activity prescriptions start with the stress that heat imposes on that resting body and specifies the allowable levels of activity given that initial stress. Heat in this model delivers a blow from the outside to an otherwise separate body. And the body that is impacted is defined and understood as distinct, in its natural characteristics and physiological processes, from the heat pressures that bear down on it. Heat is defined as an external pathogen that invades the body. Once heat enters the body from the outside, it sets in motion physical responses—injuries—that become visible through symptoms, scars, and even death—that become, in other words, an injury.

Historian Linda Nash, in her historical study of environmental pollution and disease in California's Central Valley, argues that this view of the body as a separate entity, distinct from the natural environment, has structured industrial hygiene and public health movements since the early twentieth century. This "modern" body, as she calls it, "the body that is defined in medical textbooks, the body that is composed of discrete parts and bounded by its skin," was removed from its lived contexts and analyzed in the laboratory. Health was defined as the absence of disease or injury, pathogens were defined as the vectors of disease, and interventions to protect against these harmful alien factors were developed. The modern body proved the triumph of humans and science over nature. Nash contrasts this definition of the body with the older one that it replaced, which she terms "the ecological body." She explains that this earlier understanding of the body saw it as being deeply permeable: the body was continually being traversed by nature along with its winds, miasmas, and moods; it existed in a constant exchange between inside and outside; and it was profoundly intertwined and interpenetrated with the flows and rhythms of the natural life that surrounded it. Bodies could only be understood in context. Their manifestation was a product of the "dynamic relationship between bod[ies] and [their] environment," and their health was an expression of "the state of balance, or harmony" of bodies within their larger world.[51]

The understandings of heat's effect on the body and the protocols for working in high temperatures all draw on the modern definition of the body. With prescriptions for activity levels and water intake, these protocols prescribe the dosage of heat that is safe, beyond which heat becomes a toxin, and in so doing, assert the triumph of scientific knowledge over even extreme environments while underscoring the ability of human actors to stand apart from the hazards of the environment.

The reliance on the modern definition of the body in heat injury protocols is not an artifact solely of the way that heat is represented. It also grows out of historical debates over who should bear responsibility for injuries sustained at work. The use of the modern definition of the body in this arena is an outcome of the pitched battles over occupational health and worker safety that roiled the industrial sectors of the United States and Europe in the late nineteenth and early twentieth centuries. The representation of occupational injury and illness external to the normal life of the body as well as unnatural was a victory for the labor movements and their advocates, which pressed governments to take steps to protect workers from the occupational injuries that were killing and disabling them in unprecedented numbers.[52] In factories and mines, workers were exposed to chemicals and materials in new ways, compelled by mass production methods into intensive contact with phosphorous, lead, asbestos, silica dust, and other industrial poisons.[53] Workers and their advocates mobilized in response to the strangeness of their injuries. They contended that workers' symptoms—the pulmonary damage, necrosis of the jaw, and skin and vomit that glowed in the dark from phosphorous handling; the muscle weakness, seizures, organ failure, and cognitive devastation of lead poisoning; and the slow suffocation, as silica dust hardened lungs and made them unresponsive to the need to breathe—were unnatural, and not part of the normal range of experience of disease and death.[54] This strangeness—not to mention the gruesomeness of the injuries—catalyzed progressive efforts to identify the causes of occupational illness and death as outside the natural— modern—body.[55] The definition of industrial poisons as external to the body was an important achievement for organized labor. It meant that the new regulations affirmed that worker injuries were caused by new chemicals, and more broadly, the industrial practices that exposed workers to them—and not, as many industrialists claimed, by workers' physical susceptibility or moral weakness. Their bodies, modern and self-contained, were not the cause of injury. They were only the site of the pathogen's effects.

The research on heat as an occupational hazard under new conditions of climate change has only doubled down on this conception of the modern body. Heat is still viewed as an impact factor external to the body, a vector for injury—one to add to the list of existing workplace hazards, against which occupational health protections need to be designed.[56] Whether it is research documenting the high incidence of nephritic disease among sugarcane workers in Central America, the rise in accidents on construction sites due to heat stress, or the correlation between heat and occupational injuries of multiple types, the focus has been on identifying the protective measures that could shield workers from heat exposure.[57]

But as the science on heat injury has long established, heat is not purely external to the body, nor is exposure to it strange to the life of the body. Industrial processes and workplace exploitation may intensify exposure, but the body responds to integrate the heat it encounters, generating heat of its own in the process. The complex, dynamic, nonlinear biological and cognitive processes through which the human body protects itself against heat stress also augment the effects as well as dangers of heat. Through its responses, the body becomes an active participant in shaping the consequences of heat and determining whether heat will injure.

In this sense, the older "ecological" view of the body is more accurate for understanding the body's interaction with heat. Nash, in her reflection on environmental toxins, notes that the skin is "less a boundary than a zone of transfer and connection."[58] Heat acts on skin and delivers itself through this human membrane to the body's core. It blisters and burns the skin. The skin opens its pores wide and flushes out sweat to dispel heat. When the sweat evaporates, it helps the body cool. But it may also, if compounded by humidity, slick the sweat into an insulating glaze that keeps heat in the body. Heat extends into the body. It can heat up the core, strain the body's organs, and compromise the brain. But the body, taxed, ignites from within as it works to cool itself by expelling the heat it has produced internally. The person who inhabits the body acts deliberately to alter the environment in which they move by taking a rest, finding refuge in the shade or water, or refraining from activities that generate heat, like cooking, welding, or even extraneous movement. Those adaptive responses too are shaped by heat, with heat melting cognition in ways that put the understanding of how to shelter from the heat or adjust the environment out of reach.

In her exploration of the transition in the conception of the body from an ecological to modern view, Nash explains that the understanding of the environment was also transformed. "Local environments," she writes, "were no longer understood as active components in the production of health and disease; instead, they were recast as homogeneous spaces that were traversed by pathogenic agents."[59] In a reflection of this modern view of the environment, heat, in safety protocols and analyses of heat as an occupational hazard, has been lifted out of the environment in which it occurs. It has been perceived as a pathogen or menace that traverses the spaces where workers are active—a hazard that bears down on the sugarcane fields of El Salvador, or slithers atop the desert flats on which high-rises and stadiums were being built in Qatar. Within this framework, safety protocols address heat as separate from the environment—an isolatable threat that moves across the stage that different environments provide. In the grammar of injury, heat becomes the weapon that causes damage to the body.

This flattened depiction of the natural world is, of course, only a depiction of the environment, but it is one that is deeply involved in the process of injuring. Casting heat as the stand-alone culprit of damage to the body exonerates the practices through which the environment is transformed into a weapon or cause of injury. Like the body, which is shaped moment to moment through its interaction with the environment, the environment too is cocreated through the practices that unfold in each specific context. The environment at the worksite specifically is shaped through practices of production, power relations, social connections among workers, and the production of knowledge. These elements all structure the environment that workers encounter, and refract the heat that they experience and are wounded by.

In Qatar, heat injury was the result of the ways that the physical effect of heat on the body interacted with managerial responses to heat as an occupational hazard. Firms in the construction industry relied on a modern definition of the body as separate from the environment and construed heat as an external pathogen, extrinsic to the production process, against which the body could be shielded. They specified protocols and procedures for workers to follow to protect themselves from heat while they worked in extreme temperatures. Meanwhile, the bodies of workers suffered heat, responded with heat of their own, and interacted with the environment seamlessly and porously until they began to shut down. The tension between the managerial definition of heat injury and workers' experience of heat damage is what turned heat into a weapon that injured.

Injuring

To protect against heat injury, Qatari law stipulated that outdoor work should be suspended between the hours of 11:30 a.m. and 3:00 p.m. for the calendar period between June 15 and August 31.[60] The law provided no additional safeguards against heat stress. This omission was glaring given the detail with which construction processes were regulated in Qatar. The Ministry of the Municipality and Environment issued the ample Qatar Construction Specifications of 2010, which cataloged the procedures that contractors seeking official approval should follow.[61] The section on health and safety ran over a hundred pages, but the danger of heat injury was mentioned only once as a fraction of a single bullet point.

The law, terse as it was, conceived of heat as an external and aleatory threat that companies could shield against by temporarily suspending operations during the hottest part of the day. Even so, proscriptions against outdoor work were not indexed to atmospheric heat conditions or the level of physical activity. Temperatures during the periods of allowable outdoor summertime work, even early in the day or late in the afternoon, regularly surpassed those at which international organizations deemed physical work safe. During my span of research (temperatures have risen since) in the period between June 15 and August 31, temperatures at 5:00 a.m. in the moments before dawn had already pushed past 95°F. By 11:30 a.m., when workers could legally put down their tools and seek protection from the heat, temperatures breached 105°F, regularly broiling past 115°F. Temperatures rarely dropped below 90°F even in the dead of night. Doha would have to wait until the end of September for temperatures that remained below 100°F.[62]

To make up for the gap in Qatar's occupational health and safety regulation, some companies provided training on heat safety. Those that did tended to be larger, compelled by their insurers to extend a layer of protection over and above the calendar prohibition against midday work. Company training rubrics were comprehensive and generally followed international standards for heat safety protocols. The formal training curricula that I was able to review contained information on heat stress and preventive measures: strategies to minimize the risk of heat exposure with guidelines for rest and hydration, the symptoms of heat illness and how to identify them, the proper use of protective gear, and the procedures for alerting supervisory staff to cases of heat illness and seeking medical care. They codified the skills required to complete physical labor under extreme temperature conditions as well as respond effectively to symptoms of heat stress and heatstroke.

The trainings based on these briefing books—called heat safety inductions—were rolled out at the end of April and beginning of May. I was able to attend a number of them at the different sites I visited. While the safety protocols were exhaustive, the trainings sessions themselves tended to be short, even cursory. They did not cover the full range of information included in the training briefs. Some companies supplemented heat safety training by distributing checklists of heat safety procedures to foremen and charge-hands, and directing them to review the protocols with workers in daily stand-downs—morning huddles when supervisors reviewed instructions for the day's work with their crews. But neither in the larger heat induction session nor the smaller briefings on heat safety was meaningful guidance provided on how to translate the standardized protocols, derived from international regu-lations, to the specific operational and environmental challenges that workers and supervisors encountered on Qatari sites on any given day.

The first of the heat safety inductions that I attended was at the ABC Builders stadium site. In batches of thirty to fifty men, workers were pulled off the site and directed to the air-conditioned trailer that housed the health and safety staff. Rows of chairs had been set up in the main room, facing a screen at the front. As the men walked in and found a seat on one of the plastic chairs, I took photos of the educational posters that hung on the walls. The poster that illustrated the dangers of heat injury featured a red-haired clip art man in shorts and sneakers, panting and hunched over. Under the drawing's oversize sun, right above the row of green cartoon trees, the text read, "If you feel symptoms of heat stress, stop and tell your supervisor."

Once the workers took their places, the lights went out and a slideshow began. The health and safety director narrated the slides in English, pausing from time to time to let his Indian staff member translate into Hindi. The presentation, which featured the same stock images that hung on the walls, covered the basic process changes that would be implemented as protec-tion against high temperatures. The health and safety director flagged that supervisors would explain hourly rest rotations for work, and informed the workers that shaded cooling areas, misted with water, would be provided at the base of the construction site. Against a slide with a chart of graduated shades of yellow, he stressed the importance of drinking water. I had noticed the same chart tacked up in the bathroom. The chart correlated the colors of urine depicted in the stacked rectangles with different stages of dehydration. Alongside straw-colored yellow, the poster read, "You are drinking enough water." Deep marigold yellow was a signal that the reader needed to hydrate; "remember to drink water," it reminded the viewer. And next to the rust-colored square, the poster ordered, "Drink water now!"

I looked around to gauge reactions to the presentation, and in the twilight of the darkened room, I saw that a few men had slumped over in their chairs and heads were nodding with drowsiness. The men had already been work-ing since early morning in temperatures that pushed past 90°F—or a WBGT of 28°C or 82°F. At that temperature, international standards recommend that a person engaged in moderate physical activity, such as hammering nails or sorting materials, should take a ten-minute break and drink three cups of water every hour. Any activity more intensive than that requires a minute of rest for every minute of activity and four cups of water per hour. The lights went up after half an hour. The men rubbed their eyes and shook off their tiredness. In the cool dark room, the men, already exhausted by heavy physical work with few protective breaks, had stolen a few moments of rest and sleep.

After the heat induction training at the ABC Builders stadium site, Matty, the scaffolder manager for the site, escorted me from the health and safety trailer back to the active construction site. As we walked, he explained that the heat inductions had to start in April as soon as the heat conditions began to intensify. "In a few weeks," he said, "the men will start getting very short tempered. There'll be fights breaking out all over the place. It settles down eventually, as the men get acclimated. It's just the breaking in period that's tough"—tough on the bodies of workers too. Irritability and volatile emotional reactions are symptoms of heat injury. By the time these indicators manifest, the body has already begun to ration blood flow to any organ not involved in dissipating heat. The brain is already oxygen deprived, and the heart is already taxed. Matty's comments suggested that safety protocols notwithstanding, the company allowed that a certain level of heat injury was unavoidable and even unremarkable.

Much has been written about the ways in which safety training and practices can be performative and exculpatory. Sociological and historical analyses in particular have shown the ways in which the provision of safety training and equipment has provided firms with an alibi for the occupational injuries that occur on their sites.[63] Once industrial materials were identified as the cause of the workers' injuries—once injuries were established as having been created by external pathogens rather than the workers' own bodies—workers who came into contact with lead, phosphate, silica dust, and others hazardous materials were given safety equipment to use. The equipment offered little protection against industrial toxins, but it did supply firms with protection against legal and moral culpability for worker injuries.[64] Workers handling asbestos in midcentury Britain and the United States, for example, were given cheap masks that did not filter out asbestos fibers, but did make it difficult for workers to breathe in their dusty work environments; when workers ripped off the masks to catch a breath, or simply avoided using the masks, their noncompliance was used by employers to discredit their claims for compensation when they contracted mesothelioma.[65] Accounts of contemporary safety practices note that the performance of safety has shifted from the donning of external safety equipment to the creation of a so-called safety culture. Although less tangible than a mask, these worksite practices—codified through checklists and safety protocols—still provide cover for employers against accusations of carelessness with workers' health.[66] Once an organization defines safe practices, any injury becomes proof of worker noncompliance.[67] The safety systems set by management fail because workers have disobeyed them outright or else neglected to address the continued existence of unsafe conditions.[68]

While the consideration of the ways that safety training can shift blame onto the injured has shone a bright light on its role in reproducing power dynamics at a worksite, less attention has been paid to the function of safety training in deciding what counts as an occupational hazard and what does not. Risks left unaddressed by safety protocols, in some operational sense, do not exist; injuries not anticipated by safety training are not acknowledged.

The definition of risk occurs through the definition of the skill required to protect against that risk; the occupational hazard comes into existence as an identifiable danger when the safety practices to shield against it are codified. Both the definition of the occupational hazard and the procedures required to respond it become authoritative by drawing on claims to expertise; for example, heat safety protocols derive their credibility from the physiological studies and technocratic proposals behind the indexing of heat levels to health hazards, and the precise and standardized steps to protect against bodily damage.

Safety protocols are designed like toolboxes, with clear directives, checklists, and standardized procedures all directed at the hazard they define. In this way, they reflect a particular understanding of skill: skill as knowledge that can be codified, a series of methods that can be systematized, or a fixed asset that can be parsed out of practice. The conceptualization of skill that underpins safety protocols is what creates the possibility of shifting the blame for injury onto the injured. If skill is defined as an external resource that workers can adopt—a tool that they can pick up—then any injury is evidence that the injured decided not to adopt the skill set imparted in the safety protocol. If skill can be isolated from embodied practice, then the conditions that shape embodied practice—that support, direct, or constrain it—matter little in the assessment of whether injury was due the injured's failure to adhere to skill specifications in safety protocols.

In Qatar, heat safety protocols performed the dual role of defining risk and the skill required to deflect it, but they also framed heat safety practices as a stand-alone skill set, specified independently of skillful, embodied practice. Heat illness was thus drawn into the skill politics that shaped production practices in Qatar's construction industry. Heatstroke could be redefined as proof that the worker had not applied the skills imparted in the safety protocols or training. The failure to do so indicated either that the worker had chosen to disregard the guidance or the injured worker had lacked the capacity to learn. The seizures, fainting, or severe cardiac stress that were the immediately visible symptoms of heat injury could become reframed as proof not just that the worker was unskilled but also that the worker did not possess the dimensions of personhood required to develop skill. Because after all, what worker would choose to harm his body by refraining from applying the skill set delivered in one of the many sessions of heat induction training on-site?

THREE KINDS OF INJURING

On construction sites in Qatar, safety protocols participated in three kinds of injuring through heat: control over worker actions on-site, the neglect of workers' bodily welfare, and damage to workers' cognition. At each of these levels of injuring, safety procedures became a means to constrain, undermine, or discount workers' ability to enact their embodied skill. Protocols made clear the importance of protective measures against heat, and yet at each level, workers were either prevented from taking steps to protect themselves or their access to the resources they needed to protect themselves was constrained. This juxtaposition between the provision of safety skill and lack of ability to exercise it reaffirmed to workers the extent of managerial control over their bodily integrity. Instead of standing outside injury, providing a kind of cover or merely displacing accountability, safety protocols, as extensions of managerial practice, were in fact deeply involved in the practices of injuring.

By providing safety knowledge while also limiting workers' ability to act on it, management undermined workers' ability to avoid injuries that did not make it onto the safety protocols checklist of the bodily damage that heat could cause. In construction, occupational skill is what allows workers to work safely.[69] The work is often high risk, and workers draw on the same trade expertise, skillful practice, and competent exercise of autonomy that they use to complete tasks in order to minimize injury.[70]

In Qatar, construction workers depended on their embodied cognition to stay safe. They relied on their physical dexterity and the sharpness of their cognitive reflexes, not just to complete complex and nuanced building tasks, but to avoid falls, cuts, and other workplace accidents. For workers who welded with a blowtorch while leaning out of a scaffold many stories up in the air, constructed scaffolding frames while perched on cantilevered tubes a hundred feet above the floor, or hung by ropes as they used silicon guns to seal roof cladding panels, access to this embodied cognition could be a matter of life and death. Even for other workers on the site who performed tasks that were lower risk, such as laying tiles or painting walls, the ability to draw on their embodied skill and trust that their bodies would respond in ways that were reliable was core to their capacity to complete tasks without injury.

At each of the three levels of wounding, workers' skillful practice was constrained and damaged. Heat's assault on embodied cognition was magnified. Safety training—through its codification of safety skill—recast workers' inability to protect themselves as an act of self-betrayal. Workers were made the cause of their own wounding. An examination of the practices at each of these three levels reveals how this inversion took place.

DENIAL OF WORKSITE AUTONOMY

One of the slides in the safety induction presentation featured a chart that outlined the rest periods and water intake required per hour at different temperature levels. The health and safety director went through the chart line by line in a perfunctory fashion. He told the audience of workers that their supervisors would let them know what rest quotient was required each day and remind them of the quantity of water they needed to drink. He also underscored that workers needed to take responsibility for their own safety, and rest and hydrate as they felt they needed to.

In practice, however, workers' ability to self-regulate—to adjust the pace of their work or decide when to get water—was highly constrained. Their managers directed them to protect themselves from heat by drawing on an autonomy that they did not have, and in many cases, were actively prevented from enacting. Workers were compelled to act in ways that would be dangerous, as the company's own safety induction had demonstrated, and could result in life-threatening harm.

The pace of work on the projects I visited was grueling. Many were fast-track projects with accelerated timelines and extended workdays. Working in teams that strained daily to meet production goals, workers could not take rest breaks as they felt they needed them, to say nothing of the thirty to forty-five minutes of rest per hour recommended by international safety guidelines when working in high temperatures. Doing so would likely have resulted in penalties, which ranged from verbal sanction to docked pay for the individual worker or his team. Moreover, on all but international oil and gas projects, where an error could mean an exploding gas line, and safety procedures were heightened as a result, supervisors and foremen, in the periodic morning safety huddles or stand-downs when safety procedures were reviewed, rarely authorized workers to follow a work-rest cycle appropriate for the day's environment conditions. In my observation, the shaded areas, cooled with mist on the better sites, and air-conditioning on the oil and gas sites, went mostly unused. The benches in the rest tents and cooling trailers were empty, except for a handful of workers, most of them, as they told me, waiting for new task assignments.

Hydrating as directed was similarly challenging. On all the sites that I visited, it would have been impossible for workers to access the amount of water that their managers recommended. On some sites, this was due to the fact that water stations were not regularly refilled, and water points, clearly marked with large and flashy signage, remained empty for days at a time. On other sites, water stations were located some distance from the work area itself. At ABC Builders stadium site, for example, water points were located at the base of the structure being built. For scaffolders, who worked at a fifteen- or twenty-minute climb off the ground level, a strenuous trip up ladders and staircases carrying up to twenty pounds of personal safety equipment, the water points were as good as inaccessible. As part of their protective equipment, they were fitted with insulated water flasks that could hold six cups of water. To drink the amount of water specified by international heat safety guidelines as well as recommended by their own health and safety department, scaffolders would have had to climb up and down the structure once every hour to refill their flasks. This would have left less than half an hour for work between trips, which they could only have used if they forfeited their rest breaks, mandated by international regulations, for work in the heat. In practice, scaffolders rationed their water, stretching out their six cups of water over the course of the morning or afternoon, and refilling their flasks only when they went down for their lunch break.

Another reason that workers limited their fluid intake was the scarcity of bathrooms on-site. Not only were bathrooms located as far from the work areas as water points were but there also simply weren't enough of them. Lines of workers snaked out from the portable urinals on the sites I visited, and the men stood for many minutes, unshaded, waiting their turn. In response, many workers restricted their daytime water consumption. Others resorted as discretely as they could on the crowded sites to public urination. Scaffolders carried up disposable plastic water bottles scavenged from the managers' row of trailers and filled them with what they called "scaffolders' lemonade," or sometimes, "scaffolders' tea." Scaffolders who needed to move their bowels during the workday used masonry buckets. The bottles and buckets were scattered throughout the maze of scaffolding platforms, and although they were ubiquitous, they were a source of shame to some. On more than one occasion, I noticed that when I stepped onto a given scaffolding platform, a worker would take a discrete step to the left or right so that he could block the bucket from my view. Moreover, in the often confusing lighting on the scaffold, when the sun filtered through the grid or deflected off the half-built stadium dome, the makeshift toilets became occupational hazards in the own right—potential projectiles kept by scaffolding teams that were otherwise careful not to leave the tools anywhere on a platform where they could be accidentally knocked off.

Companies delivered safety training to workers, but did not allow them the discretion to enact the protocols or provide them with the resources to follow the safety directives. Supervisory practices, the pace of work, and the lack of basic services all prevented workers from integrating safety guidelines into their skillful practice. The disjuncture between safety protocols and the latitude that workers were granted to apply them turned vulnerability to heat into an expression of managerial power: management supplied workers with the information about how to stay safe, but also determined whether or not workers would be able to use it. This tension performed a disciplinary function at the worksite: workers were expected to comply with all work demands, even when compliance required them to disregard the company's own safety guidelines and open their bodies up to injury.

LIMITING BODILY CARE

Worksite safety protocols defined heat as an occupational hazard. They addressed the danger that heat represented to workers at the worksite while they were engaged in work tasks. They did not address the dangers that heat represented to workers on the worksite when they were not performing work functions, nor the way that heat threatened workers' well-being when they were off-site. In this way, safety protocols defined the hazard that heat represented as a product of the way that work tasks exposed workers to heat and considered workers in terms of the labor function. But the danger of heat stemmed not from workers' performance of work tasks but rather the vulnerability inherent in being embodied. The damage that heat did to workers' bodies when they were not performing work tasks—during times not covered by the safety protocols—compromised their ability to enact safety guidelines and work safely.

Companies were responsible contractually for the bodily care of workers beyond when they performed work tasks at the jobsite. They were required to provide housing to their workers and supply their meals or meal allowances. Yet they often failed to provide workers with the living conditions that were protective of workers' bodies under conditions of extreme heat—even as regulations associated with the kafala system prevented those workers from seeking alternative housing and meal accommodations, or taking steps to seek redress for poor living conditions.

Because exposure to heat requires the body to perform additional coping functions, the caloric requirements of a body active in heat conditions rise. As part of heat safety training, supervisors advised workers to eat a hearty breakfast and lunch, even if heat suppressed their appetites. Yet most firms did not provide meals to their workers, especially meals consumed off-site. Instead, a food allowance was tacked onto their monthly pay, and workers were expected to purchase their food and prepare their own meals. Workers were expected to cook their dinner and pack their meals for the next day at the end of shifts that when transport back and forth to the worksite was added in, could extend to twelve hours.

The kitchen at most labor camps was not air-conditioned, and cooking over a hot stove after a long workday, in temperatures that even at night frequently did not dip below 85°F, was experienced as exceptionally taxing. Heat-exhausted workers often chose to forgo full dinners or hot breakfasts, reducing the caloric bank on which they could draw to cope with the heat and recover from its effects. In many cases, even when they did prepare protective meals, their employers failed to support them in this effort. Few companies provided refrigeration for the lunches that workers prepared at their labor camps and brought in tiffin boxes to the jobsite. By lunchtime, meals left out in the intense morning heat were spoiled and inedible, and if consumed, compounded the gastrointestinal distress caused by heat pressure. At one site I visited, the lack of refrigeration for meals led to a brief wildcat strike by the cladding crews. Two large cladding contractors operated on-site, but only one provided cooled storage for packed lunches. With the body requiring greater caloric intake to metabolize heat, this caloric shortfall made these workers more susceptible to heat stress. Workers at this company complained to their supervisors for several weeks. After two workers on their crew fainted on-site, several cladders walked to the supervisors' rest area to dump their lunches in the trash cans at the entrance, in full view of the managers and engineers gathered there. After a cladding accident when a rope was dropped by a disoriented worker and the team lost control of the panel it was hauling up to the top of the structure, workers at the company that provided refrigeration joined their colleagues in protest. Workers at the better company refused to work, arguing that their colleagues distracted by a combination of hunger and heat, and thus unable to concentrate, were making working conditions unsafe. The strike, like all forms of labor organizing by migrants, was against the law in Qatar, and the striking workers risked deportation. After a tense day when none of the cladders on-site climbed to the cladding platform, bringing cladding production to a halt, the two cladding companies reached an agreement allowing all workers to use the better company's refrigerators.

In addition to sufficient caloric intake, minimizing the physical impact of exposure to heat depends on recovery in a cool environment so that the body can return to its natural set point. Nighttime recovery and sleep have been shown to be particularly important for bodies to repair heat damage.[71] For workers in Qatar, this meant that access to climate-controlled housing was critical to their ability to cope with daytime heat levels. The reliability of air-conditioning systems in worker lodgings, however, was uneven.

In the labor camps I visited, workers were housed several to a room, generally with a mini-split air-conditioning unit perched above the stacked bunks. But the maintenance of worker housing was frequently poor, including clogged plumbing, overflowing toilets, and short-circuiting air-conditioners. Moreover, it was often unclear who was responsible for the upkeep and repair of the facilities. Some companies owned their own labor barracks, but most rented out labor accommodations, leasing a building or sometimes just a suite of rooms. The building owners hired management firms to handle the rental agreements and maintenance of the camps. Because the contractual layers made identifying accountability difficult, it could take days for the employer to corral the landlord into repairing or replacing a broken air conditioner. "Look, when the air dies, we understand that it's serious," explained Brett, the health and safety manager at a company working on the ABC Builders stadium site. "It goes to the top of my list of to-dos, but it takes a while to get sorted, and there is nothing I can do about that."

Workers generally were not able to change accommodations even when the conditions were substandard and appalling. Because bunks were packed tightly into rooms, it was often not possible for men in rooms with broken units to sleep in other rooms where the air-conditioning was still functioning; there was simply not enough space on the floor. As a result, a broken air conditioner meant that workers in that room might have to endure daytime heat exposure without the possibility of nighttime recovery for several days—a situation that had the potential to dramatically increase their vulnerability to heat injury and lasting organ damage.

The injuring practices that took place through control of workers' autonomy on-site and the neglect of their bodies off-site exposed workers to heat injury. But the most dangerous and consequential effect of these two layers of injuring is the ways in which they produced the injuring that occurred in the last, most intimate layer: the injuring that took place through the workers' own embodied cognition.

DAMAGING EMBODIED COGNITION

Confusion, dizziness, and the loss of subtle motor control—early symptoms of heat stress—appear with even mild exposure to heat or exposure of short duration. For embodied expressions of cognition, where cognitive processes are reflected in physical movement, the effects of reduced oxygen supply to the brain during moments of heat strain are magnified by light-headedness along with related vestibular impacts caused by dehydration and changes in blood viscosity.[72] Workers I spoke with talked about how heat affected their embodied cognition. "You are not yourself," "Your mind is squeezed," and "Everything becomes very slow" were some of the ways that workers described the feeling. One noted how his body became unresponsive to his commands; he said it was as if his limbs had like "a wet towel."

Workers also spoke of the way that heat stress dissolved the social connections among between them and disrupted the social interactions that were part of skillful practice on-site. "If someone is unwell, they are not paying attention to anything around," said one. One scaffolder I spoke with explained that heat made reaction times slower and grips less sure. A dropped tube could result in serious injury for those working below the scaffolding frame, and on hot days, he said, he had to double-check that his teammate had a tight grip on the tube before he released his own. Safety on the worksite depended on workers remaining aware of each other's movements, anticipating each other's actions, and compensating in real time for small errors that coworkers make. But heat stress made that interpersonal awareness unreliable.

In speaking about their confusion, disorientation, and disconnection from one another as well as their own bodies, workers described a manifestation of heat injury that safety protocols did not address: heat injury from within.

At the most basic level, heat damaged the cognition that workers needed to enact the heat safety guidelines repeated in the heat inductions that workers received. But more profoundly, heat compromised the cognitive resources that they needed to connect and interact with coworkers, and interpret changes in their surroundings.

Even though heat was the defining feature of their work environments for months out of the year, workers' found the experiences of heat injury difficult to talk about. They strained to find the words to describe the felt sensation of cognitive impairment. Some felt shame at their confusion or the disconnection with their own bodies. On one of my later visits to the ABC Builders stadium site, I came to understand why.

Because my fieldwork involved physical activity, I was careful to schedule site visits in the early morning or late afternoon. By the beginning of May, though, temperatures had already become oppressive at those times of day, and an afternoon that initially felt like any other became unexpectedly and suddenly perilous. I was climbing up a zigzag scaffolding structure with staggered platforms connected by ladders. About two-thirds of the way up, after fifteen minutes or so of climbing, I tried to pull myself through the opening in the platform above me, through which the ladder had been threaded. Because of the ladder's position, the last step involved a hike up with one leg and forceful push down on the last rung of the ladder with the opposite hand. This gesture, which I had completed many times before and many times that day, all of sudden felt unachievable. The effort left me bent over and panting, my heart racing, and a cold sweat prickling on my lower back. When I stood back up, I experienced a strong head rush and felt for a few seconds as if I if might pass out. I regained my composure and tried to proceed with my fieldwork, but the foreman's voice along with the constant banging noises of the site sounded distant and distorted, as if they were trapped and reverberating against the edges of a tin can. The activity around me seemed to recede to the periphery of my experience, and maintaining my balance as we walked along the platform required my entire focus. I could no longer be aware of the physical movements of workers around me. The concentration I applied to taking step after step on the scaffold was broken only by waves of panic about the need to rip off the safety harness I had been comfortably wearing all day; the straps seemed to be digging into my shoulders, the thick metal safety hooks, the size of my open hand, felt as if they were rubbing my bottom rib and the top of my hip raw, and the weight of the harness made it difficult to breathe. The air was suffocating me.

When I suffered from heat stress, I experienced how the cognitive and physical impacts of heat interact in ways that can increase exposure to injury. I rapidly became certain that my safety—my very survival—depended on removing my safety harness. On other days, when I had not been affected by heat, I understood clearly that my safety harness was essential to protect me from serious injury or death in the case of a fall off the scaffold. But when heat stress affected my movements, coordination, and balance—increasing the possibility of a fall—I felt an urgent need to remove the harness in order to breathe. Even so, I was not aware of how severely heat had affected my cognition. I was too confused to understand that I wanted to act against my own safety. If it had not been for the actions of a foreman on-site who noticed my unsteadiness, and encouraged me to sit and drink water until I recovered, I suspect I would have fallen. The climb up the series of interlocking scaffolding ladders was complicated and required concentration, but my attention was wholly consumed with the need to tear off my safety harness and lanyards so that I could breathe.

As I learned, the heat-afflicted person no longer has access to the ability to appraise how cognition has been damaged. For a worker (or researcher) affected by heat stress, the desire to be safe may remain, but the understanding of what safety is may be dangerously distorted. Even if a worker's understanding of safety remains sound, the body may not respond in ways that allow a worker to move safely and adeptly in a construction environment. Limbs become clumsy, fine motor movements become blunt, and balance becomes unsure. Heat stress causes injury that makes the injury itself difficult to perceive, understand, or describe. The inability to describe injury is in and of itself a product of heat damage.

In a context where safety protocols defined heat as an external threat, these internal expressions of injury allowed workers to be represented as the agents of their own wounding. Their own impaired cognition made them vulnerable to falls and injury. The physiology of heat injury allowed exposure to extreme temperatures on-site to be recast into a hazard from within, originating and playing out in the body, beyond the reach of company safety protocols.

The unpredictable physiological responses of any given body to heat abetted this displacement of blame. For reasons still scientifically undetermined, the same person can engage in the same level of activity at the same WBGT, with the same level of hydration, nutrition, and rest, and can have dramatically different physical responses on different days, coping well on one day and succumbing to heat injury on another.[73] Nowhere in the safety training on the sites or in the safety protocols was the variability of heat injury addressed. Instead, the capriciousness of heat's effect on the body created room for the claim that safety protocols ensured safety and therefore injury had to be the result of workers' own bodies acting against them.

If safety protocols were the skills required to protect against heat, codified in clear and standardized rules, workers' cognitive impairment could be enlisted as proof that workers did not have the capacity to apply them. Workers' confusion, troubled focus, and compromised dexterity in extreme temperatures were not regarded as evidence that safety protocols were insufficient, or that the conditions that would allow them to apply them were missing. Rather, injury to their embodied cognition could be used to call their embodied skill into question—to confirm that workers were unskilled. After the incident in which the cladding team dropped the guide rope and left the cladding panel swinging dangerously along the structure's shell, the cladding manager on call at ABC Builders did not address the effect of heat on the workers. He complained instead that the workers were "poor quality," "unskilled labors [*sic*]," and required more supervision than he had budgeted for.

Climate Change and the Grammar of Injury

As the temperatures rose, many of the workers I spoke with went to work knowing they would feel unwell. Before they boarded the bus in the morning, they knew that their muscles would cramp, their bodies would feel heavy, and for stretches during the day, it would feel unbearable. They knew before they climbed the scaffold or picked up a blowtorch that they would have a hard time connecting to their sense experience and embodied cognition, and would be less safe as a result. They knew also that the steps that their supervisors said were crucial for their own safety, things like rest breaks or frequent trips to the water points, would be difficult to take. They knew, but tried not to think about, what an injury might mean for them and their families. Knowing this and still being compelled to work was how workers experienced the power that managers had over them. And this too was part of the process of injuring.

This process occurred primarily through three layers of managerial practice detailed here: wounding by limiting workers' autonomy, restricting their ability to care for their bodies, and damaging cognition. These practices reinforced one another, amplifying the harm to workers' bodies and their personhood. They caused injury to workers' cognition, and in so doing, collapsed the grammar of injury into the body of the worker. The elements required for the syntax of injury—damage to the body, a weapon, and an agent that wields that weapon—were all representationally placed on the worker's body. The body was damaged; the body was the source of physical distress for the worker; and the body had turned against its owner. The body swelled to occupy all aspects of the politics of injury. No room was left for heat, managerial practice, or the skill politics reflected in safety protocols to be involved in harming. The grammar of injury crumpled; wound, weapon, and agent became indistinguishable, melted together by heat, muddled by the representation of workers as unskilled or irresponsible, and filtered through formulaic and prescriptive safety protocols.

Ganesh's father, on receiving his son's coffin, had asked, "Was it the climate? Or was it something else? These are the questions that are weighing on my heart." The answer to his question is that his son died because on Qatari worksites, the climate *became* something else. Injuring occurred when the climate—Qatar's extreme heat—was drawn into workplace power dynamics, managerial practices, and skill politics. Through its impact on embodied cognition, the climate created effects in the body that could be enlisted to represent workers as unskilled or uncooperative, and the political definition of skill as an abstract resource, separate from workers' embodied practice, created room for heat to continue to press down on workers' bodies. The climate interacted with the politics of production and bodies of workers in ways that allowed for the erasure of injury, leaving the families that received coffins desperately seeking to understand what had happened. The climate became an alibi, and injury became accident.

As climate change accelerates, Ganesh's father's question will only become more urgent, and we will need to look more intently at how climate becomes something else. As temperatures rise and heat becomes more dangerous to bodies at work and at rest, the only way to protect against heat injury will be to attend to the ways that climate and power interact in the process of injuring. A meaningful response to the threat of heat injury—a response that protects kidneys and hearts, but also cognition and dignity—will require us to examine the ways that heat shapes power relations and that political power represents the damage that heat does to bodies. A politics of labor justice in a time of global warming will require us to pay attention to the kinds of politics—like the politics of skill—through which climate is drawn into workplace practices. How climate becomes something else will need to be the question that weighs on our hearts.

CHAPTER SIX

Earth

HOW THE POLITICS OF SKILL SHAPE
RESPONSES TO CLIMATE CHANGE

WHEN QATAR WON THE 2022 World Cup hosting rights in 2010, the state funneled billions of dollars from its hydrocarbon revenues into infrastructure projects, supercharging the construction industry. The labor force for the industry ballooned. In 2010, there were just over a half-million construction workers in Qatar. By 2015, there were close to nine hundred thousand.[1]

For construction companies, the boom was a bonanza, but for Majid, a Syrian engineer, the industry expansion caused personal strain. By the time we met in late 2014, Majid had worked in the human resources department of his construction company for close to a decade. His company, Arab Earthmover and Aggregate (AEA), a midsize earthmoving firm, had been contracted to complete portions of the peripheral boring work for the Qatar metro, QRail. Majid was responsible for overseeing the manpower recruitment required for the project. "The time pressures are very strong," complained Majid. "We are bringing four or five hundred workers every three months. That's as many as we used to bring over a twelve-month period, so it's a significant increase."

When his company was first awarded the QRail contract, it turned to the recruitment networks that it had already established in a half-dozen countries in South Asia and East Africa. "We found this to be very unsatisfactory," explained Majid. In the past, the recruitment agencies that his team had worked with would ship on average a hundred or so workers to AEA per year. When AEA was awarded the QRail project, the agencies had difficulty ramping up their recruitment activity to meet the increased labor demand from the Qatari firm. The capillary recruitment networks of uncles, return migrants, and local leaders that they often turned to stretched from the agencies' storefront offices in Kathmandu and Lucknow into the flatland villages of southern Nepal and northern India, along with newer recruitment networks that extended from neon-lit backrooms in Addis Ababa into the arid stretches of the Ethiopian lowlands. As construction boomed in Qatar, these networks strained to deliver the numbers of young men that AEA requested. The orders that AEA placed with its recruiters for workers went unfilled. "We had visas for two hundred [workers], and maybe we would get eighty or even fifty," reported Majid. He pulled off his glasses, pinched the bridge of his nose, and leaned his head against his hand. "It has been difficult," he said.

A few moments later, he resumed. "Because the QRail project is priority, we were able to negotiate with the Ministry of Labor to give us a block of visas for Bangladesh." All requests to bring in migrant labor had to be authorized by the Ministries of Labor and Interior before any company could begin to recruit workers. The ministries had a vested interest in ensuring that solidarity among workers was kept to a minimum—so they usually awarded visas strategically, using diversity in nationality to undercut labor organizing and effectively creating quotas for each nationality represented on-site. Because the QRail project was designated as "fast track," funded and contracted by the Qatari Public Works Authority, Ashghal, the company was able to secure an exceptional approval from the Ministries of Labor and Interior allowing it to source the bulk of its workers from a single country.

"We are working now with an agent with good networks in the south, in the Khulna area." Majid explained that AEA was sourcing its Bangladeshi workers through this agent, and the agent was able to supply workers in the numbers that AEA required without significant or unplanned delays.

"Overall, I am happy with the supply," concluded Majid. "The problem is that the quality is not always good." I asked him what he meant by quality, expecting an answer that had to do with skill levels.

"Many of the workers are very weak when they arrive—look, frankly, [like] they are malnourished. We spend the first weeks just feeding them. After two weeks, we have them start digging." "Digging?" I asked, unsure what task in the technical excavation process he was referring to. His answer surprised me.

"Yes, we give them a shovel and we have them dig. For three or four weeks, to see if they can manage the work and the heat. If they don't regain their strength, we send them back. Only if we see that they are strong and that they will manage do we invest in training."

"Where do they dig?" I asked, still perplexed by the notion that workers would be made to dig by hand with shovels, especially given the industry-wide safety practice of avoiding the use of manual techniques for earthmoving and well-documented risk that the walls of any excavated trench might fail. Strenuous digging in high temperatures also put workers at elevated risk for heat injury and collapse, and not, as Majid would have it, because of their physical condition.

Sewage trenches mostly. It doesn't matter what they dig. They can dig a hole behind this trailer. We are testing to see if they will become strong.

Their fields are failing, and they arrive weak. So we give them a chance to see if they can recover, and if they do, they are good and they learn quickly. But if they collapse on the job, we can't use them. On two hundred, we send twenty or thirty back. But the agent is good and we are able to renew the supply quickly.

The reason that the agent was able to renew "the supply" quickly, though, had perhaps less to do with the agent being good than migrants' fields being poor.

In Bangladesh, saltwater intrusion from the Bay of Bengal, whose waters had been rising at a rate of two centimeters a year, had changed the chemical composition of both the soil and shallow groundwater over the last few decades.[2] The increasingly violent and frequent cyclones whipped up seawaters. The resulting storm surges caused severe and sometimes catastrophic flooding. Embankments designed to direct floodwaters away from villages, called *podlers* in the delta, were built with the help of the World Bank in the 1970s and 1980s. But one of the side effects of these podlers was that they held the brackish water back. With nowhere for the salty water to go, the loamy soil was forced to absorb the salt that arrived during the cycles of seasonal cyclones and tidal flooding.[3] The monsoons, which once upon a time reliably cleansed the salt from the fields, became increasingly irregular, and some years did not produce enough rain to flush out the salt. By 2010, a third of the land in Bangladesh's coastal region was already compromised by high salinity, and the salt poisoning of the land was accelerating. In the southwest quadrant of the delta, the area in and around the city of Khulna, the salinity of the soil was depressing crop yields and reducing the yield for rice—the staple crop in the region and 70 percent of the agricultural produce—by more than 15 percent.[4] In order to survive, farmers began swapping out rice and other crop cultivations for shrimp and crab farming, flooding their fields with river water, which had also become too briny to irrigate crops, but was still acceptable for growing shellfish for export to China and Malaysia.[5] The salty and contaminated water in those human-made pools further poisoned the soil and salinized the groundwater.[6] Smallholders whose plots were not large enough to support shrimp farms started selling their plots to capital-intensive commercial aquaculture outfits.[7] As these former farmers moved from rural to urban areas, regional cities like Khulna swelled. Some cities saw population increases of close to 5 percent a year.[8]

From the vantage point of AEA and its recruitment agency, men from these regions were ideal candidates for jobs in Qatar—and not just because there were so many of them. They were attractive because they were newly poor. In the recent past, they had benefited from investments in education, nutrition, health, and other aspects of human development. Until salt turned it, Khulna had been one of the wealthier regions of Bangladesh, with per capita incomes that were on average slightly higher than for the country as a whole.[9] The region also had educational outcomes that were better than average.[10] Its rates of school attendance, for both primary and secondary school, were the highest in the nation.The secondary school enrollment rates, for boys in particular, were markedly higher than in the capital city—in 2007, some 10 percentage points higher. But since the region's soil had been poisoned, and its crops had failed, people had been displaced and impoverished. They'd been forced to move or look for other forms of livelihood.

AEA's recruitment agency stepped in. They recruited young men whose families were newly poor, but still had some resources from better days to pay the agency fee that gave them access to jobs in Qatar's construction industry. Families borrowed against land that they could no longer cultivate, though could still mortgage, to pay the cost of migrating, which in Bangladesh ranged from US$1,000 to $2,100.[11] The jobs on offer were not well paid; the wages for general laborer or construction helper jobs hovered around 750 Qatari riyal per month, or approximately US$200. It took many migrants a full year to recoup the costs of migrating, but still, for many families, it was worth it. Climate change pressures displaced and impoverished what were once well-to-do smallholding families, and AEA was able to hire their literate sons at bargain prices.

The educational level of its recruits mattered to AEA because the workers who made it through the first month of grueling and, given what Majid told me, gratuitous physical labor went on to receive intensive on-the-job training in excavation and boring support. And the educational levels of the new recruits—their literacy, math, and spatial competence—helped them learn these new skills. AEA trained them in the techniques of building the shoring and bracing structures required to keep recently bored trenches open as well as solder together the complex rib cages of steel, aluminum, and wood designed to keep the earth from falling back in on itself. The workers learned to drape the exposed soil with nylon and metal netting to keep it from collapsing back down. They were taught the skills to assist in loading and discharging excavated earth from hauling trucks and learned how to complete the smaller and more detailed tasks that the mammoth earthmovers, with their massive bores and clawed flat shovels, could not do. It took a year, according to Majid's estimates, for new recruits to acquire basic competence in excavation, shoring, and trenching. "After the first year, the workers help advance the project. Before that, we are investing in them."

At the end of the workers' contract, which was on average two to four years long, AEA sent the workers that the company had trained back to their countries of origin. This, explained Majid, was to prevent their competitors from poaching AEA's investment in skill development—"stealing" their skill, as Majid put it, and using the workers AEA had already trained to underbid the company in the Qatari market. Workers sent back to Bangladesh, now with specialized expertise in boring and trenching technologies, had few opportunities to capitalize on their skill in the salt-choked villages and towns to which they returned. Those who sought to emigrate to Qatar once more or other countries in the GCC perhaps would likely have to use the same recruitment agent they had relied on before. But that agent was focused on filling bulk orders of low-cost labor. Already skilled workers were akin to higher-priced specialty items that AEA and firms like it, with their own in-house training system, did not request or need.

The story of AEA and its recruitment strategies was not unique in Qatar's construction industry. Firms throughout the industry were evaluating the benefits that climate change pressures offered them in their recruitment of migrant workers. The locations and climate pressures they explored were different: drought in the horn of Africa, fickle and volatile monsoons in Nepal and India, and sea level rise in Indonesia. But several firms, recruitment agencies, and industry representatives I interviewed spoke about the opportunities that global warming created for labor recruitment. They commented explicitly about the fact that climate change pressures turned relatively well-off people into the newly poor and made them available to migrate. They viewed these people as good recruits because they had benefited from long-term investments in education, nutrition, and health, but were now willing to accept lower wages than they would have before. The recruits were also cheap enough that companies could treat them as low-cost "single-use" workers: recruited, used, and even trained, and then dumped back into labor markets where their prospects were limited, and the institutions that might have capitalized on the skills they acquired in Qatar were missing or fragmented.

Through their recruitment practices, companies in Qatar engaged with climate change from the vantage point of skill; they looked to climate-damaged areas because that was where they could find workers who could be trained quickly and hired at low wages. Upskilled in Qatar, these workers would be categorized as unskilled regardless of the competence they acquired. But trained into anything that the companies needed, instructed in any one of a variety of trades, these workers provided firms with production flexibility. As companies in Qatar increasingly sought out this edge, they began to drive the transformation of the recruitment networks. To exercise greater strategic control, they pushed for tighter partnerships with their recruiters and modeled the business practices of the agencies they used. In the process, they shaped the economic meaning of migration: they determined who migrated and under what terms; structured working conditions and opportunities for skill development; measured out the remittances that workers could send home by setting wages; and decided whether and how migrants could commodify their labor and skill once their jobs in Qatar were over.

But they also shaped the ecological meaning of migration. Through their recruitment practices, construction companies in Qatar connected an industry bankrolled by hydrocarbon revenues to land and communities devastated by the release of carbon into the atmosphere. Construction is itself a highly polluting industry, producing nearly 40 percent of all carbon emissions worldwide.[12] The construction industry in Qatar had an outsized carbon footprint, producing about four times the amount of carbon as construction in the United States, after adjustment for population size.[13] In this sense, firms in the industry benefited doubly from the carbon economy: they built buildings paid for by profits from fossil fuel extraction, emitting large amounts of carbon in the process, and at the same time were able to extract labor at low cost from areas damaged by the fossil fuel and carbon emissions that they contributed to.

Even as firms took advantage of climate damage in distant communities, their main worry was the construction challenges that they faced in Qatar. The volatility of demand in the industry, capriciousness of government regulators, and technically challenging and often pathbreaking design specifications of buildings—all these were factors that pushed companies to prioritize the sourcing of workers with the capacity for skill development. Their skill concerns shaped how they responded to the slow-motion displacement caused by global warming.[14] To deal with the turbulence of construction in Qatar, companies were beginning to pull climate change into their production strategies. They were using ecological damage as a business resource.

The response of Qatari firms to climate change in recruitment practices is still evolving, taking shape as the dislocations caused by the climate change emerge. These new patterns are still hard to see clearly. But this is not the only reason that the way recruitment has started to capitalize on climate damage remains invisible. In both advocacy and scholarly analyses of migrant recruitment, recruitment practices are widely represented as being produced in countries of origin, carried out by profiteering agents with few scruples. Recruitment agents are represented as producing labor for export, turning migrants into commodities that can be sold to firms abroad. The ways that those firms themselves shape the practices of migrant recruitment, even before they place their orders with recruiters, receives far less attention.

The view of recruitment as an activity driven by actors in countries of origin has shaped attempts to regulate the industry. It has also shaped efforts by Qatar to off-load the responsibility for the worst abuses of labor recruitment onto the governments and recruitment agents of other countries. Qatar has argued that recruitment abuses occur before workers arrive at its borders and therefore are not its problem. But migrant recruitment is not a straightforward matter of sourcing labor. It is a set of practices through which relations between countries and places are forged, strengthened, and amended. And today, these relationships knit together places that are being altered in irrevocable and unprecedented ways by climate change. Recruitment practices, designed in Qatar and other countries that bring in migrant labor, increasingly capitalize on ecological crisis, sharpening global inequities and heightening the uneven distribution of the consequences of climate change.

Recruitment and Responsibility

After Qatar was awarded the 2022 World Cup hosting rights, the practices associated with the recruitment of migrant workers came under the same scrutiny as other labor practices in Qatar. Human rights and advocacy organizations pointed to the high fees that migrants paid to access jobs in Qatar. Investigative and press reports found that these fees ranged from several hundred to several thousand dollars.[15] To raise the funds, workers incurred large debts, often borrowing from local moneylenders at exorbitant interest rates, and they offered up their family land or homes as collateral.

These debts emerged as a focal point of global human rights advocacy because of the concern that they created conditions of debt bondage. The recruitment fees that migrants were charged turned their wages into a security against the debt they had taken on, and this financial liability compelled migrants to tolerate exploitative labor conditions. If they were fired and deported back to their country of origin, they would be forced to forfeit family property and, even in extreme cases, would be pressed to enter into direct debt bondage relations with the original moneylender.

These reports also cataloged widespread misinformation and deception in the recruitment process: workers were misled about the salaries they would receive and jobs they would perform in Qatar; once they arrived in Qatar, the contracts they had signed in their country of origin, if they had had the opportunity to view a contract before migrating, were routinely swapped out for different ones with worse conditions and less pay, and migrants often learned that their employer and sometimes even the industry they were hired for differed from those listed in the contract they had seen before migrating.[16] Amnesty International in a 2011 study of Nepali return migrants, for example, found that 111 out of the 120 workers who were interviewed reported being deceived predeparture about their wages, working conditions, or the nature of their jobs.[17]

These reports also suggested that employers were displacing the cost of recruiting labor onto their workers. Employers paid the recruiting agents a fee for supplying them with workers, and investigative accounts noted that employers regularly deducted those fees from the workers' wages, without the workers' prior knowledge or consent. In some cases, employers demanded that recruiters pay them kickbacks for having given them the recruitment contract. Recruiters in turn jacked up their recruitment fees to compensate, passing the cost of the bribe down to workers, who had to take on larger loans to cover it.[18] The World Bank estimated in a 2011 study that Nepali recruitment agencies paid between $17 and $34 million in kickbacks, through informal and untraceable transfers, to their counterparts in Qatar.[19]

A survey conducted in 2012 by Garner, Pessoa, and colleagues through Qatar University confirmed the claims that these investigative reports made about indenture.[20] The survey queried 1,189 low-income workers, defined as workers who earned less than 2,000 Qatari riyals a month, or US$550, and found that 71 percent had paid recruitment fees. The fees that migrants had paid varied by their country of origin, ranging from a low of US$650 for workers from the Philippines, to US$1,100 for Indian migrants, to a high of about US$1,600 for Egyptian and Bangladeshi migrants. In many cases, these fees included the cost of travel to Qatar. Overall, the average cost to access a job with a two-year contract was US$1,031. This meant that on a monthly salary of 800 riyal, or about US$220—a typical wage for a laborer in Qatar—a worker on a two-year contract would have to use more than four months of salary toward paying back the recruitment fees.

The survey found that almost half the migrants queried covered this expense through loans secured from third parties, with the remainder secured by drawing on either familial or personal savings. Moreover, the survey found that the practice of contract substitution, along with other forms of misinformation about employment and working conditions, was widespread. Less than half those surveyed (44 percent) had signed a contract before migrating, and the large majority of those who had (78 percent) were forced to sign a different contract on arrival in Qatar. Fifteen percent of the workers surveyed were dispatched to a job different from the one they had agreed to, and 20 percent were paid at salary rates that differed from the wages they were promised. The survey data also captured, with somewhat less definition, the employer practice of docking workers' wages to pay recruitment costs; of the 20 percent who "sometimes, rarely, or never" received their wages on time, many indicated that the cause was deductions for recruitment fees.

In response to evidence of these troubling recruitment practices, global advocates for migrant labor in Qatar called on the Qatari government to act. Human Rights Watch's call in a 2012 report on working conditions in Qatar was emblematic: "Because recruitment fees trap thousands of workers in jobs they may not have agreed to before migrating, in abusive conditions, or conditions otherwise unsatisfactory to the worker, the Qatari government has an obligation to regulate these fees, and to prohibit practices which could lead to workers' exploitation."[21]

The Qatari government initially rebuffed these calls, noting that its labor law (Law No. 14 of 2004) prohibited any person who was licensed to recruit foreign workers from charging the worker any fees. It argued that the regulation of brokers' malfeasance fell to the countries in which they operated, that the monitoring and control of recruitment practices outside its territory was beyond its formal regulatory purview in any case, and that the government of Qatar could not be expected to be responsible for the failure of other government entities to regulate corruption and malpractice in their own countries. In response to well-documented instances of exploitative recruitment practices, the Qatari government clarified the limits of its regulatory reach, as it did in the reply it sent from its Ministry of Labor to Human Rights Watch: "Regarding the levying of fees by some manpower firms in labor-exporting states, this may indeed happen because it is outside the control of the Qatari Ministry of Labor, although the Ministry does work to limit this by asking the governments of these countries to supply it with the names of licensed, authorized recruitment firms, in order to direct employers to deal with them."[22]

Whatever half-hearted steps Qatar did take to prevent recruitment fees were ineffective. A 2017 independent audit of contractors building World Cup facilities, which were covered by the Supreme Committee for Delivery and Legacy's recruitment code of conduct banning all recruitment charges, found that 79 percent of their workers had paid recruitment fees to access their job in Qatar.[23] In March 2018, the Supreme Committee announced that contractors would reimburse more than fifty-five hundred workers from across South Asia for the fees that they had paid to recruitment agents to secure jobs in Qatar, and that the Supreme Committee was working to persuade companies it had subcontracted with to reimburse an additional thirty thousand workers who had also paid for their visas.[24] The unprecedented move was hailed as "a positive step" by the International Trade Union Confederation (ITUC), one of the leading global advocates for workers in the Qatar construction industry, which added the generous caveat that "cleaning up the recruitment process for migrant workers so they get the jobs and wages they signed up for and stopping unlawful recruitment fees which force migrant workers into debt bondage is a global challenge."[25]

The government paid the recruitment fees of migrants working on high-profile stadium sites in an attempt to make a public relations headache go away. But at base, the government agreed with the ITUC that recruitment practices were "a global challenge." It was a problem that unfolded outside Qatar. Whatever exploitative and fraudulent practices recruiters relied on to send workers to Qatar was, in the opinion of Qatar's regulatory bodies, a matter for other governments to address.

THE PRODUCTION OF LABOR FOR EXPORT

Though self-interested, Qatar's take on recruitment was in line with most scholarship and advocacy research on recruitment practices, where labor recruitment is viewed as functionally separate from the industries that use the labor supplied. In other words, companies that use migrant labor are represented as depending on recruitment agents, but not as participating in the actual process of sourcing workers, even if they sometimes influence it.[26] Whatever exploitative or usury conditions that migrants suffer in the migration process are thought to be created by recruiters and not their employer.

This industry has been characterized as "a global business" that moves unskilled labor from one country to another, and recruiters have been described as part of a "migration industry" organized around the production and commodification of labor delivered to companies operating abroad.[27] The recruitment "industry" is anchored in developing countries, where it facilitates and mediates the access to "scarce and desirable low-wage job[s] abroad."[28] In this sense, the industry engages in and profits from a form of "global wage arbitrage" powered, in these accounts, by the wage differential between countries, and more pointedly, "the waves of neoliberalization that have dispossessed millions in the global South," driving them toward "coercive labor markets in cities or in the global North."[29]

The wage differential is not enough on its own, however, to get large enough numbers of migrants to move and meet the global demand for their labor. To find people to deliver from rich countries to poor ones, the scholarship on the recruitment industry explains that recruitment relies on a complex and multilayered structure. Local brokers spread the word about jobs abroad and encourage people to sign up for them. Multiple tiers of recruitment agents shuttle potential migrants from their villages to the principal recruitment agent in the urban center. In the city, often the port of departure, agents pull migrants through an array of regulatory controls and ready them for transport to the employer that contracted the recruitment agency. Also frequently involved are lawyers, fixers, and brokers of all sorts, travel agents, and petty bureaucrats. The industry built out of this often fragmented constellation of intermediaries, described by sociologist Rubén Hernández-Leon as an "ensemble of entrepreneurs who, motivated by the pursuit of financial gain, provide a variety of services facilitating human mobility across international borders," has grown so substantial and lucrative, note many policy observers, that it "may go beyond facilitation to driving migration."[30]

Recruiters charge employers for the workers they deliver, but they also charge migrants fees for the jobs that they deliver them to. At each of the many points between their home in their village or city to their seat on the airplane heading toward their job, migrants are pressed, sometimes coercively, to pay for recruitment services. Frequently, the fees are for the costs involved in migration—for transport, visas, permits, and so on—but just as often migrants are charged additional nontransparent and predatory fees in order to access jobs abroad, including fees that have been described as "a bribe for the jobs" or even "extorted payment" for the placement, with deception about the wages and job category used to ratchet up prices.[31] Recruiters use information asymmetries to inflate their fees even further; they capitalize on the migrant's isolation and lack of information about jobs abroad, and how to access them.[32] These recruitment fees end up being substantial—hundreds, thousands, and even tens of thousands of dollars depending on the job, destination industry and country, and prospects for long-term residence.

Analysts of the recruitment industry argue that the fees that the industry charges workers are not just about profits; indebting migrants is at the core of a business model designed to produce cheap labor for export.[33] Debt is what recruiters use to discipline migrants and turn them into workers who are unable to contest their working conditions at the companies to which they are delivered.[34] Workers who need the job to pay back the debts they took on to get that job are unlikely to challenge the working conditions they experience. The deceit, abuse, and exploitation described in the analyses of recruitment are not the result of a few bad actors but instead the "systemic misconduct" around which the industry is organized.[35] Legal scholar Jennifer Gordon contends that the practices that create debt "occur at the employer's behest *before* the migrant arrives on the job," and are the reason that recruitment networks can be thought of as "human supply chains."[36] Like global supply chains organized for the production of goods, recruitment networks are supply chains that produce low-wage labor, and debt is how migrants are turned into commodities.

Although accurate in the details they lay out, these analyses all share a set of working assumptions about how recruitment functions. They start with the view that the recruitment industry follows the same business logic regardless of the country it operates in. As recruiters draw people from their cities and villages, the industry extracts people out of their communities and turns them into labor. It produces workers for—but not *with*—employers abroad. Before migrants even reach the border, recruiters will have turned them into labor commodities with characteristics that are attractive to foreign companies: inexpensive, pliable, and disposable. They then turn over these newly produced labor commodities to employers for a commission—in essence, selling workers. The commercial transaction effectively ends there. Importantly, what is being sold are individual workers, even when supplied in bulk. The workers are lifted out of context; they are no longer migrants from a specific place, community, or ecology. Once they reach the border, clear customs, and board the plane or bus, migrants have already transformed into undifferentiated labor inputs.

Because the focus has been on how recruiters turn people into labor commodities, less attention has been paid to how employers structure recruitment to get the workers that they want. Employers are assumed to all want labor that is cheap and compliant. This literature engages in a far less robust exploration of the additional or competing attributes of labor that employers look for. These include job- or industry-specific attributes like vocational skill, technical literacy, or language ability, but often also socially defined attributes that employers may associate with job performance, such as gender, race, ethnic or national origin, and religion. How those requirements, legitimate or not, shape recruitment practices in the country of origin factors only peripherally into most analyses of the recruitment business and structure of its networks.

Regulatory interventions to try to curb the excesses of the recruitment industry have by and large been based on the standard view of recruitment, with its emphasis on the use of indebting practices in the country of origin to create low-cost and pliable labor. As a result, the first regulatory move has almost always been to outlaw or cap recruitment fees.[37] As a corollary to debt, many of these regulations have targeted deceitful recruiting practices. They have required that migrants receive full information about the services that they are purchasing, specifically the jobs they are offered and schedule of fees they are changed. Additionally, regulatory interventions have mandated clarity of contract as well as an enforceable transparency around pay, working conditions, and job category. These are meant to ensure that the migrant acts as a free agent, giving informed consent to the work and wages stipulated in his contract.[38]

Critics of these regulations have focused not on whether their underlying model of recruitment is sound but rather on whether the regulations are adequately enforced. Their evaluators have noted that they are often weak and poorly administered.[39] Some have even dismissed them as being performative—a kind of regulatory playacting. Gordon notes, for example, that government agents are frequently distracted from their regulatory obligations by the remittance flows generated by temporary migration programs.[40] Still others have cautioned that the dizzying arrays of requirements that many governments have put in place—mandatory required medical exams, formal registration of the migrant with the relevant government agencies, contract certification, predeparture training, biometric data extraction, and so on—hurt more than they help. And at each stage, with each regulatory hurdle the migrant needs to clear, fees to expedite the process—both above and under the table—have created new commercial opportunities for the very actors these regulations seek to eradicate.[41] Jurisdictional issues also allow agents to wriggle out of the controls. Recruitment regulations and other labor laws apply, with few exceptions, only to the nation over which the government has jurisdiction, and because recruiters send workers across a national border and are never the employer of record, they escape sanctions and regulatory penalties when workers or their advocates complain about recruitment practices and the exploitative conditions they produce at the worksite.[42]

To be sure, the standard view of migration helps us understand the way that debt is created, the disciplinary purpose it serves, and the reasons that regulation of the industry often fails to prevent recruitment from producing forms of debt bondage. But what this take on recruitment leaves out are the ways in which employers shape recruitment practices in the countries from which they source their labor. The emphasis on recruitment industry tactics and the effectiveness of regulations designed to clamp down on them makes it hard to see the ways that employers influence recruitment practices, but even more pointedly, it makes it difficult to see that employer intervention in recruitment is a core component of their business strategy. When employer involvement in recruitment is edged out of the picture, the ways in which employers direct recruitment in order to exploit regulatory opportunities, even pitting recruiters from different countries against one another as a form of regulatory arbitrage, is left out of the analysis.

We also miss the ways in which employers' intervention in recruitment shifts as their business strategy does. We may not perceive how employers adjust and often ratchet up their involvement with recruiters when they adopt new production approaches or attempt to dodge new regulatory pressures. Additionally, we may miss the ways that employers use recruitment networks to gain access to resources other than labor, such as locking down long-term access to places where they can source workers with specific attributes and developing political channels to influence local governance practices in those communities. We may fail to see how employers have started to respond to emerging ecological changes in those places as well, and how they have pushed their recruitment agents to use the social and economic dislocations that global warming is causing.

To see how employers shape recruitment in the countries of origin, we need to change the direction of analysis. Instead of starting in the communities of origin—source countries—and following the workers' trajectory to the destination country, as most studies on recruitment do, we need to start with the firms that hire migrant workers. To understand recruitment in the countries that provide workers to Qatar—recruitment practices in Bangladesh, Nepal, India, Kenya, and many other places—we need to begin in Qatar, in the offices of managers like Majid at AEA.

Manpower Planning in Qatar

For construction firms in Qatar, access to labor was an existential concern. As managers like Majid were acutely aware, firms lived and died based on their ability to recruit workers. Qatar's construction industry was extremely labor intensive by international standards—using almost seven times as much labor as the construction industry in the United States for the same level of output. More than any other resource required for production—more than raw materials, machinery, or financing—the availability of labor determined whether firms could meet their production targets.

Companies on large construction projects—where workforces totaled several thousand men—needed armies of workers and needed them immediately. Construction is a project-driven industry, and construction firms in most economies have to recruit and hire workers when they are awarded contracts, but in Qatar, where the industry was driven by megaprojects, as described in chapter 2, firms that between projects existed as contracting offices with limited managerial staff had to ramp up their production capacities virtually overnight. They had to recruit hundreds or thousands of workers within a matter of weeks. Their demand for labor was lumpy and volatile—and always urgent.

Because the kafala system tied residence in Qatar to employment, all workers in Qatar were already employed and tied to a specific sponsor. There was no standing pool of labor from which employers could pull. This meant that hiring workers always involved hiring them from abroad. (This remained generally true even after the reforms of 2017 that allowed workers to change jobs following an agreed-on period, usually a year. Workers had no legal right to remain in Qatar between jobs and, while employed, had limited possibilities for seeking out alternative employment.) Because of this, firms engaged in detailed evaluations of different construction phases and tasks in an effort to plan out the number of workers they needed to source.

Companies used a convention called a manpower histogram to plot out how many manhours were required at each stage of the project so that they could budget out the number of workers they needed to recruit. These manpower histograms were an important topic in all the interviews I conducted around labor recruitment. "Any project has a manpower histogram," Majid explained when we spoke. With his hand, he drew the hump of the histogram in the air above his desk as he spoke. "It starts low, here, when the project starts, then it increases as production increases, like this, and then it drops down as the job finishes. You cannot just have workers arrive any time. They have to follow the histogram of the job." At ABC Builders, Saad, the manager responsible for recruitment, laid out a stack of poster-size manpower graphs on the conference table:

> The manpower histogram is king. We plan our manpower needs down to the manhour. We review our productivity levels and manpower calculations daily to see if our projections were correct. Did we overshoot? Do we need to plan for more labor? You can see here on this dashboard that we have some variances [between the manhours allocated and used]. For example, here for this time period [ten days in fall 2014] for package two, which is this back portion of the building, we have, yes, here, a variance of 1,572 manhours in masonry for this work package.

"Here, you see," continued Saad, tapping the line he spoke about, "we had budgeted 102,849 hours, but we used 104,421 hours. And of course, this has affected the plasterwork. We budgeted 147,997 hours, you see, here," he noted while pointing to a number farther down the column, "but we only used 131,699.88 hours, because we could not plaster where the masonry was delayed. We have already more manpower here for the next time period." The degree of precision in these calculations—down to the decimal—seemed strange and almost performative, especially given that the actual factors that shaped worker productivity and effort on-site were much more approximate. When I asked about this, Saad emphasized the interdependence of the different tasks that different trades would perform on a project. "If you don't plan sufficient manhours for scaffolders, then they cannot advance, and it doesn't matter how many manhours you calculate for the welders. They cannot weld if they cannot access the steel skeleton. And if the welders don't work, then your budget for the cladders [who install the glass external panels on this project] is completely off. The calculation errors get compounded," explained Saad. Majid had been more direct: "If you send me workers at the end of a task, how can I use them? If the workers don't arrive at the peak, when I need them, we will have delays, and who will compensate the company?"

Manpower dashboards like these, with histograms plotted on large sheets, papered metal desks in management trailers on every project I visited. They curled into heaps on the floor at the foot of the desks. They were tacked to cubicle walls. They filled trash bins. They were the detritus of meticulous manpower planning, acts of simulated order with variances carefully recorded, sloughed off in sheets work period after work period like old skin. They spoke to the significance of labor management and recruitment for companies. If they were unable to secure workers for their projects in the time frame they planned out, the trades they required, and the numbers they needed, production would stall. They would be forced to burn through the company's cash reserves while they waited, fending off fines imposed by the client for production delays. The cost of slowdowns produced by manpower shortages were significant for firms in the industry; study after study of the Qatari industry documented that project delays due to insufficient labor were the most frequent and expensive for companies, totaling an average of 15 percent of their operating budget on projects of US$10 million and above.[43]

The graphs, in all their extraneous and irrelevant detail, were plans that managers could cling to as they agonized over whether they would be able to obtain workers in the quantities they needed, when they needed them. In the midst of unpredictable contracts, accelerated workflows, delays in equipment delivery, and financial disputes with clients, the manpower histograms were companies' best attempt to create order in the midst of industry turmoil. For all of them, though, the greatest cause of chaos and uncertainty in the sourcing of labor was the Qatari government, and the regulatory hurdles it required that they clear before they could reach out to recruitment agents abroad—hurdles that were sometimes unofficial, often political, and always changing.

VISAS, WAGES, AND NEGOTIATIONS

In Qatar, construction companies had to begin the process of securing labor by first applying to the government for worker visas. The application process involved several steps, some formally stipulated by government regulations, and others informal and unforeseeable. Construction firms' dependence on government authorization to import workers turned the regulation of visas into a powerful lever of industrial policy and political control for the Qatari government.

For firms, the most direct exposure to government pressure through the regulation of recruitment occurred during the first phase of the visa application process. Companies drafted a formal proposal to the government to recruit workers for the project. This document, colloquially called a "labor demand letter," specified the number of workers requested by country and occupational skill, and addressed the salaries, overtime expectations and payments, accommodations, and food allowances or provisions. This letter was addressed to the Ministry of Labor. (When the ministry restructured itself as the Ministry of Administrative Development, Labor and Social Affairs in 2016, it created an online application portal that collected the information solicited in the letter.) After a review by the Ministry of Labor, the letter or application was sent to the Ministry of Interior for approval, and for large orders, the Ministry of Foreign Affairs and Qatari Chamber of Commerce for endorsement.

The letter was in many cases just the opening salvo in an extended discussion between the company and government over the source country as well as wage levels. "The letter is where the negotiations start," explained Abdulrazahk, a manager at Burg JV, a company that specialized in the framing structure for skyscrapers. "We check the system to see our approvals and then we get the shock—we get approvals for trades we didn't ask for, for countries we didn't ask for, for wage levels we didn't ask for."

The companies I spoke with reported that this initial response typically led to a consultation with officials at the Ministry of Administrative Development, Labor and Social Affairs (henceforth Ministry of Labor). Well-connected companies or those working on marquee projects also occasionally met with officials at the Ministry of Interior, which not only made the final determination for all visa applications after they were processed through the Ministry of Labor but also rigorously monitored and controlled the allocation of visas by country, occupation, wage level, and religion, sequestering the data on visa allocation from other parts of the government, most notably the Ministry of Labor, which technically operated as the window for visa applications.

This informal negotiation was the most critical stage of the labor-sourcing process.[44] But it was not officially depicted or detailed anywhere—not on the flowchart that illustrated the application procedure on the Ministry of Labor's web page or in visa regulations. "We go to meet a committee to negotiate why it is important to have the nationalities requested," recounted Osman, regional manager for business processes at ABC Builders, as he described the bargaining between the company and government.

I can apply for five hundred carpenters from Tunisia at such and such a wage, and I can make a case that I want Tunisian carpenters because the project requires some detail work and I know I can find skilled carpenters in Tunisia. And the person at the ministry will say, "Fine, you can have a block visa for five hundred Tunisian carpenters, but the wage will be one thousand [Qatari] riyal [a month]. Well, I am never going to get Tunisian carpenters, not anyone who knows what they are doing, for one thousand riyal. When we tell this to the ministry, they say, "*Inshallah kheir*" [God willing, it will work out]. So you are left with two choices: you can either try and recruit carpenters from Tunisia knowing that you will never get five hundred, or you can ask for the block grant to be allocated for another country. But you can be badly surprised to discover the country they give you is some country you have never heard of or you have never worked with. They will come back and say you can have visas for Mozambique, just to take one example, but you don't have an agent in Mozambique. And it is not easy to find an agent and create the networks. It's very expensive. Or they could say you can have Thai workers, but Thai workers make problems. Lots of drinking and gambling, and we have decided to avoid them. At that point, you have to bring the company's [Qatari] sponsor into the conversation and come to a better solution. This back and forth is crushing; it slows the whole process down. But in this case, you have to just trust in God's help, because you cannot work without workers.

In addition to defining wage levels and the country of origin for migrant workers, the government approvals process determined the trade and skill levels of the workers who could be recruited. "We try to get our workers in bulk, and we have found that it is easier to get approvals for helpers and laborers than it is for Class C scaffolders or a Level II welder," noted Osman. Requests for workers at higher skill levels often required that extra justification. The negotiation frequently required detailed descriptions of the multiple tasks and processes involved in each construction element. The success of those appeals was uneven. "You give them the information on everything, and you get the feeling that it doesn't matter," Osman gripped. In response, employers usually settled for shorter visa durations. Castle Contractors, for instance, accepted six-month visas for the Romanian rope specialists it needed for scaffolding and ceiling work, even though the company estimated that they would be required for at least a year. More typically, however, companies swapped in skill categories that they judged were easier to get. The most frequent substitution reported was to replace specialized trade visa requests with bulk applications for laborers or helpers. "It's much easier to apply for 300 laborers than it is to apply for 150 laborers [and] 100 scaffolders. I bring the scaffolders under the laborers visa and promote them after they arrive, and if I still have it in my budget, I'll pay them a bit more," explained Castle Contractors' regional manager.

The logic behind the government decisions was often opaque to companies. The stock explanation given for the rejection of an application or reallocation of the visa block to another country was national security—a rationale
that companies like ABC Builders found too risky to challenge. "For political
reasons, we have to back off immediately," remarked Osman, conceding that
the government, in his view, had a point. "We need a nationality balance in our
company—we don't want to be under pressure by any one nationality—and
in Qatar, as a country, it is the same. The government has to prevent any one
nationality from dominating," observed Osman. This government rationale
seemed long-standing; in an interview with me, a staff member at the Ministry of Labor recalled a period in the late 1990s when 80,000 out of the 400,000
foreigners in Qatar were from the Indian state of Kerala.[45] The concern of the
Qatari security apparatus then was that a social movement or labor protest
by Malayalam workers could quickly destabilize the small kingdom, with its
150,000 citizens and a greedy Saudi Arabia to its west, for whom unrest could
provide a pretext to make territorial claims on the peninsula. "One big protest
and Qatar becomes India," he recalled worrying.

Several company representatives I spoke with discretely speculated that
domestic political considerations came into play too. The political sway of the
Qatari sponsor and his proximity to the inner circles of the royal family were not
inconsequential factors in determining visa approvals. "Having a good sheikh is
the most important thing," conceded one human resource manager. "Our sponsor comes from an important family, and this keeps our applications moving."

Regardless of the factors that companies believed had most affected their
applications, those I spoke with flagged the fact that the government had a
vested interest in imposing a ceiling on wage levels. On large projects, the government was either directly or indirectly the client for whom the structures were
being built. The push to keep wage levels low also stemmed, according to several
firms I spoke with, from a misunderstanding about the contribution of workers
to productivity. "We increase manpower for two reasons," confided Saad.

> One: production requirements. Two: political. The client asks us to
> increase manpower. For them, the more men working the better and
> the quicker the project will be done. We do not add as much as they
> want us to because then it's counterproductive. Too many men slows
> down the project; it is not how many, but how well [they work]. But
> even if it creates problems and slowdowns, we have to keep adding
> them so that they can see that we are working hard. It's the client men-
> tality. But the wage bill does not increase. And we see the client joining
> hands with the government to keep salaries low.

Compared with wage bills for construction projects around the world, the
proportion of project budgets allocated for salaries in Qatar were in fact
low. In most economies, the average labor bill on construction projects was

somewhere between 30 and 50 percent of the operating costs. In Qatar, according the Qatar Statistical Authority, firms with fifty direct employees or more allocated about 20 percent of their operating costs to labor in 2015—somewhat lower than the 35 percent average for US firms. Moreover, half of the wage bill went to cover the salaries of engineers, managers, and clerks, leaving about half to pay the salaries of the 85 percent of workers who did the hands-on construction work and could be considered blue collar. But even at low wage rates, firms needed those workers to be sourced quickly so that they could remain on track with their production targets. In the Qatari construction industry, fast meant a three- to six-month window to plan out workflow, translate the manhours into the number of workers, apply for visas and regulatory clearances, and then recruit the workers needed for each of the different phases of production.

The informal negotiations over visa terms could go into repeated rounds over a period of several weeks or even months, and when they were finally complete, another round of approvals began, this time formal and clearly specified. The Ministry of Interior, Ministry of Foreign Affairs, and Qatari Chamber of Commerce each separately endorsed the final visa request. The labor demand letter was then sent on to the embassy of the origin country in Qatar for attestation as well as nominally for verification that the conditions of work met the sending country's own requirements. Once the embassy returned its approved copy to the sponsor, the firm was then free to start the process of recruitment with an agency abroad.

The Qatari government's stonewalling ground firms down because it was repeated multiple times over during the course of a project. The larger the project, the more times that firms had to go through the convoluted process of visa approval. On large projects, a lead firm coordinated the work of layers of subcontractors with different specializations, capacities, and sizes. Each subcontractor in this chain had to go through the process of getting approval for importing labor individually, and its success in obtaining a speedy and satisfactory approval was informed by the political importance of the project along with the political connections of its sponsor. On project sites, the work of firms in the subcontracting system was interdependent, and any delays imposed on one firm's ability to secure the workers it needed could have a cascading effect on other firms at the site and the project as a whole. As Saad had insisted as he guided me through his manpower histogram, if the scaffolding firms could not get approval to source workers, then the welders on-site would have no scaffold to climb, and so forth. In other words, the ability of a project to recruit workers was often only as good and fast as the slowest and most frustrated visa approval process on the site.

To cope with this heavy-handed government intervention, firms shunted the pressures created by government regulation onto their recruiters. They demanded faster turn-around times in order to make up for the delay caused by regulatory bottlenecks in Qatar. At the same time, they ratcheted up their requirements for the kind of workers that was recruited. They insisted on workers malleable enough to be upgraded into scaffolders or welders, or workers in whatever other trade was needed when they were finally delivered. But in pushing the contraints they faced onto their recruitment agencies, Qatari firms also ended up restructuring the recruitment agents they worked with within India, Ethiopia, Nepal, and other places, and ultimately compelled them to reconceptualize what the business of recruiting actually involved.

Sourcing Labor and Restructuring Recruitment

Like Majid at AEA, management and human resource teams at large construction firms across Qatar turned to larger, more established recruitment agents who had the capacity to process their large orders quickly. They looked for agents who could access potentially hundreds of recruits, process their visas and other paperwork, and put them on a plane to Qatar within weeks of receiving the order from Qatar. They sought out agents good at finding workers who could be trained for any number of roles on construction sites, irrespective of the occupation specified on their recruitment visa. In practice, this meant they favored agents who had deep networks in places where people already viewed migration as a livelihood option, but where local changes were pushing more and more people to seek it out. As a result, construction firms in Qatar, through their demands and involvement, ushered in a transformation of recruitment from the business of supplying workers to that of supplying places.

The influence on Qatari firms was more directly visible in some places that in others. In part this was because Qatar, for all its financial clout, was a small country. The labor needs of the construction industry were intense, and firms recruited workers from all over the world, but migration to Qatar, a city-state with a population of two and half million, represented only a tiny fraction of the total emigration from the many countries that sent workers to Qatar. But the influence of Qatari firms was also difficult to perceive at a distance because in most of the countries that sent workers to Qatar, recruitment was an industry that relied on a mix of formal and informal practices, many of which straddled the line between legal and illicit activity. Where agents were required to register, those ledgers were in their country of operation, not the country to which they sent labor. Documentation requirements, imposed by the government of the country of origin, did not consistently require information about the destination country, industry, or firm. Moreover, the reporting requirements for agents were uneven across countries, and where information about recruitment agencies was collected, it was either not publicly available or pockmarked with data gaps, because agents often did not comply with requirements to register or report on their activity.

Recruitment agents, however, perceived the pressures applied by their clients in Qatar clearly, and described them as influential. Agents I spoke with in Nepal, India, and the Philippines explained that to respond to the demands that they received from Qatari firms, they had begun to change the way they did business. Qatari firms' demand for bulk labor that was cheap but highly trainable had been a boon for firms large as well as established enough to fill these specific orders, and it had been a death knell for others. The pressures from abroad were dividing the local recruitment industry into a segment of winners and a segment of losers.

These changes were most visible to me in Nepal. Every single construction firm I observed in Qatar recruited migrant workers from Nepal, whether as laborers or more experienced tradesmen. In Kathmandu, I interviewed the directors and staff at the main recruitment agencies that my Qatari contacts used and observed the practices through which they selected recruits and expedited their visas. I followed the recruitment networks that those companies used to small towns and villages in the southern belly of Nepal where they recruited migrants. During my fieldwork, a manager from one of the companies I had studied in Qatar traveled to Kathmandu on a recruiting trip. I was able to observe firsthand the interactions between the representative of the Qatari company and the recruitment agency in Nepal as they discussed the attributes they sought in their recruits, number of workers and other order specifications, and additional business matters.

I also conducted interviews at recruitment agencies that my contacts in Qatar did not use, although some of those agencies did supply migrant workers to Qatar. I visited twelve agencies in total. I spoke with the government agencies that regulated the recruitment industry and tried to link emigration with national development, especially the Ministry of Labor and Employment and its Department of Foreign Employment. I followed up with local and international nongovernmental organizations that were seeking to improve recruitment practices and protect workers from indenture and disinformation in the recruitment process.

For the recruitment agencies I studied, Qatar was an important market—almost always their most important one—and the preferences of their Qatari clients changed how they did business. This was a reflection of the fact that for Nepal, Qatar was the second most important destination for migrants emigrating on a worker visa, right on the heels of Malaysia, which was the top destination.[46] Between 2008 and 2017, 22 percent of Nepalis emigrating for work went to Qatar, and the number of labor permits for employment in Qatar that were issued by the Nepali Department of Foreign Employment, a requirement for labor migration, surged, tripling from 50,000 to 130,000 per year over the course of the decade. When it came to the renewal of labor permits, Qatar beat out Malaysia; contract extension for Qatar represented a third of all applications.

Migrants from Nepal had a common sociodemographic profile. Most migrants were men; 95 percent of the exit permits for labor emigration that the government issued between 2008 and 2017 went to men. Approximately 62 percent of those men emigrated for construction jobs, and another 16 percent worked as drivers or security personnel—jobs that were in high demand on construction sites in Qatar. Emigration from Nepal was also highly concentrated geographically. While government data on Nepali emigration do not break down migration to a specific destination country by the province or district that migrants are from, the information available is suggestive: 65 percent of all migrants between 2008 and 2017 heralded from the Terai region, the plains at Nepal's border with India, and the vast majority of those came from only ten districts in that region, with Dhanusha topping the list. More than 70 percent of the migrants from Dhanusha, most from the villages around the temple city of Janakpur, traveled to Qatar or Saudi Arabia, with the remainder traveling to Malaysia or crossing the border into India.[47] The recruiters I interviewed sourced workers from Dhanusha. The prevalence of recruitment activity in Dhanusha was everywhere; in the towns and small cities that I was able to visit, every other storefront seemed to offer a service related to migration, such as long-distance cell phone services, vaccinations, photos for passports, and money transfers.

PROFESSIONALIZING RECRUITMENT

On paper, it looked as if the recruitment industry in Nepal was booming, with recruitment agencies proliferating to take advantage of the growing business of out-migration; 752 recruitment agents were registered with the government of Nepal in 2014.[48] But a closer look at contracting patterns suggests that only a fraction of these hundreds of recruitment firms was thriving. The recruiting industry, undifferentiated in analytic reports on migrant recruiting and characterized as following a uniform set of business practices, was actually two separate industries: a top tier with large professionalized agents in Kathmandu, and lower tier populated with small, semiformal outfits throughout the country.

Bulk labor orders increasingly went to the professionalized recruitment companies in the capital, likely no more than a dozen in Nepal, each of which processed hundreds and in some cases thousands of workers a year. They had strong and often exclusive contractual relationships with a handful— sometimes no more than two or three—large construction companies, many of which operated in several international markets in addition to Qatar and requested labor for those projects as well. By their own account, these recruiters made their profits off the volume of workers they supplied rather than through extractive pricing directed at workers. They operated as principle agents, aggregating smaller batches of recruits from subagents and processing them for delivery to a single employer. They tended not to charge workers any direct fees over the legal maximum in their country of operation (capped at 20,000 Nepalese rupees, or about US$175, and lowered to 10,000 rupees in 2016, or approximately $90).[49] Most of their profits were derived instead from the fee they charged the Qatari firms that retained their services; the industry standard for the base charge was one month of salary per worker at the rate stipulated in the contract. They also frequently bundled in the costs of processing the visa and fulfilling other regulatory requirements, like a medical exam and the costs of travel. The owner of a large recruitment agency in Kathmandu explained his fee structure in the following way: "I move ten thousand workers a year, minimum, mostly to Qatar but other countries also. I have a staff of five people here in Kathmandu. If you understand what your product is, it is easy to make money in this business. I am not selling visas. I am selling workers. Why would I charge workers? Why would I charge a fee that would make it difficult for me to get my product? It makes no sense." Another agent compared overcharging migrants for their recruitment to charging biscuits for the privilege of sitting on a grocer's shelves.

Meanwhile, small and medium recruiting firms housed in storefronts on the outskirts of Kathmandu or in smaller provincial cities still made most of their money off the fees they charged migrants. These agencies were set up by anyone who could raise the 3,020,000 rupees, or approximately US$30,000, in combined registration and bank guarantee fees. According to the membership records of the National Association of Foreign Employment Agency, where agencies were required by law to register, these types of agencies had doubled in the decade since 2005.[50] Recruitment agencies that had once been midsize and established scrambled against this new competition for scraps of orders, barely more than tens of workers at a time, and struggled to stay afloat. The orders that came into this lower segment of the recruitment market were also from smaller overseas clients, many of which, according to interviews with firms in this segment, haggled doggedly to bring down the recruitment fees that they would pay. To get an order, any order, some recruitment agencies in this lower tier paid kickbacks to the firms that hired them—or rather the specific manager in those firms—in exchange for business. The costs of these bribes for business were passed onto the migrants, tacked onto the high recruitment fees they were already facing.

In the upper layer of the recruitment industry, meanwhile, recruitment agencies used their revenue inflows to increase their internal capacity. They upgraded their operations. They hired staff fluent in the languages in which they conducted business—primarily English. They retained lawyers or paralegals who could draft commercial contracts written in legal language that made them seem binding, even though they often could not be enforced, and invested in high-end teleconferencing facilities and data management programs. Their offices typically had well-appointed reception areas and workspaces that their foreign clients could use when they were in Kathmandu on trips for recruitment.

Most important, though, recruitment agents in the top tier strengthened their ability to move visas quickly through the regulatory process. As one agent explained,

> Delays in the process are very costly for us. We buy plane tickets, and then they get annulled because of delays, so we have to buy them again. And companies blame you and will not return to work with you if you have these delays. So you cannot pass along the costs to them and hope to stay in business. The client is coming to you because he requires workers, and if you cannot deliver them, he will still need workers. He will not wait. He will go to someone else.

The regulatory process for emigration approval involved the completion of several steps, including a medical exam or attendance at a predeparture training. Because of legal restrictions, recruitment agents could not bring these services in-house—the predeparture training had to be delivered by one of the 147 centers registered with the government's Department of Foreign Employment, for example—but to ensure that they had privileged access, allowing them to jump the queue if necessary, they formed exclusive or priority partnerships with the organizations or medical personnel that provided these services. Each of these regulatory steps required government attestation that they had been completed. Larger agencies addressed these delays in the approvals process by paying formal and informal expediting fees to both the bureaucracies and individual bureaucrats charged with reviewing visa applications. Cash bundles that I saw paper-clipped to stacks of applications undoubtedly sped the approvals process along. Ultimately, however, the larger contributions that firms made to political candidates and government executives may have been more consequential. "We support political parties that are in favor of the recruitment agencies—it is part of the cost of doing business—but there is a return on this investment in parliament," said one firm owner.

Yet no matter how professionalized, efficient, or urbane larger recruiters became, their business still relied on networks of informal brokers in small towns and villages far from Kathmandu that delivered the migrants they needed to fill their orders. The local agents were not officially in their employ, nor did the large recruitment agencies typically pay them a commission (although some reported that they did pay informal retainers to motivate the brokers and guarantee that any potential migrants would be directed exclusively to them). But these brokers, deeply embedded in local social networks, were an essential link between the centralized operations of large recruiters and communities where the workers were sourced. Large recruitment agents simply could not function without the everyday scouting, cajoling, and coaching of the brokers who delivered migrants to them. The owner of the

Bright Futures recruitment agency noted, "We run newspaper advertisements for seven days as required by law, but this is not how we find workers. You need local connections to let people know that there is a call for workers." The owner of Horizons recruitment agency recounted that his father started out as a local broker before establishing the firm in Kathmandu. "My father started out thirty years ago. He helped connect a businessman in Oman with people he knew wanted to go abroad for work. He was the bridge for people to their futures. This is honorable work." He added that the local knowledge and social connections that brokers brought to their work was a crucial resource without which Horizons could not operate. "They know the local area. They know which family has someone ready to leave for work, and the families know them. They know whether the person who wants to leave is really ready. They know who has the right mind for the work [in] a place like Qatar. This is important."

These local brokers—small town notables, respected uncles, well-connected hustlers, self-styled "social workers," and village youths who made good through migration—connected potential migrants to the principal recruiter and facilitated any logistics that the main recruiter did not resolve. They arranged travel from remote villages to city centers and secured lodging for migrants through their transit. They helped villagers obtain the government documents they would need to migrate, such as birth certificates and passports, and navigate the bureaucratic processes they needed to secure them. They referred them to moneylenders who could finance the recruitment costs and showed them how to transfer remittances back to their families. Community members turned to brokers for these services because they were known and often trusted. Data from a 2013 study by the Asia Foundation tracked these social connections, reporting that 35 percent of the Nepali migrant workers surveyed were personally acquainted with their broker, and another 57 percent were introduced to their broker through a family member, neighbor, or friend.[51]

Still, local brokers charged for the connections they made and logistical services they provided—sometimes at a remarkable premium.[52] The average fee that Nepali workers paid for migration to Qatar was 103,000 rupees, or about $905.[53] While the research on the costs of emigration does not break down these charges by the actor that charged them, studies on brokerage in Nepal suggest that local brokers were behind a thick slice of these fees, if not the lion's share. Brokers often skimmed additional profit off the loan that more than 80 percent of recruits took to finance the cost of migration, taking a commission from the moneylenders who charged cash-poor recruits an average of 35 percent interest (as opposed to the 17 percent charged by formal institutions), if they did not provide the loan themselves.[54] Though lucrative for the individual broker, these fees made migration less affordable to families contemplating sending one of their members abroad.

Thus, even though large recruiters could only operate thanks to their local, informal brokers, they were also constrained by this dependence. Principal recruiting agents received bulk orders for hundreds of workers at a time—orders that almost always needed to be filled within a short time frame—but brokers delivered workers one by one, inconsistently and opportunistically, whenever someone in a local community decided to migrate in search of work and could raise the funds to do so. Principal agents might have been able to increase the yield of their brokers by offering jobs that paid higher salaries, but wages were set by their clients in Qatar and elsewhere. Recruiters I spoke with complained that they struggled to attract workers in the numbers their clients requested and at the speed they demanded given the wage rates those clients specified. "There is a general shortage of workers. They are difficult to find because there is a lot of competition. If the hiring company is offering a good salary, we find workers. Now, that's eight hundred to a thousand QR [Qatari riyals] minimum (about US$220 to US$270) with an additional food stipend. Anything less than eight hundred, we don't bother. We cannot find workers," said the director of the Gulf Connections recruitment agency. With salaries for most construction work in Qatar no longer competitive in Kathmandu or even secondary cities, recruitment agents increasingly relied on their brokers working in rural areas for workers. Yet even the recruits yielded by those networks only dribbled in. The only way to increase the supply of workers was to increase the demand for their brokers' services.

Recruiting Places

Recruiters, straining to fill bulk orders for workers, commented that they had begun to explore new place-based strategies for recruitment to increase the number of workers their brokers could send in. They focused on brokers in the remote areas that still yielded workers at the price their clients would pay and deepened their networks there, increasing the number of brokers working for them. They offered their existing brokers financial incentives to draw people into brokerage and promoted them, unofficially since brokers were not formally employed by the principal agents, into the role of subagents who were responsible for the network of brokers below them. They paid them for workers that the networks below them yielded.

But this was not sufficient. Principal recruiting agents expanded their operations into areas that were similar to the places where they already worked but where brokerage networks were still thin. To expand their outreach to new territory, they used the same professionalized approaches they applied to the rest of their business. They evaluated new regions based on geographic contiguity, but also based on indicators such as the prevailing wage levels, relative rurality of economic activity, and existence of migration patterns, primarily rural to urban, that they could connect with and draw from. A manager at Big

Sky recruitment agency explained, "We know what places give us workers. We look for places that look like those we already work in—same villages, same economy, same culture." Once they identified new places for recruitment, they dispatched staff or subagents to do the delicate work of identifying community members who were trusted and esteemed, and could be recruited into the brokerage network.

As recruiters shifted from a focus on recruiting persons to a strategy of recruiting places, they paid attention to the social and economic changes in those places. By extension, they engaged with any ecological changes those places were experiencing. Unlike construction firms in Qatar, whose managers made an explicit connection between climate damage and recruitment prospects, agents in Nepal did not deliberately modify their recruitment strategy to capitalize on climate damage; no recruiter I spoke with described selecting places solely or primarily based on the impact of climate change. They did, however, refer to the social and economic dislocations that those places had suffered, sometimes as a consequence of ecological pressures, in explaining why they targeted them for recruitment. The manager at Big Sky remarked, for example, "We are not seeking to convince anyone to go abroad. We want to go to places where people already need to go abroad and connect them with opportunities." The owner of the Horizons agency similarly reflected, "There are places where people understand that they have no future. Sometimes those places never had a future, and sometimes the future has moved elsewhere. We can offer a future."

The recruiting agencies I studied all had begun to reorganize their businesses to prioritize this place-based approach. Those that recruited from the Terai plains, in and around Dhanusha, for example, doubled down on their operations there, extending their networks of subagents further outward to more remote towns and villages where they could find workers still willing to migrate for the wages Qatari firms offered. They drafted additional uncles and middlemen to recruit workers, and sought out local moneylenders, prized for their information about who needed a job abroad and who could borrow to pay the fees associated with getting it.

Not coincidentally, the Terai was increasingly straining under the effects of global warming, and people in the villages like those the recruiters invested in were already using migration to cope. Beginning in the 2000s, when emigration to Qatar and other places first picked up momentum, the Terai had suffered the lashing of unusually forceful monsoon rains. According government records, monsoons since the 2000s frequently arrived days late, and when they did, the rainfall was exceptionally and even violently heavy, breaking records for rainfall during a single-day period. The extreme downpours caused rivers and their tributaries in the flatlands of the Terai to breach their banks, producing catastrophic floods and landslides. Generally the damage was localized, but it was still severe, sweeping away hundreds or thousands of homes, year after year, and leaving dozens dead. The change in monsoon patterns, especially newly abrupt and violent rainfall, destroyed livelihoods and family assets. Migration along with the income that a worker could earn abroad was becoming a hedge that more and more families used against weather that was growing unpredictable and unrecognizable.[55]

Although Nepal was designated as a "white spot" by the Intergovernmental Panel on Climate Change, for the first time in its 2001 report as well as its subsequent reports, because of the paucity of data about observable and projected climate change effects in the country, the available information suggested that the country was highly susceptible to climate change impacts.[56] Nepal was ranked as the fourth most vulnerable country to climate change in the world and had already experienced a marked increase in hydrometeorologic extreme events such as droughts, storms, floods, landslides, soil erosion, and avalanches. In part, Nepal's vulnerability to climate change stemmed from the interplay between the diversity of its ecosystems and reliance on agriculture.[57] In its steep descent from the Himalayas, the small sliver of a country moved through three distinct ecological layers: snow-covered mountains in the north, forested hills in the midcountry, and the Terai plains in the south. Each of these different ecosystems is a patchwork of microclimates, with distinct flora and fauna. As a result, the 70 percent of the Nepali population that in the 2010s lived off subsistence and small-scale agriculture had developed highly localized and specific agricultural practices. These were fragile and vulnerable to even small changes in the climate.

But the changes were not small. By 2015, the mountainous north of Nepal had already lost more than a quarter of glacier mass in the three preceeding decades, and glaciers continued to retreat at a clip of forty kilometers squared per year, with consequences that were felt through each of the country's ecological layers and hurtled down all the way to the lowlands of the Terai.[58] In the north, the accelerated rate of melt destabilized ice sheets, triggered avalanches, and increased the risk of catastrophic flash floods from glacial lakes, which breached their banks and released massive waves that mixed with gravel and mud from the demolished moraines in their path.[59] The flood outbursts had calamitous impacts on downstream communities, washing away topsoil, and destroying hydropower installations and infrastructure.[60] In the middle hills region of Nepal, forests started to dry out, and farmers had begun to observe that their water resources—springs, streams, and wells—had become more meager.[61] Increasingly erratic monsoon patterns hurt rain-fed agriculture in the hills, and when the monsoons did arrive, sometimes weeks after they were anticipated, the rains fell in torrents, often washing away the terraces painstakingly carved into the hillsides to provide beds for the crops.[62]

The Terai arc, at the bottom of the country, was where the changes were most pronounced. The temperatures there had climbed twice as fast since the 1980s as in the rest of Nepal. The summer monsoon rains became unusually heavy, but they also started to arrive several weeks off phase, dessicating seed-lings or drowning them after they had taken root. Long droughts interrupted the erratic rains, causing water reserves at the surface to dry out and under-ground water tables to plummet. Rains that failed to arrive in the hills shriv-eled rivers that carried water down to the lowlands, so that some years they had run completely dry by April or May, leaving the Terai parched and without relief.[63]

Because the lowlands of the Terai comprised close to half of the arable land in Nepal, with more than 80 percent of the land under cultivation, these changes to the climate had important impacts on the livelihoods of the nine million Nepalis who lived in this narrow arc—and turned some of those nine million into potential recruits for agents like Bright Futures, Horizons, and others.[64]

The variable precipitation patterns strained customary cropping practices, and faced with yields that dropped by as much as 30 percent during flood or drought years, farmers began to move away from traditional staples such as rice toward crops that required less water or were more resistant to extremes in water availability.[65] In the Dhanusha district, where I followed Horizons' recruitment networks and trailed brokers in local villages, farmers were cop-ing with increasingly variable rainfall by shifting from rice to wheat cultiva-tion.[66] To change over to new crops, families needed cash. Wheat and other new crops were often out of sync with environmental cycles like the availabil-ity of pollinators and required investments of seed, fertilizer, or other inputs.[67] Additionally, residents faced new pest- and vector-borne disease burdens, such as malaria, Japanese encephalitis, and dengue fever, and had to buy new chemicals to protect the health of their families and crops.[68]

These climate change effects only magnified the significance of migra-tion as an economic coping strategy in an area where families had historically relied on it.[69] The Terai was a place with a long tradition of migration—both in-migration and out-migration.[70] Partly as a result of those population flows, the plains emerged as the site of some of the fastest economic growth and development in the region, with infrastructure development and agribusiness efforts booming in relative terms.[71] The Terai became more prosperous than other regions in Nepal, with poverty rates 15 percentage points lower than the national average.[72]

The migration of one or more family members was a common livelihood strategy, even for families with good incomes, used as a source of capital for agricultural investments or insurance against a bad harvest, and as the earth began to fail them, families relied on it more and more.[73] Recruiters for the construction industry in Qatar entered into these plains where fields and families faced new climate stress and offered a ready pathway for households to send a brother, father, or son abroad. To fill the massive labor orders they received from their clients, agents like Horizons and Blue Sky drew the Terai even further into their operations, pulling in stretches of territory where the demand for foreign jobs grew with each failed crop and each purchase of fertilizer for overtired fields.

The recruiters I studied also followed the migration patterns they drew on in the Terai into places when they had no previous recruitment operations, including beyond Nepal. Migration patterns in the Terai had for decades stretched across the frontier with India, which for all intents and purposes remained an open border since the two countries signed the Nepal-India Treaty of Peace in 1950. Because the treaty allowed for free movement, no formal tabulations of exits to India were recorded, but the Nepali government estimated in 2011 that close to 40 percent of all emigration was to India. Families used migration to India to supplement their household income, sometimes seasonally and sometimes indefinitely. Almost 90 percent of the men migrating to India reported to the Nepali National Demographic and Health Survey of 2011 that they were seeking work.[74]

As agents turned to place-based recruitment strategy, they began to plug into these migration patterns and expand their Nepali operations south across the border. They extended their recruitment networks and infrastructure into Bihar and Uttar Pradesh. The owner of the Horizons recruitment agency explained why he had recently started recruiting in border areas of Bihar. The landholding patterns there were similar to those in Nepal, if somewhat more precarious, with the vast majority of farmers (90 percent) holding less than an acre of land. "We have had success [in Bihar]. It's very rural, and very similar in economic structure to rural areas here in Nepal. It's an open border; people have been going back and forth for a long time," he explained.

And just like in Nepal, climate change effects were making family incomes more variable.[75] The wetlands of North Bihar, long fed by the meandering tributaries of the Ganga River, had begun to dry out due to a decline in rainfall, compounded by human-made attempts to direct the river.[76] Families were responding to these new pressures by migrating; the region had seen an uptick in population mobility.[77] The owner of Horizons explained that the rise in migration had been a boon to his company, observing, "We can get workers in Bihar at salaries that we sometimes have difficulty finding Nepali workers. We escape some of the controls [regulatory requirements] here in Nepal, and that also allows us to reduce costs." He added that the main challenge of extending operations in Bihar was building a network of brokers: "These local agents [in Bihar], they act on their own account. We have a representative in Lucknow and we are working now to connect with them."

In plugging into migration patterns, the recruiters I studied were using a place-based strategy where place was defined by economy and ecology, not by nation and regulations. Their recruitment activities across the border were legally liminal, to be sure, but it allowed recruiters to provide their Qatari clients with both Nepali and Indian workers. This gave Qatari firms more flexibility in dealing with their government's visa approvals process. If the Qatari government limited the number of Nepali visas on a given project site, for example, the Qatari construction company could ask for visas for Indian workers instead, knowing that they could rely on the same recruiter they used in Nepal to fill their request for Indian workers.

Seeking Absorptive Capacity

This place-based strategy allowed recruiters to fill the large orders for low-cost workers that they received from their clients and do so quickly, within a matter of weeks. But the real value of that strategy was that it enabled recruiters to provide Qatari companies with workers that had the specific attributes that they sought. While the scholarship on recruitment may emphasize the role that recruiters play in *making* workers for their clients, and highlight their use of debt to transform migrants into compliant and exploitable labor, the recruiters I interviewed in Nepal stressed instead that their clients wanted to be the ones to make their workers. Their Qatari clients wanted migrants who they could import under the easily available visa categories of "laborer" and "helper," but who they could train into scaffolders, steel fixers, or carpenters— migrants that they could make into whatever kind of worker they needed when their labor order finally arrived. Qatari employers wanted migrants who had what business analysts have called "absorptive capacity": the capacity to understand new information they were provided on-site, assimilate it, and apply it unquestioningly to their construction tasks.[78]

Qatari firms assessed absorptive capacity as stemming from two sets of attributes. The first was a basic level of formal schooling. They requested workers who had arithmetic ability, functional literacy, and spatial awareness. Reading and counting were essential to the everyday work on construction sites in Qatar, but firms also viewed these school-taught abilities as providing the foundation for learning the technical tasks involved in scaffolding, steel fixing, cladding, and so on, and especially for understanding how specific tasks fit into the overall building process. Qatari firms wanted workers who could learn to identify the relationship between building tasks and elements—to understand how tightening joints on a scaffold led to its stability or that a foundation supported walls.

In the Terai region, recruiters could find workers with this basic level of schooling. Educational coverage and outcomes in Nepal as a whole were somewhat weak, undermined by more than a decade of social unrest due to Maoist insurgency (brought to a close with the Comprehensive Peace Accords in 2006). Yet they were better in Terai than in any other region in the country, save for the Kathmandu area. Literacy in the Terai was several percentage points higher than in the rest of Nepal, at 65 percent compared to 60 percent in 2011, and 72 percent compared to 69 percent in 2019.[79] Likewise, access to school was better in the Terai. In 2010, 98 percent of the children in the Terai had a school within a thirty-minute walk versus only 90 percent of the children in the country overall.[80] Most labor emigrants from Nepal, to destinations other than India, had between six and ten years of schooling, according to a World Bank analysis covering 2010 and 2011, and the recruiters I spoke with reported having no difficulty finding candidates with that level of formal education or more in the Terai.[81]

The second attribute Qatari firms sought was the more subjective quality of being "good learners." While descriptions of this quality were somewhat vague, both employers and recruiters seemed to view it as the capacity to understand and follow directions, and adapt them to the setting where the task was taking place and the materials being manipulated. Employers deemed this attribute as crucial to absorptive capacity and required the larger professionalized recruitment agencies they used to test for it before they sent migrant recruits onward to Qatar. Specifically, they pressed them to develop a highly prospective version of trade testing.

In general, trade testing is the process of evaluating proficiency in a given trade against a standardized set of competencies. The assessment normally considers the skill that the worker taking the test has already acquired. So, for example, a trade test for welders aks job candidates to weld metal pieces together, and the soldered seam will then be evaluated for soundness; a trade test for carpenters asks candidates to build a wood frame, which is then tested for structural integrity; and so on, based on the trade. But Qatari firms directed their agents to design the tests to screen for absorptive capacity as opposed to acquired skill. They wanted recruitment agents to evaluate whether candidates had the foundation to interpret and follow orders in contexts that were unfamiliar to them.

For recruiters, trade testing—especially testing for subjectively defined potential as opposed to demonstrated competence—was an extra and unwelcome expense. It meant that in addition to the intricate systems they developed to draw people up from villages in the Terai and move them through a convoluted regulatory gauntlet, they had to develop an entirely new array of business practices to assess whether their recruits had the qualities that Qatari firms viewed as making them trainable. The evaluation required the agency to rent out a facility that could hold large numbers of potential recruits, hundreds at a time, for one to several days. The facility had to come equipped with the materials that firms used to evaluate potential recruits—soldering equipment for welding, tubes and planks for scaffolding, and wood or steel along with basic architectural plans for carpenters and steel fixers as well as any other materials that employers requested to run their tests. Most difficult for recruitment agencies was finding evaluators who could judge absorptive capacity. They had to find evaluators able to assess process and not just the finished product—evaluators who could, for instance, assess the potential of a welder by how he handled the torch and not just by the finished seam that he had welded.

This absorptive capacity was so critical to production on construction sites in Qatar that client firms frequently stepped in to evaluate candidates themselves. They sent company representatives to observe the trade tests and make the final selection of the candidates they would hire. When I asked human resource managers and trade supervisors at Qatari companies about trade testing as well as the criteria they used to select workers, they described a quick and somewhat chaotic evaluation. Stephen, a human resource manager at Castle Contractors for scaffolding, described asking candidates to walk on a beam raised a foot off the floor while carrying scaffolding pipes to test their balance. The trade test also included some technical assessment—such as how to create a right-angle brace—but as Stephen explained, these trade-specific components were marginal to the evaluation. "The trade test has a theoretical part and a practical part, where we see if they can use tools, electrical rods, machines and so on. If a worker fails the practical part, we still give them a grade A if they have the correct attitude. We take all the As first, and then we move down the line to the Bs and the Cs." Similarly, when ABC Builders' scaffolding manager, Robbie, went on recruiting trips, he asked candidates to build a scaffolding frame on the ground. "It doesn't much matter if they can do it; most can't. I am just trying to get a sense of whether they have a feel for the material, whether they have a feel for how to build something that is solid. Do they understand what an angle is, and how to brace a structure?" The assessment itself was fast—a matter of minutes. "You get a feel for who is going to work, by the way they move, and by the way they respond. You can see if they are listening and bright, or if they are just going through the motions," added Robbie.

This "testing by feel" approach to evaluating candidates resulted in a high failure rate. The recruitment agencies I studied reported that their clients did not explicitly define the exact traits that they wanted, and that as a result, fully one-third to one-half of all the candidates evaluated in any given trade testing session would fail to meet the employer's threshold for absorptive capacity. Robbie concurred, although his take was more sanguine than that of the recruitment agencies, which had to absorb the business costs of the high failure rate: "When I go on recruiting trips to Nepal, I feel like a rock star," said Robbie. "Wherever I go, there are hundreds of workers waiting for me. For three hundred slots, they'll be fifteen hundred guys waiting, and I have to trade test them all in three, really two and a half, days." To bring those fifteen hundred men to Kathmandu for Robbie to evaluate, the recruitment agency would already have had to make a significant investment: it would have already paid the costs associated with its intricate brokerage network, the fees for multiple bureaucratic transactions, and the charges for the transport and lodging of candidates. To manage these costs, some agencies redirected candidates who failed the trade tests to ones they ran for other clients. Gulf Connections reported using the recruits who flunked trade tests to fill orders for manpower agencies, which typically had lower requirements for absorptive capacity, if any. Still, as the owner of Blue Sky observed, this was a partial response at best. "When a worker is not good for one company, he is [just] not good."

To survive the high failure rate of their trade tests, companies like Blue Sky relied on the high yield of their place-based recruitment strategies. For the investment they made in their recruitment infrastructure in the Terai and neighboring Bihar, they were able to pull in good numbers of workers. The economies of scale that place-based strategies offered them, especially in places experiencing ecological dislocation, positioned them to absorb the business risks that their Qatari clients lobbed at them with each new trade test they demanded.

Some Qatari companies off-loaded even more of the uncertainty involved in assessing absorptive capacity onto the recruitment agencies that they used. They worked with their main recruitment agents to design and set up predeparture training systems, patterned on the specific and proprietary model of training used in the Qatari firm. These were short in duration—no longer than a few days—but they allowed for a more fine-grained assessment of a candidate's ability to learn. In this sense, these predeparture training courses enabled Qatari firms to outsource the probationary period during which they evaluated workers for absorptive capacity after arrival, and to avoid the logistic outlays and time delay involved in sending back the fraction of their labor order that did not meet their standards.

ABC Builders, for example, collaborated with the Blue Sky recruitment agency to set up a predeparture training course in Kathmandu for scaffolding recruits. As part of this initiative, the Qatari company invited the owner of the agency to its training center near Doha, described in the previous chapter, to observe the methodology that the company had developed to deepen the scaffolding skills of its workforce. This field trip involved a detailed analysis of the curriculum, real-time participant observation in the training process, and a basic introduction to scaffolding engineering. A scaffolding engineer from ABC Builders subsequently traveled to Kathmandu to help structure the training center for Blue Sky, advising the agency on the physical design and layout of the training site. The engineer also worked with the agent to develop the tests to be administered at the completion of the short training. In a distinction that the owner of Big Sky found frustratingly nuanced, the engineer insisted that the tests be designed not to measure technical competence but rather to assess absorptive capacity by tracking how much each candidate had been able to absorb over the course of the training module. Big Sky was being asked, in the estimation of its owner, to measure as well as absorb the costs of measuring "the minds of people."

CAPACITY BUT NOT COMPETENCE

It wasn't just that Qatari firms wanted workers who had the ability to acquire skill; they actively did not want workers who had already acquired skill. Some of the reluctance stemmed from the fact that it was difficult and costly for the recruiters as well as their clients to verify vocational competence. "Brokers will send people they say have the qualifications, but when you see them, you realize that they don't. They'll send you someone who they say is a master carpenter, for form building, and they will ask for thirteen hundred Qatari riyals [as a monthly wage]. But you find that he is a village carpenter, who builds tables for his neighbors," gripped the owner of Gulf Connections. Additionally, Qatari employers viewed the trade skill offered in Nepali vocational training programs as maladapted and inadequate to the advanced construction methods used in Qatar. Data on the performance of national programs in technical and vocational training in Nepal lend credence to employers' complaints; even though 120,000 people passed through the Nepali TVET system annually as of 2014, less than 4,000 workers received technical training as a preparation for skilled or semiskilled positions abroad. An evaluation of TVET programs, conducted by the Centre for the Study of Labour and Mobility in Kathmandu, found that the training was in any case useless to recruitment agencies and the international clients. "Recruitment agencies are of the view that . . . the training provided in operating machinery/equipment is hardly adequate in the countries of destination which are technologically more "advanced" or "modern" than Nepal. . . . That is one of the primary reasons why recruitment agencies routinely conduct skills tests for technical positions, even when workers possess CTEVT certification," concluded the report.[82]

Qatari firms' reluctance to hire trained workers stemmed from a skills mismatch, to be sure, but it also grew out of a concern with worker compliance and a definition of skill that prioritized rote obedience to directions over the development of deep technical fluency. In describing the absorptive capacity they sought, human resource directors and trade testers at Qatari firms explained that they were looking not just for the difficult-to-define quality of the "ability to learn" but also for clear evidence of a "willingness to learn" and "ability to take direction"—"people who will follow orders," quipped Stephen of Castle Contractors. ABC Builders internal recruiting policy documents explicitly specified that evaluators should take into account "the applicant's personality, attitude, and character."

While in Kathmandu, I was able to observe how concerns about worker discipline got folded into the assessment of workers' ability to learn. I accompanied the scaffolding manager from ABC Builders, Robbie, on a recruiting visit to a training center set up in 2011 by Helvetas, a Swiss development organization, to provide vocational training specifically designed for aspiring migrants. The program, called the Safer Migration Project—or SaMi as it was colloquially known—targeted rural residents who had some secondary education—propective migrants who had the profile that recruiters for Qatari firms were sourcing from Terai. By the time I visited in late 2014, the program had enrolled two thousand participants. It gave them forty-five days of intensive training in one of eight different construction occupations: "Steel Fixer, Shuttering Carpenter, Scaffolder, Plumber, Electrician, Mason, Aluminum Fabricator, [and] Welder" as well as lessons in basic English and tips for managing the intense heat of the Arabian peninsula. The explicit goal of the training was to improve the bargaining position of young men migrating for the first time, enabling them to push for higher wages and working conditions. "Workers that have been trained through our program can refuse lower jobs: they say, 'I am not a laborer. I am a scaffolder.' Scaffolding is where we see the highest demand. Or 'I am electrician, a steel fixer,' and so on. They can now argue," noted the program manager.

In the courtyard that flanked the SaMi training center, teams of men were building basic one- and two-story scaffolding structures with reclaimed scaffolding planks and tubes. Their trainer, dressed in a white puffer coat and jeans that Robbie loudly derided as ostentatious in color for a construction school ("Anyone with an outfit that clean and shiny has not worked construction a day in his life"), was a scaffolder who had gotten the gig after a little over a decade working in Qatar, and he wandered from team to team giving them directions. Robbie was unimpressed. "Look at this!" he said as he walked through the courtyard and pointed out elements of the structures that the students had built. "Look at this joint right here. The bracing here is incorrect. You'll have to teach them all over again, except they won't listen, will they, because they'll already know what they are doing." Later, after checking out the storage area for scaffolding materials in the shed at the far end of the yard and scoffing derisively at the heap of mismatched tubes on the concrete floor, he added, "They develop bad habits. The work is sloppy, and let me tell you, sloppy on top of sloppy equals dangerous—and expensive. Worst thing you can do is to hire bad habits."

According to SaMi's own reports, Robbie's reluctance to hire workers' from the SaMi program was widely shared. "Our completion rates are not what we would like," said the SaMi program manager. "Recruitment agents come to us, asking for trainees, scaffolders, steel fixers, and masons, but they will take them before they complete the training. We are trying to work with recruiters who will respect the duration of the program," she added as she listed the agents, all large agencies, that SaMi worked with, "but unfortunately, even in these cases, we cannot compel them to let workers finish the training." SaMi's mission was to empower workers by equipping with them with measurable and certified trade skill, but Qatari construction companies had no interest in workers who could invoke their skill as leverage.

The ambivalence of Qatari firms toward workers with vocational skill played out in other source countries in ways that were even more pronounced than in Nepal. The association that employers made between skill and insubordination was clearest in places where workers had access to the most advanced construction skill. The training that many Filipino workers received before emigrating, for instance, was considered particularly unnerving among the managers I spoke with in Qatar. The skills were deemed superior or even exceptional, but the workers were described as "problematic" or "difficult."

The Filipino workers who received training prior to emigrating received it through the Filipino government's Technical Education and Skills Development Authority—or TESDA. Established in 1994 and operational in various cities throughout the Philippines, TESDA funded and oversaw training institutions that provided vocational training and technical education to Filipino workers, irrespective of whether the training was for employment in the Philippines or abroad. TESDA developed competency standards and qualifications, as well as instruments used to assess competencies, and ensured that the training delivered at the various training centers under its umbrella was robust and current.[83] As part of this mandate, TESDA engaged with various international accrediting organizations such as the International Organization for Standardization and ILO and worked with global companies to update the skills required for given trades. For training programs in the construction trades, TESDA regularly consulted, for example, with global construction companies, international engineering firms, and large oil companies, such as Aramco and Shell, to hone its curriculum for skilled as well as semiskilled positions in construction and refine its trade testing.

The vocational training centers under TESDA offered high, internationally recognized levels of technical competency, but they also augmented these practical skills with soft-skill training such as interpersonal communication and problem solving. As I was able to observe during a 2013 field visit to a vocational training center for building trades outside Manila, lessons on how to identify problems, and more important perhaps, bring the problems and potential solutions to the attention of supervisors, were folded into the vocational training. I attended a training session for electricians, and as the students were putting together their circuit boards to match the diagrams on worksheets, the trainer explained his approach. During our conversation, he reached over and took the notebook where I had been jotting down notes from our interview. He drew a square with four equal quadrants, then an arrow from each of the first three quadrants and at the arrow's end, and wrote down a category of technical competencies he covered in his course. He shaded in the last quadrant and said, "This is the most important one. Without this one, none of the other parts matter. This is for problem solving. This is how to tell your supervisor there is problem, how to tell him so that he can see it, and so that he will respect you after you tell him, and maybe also so that he can hear your suggestion."

Filipino workers, whether or not they had gone through TESDA training, were widely associated with these soft skills. They were viewed as having a clear understanding of the technical ability they brought to the project too. As a result, managers in Qatar by and large viewed them as disruptive, and the human resource managers preferred to direct their recruiting contract to countries where they could source workers with absorptive capacity rather than acquired competence. According to the Ministry of Labor in Qatar, the visas issued for Filipino workers were the only national class that went unfilled, with more a third of the visas allocated left unclaimed in 2013. Castle Contractors' human resource manager, Stephen, whom I interviewed in Qatar after he had just returned from a recruiting trip to Kathmandu, put it this way: "Look, it's a trade-off. Filipino workers are very good. They arrive with excellent training. But they are very stubborn in wanting to do things their way. Give me a Nepali over a Filipino any day, if you ask me."

Not all human resource managers shared Stephen's reservations about Filipino workers. At one masonry firm I visited in Qatar, the human resource manager, Mustafa, explained that the company was trying to take advantage of the surfeit of unclaimed visas for Filipinos. The company had explored partnerships with recruiting agencies that bypassed the TESDA vocational training systems. "We provide training here [in Qatar]. It's more economical for us to hire a laborer and develop him on-site." He also mentioned that the company was working with a recruitment agency in Tacloban City, in the eastern Visayas region of the Philippines. "This is a new agency for us, but they have been good. On time delivery. And the workers have been good. Good character—they don't make problems." At the time of my interview in fall 2014, the company had been working with the agency in Tacloban for four months and had received their first order of fifty workers. In 2013, the Visayas were devastated by Typhoon Haiyan, known as Typhoon Yolanda in the Philippines, one of the most powerful cyclones ever recorded. The storm affected eleven million people, leaving an estimated ten thousand dead and many more homeless. The storm surges demolished wide tracts of Tacloban, and turned many outlying areas into wastelands of mud and debris.[84]

The recruitment agency that Mustafa praised may have been leaning on the same place-based approach that agencies in Nepal had been using in response to Qatari companies' demands, specifically their urgent orders for large numbers of workers with absorptive capacity. In the Visayas, just like in the Terai, climate pressures had damaged livelihoods, and a climate disaster, fast moving in the Philippines, had dramatically impoverished people who had solid incomes and family assets, and who had, before the storm made landfall, been able to invest in their own development.

In the Philippines, the Terai, Bihar, and many other places, global warming was causing economic and ecological shocks that people tried to manage with migration. Recruitment agencies, guided by their clients in Qatar, drew on these dynamics to provide Qatari companies with the kind of workers that they sought: cheap, compliant migrants whom they could train into the workers they needed at any given point in a construction project—workers whom they could use to fill the labor needs sketched out in the manpower histograms that papered management trailers on every single Qatari construction site.

Skill, Recruitment, and Climate Change

In the swelling literature on climate change and migration, the emphasis has been on the ways that climate change has pushed people to migrate, with natural disasters or slow-moving climatic shifts creating "climate migrants," or the even more sensationalist "climate refugees."[85] An examination of the recruitment practices through which Qatar's construction industry secured its labor suggests that there may be more to this story, and the actions of employers and recruiters may be at least as relevant to understanding climate-related migration patterns as the monsoons that have failed to arrive or the typhoons that have ripped through settlements.

The conventional view of recruitment is one in which recruiters operate in faraway countries and produce labor that they export to firms abroad, often taking advantage of lax regulations along the way. But this take on recruitment is a partial one at best, abstracted out of context and inattentive to the ways that the firms that hire migrants shape the practices through which migrants are recruited. Qatari firms determined the practices of the recruitment agents that supplied them with labor and structured the recruitment industries of the countries they sourced from. Their urgent demand for large numbers of low-wage workers and appetite in particular for workers who were unskilled but assessed as trainable strengthened the position of large recruiters in their local markets, and pushed them to source from areas with the specific socioeconomic and ecological profiles that allowed them to fill these orders.

The story of Qatar's influence over recruitment practices is about the way that recruitment draws ecological places into economic exchange. The recruitment practices that Qatari firms helped shape not only pulled in places that were being increasingly affected by climate change pressures into recruitment networks but also turned drowned fields and flood-destroyed homes into assets that recruiters could draw on as they sought to fill orders from Qatar. The people sourced from those climate-damaged areas were attractive because they were newly poor, and before salt intrusion, late monsoons, or drought eroded their livelihoods, their communities made investments—in areas such as health, nutrition, and education—that equipped the recruits with the absorptive capacity that Qatari construction firms were so keen on.

In this way, recruitment practices may be creating a closed loop of climate damage. With their livelihoods made fragile by climate change effects, households have used land damaged by climate change to finance migration to take low-wage jobs in economies powered by the extraction of the hydro-carbons that are causing the global warming. Climate change effects in countries from which Qatar sources labor have set the stage for similar cycles—in Bangladesh, where Majid from AEA worked with recruiters who sourced labor from the salt-strangled Khulna region; in Thailand, where migration pathways have emerged in response to changing precipitation patterns and their impacted rain-fed farming; in Ethiopia, where climate change pressures have led to a steady rise in the use of migration as a hedge against drought; and in many other others.[86] To be sure, these patterns are emergent. Their outlines are not as clear as in Nepal and are still being defined. Though still difficult to discern, their authors are not anonymous. Recruiting firms and recruitment agents are likely to play an increasingly important role in defining the shape that climate change migration will ultimately take. The labor politics in destination countries—and skill politics in particular—may shape the implications of climate stress for migration.

In a broader sense, the story of labor recruitment for Qatar, racing to turn hydrocarbon revenues into a global city, is one that we will increasingly tell about all economic exchanges and connections. As climate change reshapes ecologies and communities, and global warming heightens inequality between places, it will become impossible to consider the significance of economic functions and interactions without taking into account the ecological spaces in which they occur and that they tie together. Work, production, migration, and regulation—all these are already being remolded by climate change pressures. Climate pressures are already reshaping implications for economic opportunity, economic marginalization, and the distribution of economic power. They are already redefining the meaning of skill and its relationship to power. As climate change alters our world in ways that are unprecedented and fundamental, and as migrants recruited to work in Qatar can already tell us, all matters of the economy—with their consequences for equity, justice, and dignity—will be matters of earth.

Conclusion

THE ARGUMENT THAT skill is political is, in some ways, an obvious one. The claim that the way we assess skill is both subjective and refracted through social constructs has been well documented and well developed by a variety of scholars. Regardless of whether that claim rests on the limitations of the indirect indicators used to capture skill—things like years of education or occupational certification—or homes in on the way that social categories—like race, gender, religion, and national origin—bias its assessment, the conclusion is the same: an objective measure of skill proves impossible. Definitions of skill are thus inimically informed by the structure of economic systems, social stratification, and political power. The distinction between skilled and unskilled, in other words, is always political.

This is not the argument that I am making in this book. The notion that skill is political provides a starting point, to be sure. But the core of the argument presented here is not fundamentally about skill and its assessment. Rather, it is about the political definition of personhood. More specifically, it is about the use of skill as a political language to render questionable the humanity and capacity for freedom of those who are described as unskilled. This book is not about why some people are defined as skilled or unskilled, or even the validity of those distinctions. It is instead about the political implications of skill classifications—and most pointedly, the political disenfranchisement and dehumanization of those people who are categorized as unskilled.

The difference between these two arguments—between the argument about the political *assessment* of skill and the argument about the *use* of skill—is not a matter of degree. Instead, the difference between these two lines of inquiry hinges on the observable role that skill plays in the social and political organization of capitalist economic systems. Implicit in the claim that evaluations of skill are subjective and political is the notion that these assessments are inaccurate and distortionary. They are mistakes, even when they are deliberate and ideological, even when they are designed to marginalize, and as mistakes, they are defined as external to the functioning of the economy. A misappraisal and especially devaluation of skill can lead to the undercompensation or theft of competence, but if that mistake is corrected and skill is evaluated accurately, without prejudice, without the thumb of political power on wage scales, then the assumption is that skill will be compensated in a way that is roughly commensurate with the contribution of that skill to the functioning of the economy.

The argument about the political use of skill—the one I have made in this book—differs in that it views the conflation of skill and political personhood as internal to the economy. My claim is that the political use of skill assessments to divest the unskilled of their political personhood is a structural feature of capitalist systems. The equation of lack of skill with lack of the full capacity for freedom and subjectivity is not an aberration. It is not a mistake or a distortion. Instead, it is an ordering principle of capitalist economies; it shapes their social organization and political justifications. More specifically, skill as a political language that apportions human dignity is primarily, fundamentally, and foundationally a method of labor coercion and social control. In denying those described as unskilled the full rights associated with political personhood and full capacities for freedom, the political use of skill exposes the so-called unskilled to forms of violence, exclusion, and compulsion, even as it seems to affirm political narratives about freedom from which market economies derive so much of their legitimacy.

As an organizing principle, the political use of skill is at once invisible and all pervasive. Skill masquerades as a technical question that is politically neutral, and concerned with those competencies that favor the sophistication of economies and deepening of the associated knowledge base. But in fact the political use of skill, with its adjudication of personhood, shapes all aspects of social, political, and economic life. Political narratives about skill define the structure of the political rights to which people have access depending on whether they are described as skilled or unskilled. Skill politics draw the spatial organization of societies and imprint the patterns of our urban fabrics with lines that segregate. The language of skill influences the political definition of the body, confining the unskilled to the parameters of a brute corporality, even as those viewed as skilled are afforded an embodied existence that is expansive enough to include imagination, desire, abstract cognition, and personal will. The politics of skill even bend the relations between nations, with skill categories increasingly shaping the international agreements, national politics, and pressure campaigns through which the global movement of labor is managed.

The Politics of Skill in Qatar

In order to explore the politics of skill—to listen to many registers of its language—this book turned to Qatar as a prism. Because more than 90 percent of the country's residents are migrants residing in Qatar as workers, their political status is a sole product of their economic function. As a result, the language of skill, with its economistic tone, has been more audible in Qatar than in other localities. This book considered skill politics in Qatar mostly during the country's heady expansion in anticipation of the 2022 World Cup, for which the small peninsular nation unexpectedly and controversially won the hosting rights. Qatar's reinvention as a hub for global culture was a thoroughly international endeavor, with companies from around the world pouring in to build the stadiums, infrastructure, and hydrocarbon mining facilities on which a collective vision for national development depended. The political use of skill and skill categories to define personhood in Qatar was only a local expression of a global practice. Local skill categories—and in particular the thick dividing line between skilled and unskilled—were produced through a long history of global economic exchange that crisscrossed Qatar since the early nineteenth century and that still does. The use of skill categories as a means to limit political personhood has reverberated outward through those global networks; meanings attached to skill in Qatar have traveled out folded into the international business practices of global construction firms, written into migrant recruitment contracts, and even tucked into the frameworks used in human rights activism to advocate for the unskilled.

Does Skill Make Us Human? explored the ways in which the question in the title was asked and answered in Qatar. The beliefs about skill and personhood woven into the answer shaped reality across multiple social, symbolic, and material registers. The response to the question came in many versions, and each chapter of this book took on a different rendition. "Regulation," chapter 1, looked at the political lexicon through which the answer was articulated, and examined how skill was used to parse definitions of freedom and rights, confining the rights of the unskilled to their bodily welfare while allowing the skilled a fuller spectrum of freedoms, including rights that encompassed their entitlement to creativity, desire, mobility, and agency. "Production," chapter 2, depicted the place where the answer to that question was delivered, and how the answer itself came to make the place. The chapter looked at Qatar's modernist planning and revealed skill's imprint on both the capital city of Doha, with its formal hypersegregation by skill category, and the organization of the construction industry that built it. In chapter 3, "Skill," the book turned to the way the answer to the book's title was used. It showed how the political definition of skill was used to pry skillful embodied practice out of worker's bodies and redefine it as an abstract asset introduced into production by management. It also detailed the disciplinary control of workers, including through physical coercion, and its role in enforcing the myth that the unskilled did not have the capacity for freedom. "Protest," the following chapter, listened to the rebuttals that workers lobbied against claims about their lack of skill and personhood. It showed how workers, in a context where protests, strikes, and labor organizing were illegal, used their skillful practice to resist their utter subjugation. Workers nurtured and affirmed the qualities of connection, imagination, and sociality that were denied to them in the debased form of political subjectivity that Qatar's skill politics allowed them. Chapter 5, "Body," showed how much the answer to the question about workers' humanity hurt, and revealed that skill politics were deeply implicated in workers' exposure to life-threatening heat injury. The political language of skill meant that injury, and in particular heat's damage to cognition, could be twisted into proof that workers were ontologically unskilled, or even resistant to skill and learning, thus confirming the claim that they did not have the capacities required for full political personhood. "Earth," the book's final chapter, explored how the equivalence made between skill and personhood sharpened the consequences of ecological damage for those defined as unskilled. It looked at the recruitment of migrant workers, and the way that the political definition of skill was reframing ecological damage as a business opportunity for the recruiters that delivered workers and the companies that hired them.

In its progression, this book's attention to the claims about skill and personhood moved from more explicitly political realms where rights were defined, cities were designed, and production systems were organized, down to more material practices through which migrants were controlled and detained, bodies were injured, and the earth was damaged. This progression was deliberate; the more material the plane, the higher the stakes of skill politics. Where skill politics meet the materiality of the body, they can become quite literally a matter of life and death.

Life and Death through the Politics of Skill

Perhaps nothing has illustrated the stakes of skill politics in Qatar as dramatically as the country's management of the coronavirus pandemic. By early March 2020, the pandemic had already established itself decisively in Qatar, and on March 11, with 239 registered cases of COVID-19, the government responded by drawing a strict cordon sanitaire around the industrial area, the zone on the outskirts of Doha where migrant construction workers were housed.[1] The government set up roadblocks and built a concrete barrier around the perimeter of the industrial area to mark out the boundaries.[2] The cordon sanitaire was strictly enforced; the government did not permit residents to leave the zone for any reason, including seeking out medical care.[3] The few big-box grocery stores in the industrial area that workers relied on to purchase food were not restocked. News media and human rights observers were prohibited from crossing into the industrial area, and the Qatari government maintained a ban on the use of Voice Over Internet Protocol platforms for voice and video internet calls, despite criticism from human rights and media groups around the world.[4] Still, workers sent messages on encrypted apps to journalists and human rights organizations describing the heavy police presence enforcing the lockdown as well as reporting that they were unable to access food.[5] "There are a hundred workers in my camp and we ran out of food days ago," one said.[6]

Even as the government cordoned off the industrial area, it mandated that construction work on the large projects leading up the 2022 World Cup continue apace. Workers were transported daily to construction sites on packed buses. Once at construction sites, they labored in close physical proximity with thousands of other workers. They worked elbow to elbow, shared tools and handled the same materials, and communicated as well as coordinated their physical movements. This physical interaction favored the spread of the coronavirus, producing infections that could then be transmitted to others in the close quarters of the labor camps where physical distancing was impossible and protective hygiene extremely difficult. How much the coronavirus spread within the industrial area was unclear. Qatar rolled out an ambitious testing program, but after its data revealed that cases were highly concentrated in the industrial area, the government stopped publishing locational information for its running case count.[7] Still, through to the end of 2020, when this manuscript went to press, Qatar ranked, as it had since the beginning of March, as the country with one of the highest rates of COVID-19 cases per capita in the world.[8]

On some level, though, the rate of infection in the industrial area didn't matter. The purpose of a cordon sanitaire, in Qatar and elsewhere, was and is not the prevention of contagion in a society. It is to cut off the portion of society perceived as diseased from the rest of the social body. How diseased that portion of society ultimately becomes is irrelevant; it has already been amputated.[9]

Qatar drew its sanitary line at its skill line, and the segment of the population it chose to abandon to the virus was the one that the politics of skill had classed as unskilled. With cement barriers and police enforcement, the government of Qatar hardened its existing skill-based spatial segregation and turned the industrial area into a vast carceral tract. The cordon wiped out migrant workers' identity as juridical beings. Not only did skill politics deny them their full personhood and the capacity for freedom, but amplified by the coronavirus, those politics were further used to deny migrant workers tagged as unskilled the basic right to life. Workers were transported to construction sites not as men but instead as labor to be used instrumentally while their health permitted it, and then abandoned to illness and in some cases death from COVID-19.

The contours of exclusion in contexts other than Qatar are defined by skill too, especially as they bear down on migrants, and although they sometimes divide less explicitly based on skill categories than in Qatar, the material stakes are just as high. Migrants who are detained and deported in the United States, Europe, and Australia are widely portrayed—in press coverage and policy—as unskilled. The migrants who are rounded up on neighborhood streets, yanked from their families, and held in carceral conditions are assumed to be unskilled; in accounts of migrants transported in handcuffs and shackled ankles, it is almost unthinkable that they should be skilled professionals. The migrants who are confined to refugee and other holding camps on the edges of countries refusing to let them in, abandoned in dinghies on the Mediterranean, and denied basic access to housing and health care—these migrants are all implicitly represented as unskilled. They are not presumed to be doctors, lawyers, scientists, or entrepreneurs. In a ruthless tautology, the material constraints imposed on them confirm their status as unskilled, irrespective of their expertise, and reinforce their position as people divested not of competence but rather political personhood, judged as lacking the full capacity for freedom.[10] If migrants are detained, subject to bodily controls, then they must be unskilled. And if they are unskilled, then they are deeemed less than full persons, and can be injured, sometimes fatally, without political consequence. The spread of COVID-19 has only amplified this political equivalence. In their response to the pandemic, governments around the world have applied the designation of essential workers to those defined as unskilled, many of whom are migrants, sanctioning their continued presence in public workspaces, frequently without the provision of adequate protection against infection. In this way, pandemic responses have only amplified the politics of skill by recasting unskilled workers as workers whose *labor* is essential, but whose lives are not.

As the immigration policies of countries around the world have become more restrictive and exclusionary, the salience of the politics of skill has only increased. Governments have invoked "merit-based" migration criteria as means to limit immigration and turned to skill-based standards as a way to define the social character of the migrants they choose to allow. Because the political definition of skill is only loosely tethered to actual expertise, skill categories provide a versatile mechanism to achieve other policy goals. Governments or advocates can use skill—or merit—as a stand-in for other bases of exclusion, such as race and national origin. Similarly, because the line between skilled and unskilled delineates social categories rather than competence, it can drift or be redrawn in response to new nationalist priorities or economic ideologies, and those classed as skilled today and endowed with the political personhood that such a status affords may be recategorized as unskilled at some time in the future, and so shorn of their political rights. Global crises, whether fast moving like the coronavirus pandemic or slow but existential like global warming, may shift the line even further and will undoubtedly sharpen the material implications of having one's full political personhood denied. Those crises may make skill politics even more a matter of life and death than they already are.

Skill and the Politics of Embodied Imagination

The trouble with skill as a political language is that it traffics in simile: it draws an equivalence between two unrelated things. It uses competence, expertise, and even mastery to talk about political personhood and its absence. It equates lacking skill with lacking the capacities required for learning and, by implication, freedom—agentic will, aptitude, desire for social connection, and imagination. This reliance on simile is what makes the politics of skill so difficult to contest. Challenging the way that skill politics apportion political personhood can easily be dismissed as a disregard for expertise for its usefulness and authority, and the effort, dedication, and investment that the development of mastery requires. It can even be brushed off or derided as veering recklessly toward a denialism of knowledge, science, and the importance of education. Through the political alchemy of simile, questioning the politics of skill can be equated with questioning the value of skill, and even sloughed off as some naive and saccharine claim that we are all skilled in some way.

As a result, the only way to challenge the politics of skill is to break apart the simile between skill and the capacity for freedom. Shattering this equivalence requires an affirmative politics that emphasizes that the human capacities associated with skill belong to everyone. The agentic creativity, social empathy and collaboration, and desire and even pleasure on which learning depends have to be claimed as a birthright that we possess—declared features of our embodied humanity that are essential and inalienable—regardless of whether or not we are skilled, or to what degree we are skilled, and that we enact at all points on our journeys from novice to master. Breaking apart the simile requires, in other words, that we affirm that our capacities for freedom do not depend on our skill, and we do not require skill as evidence that we are endowed with the capacity for freedom. It calls for an affirmative claims making to the right to imagination, desire, connection, and expansive creativity.

Breaking apart the simile of skill politics in this way also breaks open space for a generative kind of politics that draws on skill in most responsive and embodied expressions. It allows for a politics that views skill not as a fixed and knowable asset, an economic resource separate from the body, but rather as part of our embodied flow of creativity, a resource continually renewed through learning, changing and developing moment to moment as we engage with the world around us. It allows us to view skillful practice as a resource for the envisioning of new political possibilities—ones that privilege more expansive definitions of work, political personhood, and dignity. It allows, for example, for a politics in which we perceive the stadiums and gleaming high-rises of Qatar not only as hyperdesigned concrete structures but also as the accumulation of thousands and thousands of everyday moments of embodied imagination and connection. Reframed in this way, the buildings become monuments to the freedom necessarily exercised in learning. They stand as reminders to us all to turn to the creativity practiced in everyday embodied moments of learning as a means of responding to the material and political crises on the horizon. Breaking apart the simile between skill and political personhood does not simply dissolve the long-standing interplay between the definition of skill and forms of degradation and bondage; it affirms embodied imagination as the essence of individual and collective freedom.

Postscript

ON SEPTEMBER 4, 2014, about halfway through my planned fieldwork in Qatar for this project, the BBC reported that two British researchers investigating the treatment of migrant workers in Qatar had gone missing. The organization with which they were affiliated, the Norway-based Global Network for Rights and Development, issued a statement indicating that the two researchers had been in Qatar since August 27, and it was "deeply concerned that these employees, both British citizens, may have been subject to enforced disappearance."[1] The evidence for this, on September 4, was still circumstantial: Krishna Upadhyaya had sent several text messages to friends in Norway claiming that plainclothes police had been following him and his colleague, photographer Ghimire Gundev, since the weekend. For several days, the researchers had begun conducting interviews with the trickle of Nepalese workers who had come to collect visas at their embassy, having been advised that it would be impossible to gain access to labor camps. The men had checked out of their hotel, but had never arrived at the airport for their scheduled departure on August 31. The Qatari authorities denied having any information, but promised to look into the case.

Within days, however, the Qatari government confirmed that it had detained the men, and they were, according to a statement issued by the Foreign Ministry on September 7, "being interrogated for having violated the provisions of the laws of the state of Qatar."[2] The men were interrogated and held in solitary confinement without access to consular support for ten days, at which point they were released, but prohibited from leaving the country for an additional eight days. After his return to the United Kingdom, Upadhyaya reported that he and his colleague had been compelled to surrender passwords to their personal and professional email accounts as well as all the interview and photographic data they had collected. "There were very concerned to learn exactly what we had been doing and why I was focusing on Qatar and why, as they saw it, I wanted to portray a negative image of their country. They were particularly sensitive about anything linked to the World Cup," he said of his interrogators.³ Ultimately, the two researchers were formally charged with having wrongly entered Qatar on tourist visas and holding "illegal documents," believed to be a reference to their videos and research notes.

Some months later, on May 5, 2015, a BBC crew, invited by the Qatari prime minister's office to participate in a tour of newly constructed housing facilities for migrant workers organized by the London-based public relations firm Portland Communications, was roughed up and detained by the Qatari authorities. According to the Qatari government's head of communications, the crew of four was arrested because of its reporting activity after it departed from the official press tour: "The BBC crew decided to do their own site visits and interviews in the days leading up to the planned tour. In doing so, they trespassed on private property, which is against the law in Qatar just as it is in most countries. Security forces were called and the BBC crew was detained."⁴ As in the case of the two British researchers, the crew was stopped on a road on the outskirts of the capital. The four men were handcuffed, detained, and subjected to insistent interrogation about what they had done and whom they had met, and had their equipment and hard drives confiscated. During their interrogation, the lead journalist, Mark Lobel, was shown a photographic record of his activities since his arrival in Doha several days prior, including activities as mundane as "lying next to a swimming pool with friends," suggesting that the interrogation about his activities was superfluous and performative. As he recounted after his returned to the United Kingdom, "One of the interrogators snapped. 'This is not Disneyland,' he barked. 'You cannot stick your camera anywhere.'" After two days, the crew was released and allowed to rejoin the formal press tour that was still ongoing. Lobel described his team's encounter with the Qatari authorities as "Qatar's Jekyll-and-Hyde approach to journalism." In their experience, just as in mine, repressive actions were followed by bureaucratic procedures and overtures that were innocuous, ordinary, and even friendly; Lobel remarked that after his treatment in detention, the BBC crew was reintegrated into the choreographed press tour after their release, "as if nothing had happened."⁵ A few days afterward, the men were allowed to leave the country. Their equipment, footage, and interview notes were not returned, despite numerous formal appeals from the BBC.

The arrest of Upadhyaya and Gundev marked an inflection point in my research. It signaled a shift in political climate, and the end to a moment of relative, somewhat chaotic, and perhaps unintended political aperture in Qatar after the country was awarded the 2022 World Cup hosting rights in 2010. The British researchers had been detained in order to pressure them to release the data they had collected, in raw form, to the authorities. Their detention provided the context for the measures to which I was increasingly subject as my research progressed: routine surveillance, sporadic intimidation, an abrupt change in visa category, and sustained regulatory pressure and questioning. When it became clear in late October 2014, two months after Upadhyaya and Gundev were first picked up and sent to solitary confinement, that my ability to protect the confidentiality of my informants was threatened, I left the country. The detention of the BBC team in May the following year only validated these concerns.

Any researcher worth their salt will tell you that research never goes according to plan. But the way that the field being investigated upends research also provides important insight into the phenomena being studied. These disruptions highlight the structures of power, political crosscurrents, and resources for agency and even resistance that shape the social dynamics and spaces being explored. In Qatar, the interruption of my fieldwork midstream highlighted how closely official reasonableness and even congeniality were intertwined with the menace of arbitrary as well as authoritarian interventions, and how this juxtaposition made the risks difficult to discern, especially for institutional actors outside Qatar, until they became manifest as actions against me or others. This postscript describes why the imbrication of security structures and bureaucratic processes required me to cut the field research for this project short in order to protect the confidentiality of the participants. It also explains why, to my great regret, I am unable to acknowledge by name the many people who helped me with the fieldwork that I was able to complete before my departure.

Research in Authoritarian Fields

By any standard measure in political science, the political system in Qatar at the time of my research was authoritarian. The small but lavishly wealthy country was ruled by an emir from the house of Al Thani, whose position is hereditary yet not determined by primogeniture, and had been since it was declared an independent nation in 1971. In the past, this has led to struggles at the moment of succession, but ones that were much more discrete than those in neighboring emirates or Saudi Arabia. The person of the emir was inviolable, and his authority virtually absolute. Certainly no elections were held, and there were no political parties; neither was there a right to freedom of expression or access to information, and there was no meaningful freedom of association.

Still, like Leo Tolstoy's unhappy families, every authoritarian regime is authoritarian in its own way.[6] The particular blend of practices on which the regime in Qatar relied to maintain control reflects its specific history, the source of political threats, the structure of its economy, and its aspirations on the world stage. These practices conditioned and ultimately constrained my research project. They shaped what was possible: they informed the strategies I developed to get access to people and sites; they colored how participants viewed the research project, and why they appropriated it as a space of interpretation, reflection, and even resistance; and they were the reason why much of the research was surprising and unprecedented in Qatar, even to the authorities tasked with monitoring it.

The boundaries drawn around my research by these authoritarian practices were often unstable and unclear. Indeed, the practices that drew those boundaries were diffuse, contradictory, and volatile, and they were carried out by an array of actors at different levels of government and private organizations, each of whom who had complex motivations, including fear, ambition, and even loyalty. But the capriciousness of power was not an accidental by-product of a disorganized state; rather, the unrestrained and erratic expression of state repression was a core component of the regime's authoritarian control because it affirmed the regime's assertion that it alone could determine the legitimacy of its use of power, and extend that power to places that had felt protected and private.

As recent reflective scholarship on the methodological questions of conducting fieldwork in authoritarian contexts has observed, the defining and distinctive challenge faced by researchers in authoritarian fields is the unpredictability of power, backed by the real, although not always explicit, risk of coercion and intimidation.[7] As international relations professor Marlies Glasius and colleagues note, "The feature of authoritarianism that most prominently affects our fieldwork is not its repressive aspect as such, but its arbitrariness."[8] Moreover, the implicit rules—the red lines—that determine which kinds of speech or activity are forbidden by the regime are not static; "they move, for us and for our respondents."[9] This creates a sense of foreboding and insecurity for the researcher as well as residents; "the latent threat that something can happen, to you or your respondents, is what is specific about authoritarian regimes, and hence also authoritarian fieldwork."[10] This is likely to be especially true when the researcher uses an extended case method approach to research, as I did in Qatar. Sociologist Michael Burawoy describes this approach as the use of direct observation to study strategic actions and their relation to social processes, as they are situated in a field of wider forces and the multiple dimensions of power found there. "When we participate in the life of others, we find ourselves enmeshed in networks of domination, distorting communication and restricting what we can discover," notes Burawoy.[11]

In Qatar, the sense of vulnerability to power's arbitrariness was heightened by the fact that almost everyone was in the country only provisionally, at the pleasure of the state and their employer. More than 90 percent of the population in Qatar was migrant, and lived and worked in the country, as mentioned earlier, under the kafala system, tied to a Qatari sponsor or kafeel. A migrant's sponsor had the legal right to have their charge deported for any reason, and during the time I was conducting my research, a sponsor could also prevent their migrant charge from leaving the country, denying them the exit visa required to cross the border out of Qatar. Likewise, the sponsor could prevent the migrant employee from changing jobs or even quitting. Through this sponsorship system, the regime's power was magnified even as it was delegated to sponsors and dispersed through them into all corners of the society. Sponsors regularly monitored the physical movements of their employees and surveilled their electronic communication. I met more than one senior manager who refused to email or text with me, and many would only arrange in-person meetings with me through a trusted intermediary. Any sponsor could enforce a red line, and indeed migrants in managerial positions or other supervisory roles also enforced red lines for fear that not doing so might lead to their own deportation or other more serious consequences. The threat of deportation saturated all interactions in Qatar and lent an edge to even the most anodyne exchanges.

The red lines in Qatar shifted midway through my project. After ruling for almost twenty years, Sheikh Khalifa had, in summer 2013, abdicated in favor of his son Sheikh Tamim. Over the next several months, the new emir worked to consolidate his power base and install a new cadre of young, powerful allies. The reverberations shook well-established red lines loose and heightened the uncertainty already endemic to the authoritarian regime. Because Sheikh Tamim had been behind the effort to make Qatar an international sporting destination and spearheaded the campaign to bring the World Cup to Qatar, anything having to do with preparation for the games became charged. The working conditions of the migrants who were building the facilities and infrastructure for the World Cup, or even any related construction projects, became newly sensitive. To a great extent, this was not the result of a deliberate political strategy but rather the product of the many smaller actions, each driven by a well-founded sense of vulnerability in the face of power that could be capricious, enacted by those who implemented the quotidian and mundane authoritarian practices on which the regime's control depended.

The outcome, however, was the same: research that had a few months earlier been approved and supported by the regime became threatening and provocative—and thus risky both for those who had sanctioned it and those charged with monitoring it.

Regulatory Layers

My research in Qatar began with a series of short trips to the country starting in 2011. During these preliminary trips, I spoke with a variety of institutional actors about the possibility of doing research on migrant workers in Qatar. These conversations unfolded at a time of heady optimism in the country: Qatar had just been awarded hosting rights for the World Cup and had aspirations of positioning itself as a global hub for sports and culture. Included in that ambit were ambitions to become a knowledge economy. Qatar was recruiting global universities to set up outposts in the country, and research was an activity that the government sought to advance. Nevertheless, two things became clear quickly: research interpreted as an exposé of working conditions for migrants in the construction industry would be not be possible, and research funded by external foundations and, even more so, foreign governments would be distinctly unwelcome.

To fit my project within these parameters, I sought and obtained support for my research from the Qatari government. The project was funded by the Qatar National Research Foundation, a Qatari organization under the umbrella of the larger Qatar Foundation, a quasi-governmental entity with strong royal backing. According to the terms of the grant, I was required to collaborate with a local institution that would act as my partner in the project, receiving the majority of the funding. I chose to work with Silatech, a quasi-governmental organization and royal philanthropic outfit, under the direct patronage of Sheikha Moza, the powerful wife of Sheikh Hamad, who was still the emir at the time. Silatech sponsored me as a researcher under the same terms that any migrant worker would be sponsored under Qatar's kafala system, and the business visa that it secured for me did not allow me to exit the country without my sponsor's assent. Just like the migrant workers I interviewed, I required permission from Silatech and the government—an exit visa—to leave the country. There was a loophole in this setup: if I left Qatar before the restriction on exit kicked in, I could preserve my ability to leave at will, and so I left Qatar every five weeks for the required minimum of a week. Additionally, I secured formal letters of support from powerful industry and government actors, including the Qatar 2022 Supreme Committee for Delivery and Legacy and the Qatar Foundation.

From the application process through to its administration, the grant was structured to extract compliance from the researcher. The Qatar National Research Foundation stipulated that it should be the sole funder for projects, and researchers could neither apply for nor receive funding from additional sources. The application process required an unusually detailed description of the research process, including a detailed timeline along with a highly and uncommonly specific enumeration of all the questions that would be asked during both the formal interviews and in more open-ended ethnographic research. Furthermore, the proposal had to justify each phase, set of questions, and element of the research by explaining how each would advance specific portions of the Qatar National Research Strategy—a strategy itself derived from the *Qatar National Vision 2030* development plan.

The regulatory layers were manifold and included many more than the ones described here, but the layer that would ultimately prove most and unexpectedly problematic was the requirement that the research protocol be vetted and supervised by an ethical review board that was affiliated with the funder, a foundation that was part of an authoritarian government structure. In the United States, academic research that involves human subjects is appraised by an institutional review board (IRB) to ensure that the research does not harm or imperil the people who participate. Typically, researchers involved in a project are certified by the institution that employs them or is hosting the research. For this project, my human subjects protocol was reviewed and approved by New York University. Additionally, as required by New York University for international projects, the protocol was submitted to an IRB in the country where the research was conducted. The Qatar National Research Foundation designated a board run by the Qatar Supreme Council of Health and nominally certified by Georgetown University School of Foreign Service, which has an outpost in Qatar. Silatech, as the Qatari representative of the project and its kafeel, submitted the human subjects protocol for the project to the Qatar Supreme Council of Health, and managed all correspondence and engagement with the Qatari regulatory body. Because the protocol for the use of human subjects required by New York University was more protective of research participants, Silatech, at my insistence, arranged for my research activities to be covered by the human subjects protocol approved by New York University.

Per the approved human subjects protocol, I took the indicated steps to protect the confidentiality of the informants I spoke with, but I also added additional formal measures of confidentiality protection over and above those required. My adherence to the human subjects protocol for the project was also explicit, deliberately observable, and emphatic. When I retained translators to help with worker interviews on multilingual construction sites, for example, I made sure to destroy the paper that I had provided them so that they could jot down notes during interviews in full view of the translators themselves and, importantly, company management. This was intended not only as an overt show of compliance with the requirement to maintain the confidentiality of the interview contents but a clear indication too that I was the only person who had access to any record of the interview contents. It was a strategy to protect the members of my research team and the translators who worked with us. I was also careful to indicate that the research did not center on human rights violations or migrant working conditions, and while in Qatar, I refrained from communicating with human rights organizations and monitors.

In interviews with workers, it was not uncommon for them to view me initially as a human rights researcher or journalist. Many began with an almost rote catalog of grievances, and listed off their low pay level, the substandard state of their accommodations, and the deception of their recruiter. Their body language tended to be closed, and their answers perfunctory, reflecting a sense, I suspect, that although the information would be used, it would have little impact on their conditions. In those instances, I recorded their answers, but then gently added questions about skill along with what they had learned, what they felt mastery in, and how they shared their knowledge with their colleagues. With that turn, the interview invariably opened up. The workers I spoke with were keen to describe their areas of competence, and many felt pride at describing the effort and thoughtfulness that learning those skills had required. These reflections on skill expanded to commentary about power dynamics on-site, the working conditions they produced, and the strategies of resistance that workers had begun to develop. They not infrequently also led to the sharing of more personal stories—the mother or sister who was dearly missed, the brother whom the worker was putting through school, or the child born shortly after the worker traveled to Qatar—and a more intimate unburdening.

For managers and supervisors too, skill was rich terrain. It led to discussions of manpower planning and workforce training strategies; segued into descriptions of recruitment approaches and competitive tactics based on skill; and pivoted to expressions of frustration with government control and the sponsorship system, which many managers viewed as deeply unfair to themselves and sometimes their companies. In these interviews as well, reflections on skill and its management gave way to stories of personal sacrifice, generally to support family, and sometimes, when my interlocutors had fled conflict, about exile and its heartache.

Moving Red Lines

As the political transition between one emir and another unfolded, the valence of my research seemed to have changed. Toward the end of the first phase of my fieldwork, in late spring 2014, I began to field expressions of discomfort with my research. Some of these expressions were explicit and were issued by private actors. They included occasional threats, with one threat of sexual violence from a contractor who believed, erroneously, that I had uncovered his firm's kickback scheme for contracts, delivered in such concrete and immanent terms that I sought refuge in the women's bathroom in a mall until I felt the threat had subsided enough for me to make it safely back to my hotel. Other gestures were more cryptic. One night, for example, a white man in an expensive suit and earpiece started pounding violently on the door to my hotel room at 2 a.m., and continued for close an hour. I called hotel security several times during that hour, and despite assurances that someone was on their way up, the hotel management sent no one. There were many other instances like these, disconcerting and somewhat random.

Other expressions of discomfort were implicit and subtle, and as other researchers in authoritarian settings have found, these were more jarring.[12] After a trip away from Doha, the driver I used regularly was suddenly unavailable, and his number had been passed to a new driver who claimed to be his cousin. This kind of bequeathing of cell phone numbers was not unusual, but what struck me as odd was that this happened without notice from the driver who had texted me daily. On several occasions during the late spring and fall, the belongings in my room were moved in a manner that seemed designed to indicate that a search had been conducted and communicate that I was being surveilled. To protect the confidentiality of my data, I uploaded all my field notes and interviews onto my university's password-protected server in New York, and kept nothing on my laptop. As an extra precaution, however, I locked my laptop in the safety deposit box of my room whenever I left. I returned several times to find my laptop on the desk, and once, as if to underscore the message, I found it open and running on the made bed that I had left unmade that morning.

Ultimately, the measures that made continued research in Qatar impossible were those that drew on the regulatory structures applied to the project. After the first phase of my fieldwork, I submitted a progress report to the Qatar National Research Foundation per the terms of my grant. In the report, I listed the number of sites I had accessed, number of interviews I had completed, and aspects of skill development that the interviews had addressed, and just as I did with my own university's IRB, I submitted, through Silatech, the documentation required to renew the human subject protocol for the project. I returned to New York to work on the design of the anonymized online survey on skill and recruitment that I had planned to administer to managerial staff in Qatar's construction industry.

In mid-September, just prior to my departure back to Qatar, and as the detention of Upadhyaya and Gundev was being reported in the international press, I received a notice via Silatech from the IRB at the Qatar Supreme Council of Health informing me that it did not believe I had obtained consent from any of my interview subjects for my research. The correspondence indicated that the IRB judged that I had not obtained consent because I had not used forms stamped by its Qatar Supreme Council of Health, and I had not required that workers add their names and signatures to the forms. This argument ran counter to the agreement that my research activities would be covered by the protocol approved by New York University and verified by the Qatar Supreme Council of Health's IRB. The New York University protocol, which I had insisted on the ability to use, allowed workers to be consented verbally, without providing written records of their names and participation, for their own protection and so that there would be no documentation of their involvement in the study. Several other queries followed about the research sites and interview participants themselves as well as the specific intermediaries who had helped me to establish contact. A response with the information requested would have required me to violate the very confidentiality that the human subjects protocol, with its multiple layers of review, was designed to protect, and in Qatar's authoritarian context, would have placed the participants in the research at risk.

Against the backdrop of the detention of the two British researchers, who had interviewed a handful of workers in their embassies, and had not visited construction sites or labor camps, the significance of the demands issued by the Qatari IRB was unclear. Was this a matter of bureaucratic confusion?

Were the queries simply the action of a zealous staff member, concerned perhaps about the seemingly increased political sensitivity to research on workers in the construction industry and taking proactive steps to do due diligence? Or were the requests a manifestation of a more significant political shift? Of particular concern to me was the fact that the researchers detained were held until they handed over the data that they had collected. I did not want to find myself in a position of having to choose between detention or protecting the confidentiality I had pledged to those participating in the research. I consulted with trusted contacts, highly placed in the Qatari government and in political networks connected to the royal family, and the response that I received from the people I spoke with was that everyone in Qatar knew me and what I was researching, and that the government supported the research. After consulting with my dean and sending a letter to the US State Department, I decided to return to Qatar in late September.

When I arrived in Doha, it became clear quite quickly that the political ground had shifted. The ambiguous messages of displeasure with my research were more frequent, and the government and managerial contacts that had been accessible and supportive were now impossible to reach. Silatech had been gutted. The organization's funds were slashed, and the executive director removed. Meanwhile, the Qatari IRB placed a moratorium on my research until it could conduct a comprehensive review of my protocol—a process that could take several months even if conducted in good faith.

The level of access I had been able to secure and number of people I had spoken to in the multiple social spaces I had been able to enter seemed a matter of particular concern to the Qatari IRB, with questions raised about how I had managed to secure access to the multiple arenas in which I had conducted research. While workspaces in Qatar were profoundly international and included multiple occupational strata, social spaces and social interactions were more separate by migration status and class. Casual movement across these spaces was not illegal, but it was often perceived as such. Many supervisors and foremen on construction sites, for example, had never been to the labor camps where the men they worked with, elbow to elbow, day in and day out, were housed. Several academics I spoke with in Qatar believed that unauthorized excursions to the industrial area and labor camps in particular would result in sanction. Even the production of the government data that were publicly released was built around these divisions. The data released by the Qatar Planning and Statistics Authority on the income levels of workers by occupation offers one case in point. The wages indicated for unskilled construction workers in the data published for 2013 were three times higher than the wages reported to me by the workers I interviewed at multiple different sites and that were also reported by several different investigative reports by human rights organizations. After repeated visits, I was ultimately given access to the survey instrument used to collect information about salaries.

(Survey instruments are technically public and frequently published on the Qatar Planning and Statistics Authority's website along with the statistical tables, but the reticence I encountered reflected the pervasive sense of risk generated by the kafala system.) A look at the survey methodology revealed that questions about salary were posed to the employer, not the worker, and the employer regularly added the housing and food allowances that firms were required to provide to the salary figure. Even the people administering government surveys did not cross the divisions in Qatar in order to ask workers directly about their wages.

The Qatari IRB eventually called for a full board review—a step taken when a researcher is viewed as being in breach of their approved human subject protocol and suspected of having committed serious ethical violations. As the bureaucratic gears turned at the Qatar Supreme Council of Health, Silatech informed me that since my project was stalled, it planned to move me to a tourist visa status. This was a worrying development because the two British researchers who were detained were ultimately charged with being in the country under false pretenses, entering and residing on a tourist visa when their main purpose was not tourism. At around this time, I received a couple different phone calls from some of the very same contacts who had, just a few weeks earlier, assured me that I could conduct research safely in Qatar. This time their message was quite different: one interlocutor suggested that my family in Cairo must miss me a great deal and I should plan a visit soon, and another that the research had been so comprehensive, there was nothing more I could learn and I should consider moving on to other projects. He also asked me later in the conversation if I had heard that so-and-so, a staff member working on state-sanctioned and state-promoted worker welfare codes, had been deported.

With this information, I decided to be outside Qatar on the day of the full board review meeting and left for Cairo. The Qatari IRB deemed my research to be noncompliant with its procedures and placed an administrative hold on my project, to be lifted only after I provided information that would have jeopardized the safety of my informants and research team. Instead of returning to Qatar, I flew from Cairo directly to Nepal to conduct research on the recruitment practices that supplied workers to Qatar's construction industry. Save for a transit stop through the airport on my way back to New York, I have not returned to Qatar since.

On my return to New York, New York University's IRB conducted a careful review of my research practices, confirmed that I had been compliant with the protocol it had approved, and assisted me in preparing a rebuttal folio, which it cosigned with me, and which was sent to the IRB in Qatar. After several months, over the course of which the IRB requested additional information that would have violated the confidentiality of the research subjects—even at one point asserting that the IRB should be considered part of the research team and thus have access to confidential research data—the IRB at the Qatar

Supreme Council for Health finally relented and recertified the project following a nine-month suspension.

Because of the actions of the Qatari IRB and the kind of information it
claimed the right to access, I concluded that I could no longer conduct research
in Qatar while also protecting the confidentiality of research participants. The
gestures of intimidation that had crescendoed before my departure in late
October 2014 also raised concerns for me about my personal safety and that
of members of any research team. Even if these concerns could be resolved,
the actions of the Qatari IRB irreparably damaged the project: the IRB had
placed me in the regulatory crosshairs in an authoritarian setting, nullify-
ing any support I could legitimately claim from the government through the
Qatar National Research Foundation; my departure, with no explanation that
I could offer my research participants without subjecting them to some measure of the risk I was confronting, undermined the delicate relations of trust
on which this project depended. Additionally, the investments in the research
infrastructure that I had made for the subsequent phases of the research in
Qatar had been undermined, including the recruitment, hiring, and training of a research team; the design of an industry survey, setup of preparatory
logistics, and endorsement of important industry actors; and access to new
skill certification programs.

In June 2015, a few weeks after the BBC team was detained in Qatar, and
I submitted the interim research progress report requested by Silatech, as if,
as Lobel of the BCC commented, "nothing had happened," New York University formally canceled the research contract. The Qatar National Research
Foundation subsequently launched a detailed audit of New York University's
financial management of the grant that lasted well into the following year.

Acknowledgments and Confidentiality

There was much to love about Qatar, and I did. I admired the optimism of
Qatar's ambition to reinvent itself, and its drive to fulfill its slogan for the
2022 World Cup bid: "Expect Amazing." Qatar was a riotously cosmopolitan
place, with people from around the world of different cultures, religions, and
histories working together, forging connection, and caring for one another. In
many senses, it was a hopeful affirmation of how generative and easy it can
be to form community that is multinational, multilingual, and multifaceted,
and that differences that have elsewhere hardened into divisions can be sur-
mounted as well as perhaps even revealed as political fictions.

The embargo on my research was a product of a moment in time, although
arguably all forms of repression are expressions of moments in time. In the
wake of Qatari efforts to curtail research on migrant workers, and to some
extent, alongside them, the Qatari government also instituted a number
of legal reforms that significantly increased the rights of migrant workers

in Qatar. Still, as the recent autocratic turn in countries around the world reminds us, moments of political openness are always defined by their vulnerability to closure.

The research for this project took place at a time when the red lines of authoritarian control parted for a while to allow it. Still, it could not have been completed without generous, significant, and brave help. For the reasons described in this postscript, and because I cannot predict how this research will be perceived in the future, I am unable to thank those who helped by name.

Even so, I want to thank the workers on the various construction sites that I visited. They kept me and my research assistant safe as we climbed scaffolds, observed their work at heights, and moved through areas of the construction sites where multiple functions were happening at the same time. Their attentiveness, reading of our body language, and constancy of their kindness made the field research we did possible. I also want to thank the managers, consultants, and engineers for their candor and clear-eyed assessments, help in facilitating this research, especially access, and detailed explanations of the technical challenges involved in construction. Many officials in government, both Qatari and non-Qatari, assisted with this project, and I am grateful for their help—often remarkable for its generosity and the commitment to the well-being of workers that it reflected—and thoughtful institutional analysis. The staff at Silatch, my institutional sponsor on this project, was strategic and generous in navigating the political and institutional constraints this research faced, and if there was any room to conduct the fieldwork on which this book depends, it is thanks to them.

I am deeply indebted to my research assistant, to whom I will give the pseudonym Heba, which means "gift" in Arabic, because that is what she was. She was intrepid, assertive, and compassionate, and engaged with the array of research tasks involved in this project—from detailed administrative tasks to hot afternoons in labor camps—with tremendous resourcefulness. She also made the research fun. We laughed, and it helped our hearts in the midst of the heartache we frequently witnessed. One of the best memories I have from the research is driving to a construction site at sunrise with Om Kalsoum playing on the radio and Heba's mother's dawn prayers following us with their kindness. At various points in the project, I had two other research assistants, whom I will also not name but would like to thank: C. helped design the survey that we were never able to run, and traveled with me to Nepal and met my middle-of-the-night emails about the following day's interviews with both forbearance and diligence. N. kept track of the statistical data for the project. His legal analysis of the various iterations of Qatar's labor codes was meticulous and insightful. I would also like to acknowledge the five translators we worked with, some of whom were new to the field of construction, and others who had been employed in construction themselves. All were sensitive, curious, and generous.

New York University provided significant institutional support for this project. I would especially like to thank Ellen Schall, who came to my rescue at a particularly difficult juncture of this project, along with Sherry Glied, Victoria McCoy-Constantino, Kathleen Walcott, and the entire team at the IRB for human subjects protocols, especially Alison Dewhurst, Gretchen Borges, and Marguarette Bolton-Blatt. I am grateful to Arundathi Amirapu and Nicole Vecchione, who helped with background research. New York University also supplied funding for portions of the research.

The research and writing that went into this book were also generously supported through two faculty fellowships, the first at the Center for the Advanced Study of the Behavioral Sciences at Stanford University, where Margaret Levi provided me with invaluable inspriration and guidance, and the second at the Zolberg Institute for Migration and Mobility at the New School for Social Research. I am immensely grateful for the engagement that those fellowships offered. The richness of those exchanges left their mark on the book, and it is much better for them.

The analysis that went into the book was deeply inductive, and at various points in time, I felt I was feeling my way forward in the dark. Without the North Star provided by so many colleagues and friends who read sections of the manuscript, pushed me with perceptive questions, and shared their razor-sharp insights, this book would never have found its way to becoming. My debt to them is immense. For their generous and thoughtful engagement with the book, and their discerning commentary, I want to thank Rachel Sherman, Anne McNevin, Alexandra Delano, Radhika Subramanian, Laura Liu, Paul Osterman, Susan Silbey, Thomas Kochan, Andrew Schrank, Richard Locke, Meenu Tewari, Monica Pinhanez, Janice Fine, Roger Waldinger, Hiroshi Motomura, Nicole Constable, Rachel Silvey, Rhacel Parreñas, Patricia Fernandez-Kelly, Paula Chakravartty, May Al Dabbagh, John Gershman, Jonathan Morduch, Andrew Ross, Marie Leger, Ruth Milkman, Louis Hyman, Maureen Perry-Jenkins, Loren Landau, Daniel Rodgers, and Frances Morphy. Manjula Luthria, Michael Clemens, and Theo Emery buoyed the project at various points in its development with their belief in it. Rina Agarwala found the heart of the argument and encouraged me to polish away all that didn't belong to it. Sumila Gulyani fed the project with her enthusiasm for it, and bettered it with her perceptive and keen feedback. Michael Piore was an unfailing and compassionate guide, helping me, as he has for two decades now, find what was true in the argument. Victoria Hattam vivified my curiousity with her own, and helped me immeasurably through her reading and rereading of chapters to sharpen the contours of the claims I make and the stories I tell. Miriam Ticktin embraced this project; she read and gave criticals insights on the many versions of the many chapters in this book, and the final version is much improved for her intelligent care and suggestions. I am deeply grateful to Nichola Lowe. Our longtime collaboration in the exploration of skill acted as a compass as I researched and wrote this book. I drew on what I learned through our joint examination of skill, its tacit layers and its constant evolution, and was reminded by our friendship that discerning the patterns of skillful practice can only happen through friendly dedication. Sometimes people provided support without knowing that they did; for these unknowing but invaluable gestures of help, I want to thank Nils Fonstad, Woody Powell, and the late Mary Grantham-Campbell. Additionally, I would like to thank the three anonymous reviewers whose careful assessment of the manuscript improved it immensely. Whatever errors remain after all the effort that others have poured into this book are mine alone.

In the writing of this book, I am also indebted to Emily Austin, whose skillful editing refined my prose, and Corinne Kentor, who managed my citations with awesome adeptness and gave me beautifully perceptive feedback on drafts. Thanks also to Javier Perez, who helped me tell the story of this book and its making.

At Princeton University Press, I am grateful to Meagan Levinson, a beautifully sensitive editor, and the entire editorial and publicity team, especially Jacqueline Delaney, Jill Harris, Karl Spurzem, Brigid Ackerman, Kate Hensley, and Kathryn Stevens, for their dedication to this project, and Cindy Milstein, for their mastery of detail.

The research and writing of this book was a long journey, and while I traveled it, I drew on the support and love of my family and friends. They are my good fortune. I am so grateful to Magdi Iskander, Silvia Sagari, and Yasmine Iskander for being the earth to my roots; my beloved aunts, Hoda, Mona, Samia, and Laila Iskander, for their fierce counsel; Carmen and Antonio Elosua for their warm embrace (and a place to swim and write); Robin Chalfin for the constancy and sensitivity of her friendship; Maria del Carmen Elosua, my partner and fellow traveler in the adventures of this life, for the lightness and celebration with which she reminds me to walk.

And finally, per the terms of my grant with the Qatar National Research Foundation, I need to specify that large portions of this research were made possible by NPRP grant NPRP 6-506-5-052 from the Qatar National Research Fund (a member of Qatar Foundation). The statements made herein are solely the responsibility of the author. The author acknowledges the support of Silatech.

NOTES

Introduction

1. Richard Spencer, "Asian Labourers Press Ganged into Joining Qatar Marathon Record Attempt," *Telegraph*, March 30, 2015, accessed February 13, 2020, https://www.telegraph.co.uk/news/worldnews/middleeast/qatar/11503669/Asian-labourers-press-ganged-into-joining-Qatar-marathon-record-attempt.html.

2. Ben Collins, "Slaves Forced to Run Marathon Shoeless in Qatar," *Daily Beast*, April 14, 2017, accessed February 13, 2020, https://www.thedailybeast.com/slaves-forced-to-run-marathon-shoeless-in-qatar.

3. Joey Aguilar, "Qatar Mega Marathon 2015 Set for March 27," *Gulf Times*, February 4, 2015, accessed February 13, 2020, https://desktop.gulf-times.com/story/425911/Qatar-Mega-Marathon-2015-set-for-March-27; Bhanvi Satija, "Why Were These Immigrant Workers Made to Run a Marathon, Shoeless, in Qatar?," *Youth Ki Awaaz*, April 15, 2015, accessed February 13, 2020, https://www.youthkiawaaz.com/2015/04/qatar-mega-marathon/.

4. Kit Fox, "Problems Abundant at Qatar Mega Marathon," *Runner's World*, April 6, 2015, accessed February 13, 2020, https://www.runnersworld.com/news/a20783965/problems-abundant-at-qatar-mega-marathon/.

5. Dylan Newman, "Qatari Soccer Team Forces Migrant Workers to Run Half-Marathon in Flip Flops without Water," *Soccer Politics*, April 3, 2015, accessed February 13, 2020, https://sites.duke.edu/wcwp/2015/04/03/qatari-soccer-team-forces-migrant-workers-to-run-half-marathon-in-flip-flops-without-water/.

6. Arturo Mabag, "Qatar Mega Marathon 2015," YouTube, March 28, 2015, accessed February 13, 2020, https://www.youtube.com/watch?v=ArlrlHa3oME&t=116s.

7. Spencer, "Asian Labourers Press Ganged into Joining Qatar Marathon Record Attempt."

8. Human Rights Watch, "Qatar: Take Urgent Action to Protect Construction Workers," September 27, 2017, accessed November 10, 2020, https://www.hrw.org/news/2017/09/27/qatar-take-urgent-action-protect-construction-workers#; Amnesty International, *Qatar: The Dark Side of Migration: Spotlight on Qatar's Construction Sector Ahead of the World Cup* (London: Amnesty International, 2013), accessed November 10, 2020, https://www.amnesty.org/en/documents/MDE22/010/2013/en/; Amnesty International, *All Work, No Pay: The Struggle of Qatar's Migrant Workers for Justice* (London: Amnesty International, 2019), accessed November 10, 2020, https://www.amnesty.at/media/6034/amnesty_all-work-no-pay-the-struggle-of-qatars-migrant-workers-for-justice_bericht-september-2019.pdf; Amnesty International, *Qatar: Migrant Workers Unpaid for Months of Work by Company Linked to World Cup Host City* (London: Amnesty International, 2018), accessed November 10, 2020, https://www.amnestyusa.org/reports/qatar-migrant-workers-unpaid-for-months-of-work-by-company-linked-to-world-cup-host-city/.

9. Stephen R. Barley and Gideon Kunda, "Bringing Work Back In," *Organization Science* 12, no. 1 (2001): 76–95.

10. Michael Burawoy, *Manufacturing Consent: Changes in the Labor Process under Monopoly Capitalism* (Chicago: University of Chicago Press, 1982).

11. For a review, see Paul Attewell, "What Is Skill?," *Work and Occupations* 17, no. 4 (1990): 422–48.

12. For a review, see Françoise Delamare Le Deist and Jonathan Winterton, "What Is Competence?," *Human Resource Development International* 8, no. 1 (2005): 27–46.

13. Karl Marx, *Economic and Philosophic Manuscripts of 1844* (Mineola, NY: Dover Publications, Inc., 2007), 89, 90, 87, 86.

14. For a review, see Fredrick Muyia Nafukho, Nancy Hairston, and Kit Brooks, "Human Capital Theory: Implications for Human Resource Development," *Human Resource Development International* 7, no. 4 (2004): 545–51.

15. Diane Elson and Ruth Pearson, "Nimble Fingers Make Cheap Workers: An Analysis of Women's Employment in Third World Export Manufacturing," *Feminist Review* 7, no. 1 (1981): 87–107; Ann Farnsworth-Alvear, *Dulcinea in the Factory: Myths, Morals, Men, and Women in Colombia's Industrial Experiment, 1905–1960* (Durham, NC: Duke University Press, 2000).

16. Laura Levine Frader, "From Muscles to Nerves: Gender, 'Race' and the Body at Work in France, 1919–1939," *International Review of Social History* 44, no. S7 (1999): 123–47; Erasmo Gamboa, *Mexican Labor and World War II: Braceros in the Pacific Northwest, 1942–1947* (Seattle: University of Washington Press, 2000); Phillip Moss and Chris Tilly, *Stories Employers Tell: Race, Skill, and Hiring in America* (New York: Russell Sage Foundation, 2001).

17. Evelyn Nakano Glenn, "From Servitude to Service Work: Historical Continuities in the Racial Division of Paid Reproductive Labor," *Signs: Journal of Women in Culture and Society* 18, no. 1 (1992): 1–43; Kiran Mirchandani, "Challenging Racial Silences in Studies of Emotion Work: Contributions from Anti-Racist Feminist Theory," *Organization Studies* 24, no. 5 (2003): 721–42; Ronnie J. Steinberg and Deborah M. Figart, "Emotional Labor Since: The Managed Heart," *Annals of the American Academy of Political and Social Science* 561, no. 1 (1999): 8–26.

18. Carol Wolkowitz, *Bodies at Work* (London: Sage, 2006).

19. Diana Coole, "Rethinking Agency: A Phenomenological Approach to Embodiment and Agentic Capacities," *Political Studies* 53, no. 1 (2005): 124–42.

20. Cedric J. Robinson, *Black Marxism: The Making of the Black Radical Tradition* (Chapel Hill: University of North Carolina Press, 2000).

21. Jodi Melamed, "Racial Capitalism," *Critical Ethnic Studies* 1, no. 1 (2015): 76–85; Ruth Wilson Gilmore, *Golden Gulag: Prisons, Surplus, Crisis, and Opposition in Globalizing California* (Berkeley: University of California Press, 2007).

22. American FactFinder, 2020, accessed February 21, 2020, https://factfinder.census.gov/faces/tableservices/jsf/pages/productview.xhtml?src=bkmk.

23. "World Economic Outlook Database, April 2019," International Monetary Fund, April 12, 2019.

24. Central Intelligence Agency, "Country Comparison: Natural Gas—Proved Reserves," World Factbook, accessed February 13, 2020, https://www.cia.gov/library/publications/the-world-factbook/rankorder/2253rank.html.

25. Way Lee Cheng, Ayman Saleem, and Reza Sadr, "Recent Warming Trend in the Coastal Region of Qatar," *Theoretical and Applied Climatology* 128, no. 1 (2017): 193–205, accessed November 10, 2020, https://doi.org/10.1007/s00704-015-1693-6, https://doi.org/10.1007/s00704-015-1693-6; Berkeley Earth, "Regional Climate Change: Qatar," 2015, accessed February 13, 2020, http://berkeleyearth.lbl.gov/regions/qatar.

26. Steven Mufson, "Facing Unbearable Heat, Qatar Has Begun to Air-condition the Outdoors," *Washington Post* (Doha), October 16, 2019, accessed November 11, 2020, https://www.washingtonpost.com/graphics/2019/world/climate-environment/climate-change-qatar-air-conditioning-outdoors/.

27. Ministry of Development Planning and Statistics, *First Section: Population and Social Statistics, Chapter II: Labour Force* (2015), accessed November 11, 2020, https://www

.psa.gov.qa/en/statistics/Statistical%20Releases/Social/LaborForce/2015/Labour_force_2_2015_AE.pdf.

28. Jure Snoj, "Population of Qatar by Nationality—2019," *Priya Dsouza Communications*, no. In Our Perspectives, Our Expertise (August 15, 2019), accessed February 13, 2020, http://priyadsouza.com/population-of-qatar-by-nationality-in-2017/.

29. Ismail Serageldin, James A. Socknat, J. Stace Birks, Bob Li, and Clive A. Sinclair, *Manpower and International Labor Migration in the Middle East and North Africa*, ed. World Bank (Washington, DC: Oxford University Press, 1983); J. Stace Birks, Ian J. Seccombe, and Clive A. Sinclair, "Labour Migration in the Arab Gulf States: Patterns, Trends, and Prospects," *International Migration* 26, no. 3 (1988): 267–86.

30. Ministry of Development Planning and Statistics, *First Section: Population and Social Statistics, Chapter II*, table 20.

31. Business Monitor International, *Qatar Infrastructure Report Q1 2015* (London: Business Monitor International, 2015).

32. Abdelhakim Mohamed Hassabou and Moazzam Ali Khan, "Energy Efficient and Sustainable Buildings: Integration with Solar Air-conditioning Technology in Qatar—A Step towards Grid Free Zero Carbon Living," *International Solar Energy Society* (2018), accessed November 11, 2020, http://proceedings.ises.org/paper/eurosun2018/eurosun2018-0090-Khan.pdf; Urban Times, "Carbon Heavy Qatar Roars Ahead in Green Building Innovation," *Smart Cities Dive*, accessed November 11, 2020, https://www.smartcitiesdive.com/ex/sustainablecitiescollective/qatar-green-building-innovation/122191/.

33. Adam Hanieh, *Money, Markets, and Monarchies: The Gulf Cooperation Council and the Political Economy of the Contemporary Middle East* (Cambridge: Cambridge University Press, 2018).

34. John Van Maanen, "Ethnography as Work: Some Rules of Engagement," *Journal of Management Studies* 48, no. 1 (2011): 218–34.

35. Michael Burawoy, "Revisits: An Outline of a Theory of Reflexive Ethnography," *American Sociological Review* (2003): 645–79; Frederick Erickson, "What Makes School Ethnography 'Ethnographic'?," *Anthropology and Education Quarterly* 15, no. 1 (1984): 51–66.

36. Natasha Iskander and Nichola Lowe, "Hidden Talent: Tacit Skill Formation and Labor Market Incorporation of Latino Immigrants in the United States," *Journal of Planning Education and Research* 30, no. 2 (2010): 132–46.

37. Tim Ingold, "Five Questions of Skill," *Cultural Geographies* 25, no. 1 (2018): 159–63.

38. Ministry of Development Planning and Statistics, *First Section: Population and Social Statistics, Chapter II*, table 20.

39. Michelle Buckley, "Locating Neoliberalism in Dubai: Migrant Workers and Class Struggle in the Autocratic City," *Antipode* 45, no. 2 (2013): 256–74; Bina Fernandez, "Cheap and Disposable? The Impact of the Global Economic Crisis on the Migration of Ethiopian Women Domestic Workers to the Gulf," *Gender and Development* 18, no. 2 (2010): 249–62; Rhacel Parreñas, *Servants of Globalization: Migration and Domestic Work* (Palo Alto, CA: Stanford University Press, 2015); Rachel Silvey, "Consuming the Transnational Family: Indonesian Migrant Domestic Workers to Saudi Arabia," *Global Networks* 6, no. 1 (2006): 23–40.

Chapter 1. Regulation: How the Politics of Skill Become Law

1. Marissa Payne, "Bill Clinton Reportedly Smashed a Mirror after Hearing Qatar Won the 2022 World Cup Bid," *Washington Post*, June 3, 2014, accessed January 2, 2020, https://www.washingtonpost.com/news/early-lead/wp/2014/06/03/bill-clinton-reportedly

-smashed-a-mirror-after-hearing-qatar-won-the-2022-world-cup-bid/?utm_term=
.f06ae74d38ca.

2. *PBS NewsHour*, "FIFA Announces Russia, Qatar as World Cup Hosts for 2018, 2022 (Full Presentation)," YouTube, December 2, 2010, accessed January 2, 2020, https://www .youtube.com/watch?v=YfyPi5MnPSY.

3. International Trade Union Confederation, *Hidden Faces of the Gulf Miracle* (May 5, 2011), accessed November 12, 2020, https://www.ituc-csi.org/hidden-faces-of-the-gulf -miracle-9144.

4. Brian Homewood, "Soccer-FIFA Warned to Make Sure Qatar Respects Workers Rights," *Reuters*, November 16, 2011, accessed February 19, 2020, https://uk.reuters.com /article/soccer-fifa-workers/soccer-fifa-warned-to-make-sure-qatar-respects-workers -rights-idUKB18866220111116.

5. Priyanka Motaparthy, *Building a Better World Cup: Protecting Migrant Workers in Qatar Ahead of FIFA 2022* (New York: Human Rights Watch, 2012), accessed November 12, 2020, https://www.hrw.org/sites/default/files/reports/qatar0612webwcover_0.pdf; Amnesty International, *Qatar: The Dark Side of Migration: Spotlight on Qatar's Construction Sector Ahead of the World Cup* (London: Amnesty International, 2013), accessed November 10, 20202, https://www.amnesty.org/en/documents/MDE22/010/2013/en/.

6. Pete Pattisson, "Revealed: Qatar's World Cup 'Slaves,'" *Guardian* (Kathmandu and Doha), September 25, 2013, accessed November 12, 2020, https://www.theguardian.com /world/2013/sep/25/revealed-qatars-world-cup-slaves.

7. Amnesty International, *The Ugly Side of the Beautiful Game: Exploitation of Migrant Workers on a Qatar 2022 World Cup Site* (London: Amnesty International, 2016), accessed November 12, 2020, https://www.amnesty.org/download/Documents /MDE2235482016ENGLISH.PDF.

8. Christiane Amanpour, "Full Interview: Emir of Qatar," *CNN World*, 2014, November 12, 2020, https://www.cnn.com/videos/world/2014/09/25/intv-amanpour-qatar-emir -tamim-bin-hamad-al-thani-full.cnn.

9. "Qatar World Cup: 'Squalid' Conditions for Migrant Workers," *Channel 4 News*, 2015, accessed November 12, 2020, https://www.channel4.com/news/qatar-world-cup-squalid -conditions-for-migrant-workers.

10. Leana Hosea, "Inside Qatar's Squalid Labour Camps," *BBC World News*, 2014, accessed November 12, 2020, https://www.bbc.com/news/world-middle-east-26482775.

11. Sam Badger and Giorgio Cafiero, "Kingdom of Slaves," September 12, 2014, accessed January 2, 2020, https://fpif.org/kingdom-slaves/.

12. Andrew M. Gardner, Silvia Pessoa, and Laura M. Harkness, *Labour Migrants and Access to Justice in Contemporary Qatar*, LSE Middle East Centre, November 2014; Anh Nga Longva, *Walls Built on Sand: Migration, Exclusion, and Society in Kuwait* (Boulder, CO: Westview Press, 1999); Azfar Khan and Hélène Harroff-Tavel, "Reforming the Kafala: Challenges and Opportunities in Moving Forward," *Asian and Pacific Migration Journal* 20, no. 3–4 (2011): 293–313; Radhika Kanchana, "Is the Kafala Tradition to Blame for the Exploitative Work Conditions in the Arab-Gulf Countries?," in *South Asian Migration in the Gulf: Causes and Consequences*, ed. Mehdi Chowdhury and S. Irudaya Rajan (New York: Springer, 2018), 61–79; Mutaz M. Qafisheh, "Restorative Justice in the Islamic Penal Law: A Contribution to the Global System," *International Journal of Criminal Justice Sciences* 7, no. 1 (2012): 487–507.

13. Press Association, "FIFA's Sepp Blatter Dismisses Fears over 2022 World Cup in Qatar," *Guardian*, December 13, 2010, accessed November 13, 2020, https://www .theguardian.com/football/2010/dec/13/fifa-sepp-blatter-discrimination-qatar-2022.

14. Azadeh Erfani, "Kicking Away Responsibility: FIFA's Role in Response to Migrant Worker Abuses in Qatar's 2022 World Cup," *Jeffrey S. Moorad Sports LJ* 22 (2015): 623.

15. For an analysis of the contemporary and historical ways in which humanitarian practices have narrowed definitions of freedom to bodily welfare, see Miriam Ticktim, *Casualties of Care: Immigration and the Politics of Humanitarianism in France* (Berkeley: University of California Press, 2011).

16. "Pearls Growing Scarce: Rich Are Buying Them," *New York Times*, September 14, 1906.

17. Matthew S. Hopper, *Slaves of One Master: Globalization and Slavery in Arabia in the Age of Empire* (New Haven, CT: Yale University Press, 2015); George Frederick Kunz and Charles Hugh Stevenson, *The Book of the Pearl: The History, Art, Science and Industry of the Queen of Gems* (1908; repr., Mineola, NY: Dover Publications, 1993); "J.P. Morgan Gives Pearls to Bride," *New York Times*, January 3, 1909.

18. Hopper, *Slaves of One Master*.

19. Arthur Howard, "Selling Jewels to Multimillionaires: The Duchess of Montrose's Necklace," *McClure's Magazine*, July 1913, 56–65.

20. Kunz and Stevenson, *The Book of the Pearl*.

21. "Pearls Growing Scarce."

22. Hopper, *Slaves of One Master*, 94–96; John Gordon Lorimer, *Gazetteer of the Persian Gulf, 'Oman, and Central Arabia* (Calcutta: Superintendent Government Printing, 1915), 2220–21, accessed November 13, 2020, http://catalog.hathitrust.org/Record/011590480.

23. Lorimer, *Gazetteer of the Persian Gulf*, 2220.

24. Hopper, *Slaves of One Master*, 81.

25. Lorimer, *Gazetteer of the Persian Gulf*, 2257.

26. Abed Al-Razzak Al-Maani and Saleh Alsharari, "Pearl Trade in the Persian Gulf during the 19th Century," *Asian Culture and History* 6, no. 1 (2014): 43–52.

27. Hopper, *Slaves of One Master*.

28. Patrick Manning, *Slavery and African Life: Occidental, Oriental, and African Slave Trades* (Cambridge: Cambridge University Press, 1990), 67:83; Benjamin Reilly, *Slavery, Agriculture, and Malaria in the Arabian Peninsula* (Athens: Ohio University Press, 2015), 128–29.

29. Frederick Cooper, "Conflict and Connection: Rethinking Colonial African History," *American Historical Review* 99, no. 5 (1994): 1516–45.

30. Matthew S. Hopper, "East Africa and the End of the Indian Ocean Slave Trade," *Journal of African Development* 13, no. 1 (2011): 39–65.

31. Hopper, *Slaves of One Master*; Jerzy Zdanowski, *Speaking with Their Own Voices: The Stories of Slaves in the Persian Gulf in the 20th Century* (Cambridge: Cambridge Scholars Publishing, 2014).

32. Jerzy Zdanowski, *Slavery and Manumission: British Policy in the Red Sea and the Persian Gulf in the First Half of the 20th Century* (Reading, UK: Ithaca Press, 2013).

33. Hopper, *Slaves of One Master*.

34. Zdanowski, *Speaking with Their Own Voices*, 77.

35. Zdanowski, *Slavery and Manumission*.

36. Hopper, *Slaves of One Master*; Kunz and Stevenson, *The Book of the Pearl*, 92; Lorimer, *Gazetteer of the Persian Gulf*, 2227–31.

37. Lorimer, *Gazetteer of the Persian Gulf*, 2239.

38. Hopper, *Slaves of One Master*, 112.

39. Hopper, *Slaves of One Master*, 142.

40. Suzanne Miers, "Slavery and the Slave Trade as International Issues, 1890–1939," *Slavery and Abolition* 19, no. 2 (1998): 16–37; Benjamin J. Reilly, "A Well-Intentioned Failure: British Anti-Slavery Measures and the Arabian Peninsula, 1820–1940," *Journal of Arabian Studies* 5, no. 2 (2015): 91–115.

41. Lorimer, *Gazetteer of the Persian Gulf*, 2243.

42. Hopper, *Slaves of One Master.*

43. Lorimer, *Gazetteer of the Persian Gulf*, 2231.

44. Joseph Taylor and Elizabeth Strack, *Pearl Production* (Amsterdam: Elsevier, 2008), 284–85.

45. Sugata Bose, *A Hundred Horizons: The India Ocean in the Age of Global Empire* (Cambridge, MA: Harvard University Press, 2006): 85–88.

46. Michael Field, *The Merchants: The Big Business Families of Saudi Arabia and the Gulf States* (New York: Overlook Press, 1985), 205.

47. Mohammed Alsudairi and Rogaia Mustafa Abusharaf, "Migration in Pre-Oil Qatar: A Sketch," *Studies in Ethnicity and Nationalism* 15, no. 3 (2015): 511–21.

48. Hopper, "East Africa"; Ian J. Seccombe, "Labour Migration to the Arabian Gulf: Evolution and Characteristics, 1920–1950," *British Journal of Middle Eastern Studies* 10, no. 1 (1983): 3–20.

49. Suzanne Miers, *Slavery in the Twentieth Century: The Evolution of a Global Problem* (Walnut Creek, CA: Rowman and Littlefield, 2003).

50. Hopper, *Slaves of One Master*, 194–95; Zdanowski, *Speaking with Their Own Voices*, 82–83.

51. Bose, *A Hundred Horizons*, 90–91.

52. Zdanowski, *Speaking with Their Own Voices*, 84.

53. Rupert Hay, *The Persian Gulf States* (London: Middle East Institute, 1959), 112.

54. Rupert Hay, "The Impact of the Oil Industry on the Persian Gulf Shaykhdoms," *Middle East Journal* 9, no. 4 (1955): 368–69.

55. Hay, *The Persian Gulf States*, 110.

56. "Coll 54/2 'Middle East (Official) Committee: Working Party,'" IOR/L/PS/12/4758, British Library: India Office Records and Private Papers, Qatar Digital Library, accessed November 14, 2020, https://www.qdl.qa/en/archive/81055/vdc_100000000691.0x0001dd.

57. Rosemarie Said Zahlan, *The Creation of Qatar* (London: Croon Helm, 1979), 99.

58. Frederick F. Anscombe, *The Ottoman Gulf: The Creation of Kuwait, Saudi Arabia, and Qatar* (New York: Columbia University Press, 1997).

59. Mark Hayman, "Inducement and Coercion on the Trucial Coast: The First Oil Agreements," *Journal of Imperial and Commonwealth History* 38, no. 2 (2010): 261–78.

60. Zuhair Ahmed Nafi, *Economic and Social Development in Qatar* (London: Bloomsbury Academic, 1983).

61. A' Asi, "The Arab/Persian Gulf: Oil on Troubled Waters," *MERIP Reports* (1971): 1–8.

62. "'File 82/27 VII F 91 Qatar Oil' [37r] (82/468)," IOR/R/15/1/633, British Library: India Office of Records and Private Papers, Qatar Digital Library, accessed November 14, 2020, https://www.qdl.qa/en/archive/81055/vdc_100023800656.0x000054.

63. Jill Crystal, *Oil and Politics in the Gulf: Rulers and Merchants in Kuwait and Qatar*, vol. 24 (Cambridge: Cambridge University Press, 1995).

64. "'File 10/3 III Qatar Oil Concession' [136r] (293/470)," IOR/R/15/2/412, British Library: India Office Records and Private Papers, Qatar Digital Library, accessed November 14, 2020, http://www.qdl.qa/en/archive/81055/vdc_100023550520.0x00005e.

65. "'File 10/3 III Qatar Oil Concession' [179r] (382/470)," IOR/R/15/2/412, British Library: India Office Records and Private Papers, Qatar Digital Library, accessed November 14, 2020, http://www.qdl.qa/en/archive/81055/vdc_100023550520.0x0000b7.

66. "'File 10/3 III Qatar Oil Concession' [108r] (323/470)," IOR/R/15/2/412, British Library: India Office Records and Private Papers, Qatar Digital Library, accessed November 14, 2020, http://www.qdl.qa/en/archive/81055/vdc_100023550520.0x000021.

67. "'File 10/3 III Qatar Oil Concession' [179r] (382/470)."

68. Ian J. Seccombe and Richard I. Lawless, "Foreign Worker Dependence in the Gulf, and the International Oil Companies: 1910–50," *International Migration Review* (1986): 552–53.

69. Nasser al-Othman, *With Their Bare Hands: The Story of the Oil Industry in Qatar*, trans. Ken Whittingham (London: Longman, 1984), 52.

70. Rosemarie Said Zahlan, "The Impact of the Early Oil Concessions in the Gulf States," in *The Gulf in the Early 20th Century: Foreign Institutions and Local Responses*, ed. Richard I. Lawless (Durham, NC: Center for Middle Eastern and Islamic Studies, 1986).

71. Crystal, *Oil and Politics in the Gulf*, 24, 134.

72. Crystal, *Oil and Politics in the Gulf*, 24, 134; Field, *The Merchants*.

73. Crystal, *Oil and Politics in the Gulf*, 24, 133.

74. Ian J. Seccombe and Richard I. Lawless, "The Gulf Labour Market and the Early Oil Industry: Traditional Structures and New Forms of Organisation," in *The Gulf in the Early 20th Century: Foreign Institutions and Local Responses*, ed. Richard I. Lawless (Durham, NC: Center for Middle Eastern and Islamic Studies, 1986), 101.

75. Seccombe and Lawless, "The Gulf Labour Market and the Early Oil Industry," 106.

76. Seccombe and Lawless, "The Gulf Labour Market and the Early Oil Industry," 108.

77. al-Othman, *With Their Bare Hands*, 60.

78. "Coll 30/231 'Annual Political Review of Events in the Persian Gulf' [12r] (24/33)," IOR/L/PS/12/3973, British Library: India Office Records and Private Papers, Qatar Digital Library, accessed November 15, 2020, https://www.qdl.qa/archive/81055/vdc_100060870618.0x000019.

79. Miers, *Slavery in the Twentieth Century*, 307–9.

80. Henry Longhurst, *Adventures in Oil: The Story of British Petroleum* (London: Sidgwick and Jackson, 1959), 210–11.

81. Crystal, *Oil and Politics in the Gulf*, 24, 140.

82. Seccombe and Lawless, "The Gulf Labour Market and the Early Oil Industry," 102.

83. "Coll 54/2 'Middle East (Official) Committee: Working Party'"; Seccombe and Lawless, "The Gulf Labour Market and the Early Oil Industry," 102.

84. Crystal, *Oil and Politics in the Gulf*, 24, 141.

85. al-Othman, *With Their Bare Hands*, 46.

86. "Oil in the Persian Gulf: Qatar Peninsula Terminals," *Times* (London), December 30, 1952.

87. David Northrup, *Indentured Labor in the Age of Imperialism, 1834–1922* (Cambridge: Cambridge University Press, 1995).

88. Madhavi Kale, *Fragments of Empire: Capital, Slavery, and Indian Indentured Labor in the British Caribbean* (Philadelphia: University of Pennsylvania Press, 2010).

89. Mrinalini Sinha, "Premonitions of the Past," *Journal of Asian Studies* 74, no. 4 (2015): 821–41.

90. Radhika Mongia, *Indian Migration and Empire: A Colonial Genealogy of the Modern State* (Durham, NC: Duke University Press, 2018).

91. Seccombe and Lawless, "Foreign Worker Dependence in the Gulf."

92. G. Findlay Shirras, "Indian Migration," in *International Migrations, Volume II: Interpretations*, ed. Walter F. Willcox (Cambridge, MA: National Bureau of Economic Research, 1931); Stefan Tetzlaff, "Entangled Boundaries: British India and the Persian Gulf Region during the Transition from Empires to Nation States, c. 1880–1935" (MA thesis, Humboldt Universitat zu Berlin, 2009).

93. Seccombe and Lawless, "Foreign Worker Dependence in the Gulf," 68; "'File 28/39 Roster of Petroleum Concessions Limited Employees' [43r] (85/180)," IOR/R/15/2/1736,

British Library: India Office Records and Private Papers, Qatar Digital Library, accessed November 15, 2020, http://www.qdl.qa/en/archive/81055/vdc_100023548254.0x000056; Seccombe and Lawless, "The Gulf Labour Market and the Early Oil Industry."

94. al-Othman, *With Their Bare Hands*.

95. Seccombe and Lawless, "Foreign Worker Dependence in the Gulf," 561–62.

96. Northrup, *Indentured Labor in the Age of Imperialism*; Mauritius, *Labor Laws of Mauritius or a Collection of the Laws Specially Relating to Masters and Servants at Mauritius Including the Acts of the Government of India on Emigration to That Colony* (Oxford: L. Channell's Steam Printing Establishment, 1869).

97. Rachel Sturman, "Indian Indentured Labor and the History of International Rights Regimes," *American Historical Review* 119, no. 5 (2014): 1445–46.

98. Sturman, "Indian Indentured Labor," 1454.

99. "Coll 54/2 'Middle East (Official) Committee: Working Party.'"

100. "Coll 54/2 'Middle East (Official) Committee: Working Party.'"

101. "Coll 54/2 'Middle East (Official) Committee: Working Party.'"

102. Seccombe and Lawless, "Foreign Worker Dependence in the Gulf."

103. al-Othman, *With Their Bare Hands*, 80.

104. "'File 3/21 Political Officer, Qatar and Political Affairs, Qatar' [13r] (25/94)," IOR/R/15/2/2000, British Library: India Office of Records and Private Papers, Qatar Digital Library, accessed November 15, 2020, https://www.qdl.qa/en/archive/81055/vdc_100026682295.0x00001a.

105. Crystal, *Oil and Politics in the Gulf*, 24, 122, 144.

106. Ian J. Seccombe and Richard I. Lawless, "Work Camps and Company Towns: Settlement Patterns and the Gulf Oil Industry" (working paper, University of Durham, Centre for Middle Eastern and Islamic Studies, 1987, 71.

107. Seccombe and Lawless, "Work Camps and Company Towns," 70.

108. Seccombe and Lawless, "Work Camps and Company Towns," 69.

109. David Finnie, "Recruitment and Training of Labor: The Middle East Oil Industry," *Middle East Journal* (1958): 127–43; Longhurst, *Adventure in Oil*.

110. Seccombe and Lawless, "The Gulf Labour Market and the Early Oil Industry," 113.

111. Anthony Toth, "Qatar," in *Persian Gulf States: Country Studies*, ed. Helen Chapin Metz (Washington, DC: Federal Research Division, Department of the Army, 1994), 147–96.

112. Crystal, *Oil and Politics in the Gulf*, 24, 141.

113. David H. Finnie, *Desert Enterprise: The Middle East Oil Industry in Its Local Environment*, vol. 1 (Cambridge, MA: Harvard University Press, 1958).

114. John Chalcraft, "Migration and Popular Protest in the Arabian Peninsula and the Gulf in the 1950s and 1960s," *International Labor and Working-Class History* 79, no. 1 (2011): 28–47.

115. al-Othman, *With Their Bare Hands*; Toth, "Qatar."

116. Crystal, *Oil and Politics in the Gulf*, 24.

117. Crystal, *Oil and Politics in the Gulf*, 24; Seccombe and Lawless, "The Gulf Labour Market and the Early Oil Industry."

118. Crystal, *Oil and Politics in the Gulf*, 24.

119. Zdanowski, *Slavery and Manumission*.

120. Zahlan, *The Creation of Qatar*.

121. Crystal, *Oil and Politics in the Gulf*, 24.

122. Ibrahim Shahdad, "الحراك الشعبيفيقطر 1950–1963 دراسة تحليلية [Popular movements, 1950–1963, analytic study]" (Kuwait City: Gulf Center for Development Policies, 2012).

123. Seccombe and Lawless, "Foreign Worker Dependence in the Gulf."

124. Gennaro Errichiello, "Foreign Workforce in the Arab Gulf States (1930–1950): Migration Patterns and Nationality Clause," *International Migration Review* 46, no. 2 (2012): 389–413; Finnie, *Desert Enterprise*, 1.

125. John Chalcraft, "Migration and Popular Protest in the Arabian Peninsula and the Gulf in the 1950s and 1960s," *International Labor and Working-Class History* 79, no. 1 (2011): 28–47.

126. Shahdad, "الحراك الشعبيفيقطر 1950–1963 دراسة تحليلية".

127. Crystal, *Oil and Politics in the Gulf*, 24; Miriam Joyce, *Ruling Shaikhs and Her Majesty's Government, 1960–1969* (London: Psychology Press, 2003), 51.

128. Ahmed bin Ali Al-Thani, "Law No. 2 of 1961 on the Qatari Nationality (repealed)" (Al Meezan: Qatar Legal Portal, 1961), accessed November 17, 2020, http://www.almeezan .qa/LawView.aspx?opt&LawID=2578&language=en.

129. "The Labour Law No. 3 of 1962" (Al Meezan: Qatar Legal Portal, 1962), accessed November 17, 2020, http://almeezan.qa/LawView.aspx?opt&LawID=2599&language=en.

130. Ahmed bin Ali Al-Thani, "Act No. (3) for the Year 1963 Governing Aliens Entry and Residence in Qatar" (Qatar: National Legislative Bodies / National Authorities, February 16, 1963), Article 21, accessed November 17, 2020, https://www.refworld.org/docid /3fb9f96f2.html.

131. A Nizar Hamzeh, "Qatar: The Duality of the Legal System," *Middle Eastern Studies* 30, no. 1 (1994): 79–90.

132. Ragaei El Mallakh, *Qatar: Energy and Development* (London: Croom Helm, 1985).

133. Onn Winckler, "TheI Immigration Policy of the Gulf Cooperation Council (GCC) States," *Middle Eastern Studies* 33, no. 3 (1997): 480–93.

134. Khalifa bin Hamad Al-Thani. "Law No. 3 of 1984 Regulating the Sponsorship of Residence and Departure of Foreigners (Repealed)" (Al Meezan: Qatar Legal Portal, January 1, 1984), accessed November 17, 2020, http://www.almeezan.qa/LawView.aspx ?opt&LawID=292&language=en.

135. Crystal, *Oil and Politics in the Gulf*, 24.

136. Miers, *Slavery in the Twentieth Century*.

137. World Bank, "Qatar: Oil Revenue," TheGlobalEconomy.com, 2019, accessed November 17, 2020, https://www.theglobaleconomy.com/Qatar/oil_revenue/.

138. Macrotrends, "Qatar GDP 1970–2020," Macrotrends, 2010–20, accessed November 17, 2020, https://www.macrotrends.net/countries/QAT/qatar/gdp-gross-domestic -product.

139. J. Stace Birks, Ian J. Seccombe, and Clive A. Sinclair, "Labour Migration in the Arab Gulf States: Patterns, Trends and Prospects," *International Migration* 26, no. 3 (1988): 267–86; Winckler, "The Immigration Policy of the Gulf Cooperation Council (GCC) States."

140. "Gulf States: Qatar," OxResearch Daily Brief Service, Oxford, 1989.

141. Winckler, "The Immigration Policy of the Gulf Cooperation Council (GCC) States."

142. John Connell, Jenny Want, A. K. Tripathi, and V. B. Bhatt, "Distant Victims? The Impact of the Gulf War on International Migration to the Middle East from Asia," in *Changing Environmental Ideologies*, ed. A. K. Tripathi and V. B. Bhatt (New Delhi: Ashish Publishing House, 1992), 131–64.

143. Sharon Stanton Russell, "International Migration and Political Turmoil in the Middle East," *Population and Development Review* 18, no. 4 (1992): 719–27, accessed November 17, 2020, https://doi.org/10.2307/1973761.

144. David McMurray, "Recent Trends in Middle Eastern Migration," *Middle East Report*, no. 211 (1999): 16–19, accessed November 17, 2020, https://doi.org/10.2307 /3013329.

145. J. Addleton, "The Impact of the Gulf War on Migration and Remittances in Asia and the Middle East," *International Migration* 29, no. 4 (1991): 509–26.

146. *Qatar Country Study Guide* (Washington, DC: International Business Publications, 2006).

147. Denis MacShane, "Gulf Slaves," *New Statements and Society*, 1991, 15–16.

148. Mark Fineman, "Lines in the Sand Drawing Gulf Nationals into Disputes; It's Not Just Iraq," *Los Angeles Times*, October 13, 1992.

149. Uzi Rabi, "Qatar," in *Middle East Contemporary Survey 1991*, ed. Ami Ayalon (Boulder, CO: Westview Press 1993), 612.

150. Mostafa H. Nagi, "Migration of Asian Workers to the Arab Gulf: Policy Determinants and Consequences," *Journal of South Asian and Middle Eastern Studies* 9, no. 3 (1986): 19.

151. Sooyong Kim, "Labor Migration from Korea to the Middle East: Its Trend and Impact on the Korean Economy," in *Asian Labor Migration*, ed. Fred Arnold and Nasra M. Shah (Boulder, CO: Westview Press, 1986): 163–75.

152. Robert LaPorte, "The Ability of South and East Asia to Meet the Labor Demands of the Middle East and North Africa," *Middle East Journal* 38, no. 4 (1984): 706, accessed November 17, 2020, http://ezproxy.library.nyu.edu:2105/stable/4326924.

153. Seung-Ik Chant, "Overseas Construction Expected to Be 'Dollar Box,'" *Korea Times*, March 2, 1975; Kon-ju Han, "Arab Nations Interested in Learning Technology," *Korea Times*, February 11, 1982; Nagi, "Migration of Asian Workers to the Arab Gulf."

154. "Jung Woo Boasts Hi-Fi Skills," *Korea Times*, June 23, 1981.

155. "Qatar to Open Doors to More ROK Builders," *Korea Times*, May 4, 1982.

156. John E. Smart, Virginia A. Teodosio, and Carol J. Jimenez, "Skills and Earnings: Issues in the Developmental Impact on the Philippines of Labor Export to the Middle East," in *Asian Labor Migration*, ed. Fred Arnold and Nasra M. Shah (Boulder, CO: Westview Press, 1986), 101–24.

157. LaPorte, "The Ability of South and East Asia to Meet the Labor Demands."

158. LaPorte, "The Ability of South and East Asia to Meet the Labor Demands," 705.

159. Ismail Serageldin, James A. Socknat, J. Stace Birks, Bob Li, and Clive A. Sinclair, *Manpower and International Labor Migration in the Middle East and North Africa*, ed. World Bank (Washington, DC: Oxford University Press, 1983).

160. Mary Anne Weaver, "Democracy by Decree," *New Yorker*, November 20, 2000, 54–61.

161. Jim Krane, "Gas Bubble Creates Economic Boom," Associated Press, April 25, 2005.

162. Russell Gold, "Power Play: In Qatar, Oil Firms Make Huge Bet on Alternative Fuel; Supporters Say New Diesel Is Cleaner, More Efficient; Untested on Large Scale; 'It Was Just Like Water,'" *Wall Street Journal*, Febraury 15, 2005, A1.

163. Planning Council, *Population and Housing Census (1997)*, QSA, 1997.

164. Planning Council, *Population and Housing Census (2004)*, QSA, 2004; State of Qatar, *Census of Population and Housing and Establishments 2010*, 2010, accessed November 17, 2020, https://www.psa.gov.qa/en/statistics/Statistical%20Releases/General/Census/Population_Households_Establishment_QSA_Census_AE_2010_1.pdf.

165. "Law No. 14 on the Promulgation of Labour Law" (Al Meezan: Qatar Legal Portal, July 7, 2004), accessed November 17, 2020, http://www.almeezan.qa/LawView.aspx?opt&LawID=3961&language=en.

166. Gardner, Pessoa, and Harkness, "Labour Migrants and Access to Justice."

167. Tamim bin Hamad Al-Thani, "Law No. 4 of 2009 regarding Regulation of the Expatriates Entry, Departure, Residence, and Sponsorship" (Al Meezan: Qatar Legal

Portal, 2009), accessed November 17, 2020, http://www.almeezan.qa/LawView.aspx ?opt&LawID=2611&language=en.

168. Tamim bin Hamad Al-Thani, "Law No. 4 of 2009," Article 37.

169. "Qatar GDP—Gross Domestic Product," Countryeconomy.com, 2009, accessed February 19, 2020, https://countryeconomy.com/gdp/qatar?year=2009.

170. Omer Aziz and Murtaza Hussain, "Qatar's World Cup Must Not Become a Monument to Slavery," opinion, *Globe and Mail*, December 18, 2013, accessed November 18, 2020, https://www.theglobeandmail.com/opinion/qatars-world-cup-must-not-become -a-monument-to-slavery/article16027180/; "Death and Servitude in Qatar," editorial, *New York Times*, 2013, accessed November 18, 2020, https://www.nytimes.com/2013/11 /02/opinion/death-and-servitude-in-qatar.html; Hosea, "Inside Qatar's Squalid Labour Camps."

171. Brian Homewood, "Blatter Calls Qatar Labor Situation 'Unacceptable,'" Reuters, November 20, 2013, Sports News, accessed November 18, 2020, https://www.reuters .com/article/us-soccer-qatar-labour/blatter-calls-qatar-labor-situation-unacceptable -idUSBRE9AJ0V620131120.

172. For a review, see Heidi Blake and Jonathan Calvert, *The Ugly Game: The Qatari Plot to Buy the World Cup* (New York: Simon and Schuster, 2015).

173. Qatar Foundation, *QF Mandatory Standards of Migrant Workers' Welfare for Contractors and Sub-Contractors* (Doha: Qatar Foundation, 2013); Supreme Committee for Delivery and Legacy, *SC Workers' Welfare Standards: A Lasting Legacy of Human and Social Development* (Doha: Supreme Committee for Delivery and Legacy, 2014).

174. Richard M. Locke, *The Promise and Limits of Private Power: Promoting Labor Standards in a Global Economy* (New York: Cambridge University Press, 2013).

175. DLA Piper, *Migrant Labor in the Construction Sector in the State of Qatar* (London: DLA Piper UK LLP, April 2014).

176. Tamim bin Hamad Al-Thani, "Law No. 1 of 2014 Regulating the Activities of Nursery Schools," (Al Meezan: Qatar Legal Portal, January 30, 2014 2014). http://www.almeezan .qa/LawPage.aspx?id=6115&language=en; Ray Jureidini, "Wage Protection Systems and Programmes in the GCC," *Migration to the Gulf: Policies in Sending and Receiving Countries*, ed. Philippe Fargues and Nasra M. Shah (Cambridge, UK: Gulf Research Centre, 2017), 9–33.

177. "Law No. 21 of 2015 Regulating the Entry and Exit of Expatriates and Their Residence," Official Gazette, October 27, 2015, accessed November 18, 2020, https://www.ilo.org /dyn/natlex/natlex4.detail?p_lang=en&p_isn=102231.

178. "Qatar Abolishes Controversial 'Kafala' Labour System," BBC News, December 13, 2016, Middle East, accessed November 18, 2020, https://www.bbc.com/news/world-middle -east-38298393.

179. Amnesty International, *The Ugly Side of the Beautiful Game*, 26.

180. International Labor Organization, *Complaint concerning Non-Observance by Qatar of the Forced Labour Convention, 1930 (No. 29), and the Labour Inspection Convention,1947 (No. 81), Made by Delegates to the 103rd Session (2014) of the International Labour Conference under Article 26 of the ILO Constitution* (Geneva: International Labor Organization, March 17, 2016), 18, accessed November 18, 2020, https://www.ilo.org/wcmsp5 /groups/public/---ed_norm/---relconf/documents/meetingdocument/wcms_459148.pdf.

181. Associated Press, "AP Interview: Qatar Labor Chief Criticizes Migrant Worker Housing, Vows to Improve Their Lives," Fox News, December 2, 2015, World, accessed November 18, 2020, https://www.foxnews.com/world/ap-interview-qatar-labor-chief -criticizes-migrant-worker-housing-vows-to-improve-their-lives; Amnesty International, *The Ugly Side of the Beautiful Game.*

182. Faras Ghani, "Minimum Wage, No NOC: Qatar Announces Changes to Labour Law," Al Jazeera, August 30, 2020, accessed December 27, 2020, https://www.aljazeera.com /economy/2020/8/30/minimum-wage-no-noc-qatar-announces-changes-to-labour-law.

183. Agence France Press, "Qatar to Introduce Minimum Wage for Workers," *Hindustan Times*, October 25, 2017, accessed December 26, 2020, https://www .hindustantimes.com/world-news/qatar-to-introduce-minimum-wage-for-workers/story -8hXPhSrzkJIusdeoCbj6DJ.html.

184. Hamad bin Khafila Al-Thani, "Law No. 13 of 1988 on the Temporary Expropriation and Appropriation of Real Estate for the Public Benefit" (Al Meezan: Qatar Legal Portal, 2018), accessed November 18, 2020, http://www.almeezan.qa/LawPage.aspx?id =3957&language=en.

185. "New Exit Permit Law Comes into Effect," *Gulf Times*, October 29, 2018, Qatar, accessed November 18, 2020, https://www.gulf-times.com/story/611068/New-exit-permit -law-comes-into-effect.

186. Steve Needham, "End of Exit Permits for Most Migrant Workers in Qatar Welcomed," International Labor Organization, September 4, 2018, accessed November 18, 2020, https://www.ilo.org/global/about-the-ilo/newsroom/news/WCMS_638754/lang --en/index.htm.

187. General Secretariat for Development Planning, *Qatar National Vision 2030* (Doha: General Secretariat for Development Planning, July 2008), accessed November 18, 2020, https://www.gco.gov.qa/wp-content/uploads/2016/09/GCO-QNV-English.pdf.

188. Qatar National Vision and Ministry of Development Planning and Statistics, *Qatar Second National Development Strategy, 2018–2022* (Doha: Planning and Statistics Authority, 2019), accessed November 18, 2020, https://www.psa.gov.qa/en/knowledge /Documents/NDS2Final.pdf.

189. Qatar National Vision and Ministry of Development Planning and Statistics, *Qatar Second National Development Strategy*, 204–5.

190. Gregory Walton, "Qatar to End Controversial Migrant Worker Restrictions," *AFP International Text Wire in English* (Washington, DC), October 16, 2019.

191. State of Qatar, Law No. 18 of 2020 (Termination of Employment), International Labor Organization—Project Office for the State of Qatar, September 8, 2020, accessed December 27, 2020, https://www.ilo.org/beirut/projects/qatar-office/WCMS_754882/lang --en/index.htm.

192. Ghani, "Minimum Wage, No NOC."

Chapter 2. Production: How Skill Makes Cities

1. Qatar Planning and Statistics Authority, *Population and Social Statistics—Quarterly Bulletin (2000–2018)* (Doha: State of Qatar, 2018).

2. Ashraf M. Salama and Florian Wiedmann, *Demystifying Doha: On Architecture and Urbanism in an Emerging City* (Abingdon, UK: Routledge, 2016).

3. Qatar Planning and Statistics Authority, *Population and Social Statistics*, table 9.

4. "Ministry of Civil Service Affairs and Housing Decree No. 17 of 2005 on Workers' Living Quarters" (Qatar, December 29, 2005), accessed November 19, 2020, https:// gulfmigration.org/ministry-of-civil-service-affairs-and-housing-decree-no-17-of-2005-on -workers-living-quarters/.

5. "Law No. 15 of 2010 Prohibition of Workers Camps within Family Residential Areas," in *15* (Al Meezan: Qatar Legal Portal, August 19, 2010), accessed November 19, 2020, http:// www.almeezan.qa/LawView.aspx?opt&LawID=2510&language=en.

6. Michelle Buckley, "Construction Work, 'Bachelor' Builders and the Intersectional Politics of Urbanization in Dubai," in *Transit States: Labour, Migration and Citizenship in*

the Gulf, ed. Abdulhadi Khalaf, Omar AlShehabi, and Adam Hanieh (London: Pluto Press, 2015), 132–52; Behzad Sarmadi, "'Bachelor' in the City: Urban Transformation and Matter Out of Place in Dubai," *Journal of Arabian Studies* 3, no. 2 (2013): 196–214.

7. "Qatar's 'Bachelor Ban' Makes Life Laborious for Blue-collar Workers," *New Arab*, 2016, accessed November 19, 2020, https://www.alaraby.co.uk/english/blog/2016/5/20/qatars-bachelor-ban-makes-life-laborious-for-blue-collar-workers.

8. Ministry of Municipal Affairs and Civil Planning, "Qatar: Ministry of Municipal Affairs and Civil Planning Decree No. 83 regarding Family Residential Areas" (Al Meezan: Qatar Legal Portal, August 25, 2011); *Municipality Designates Areas for Bachelor Living* (Alraya, Doha, October 3, 2011), 21.

9. Ministry of Municipality and Environment, "Doha Mun Family Zone," 2019, accessed February 18, 2020, http://www.mme.gov.qa/cui/view.dox?id=1182&contentID=1425&siteID=2.

10. Pete Pattisson, "Qatar's 'Families Only' Zones Entrench Segregation of Migrant Workers," *Guardian* (Doha), April 13, 2016, accessed November 19, 2020, https://www.theguardian.com/global-development/2016/apr/13/qatar-families-only-zones-entrench-segregation-of-migrant-workers.

11. Tom Finn, "'Bachelor Ban' in Qatar Tests Relations with Migrant Workers," Reuters (Al Khor, Qatar), May 17, 2016, World News, accessed November 19, 2020, https://www.reuters.com/article/us-qatar-labour-bachelors-idUSKCN0Y81H4.

12. James Holston, *The Modernist City: An Anthropological Critique of Brasília* (Chicago: University of Chicago Press, 1989).

13. Mauro F. Guillén, *The Taylorized Beauty of the Mechanical: Scientific Management and the Rise of Modernist Architecture* (Princeton, NJ: Princeton University Press, 2006).

14. "Qatar 2022 World Cup Stadiums: All You Need to Know," Al Jazeera, September 18, 2019, News/Football, accessed November 19, 2020, https://www.aljazeera.com/news/2018/10/qatar-2022-world-cup-stadiums-181025142408471.html.

15. Ananda Shakespeare, "Building Boom Gathers Pace in Qatar," MEED: Middle East Business Intelligence, May 13, 2014, accessed November 19, 2020, https://www.meed.com/building-boom-gathers-pace-in-qatar/; "Analysis: Qatar Projects Market Forcast and Review H1 2019," MEED: Middle East Business Intelligence, 2019.

16. Planning Ministry of Development and Statistics, *First Section: Population and Social Statistics, Chapter 1: Population* (2016), accessed November 19, 2020, https://www.psa.gov.qa/en/statistics/Statistical%20Releases/Population/Population/2016/Population_social_1_2016_AE.pdf.

17. Ibrahim Ibrahim and Frank Harrigan, "Qatar's Economy: Past, Present and Future," *QScience Connect*, no. 1 (2012): 9; General Secretariat for Development Planning, *Qatar National Vision 2030* (Doha: General Secretariat for Development Planning, July 2008), accessed November 18, 2020, https://www.gco.gov.qa/wp-content/uploads/2016/09/GCO-QNV-English.pdf.

18. Agatino Rizzo, "Metro Doha," *Cities* 31 (2013): 533–43.

19. Nadeem Hashem and Perumal Balakrishnan, "Change Analysis of Land Use / Land Cover and Modelling Urban Growth in Greater Doha, Qatar," *Annals of GIS* 21, no. 3 (2015): 233–47, accessed November 19, 2020, https://doi.org/10.1080/19475683.2014.992369; Vivek Shandas, Yasuyo Makido, and Salim Ferwati, "Rapid Urban Growth and Land Use Patterns in Doha, Qatar: Opportunities for Sustainability," *European Journal of Sustainable Development Research* 1, no. 2 (2017): 1–13.

20. Rebecca Spong, "Airport Delay Affecting National Airline," *MEED: Middle East Economic Digest* 57, no. 19 (May 10, 2013): 42–43.

21. Shakespeare, "Building Boom Gathers Pace in Qatar"; "Analysis: Qatar Projects Market Forcast and Review H1 2019."

22. "In the Crosshairs: Could the Construction Sector Be Facing a Slowdown, Lead by Sharq Crossing's Shelving?," *Construction Week*, March 3, 2015, accessed November 19, 2020, https://www.constructionweekonline.com/article-32744-in-the-crosshairs; Business Monitor International, *Qatar Infrastructure Report Q1 2015* (London: Business Moniter International, 2015); Fitch Solutions, *Qatar Infrastructure Report Q4 2018* (London: Fitch Solutions, 2018).

23. "North Field Expansion Project," NS Energy Business, accessed January 19, 2020, https://www.nsenergybusiness.com/projects/north-field-expansion-project/.

24. GlobalData Energy, "Qatar North Field Expansion to Increase LNG Export Capacity by 43%," August 7, 2019, accessed January 19, 2020, https://www.offshore-technology.com/comment/qatar-north-field-expansion-to-increase-lng-export-capacity-by-43/.

25. Fitch Solutions, *Qatar Infrastructure Report Q1* (London: Fitch Solutions, 2019).

26. Agatino Rizzo, "Rapid Urban Development and National Master Planning in Arab Gulf Countries: Qatar as a Case Study," *Cities* 39 (2014): 50–57.

27. James C. Scott, *Seeing Like a State: How Certain Schemes to Improve the Human Condition Have Failed* (New Haven, CT: Yale University Press, 1998), 112.

28. Yasser Elsheshtawy, *Planning Middle Eastern Cities: An Urban Kaleidoscope* (London: Routledge, 2004); Yasser Elsheshtawy, *Dubai: Behind an Urban Spectacle* (Abingdon, UK: Routledge, 2009); Harvey Molotch and Davide Ponzini, *The New Arab Urban: Gulf Cities of Wealth, Ambition, and Distress* (New York: NYU Press, 2019).

29. Scott, *Seeing Like a State*, 113; Holston, *The Modernist City*; C. D. Blanton, "Abstract in Concrete: Brutalism and Modernist Half-Life," in *The Contemporaneity of Modernism*, ed. Michael D'Arcy and Mathias Nilges (New York: Routledge, 2015), 17–30.

30. Holston, *The Modernist City*.

31. Scott, *Seeing Like a State*, 114.

32. Scott, *Seeing Like a State*.

33. Holston, *The Modernist City*, 9.

34. Scott, *Seeing Like a State*, 11.

35. Guillén, *The Taylorized Beauty of the Mechanical*.

36. Scott, *Seeing Like a State*.

37. Khondker Rahman, "The Qatar National Master Plan," *Sustainable Development: An Appraisal from the Gulf Region* 19 (2014): 82.

38. Lusail City, "The Vision Is Taking Shape," accessed January 17, 2020, http://www.lusail.com/who-we-are/the-vision-is-taking-shape/.

39. Stéphanie Buret, "Lusail: Sleek New City Offers Glimpse of Qatar's Post-Oil Future," *Guardian*, July 11, 2019, accessed November 20, 2020, https://www.theguardian.com/cities/2019/jul/11/lusail-sleek-new-city-offers-glimpse-of-qatar-post-oil-future.

40. International Monetary Fund, *IMF Country Report No 19/146* (Washington, DC: International Monetary Fund, June 2019), accessed November 20, 2020, www.imf.org.

41. George Katodrytis and Kevin Mitchell, *UAE and the Gulf: Architecture and Urbanism Now* (London: John Wiley and Sons, 2015).

42. Steven Humphrey, *Qatar Construction Market Outlook 2017–2030* (Crossville, TN: Plateau Group, June 2017).

43. Simeon Kerr, "Qatar's Slowing Economy Puts World Cup Spending in Spotlight," *Financial Times* (London), March 1, 2017, accessed November 20, 2020, https://www.ft.com/content/048e5762-f9a4-11e6-bd4e-68d53499ed71.

44. Florian Wiedmann and Ashraf M. Salama, "From Pre-Oil Settlement to Post-Oil Hub: The Urban Transformation of Doha," *Archnet-IJAR: International Journal of Architectural Research* 7, no. 2 (2013): 146–59.

45. William L. Pereira Associates, *New Doha Planning Studies: Concept Plan* (Los Angeles: William L. Pereira Associates, 1975), 32–33.

46. Sharon Nagy, "Dressing up Downtown: Urban Development and Government Public Image in Qatar," *City and Society* 12, no. 1 (2000): 125–47.

47. Khaled Adham, "Rediscovering the Island: Doha's Urbanity from Pearls to Spectacle," in *The Evolving Arab City: Tradition, Modernity and Urban Development*, ed. Yasser Elsheshtawy (London: Routledge, 2008), 218–57.

48. Ameena Ahmadi, "The Urban Core of Doha: Spacial Structure and the Experienced Center" (MS thesis, University College London, 2008).

49. Kelly Hutzell, Rami el Samahy, and Adam Himes, "Inexhaustible Ambition: Two Eras of Planning in Doha, Qatar," *Architectural Design* 85, no. 1 (2015): 80–91.

50. Mary Frings, "Financial Times Survey: Qatar—Economy—Heavy Reliance on State Spending," *Financial Times* (London), July 9, 1984.

51. Hutzell, el Samahy, and Himes, "Inexhaustible Ambition"; : Salama and Wiedmann, *Demystifying Doha*.

52. Nagy, "Dressing up Downtown."

53. Planning and Statistics Authority, *Window on Economic Statistics of Qatar*, July 2019, accessed November 20, 2020, https://www.psa.gov.qa/en/statistics/Statistical%20Releases/Economic/GeneralEconomicStatistics/windowonstatistics/2019/Q1/WinEconomicStat_28th_Issue_Q1_2019_AE.pdf.

54. Fitch Solutions, *Qatar Infrastructure Report Q1*.

55. Ministry of Development Planning and Statistics, State of Qatar, "Annual Bulletin—Labor Force Sample Survey," chapter 2, table no. 22, July 2018, accessed December 29, 2020, https://www.psa.gov.qa/en/statistics/Statistical%20Releases/Social/LaborForce/2017/Annual_Bulletin_Labour_force_2017_AE.pdf.

56. "Face to Face: Mark Ainger, Faithful+Gould," *Construction Week Online*, March 3, 2016, accessed November 20, 2020, https://www.constructionweekonline.com/article-37765-face-to-face-mark-ainger-faithfulgould.

57. "QPMC Contracts Ensure Materials Supply," *Construction Week*, October 13, 2015, accessed November 20, 2020, https://www.constructionweekonline.com/article-35877-qpmc-contracts-ensure-materials-supply.

58. Abdulaziz M. Jarkas and Theodore C. Haupt, "Major Construction Risk Factors Considered by General Contractors in Qatar," *Journal of Engineering, Design and Technology* 13, no. 1 (2015): 165–94.

59. Jassim bin Hamad Al-Thani, "Law No. 13 of 2000 Regulation of the Investment of Non-Qatari Capital in the Economic Activity 13/2000," ed. Council of Ministers, 2000, accessed November 20, 2020, https://ticaret.gov.tr/data/5b8882ec13b87615b0eea9d7/Law%20No%2013%20of%202000%20Regulation%20of%20the%20Investment%20of%20Non-Qatari%20Capital%20in%20the%20Economic%20Activity.pdf.

60. Safwan Moubaydeen, Julian Pope, Julie Tuck, Matthew Walker, and Natalie Mackay, "Construction and Projects in Qatar: Overview," in *Construction and Projects Multi-Jurisdictional Guide (2013/2014)*, Qatar: Dentons and Co (2013).

61. Craig Shepherd, Sean Whitham, and Herbert Freehills, *Construction Arbitration: Qatar* (2018), accessed November 20, 2020, https://globalarbitrationreview.com/jurisdiction/1005078/qatar.

62. Moubaydeen et al., "Construction and Projects in Qatar."

63. Michael Grose and Ramiz Shlah, "Construction Law in Qatar and the United Arab Emirates: Key Differences," *Turkish Commercial Law Review* 1 (2015): 189.

64. Moubaydeen et al., "Construction and Projects in Qatar."

65. "Face to Face: Amr Belal, Powergreen," *Construction Week*, June 1, 2016, accessed November 20, 2020, https://www.constructionweekonline.com/article-39318-face-to-face-amr-belal-powergreen.

66. Abdulaziz M. Jarkas and Jamal H. Younes, "Principle Factors Contributing to Construction Delays in the State of Qatar," *International Journal of Construction Project Management* 6, no. 1 (2014): 39.

67. "Late Payments Challenge Qatar Construction Sector," *Construction Week*, March 3, 2016, accessed November 20, 2020, https://www.constructionweekonline.com/article-37759-late-payments-challenge-qatar-construction-sector.

68. "In the Crosshairs": Matt Smith, "Qatar Building Boom Proves a Challenge for Foreign Construction Firms," Reuters (Dubai), June 23, 2015, accessed November 20, 2020, https://www.reuters.com/article/qatar-construction-idUSL5N0YU1BK20150623; Reuters, "Qatar Slashes Healthcare Spending, World Cup Escapes Cuts," *Arabian Business Global*, May 25, 2016, accessed November 20, 2020, https://www.arabianbusiness.com/qatar-slashes-healthcare-spending-world-cup-escapes-cuts-632971.html.

69. "Face-to-Face: Jason Morris, AECOM," *Construction Week*, October 10, 2016, accessed November 20, 2020, https://www.constructionweekonline.com/article-41164-face-to-face-jason-morris-aecom; CW Guest Columnist, "Fast-track to Delay," *Construction Week*, September 15, 2016, accessed November 20, 2020, https://www.constructionweekonline.com/article-40900-fast-track-to-delay.

70. CW Guest Columnist, "Beyond the Numbers," *Construction Week*, December 6,2014, accessed November 20, 2020, https://www.constructionweekonline.com/article-31516-beyond-the-numbers.

71. Ahmed Senouci, Ahmed Alsarraj, Murat Gunduz, and Neil Eldin, "Analysis of Change Orders in Qatari Construction Projects," *International Journal of Construction Management* 17, no. 4 (2017): 280–92.

72. AECOM, *Property and Construction Handbook: Middle East* (Los Angeles: AECOM, 2019), accessed November 20, 2020, https://www.aecom.com/ae/wp-content/uploads/2018/10/Construction-Handbook-2018_19.pdf.

73. Fitch Solutions, *Qatar Infrastructure Report Q4 2018*.

74. Fitch Solutions, *Qatar Infrastructure Report Q1*, 10.

75. Fitch Solutions, *Qatar Infrastructure Report Q4 2018*.

76. Andrew Roscoe, "Qatar Primary Materials Company," *MEED: Middle East Economic Digest* 57, no. 49 (2013): 26–27.

77. "Face to Face: Mihir Shah, KPMG," *Construction Week*, May 8, 2016, accessed November 20, 2020, https://www.constructionweekonline.com/article-38884-face-to-face-mihir-shah-kpmg; "Construction Risky Business in Qatar," *MEED: Middle East Economic Digest* 59, no. 20 (2015): 56; Joe Quirke, "Samsung and OHL fired from $1.4bn Qatar Rail Contract," *Global Construction Review*, May 9, 2016, accessed November 20, 2020, http://www.globalconstructionreview.com/news/samsung-and-ohl-fired-14bn-qat7ar-ra7il-contr7act/.

78. Fitch Solutions, *Qatar Infrastructure Report Q1*, 36.

79. DLA Piper, *The A-Z of Construction Law in Qatar* (London: DLA Piper, 2016), accessed November 20, 2020, www.dlapiper.com.

80. "Face to Face: Amr Belal, Powergreen."

81. Paul Attewell, "The Deskilling Controversy," *Work and Occupations* 14, no. 3 (1987): 323–46.

82. Peter B. Doeringer and Michael J. Piore, *Internal Labor Markets and Manpower Analysis* (Armonk, NY: M. E. Sharpe, 1985); Arne L. Kalleberg, *Good Jobs, Bad Jobs: The Rise of Polarized and Precarious Employment Systems in the United States, 1970s–2000s* (New York: Russell Sage Foundation, 2011); Paul Osterman, "Choice of Employment Systems in Internal Labor Markets," *Industrial Relations: A Journal of Economy and Society*

26, no. 1 (1987): 46–67; Michael J. Piore, "Thirty Years Later: Internal Labor Markets, Flexibility and the New Economy," *Journal of Management and Governance* 6, no. 4 (2002): 271–79.

83. "Qatar Opens 'Labour City' for 70000 Migrant Workers," *New Arab*, November 2, 2015, accessed November 21, 2020, https://www.alaraby.co.uk/english/news/2015/11/2/qatar-opens-labour-city-for-70000-migrant-workers.

84. Peter Kovessy, "Qatar Answers Call for Better Housing with New 'Labor City,'" *Doha News*, November 5, 2015.

85. "PM Inaugurates Largest Labour City in Gulf Region," *Gulf Times* (Doha), November 1, 2015, accessed November 21, 2020, https://www.gulf-times.com/story/461159/PM-inaugurates-largest-Labour-City-in-Gulf-region.

86. MarketWatch, "Sysorex Announces $2.5 Milliion AirPatrol Contract," July 1, 2015, accessed November 21, 2020, https://www.marketwatch.com/press-release/sysorex-announces-25-million-airpatrol-contract-2015-07-01.

Chapter 3. Skill: How Skill Is Embodied and What It Means for the Control of Bodies

1. Velina Mirincheva, "The Qatar Faculty of Islamic Studies by Mangera Yvars Is a Process of Continuous Learning and Enlightenment," *Architectural Review*, March 7, 2017, accessed November 22, 2020, https://www.architectural-review.com/buildings/the-qatar-faculty-of-islamic-studies-by-mangera-yvars-is-a-process-of-continuous-learning-and-enlightenment/10017755.article.

2. Mirincheva, "The Qatar Faculty of Islamic Studies"; Mangera Yvars Architects, "Qatar Faculty of Islamic Studies," Architonic, 2015, accessed January 18, 2020, https://www.architonic.com/en/project/mangera-yvars-architects-qatar-faculty-of-islamic-studies/5105543.

3. Marhaba Qatar Destination Guide, "QFIS Building Wins Award at World Architecture Festival" (Marhaba: Qatar's Premier Information Guide, November 10, 2015), accessed January 18, 2020, https://www.marhaba.qa/qfis-building-wins-award-at-world-architecture-festival/.

4. "The QFIS Challenges: Astutely Addressed by ASTAD," *Special Integration Asia* 156, no. 2 (2017): 72–77.

5. Ben Lewis, "Digitally Designed—Qatar Faculty of Islamic Studies," *Structural Engineer: Journal of the Institution of Structural Engineer* 94, no. 3 (2016): 69–76; Constantine Emmanouil Migiakis, "The Qatar Faculty of Islamic Studies" (July 11, 2015), accessed November 22, 2020, http://eeme.ntua.gr/proceedings/7th/003.pdf.

6. Migiakis, "The Qatar Faculty of Islamic Studies."

7. Francisco J. Varela, Eleanor Rosch, and Evan Thompson, *The Embodied Mind: Cognitive Science and Human Experience* (Cambridge, MA: MIT Press, 2017), 172–73.

8. Max Van Manen, "Phenomenological Pedagogy," *Curriculum Inquiry* 12, no. 3 (1982): 283–99.

9. "Qatar's Reliance on Unskilled Workers Reduced," *Construction Week*, June 26, 2016, accessed November 21, 2020, https://www.constructionweekonline.com/article-39733-qatars-reliance-on-unskilled-workers-reduced.

10. Qatar Planning and Statistics Authority, *Bulletin Labor Force Statistics, 2015* (Qatar: Government of Qatar, 2015), tables 51, 25.

11. Sherif M. Ahmed, Hassan H. Emam, and Peter Farrell, "Barriers to BIM/4D Implementation in Qatar" (paper presented at the First International Conference of the CIB

Middle East and North Africa Research Network, 2014); Nashwan Dawood and Vladimir Vukovic, "Whole Lifecycle Information Flow Underpinned by BIM: Technology, Process, Policy and People" (paper presented at the Second International Conference on Civil and Building Engineering Informatics, 2015).

12. Arthur M. Glenberg, Jessica K. Witt, and Janet Metcalfe, "From the Revolution to Embodiment: 25 Years of Cognitive Psychology," *Perspectives on Psychological Science* 8, no. 5 (2013): 573–85.

13. Margaret Wilson, "Six Views of Embodied Cognition," *Psychonomic Bulletin and Review* 9, no. 4 (2002): 625–36.

14. Michael L. Anderson, "Embodied Cognition: A Field Guide," *Artificial Intelligence* 149, no. 1 (2003): 91–130.

15. Varela, Rosch, and Thompson, *The Embodied Mind*.

16. Alva Noë, *Action in Perception* (Cambridge, MA: MIT Press, 2004).

17. Manuel de Vega, Arthur M. Glenberg, and Arthur C. Graesser, *Symbols and Embodiment: Debates on Meaning and Cognition* (Oxford: Oxford University Press, 2012); Arthur M. Glenberg, "Few Believe the World Is Flat: How Embodiment Is Changing the Scientific Understanding of Cognition," *Canadian Journal of Experimental Psychology / Revue canadienne de psychologie expérimentale* 69, no. 2 (2015): 165.

18. Xabier E. Barandiaran, "Autonomy and Enactivism: Towards a Theory of Sensorimotor Autonomous Agency," *Topoi* 36, no. 3 (September 1, 2017): 409–30, accessed November 23, 2020, https://doi.org/10.1007/s11245-016-9365-4; Autumn B. Hostetter and Martha W. Alibali, "Visible Embodiment: Gestures as Simulated Action," *Psychonomic Bulletin and Review* 15, no. 3 (2008): 495–514.

19. Alicia Juarrero, "Dynamics in Action: Intentional Behavior as a Complex System," *Emergence* 2, no. 2 (2000): 24–57.

20. Hanne De Jaegher, Barbara Pieper, Daniel Clénin, and Thomas Fuchs, "Grasping Intersubjectivity: An Invitation to Embody Social Interaction Research," *Phenomenology and the Cognitive Sciences* 16, no. 3 (2017): 491–523.

21. Hanne De Jaegher and Ezequiel Di Paolo, "Participatory Sense-Making," *Phenomenology and the Cognitive Sciences* 6, no. 4 (2007): 485–507; De Jaegher et al., "Grasping Intersubjectivity"; Daniel D. Hutto and Erik Myin, *Radicalizing Enactivism: Basic Minds without Content* (Cambridge, MA: MIT Press, 2012); Lawrence Shapiro, *Embodied Cognition* (Abingdon, UK: Routledge, 2019).

22. Wanda J. Orlikowski, "Using Technology and Constituting Structures: A Practice Lens for Studying Technology in Organizations," *Organization Science* 11, no. 4 (2000): 404–28.

23. Nuwan D. Leitan and Lucian Chaffey, "Embodied Cognition and Its Applications: A Brief Review," *Sensoria: A Journal of Mind, Brain and Culture* 10, no. 1 (2014): 3–10.

24. Hubert L. Dreyfus, "Intelligence without Representation—Merleau-Ponty's Critique of Mental Representation: The Relevance of Phenomenology to Scientific Explanation," *Phenomenology and the Cognitive Sciences* 1, no. 4 (2002): 373.

25. Thomas Fuchs, *Ecology of the Brain: The Phenomenology and Biology of the Embodied Mind* (Oxford: Oxford University Press, 2017).

26. Francisco J. Varela, *Ethical Know-how: Action, Wisdom, and Cognition* (Palo Alto, CA: Stanford University Press, 1999).

27. Lawrence W. Barsalou, Paula M. Niedenthal, Aron K. Barbey, and Jennifer A. Ruppert, "Social Embodiment," *Psychology of Learning and Motivation* 43 (2003): 43–92.

28. Shaun Gallagher and Robb Lindgren, "Enactive Metaphors: Learning through Full-Body Engagement," *Educational Psychology Review* 27, no. 3 (2015): 391–404; Tim Ingold, "Five Questions of Skill," *Cultural Geographies* 25, no. 1 (2018): 159–63.

29. Greg Downey, *Learning Capoeira: Lessons in Cunning from an Afro-Brazilian Art* (Oxford: Oxford University Press, 2005); Greg Downey, "Scaffolding Imitation in Capoeira: Physical Education and Enculturation in an Afro-Brazilian Art," *American Anthropologist* 110, no. 2 (2008): 204–13; Trevor H. J. Marchand, "Making Knowledge: Explorations of the Indissoluble Relation between Minds, Bodies, and Environment," *Journal of the Royal Anthropological Institute* 16 (2010): S1–S21; Trevor H. J. Marchand, *Making Knowledge: Explorations of the Indissoluble Relation between Mind, Body and Environment* (London: John Wiley and Sons, 2011).

30. Michael Polanyi, *The Tacit Dimension* (London: Routledge, 1966).

31. Varela, Rosch, and Thompson, *The Embodied Mind*.

32. Jean Lave, "Situating Learning in Communities of Practice," *Perspectives on Socially Shared Cognition* 2 (1991): 63–82; Jean Lave and Etienne Wenger, *Situated Learning: Legitimate Peripheral Participation* (Cambridge: Cambridge University Press, 1991).

33. Joan Acker, "Hierarchies, Jobs, Bodies: A Theory of Gendered Organizations," *Gender and Society* 4, no. 2 (1990): 139–58; Jane L. Collins, *Threads: Gender, Labor, and Power in the Global Apparel Industry* (Chicago: University of Chicago Press, 2009).

34. Ann Farnsworth-Alvear, *Dulcinea in the Factory: Myths, Morals, Men, and Women in Colombia's Industrial Experiment, 1905–1960* (Durham, NC: Duke University Press, 2000); Kris Paap, *Working Construction: Why White Working-Class Men Put Themselves—and the Labor Movement—in Harm's Way* (Ithaca, NY: Cornell University Press, 2018).

35. Julian Orr, *Talking about Machines: An Ethnography of a Modern Job* (Ithaca, NY: Cornell University Press, 1996).

36. Yogesh Malhotra, "Why Knowledge Management Systems Fail: Enablers and Constraints of Knowledge Management in Human Enterprises," in *Handbook on Knowledge Management 1*, ed. Clyde Holsapple (New York: Springer, 2004), 577–99; Hugh Willmott, "From Knowledge to Learning," in *Managing Knowledge: Critical Investigations of Work and Learning*, ed. Craig Prichard, Richard Hull, Mike Chumer, and Hugh Willmott (London: Macmillan, 2000), 216–22; Ali Yakhlef, "The Corporeality of Practice-Based Learning," *Organization Studies* 31, no. 4 (2010).

37. Alessia Contu, "On Boundaries and Difference: Communities of Practice and Power Relations in Creative Work," *Management Learning* 45, no. 3 (2014): 289–316.

38. Chun Wei Choo, "The Knowing Organization: How Organizations Use Information to Construct Meaning, Create Knowledge and Make Decisions," *International Journal of Information Management* 16, no. 5 (1996): 329–40; Catherine Truss, Edel Conway, Alesia d'Amato, Gráinne Kelly, Kathy Monks, Enda Hannon, and Patrick C. Flood, "Knowledge Work: Gender-Blind or Gender-Biased?," *Work, Employment and Society* 26, no. 5 (2012): 735–54; Beth A. Bechky, "Sharing Meaning across Occupational Communities: The Transformation of Understanding on a Production Floor," *Organization Science* 14, no. 3 (2003): 312–30.

39. Lave, "Situating Learning in Communities of Practice."

40. Richard Sennett, *The Craftsman* (New Haven, CT: Yale University Press, 2008); Allan Bird, "Careers as Repositories of Knowledge: A New Perspective on Boundaryless Careers," *Journal of Organizational Behavior* 15, no. 4 (1994): 325–44; Bill LaFayette, Wayne Curtis, Denise Bedford, and Seema Iyer, "Learning and the Knowledge Capacity of Organizations," *Knowledge Economies and Knowledge Work (Working Methods for Knowledge Management)* (2019): 171–209; Ikujirō Nonaka and Hirotaka Takeuchi, "The Knowledge-Creating Company," *Harvard Business Review* 85, no. 7–8 (2007): 162.

41. Alessia Contu, Christopher Grey, and Anders Örtenblad, "Against Learning," *Human Relations* 56, no. 8 (2003): 931–52.

Chapter 4. Protest: How Skillful
Practice Becomes Resistance

1. Amnesty International, *Qatar: Unpaid Migrant Construction Workers Left to Go Hungry* (December 18, 2013), accessed November 26, 2020, https://www.amnesty.org /en/latest/news/2013/12/qatar-unpaid-migrant-construction-workers-left-go-hungry /; Amnesty International, *Qatar: Migrant Workers Unpaid for Months of Work by Company Linked to World Cup Host City* (London: Amnesty International, 2018), accessed November 10, 2020, https://www.amnestyusa.org/reports/qatar-migrant-workers-unpaid -for-months-of-work-by-company-linked-to-world-cup-host-city/.

2. Amnesty International, *All Work, No Pay: The Struggle of Qatar's Migrant Workers for Justice* (London: Amnesty International, 2019), accessed November 10, 2020, https:// www.amnesty.at/media/6034/amnesty_all-work-no-pay-the-struggle-of-qatars-migrant -workers-for-justice_bericht-september-2019.pdf; Himalayan News Service, "Qatar World Cup Workers Unpaid for Months: AI," *Himalayan Times*, September 27, 2018, accessed February 13, 2020, https://thehimalayantimes.com/kathmandu/qatar-world-cup-workers -unpaid-for-months-amnesty-international/.

3. Amnesty International, *All Work, No Pay*.

4. Charles Tilly, *Popular Contention in Great Britain, 1758–1834* (London: Routledge, 2015), 42.

5. Charles Tilly, "Contentious Repertoires in Great Britain, 1758–1834," *Social Science History* 17, no. 2 (1993): 253–80.

6. Sidney Tarrow, "Cycles of Collective Action: Between Moments of Madness and the Repertoire of Contention," *Social Science History* 17, no. 2 (1993): 281–307.

7. Kevin Gillan, "Social Movements, Protest, and Practices of Social Change," in *The Wiley Blackwell Companion to Sociology*, ed. George Ritzer and Wendy Wiedenhoft Murphy (Hoboken, NJ: John Wiley and Sons, 2019), 301–18.

8. Charles Tilly, "Social Movements as Historically Specific Clusters of Political Performances," *Berkeley Journal of Sociology* 38 (1993): 1–30.

9. Tarrow, "Cycles of Collective Action."

10. Robert S. Jansen, *Revolutionizing Repertoires: The Rise of Populist Mobilization in Peru* (Chicago: University of Chicago Press, 2017); Aldon D. Morris, "Birmingham Confrontation Reconsidered: An Analysis of the Dynamics and Tactics of Mobilization," *American Sociological Review* (1993): 621–36.

11. Mark Traugott, *Repertoires and Cycles of Collective Action* (Durham, NC: Duke University Press, 1995).

12. Sidney Tarrow, "Social Movements in Contentious Politics: A Review Article," *American Political Science Review* 90, no. 4 (1996): 874–83; Charles Tilly, *Regimes and Repertoires* (Chicago: University of Chicago Press, 2010).

13. Doug McAdam, Sidney Tarrow, and Charles Tilly, "Comparative Perspectives on Contentious Politics," in *Comparative Politics: Rationality, Culture, and Structure*, ed. Mark Irving Lichbach and Alan S. Zuckerman (Cambridge: Cambridge University Press, 2009), 260–90.

14. Judith Butler, "Bodily Vulnerability, Coalitions, and Street Politics," *Critical Studies* 37 (2014): 9.

15. Aristide R. Zolberg, "Moments of Madness," *Politics and Society* 2, no. 2 (1972): 183.

16. Richard J. Bernstein, *Praxis and Action: Contemporary Philosophies of Human Activity* (Philadelphia: University of Pennsylvania Press, 2011).

17. Paulo Freire, *Pedagogy of the Oppressed* (New York: Bloomsbury Publishing USA, 2018), 101.

18. Markus S. Shulz, "Collective Action across Borders: Opportunity Structures, Network Capacities, and Communicative Praxis in the Age of Advanced Globalization," *Sociological Perspectives* 41, no. 3 (1998): 587–616.

19. Hannah Arendt, *The Human Condition* (Chicago: University of Chicago Press, 2013).

20. Arendt, *The Human Condition*, 180.

21. Jean Lave, "The Culture of Acquisition and the Practice of Understanding," *Situated Cognition: Social, Semiotic, and Psychological Perspectives* (1997): 63–82; Jean Lave, *Apprenticeship in Critical Ethnographic Practice* (Chicago: University of Chicago Press, 2011).

22. Jean Lave and Etienne Wenger, *Situated Learning: Legitimate Peripheral Participation* (Cambridge: Cambridge University Press, 1991).

23. Freire, *Pedagogy of the Oppressed*, 84.

24. Arendt, *The Human Condition*, 178.

Chapter 5. Body: How Definitions of Skill Cause Injury

1. Pete Pattisson, "Revealed: Qatar's World Cup 'Slaves,'" *Guardian* (Kathmandu and Doha), September 25, 2013, accessed November 12, 2020, https://www.theguardian.com/world/2013/sep/25/revealed-qatars-world-cup-slaves.

2. Priyanka Motaparthy, *Building a Better World Cup: Protecting Migrant Workers in Qatar Ahead of FIFA 2022* (New York: Human Rights Watch, 2012), 4, accessed November 12, 2020, https://www.hrw.org/sites/default/files/reports/qatar0612webwcover_0.pdf.

3. Amnesty International, *Qatar: The Dark Side of Migration: Spotlight on Qatar's Construction Sector Ahead of the World Cup* (London: Amnesty International, 2013), accessed November 10, 2020, https://www.amnesty.org/en/documents/MDE22/010/2013/en/.

4. "Qatar 2022 World Cup Risks 4000 Lives, Warns International Trade Union Confederation," ITUC CSI IGB, September 27, 2013, accessed February 15, 2020, https://www.ituc-csi.org/qatar-2022-world-cup-risks-4000.

5. Reuters, "Nepal Envoy Recalled after Qatar 'Open Jail' Remarks," September 26, 2013, accessed, November 15, 2020, https://www.reuters.com/article/us-nepal-qatar-ambassador/nepal-envoy-recalled-after-qatar-open-jail-remarks-idUSBRE98P1O020130926.

6. Robert Booth, "Qatar World Cup 2022: 70 Nepalese Workers Die on Building Sites," *Guardian* (Qatar), October 1, 2013, accessed November 29, 2020, https://www.theguardian.com/world/2013/oct/01/qatar-world-cup-2022-nepalese-die-building-sites.

7. Dovas, "People Make Anti-Logos to Urge Sponsors to Withdraw from Qatar 2022 World Cup," 2016, accessed November 29, 2020, https://www.boredpanda.com/qatar-2022-world-cup-human-rights-sponsor-anti-advertisement/.

8. Sean Gregory, "Major FIFA Sponsors Don't Want to Talk about Qatar, Either," *Time*, May 29, 2015, accessed November 29, 2020, https://time.com/3900357/fifa-sponsors-coke-visa-adidas/.

9. DLA Piper, *Migrant Labor in the Construction Sector in the State of Qatar* (London: DLA Piper UK LLP, April 2014).

10. Occupational Safety and Health Administration, "Commonly Used Statistics," accessed February 15, 2020, https://www.osha.gov/oshstats/commonstats.html; Health and Safety Executive, *Construction Statistics in Great Britain, 2019* (2019), accessed November 29, 2020, https://www.hse.gov.uk/statistics/industry/construction.pdf.

11. Jeremy S. Pal and Elfatih A. B. Eltahir, "Future Temperature in Southwest Asia Projected to Exceed a Threshold for Human Adaptability," *Nature Climate Change* 6, no. 2 (2016): 197–200, accessed November 29, 2020, https://doi.org/10.1038/nclimate2833.

12. Pengfei Xue and Elfatih A. B. Eltahir, "Estimation of the Heat and Water Budgets of the Persian (Arabian) Gulf Using a Regional Climate Model," *Journal of Climate* 28, no. 13 (2015): 5041–62.

13. Christoph Schär, "Climate Extremes: The Worst Heat Waves to Come," *Nature Climate Change* 6, no. 2 (2016): 128–29, accessed November 29, 2020, https://doi.org/10.1038/nclimate2864, https://doi.org/10.1038/nclimate2864.

14. Yann Chavaillaz, Philippe Roy, Antti-Ilari Partanen, Laurent Da Silva, Émilie Bresson, Nadine Mengis, Diane Chaumont, and H. Damon Matthews, "Exposure to Excessive Heat and Impacts on Labour Productivity Linked to Cumulative CO_2 Emissions," *Scientific Reports* 9, no. 1 (2019): 13711, https://doi.org/10.1038/s41598-019-50047-w; Richard J. Johnson, Laura Gabriela Sánchez-Lozada, Lee Scott Newman, Miguel A. Lanaspa, Henry F. Diaz, Jay Lemery, Bernardo Rodriguez-Iturbe, et al., "Climate Change and the Kidney," *Annals of Nutrition and Metabolism* 74 (Suppl. 3), no. 3 (2019): 38–44, accessed November 29, 2020, https://doi.org/10.1159/000500344; Pal and Eltahir, "Future Temperature in Southwest Asia"; Schär, "Climate Extremes."

15. John P. Dunne, Ronald J. Stouffer, and Jasmin G. John, "Reductions in Labour Capacity from Heat Stress under Climate Warming," *Nature Climate Change* 3, no. 6 (2013): 563; Joshua Goodman, Michael Hurwitz, Jisung Park, and Jonathan Smith, "Heat and Learning," National Bureau of Economic Research Working Paper No. 24639, 2019, accessed December 9, 2020, https://www.nber.org/papers/w24639.

16. Tord Kjellstrom, "Impact of Climate Conditions on Occupational Health and Related Economic Losses: A New Feature of Global and Urban Health in the Context of Climate Change," *Asia Pacific Journal of Public Health* 28, no. 2 (2016): 28S–37S, accessed November 29, 2020, https://doi.org/10.1177/1010539514568711; Tord Kjellstrom, David Briggs, Chris Freyberg, Bruno Lemke, Matthias Otto, and Olivia Hyatt, "Heat, Human Performance, and Occupational Health: A Key Issue for the Assessment of Global Climate Change Impacts," *Annual Review of Public Health* 37, no. 1 (2016): 97–112, accessed November 29, 2020, https://doi.org/10.1146/annurev-publhealth-032315-021740.

17. Pattisson, "Revealed."

18. Sarah S. Lochlann Jain, *Injury: The Politics of Product Design and Safety Law in the United States* (Princeton, NJ: Princeton University Press, 2006).

19. Jain, *Injury*.

20. Jain, *Injury*.

21. Adriana Petryna, *Life Exposed: Biological Citizens after Chernobyl* (Princeton, NJ: Princeton University Press, 2013).

22. Om Astha Rai, "A Mysterious Rash of Kidney Failures," *Nepali Times*, April 7–13, 2017, accessed November 29, 2020, http://archive.nepalitimes.com/article/Nepali-Times-Buzz/A-mysterious-rash-of-kidney-failures,3639; D. Mishra and P. Koirala, "Status of Chronic Kidney Disease Patients Registered in National Kidney Center, Banasthali, Kathmandu," *Journal of Manmohan Memorial Institute of Health Sciences* 1, no. 4 (2015): 19–23; Pradhan et al., "Heat Stress Impacts on Cardiac Mortality"; Sanjib Kumar Sharma, Subodh Dhakal, Lekhjung Thapa, Anup Ghimire, Rikesh Tamrakar, Satdal Chaudhary, Rajib Deo, et al., "Community-Based Screening for Chronic Kidney Disease, Hypertension and Diabetes in Dharan," *Journal of the Nepal Medical Association* 52, no. 189 (2013): 205–12.

23. Bandana Pradhan, Tord Kjellstrom, Dan Atar, Puspa Sharma, Birendra Kayastha, Gita Bhandari, and Pushkar K. Pradhan, "Heat Stress Impacts on Cardiac Mortality in Nepali Migrant Workers in Qatar," *Cardiology* 143, no. 1 (2019): 37–48.

24. Climate CHIP, "Your Weather: Today," 2020, accessed February 16, 2020, https://www.climatechip.org/your-area-climate-data.

25. Brenda Jacklitsch, W. John Williams, Kristin Musolin, Aitor Coca, Jung-Hyun Kim, and Nina Turner, *Occupational Exposure to Heat and Hot Environments, Revised Criteria 2016*, Department of Health and Human Services, Centers for Disease Control and Prevention, National Institute for Occupational Safety and Health, February 2016, accessed November 30, 2020, https://www.cdc.gov/niosh/docs/2016-106/pdfs/2016-106.pdf.

26. Jacklitsch et al., *Occupational Exposure to Heat and Hot Environments*.

27. William A. Latzka, Michael N. Sawka, Scott J. Montain, Gary S. Skrinar, Roger A. Fielding, Ralph P. Matott, and Kent B. Pandolf, "Hyperhydration: Tolerance and Cardiovascular Effects during Uncompensable Exercise-Heat Stress," *Journal of Applied Physiology* 84, no. 6 (1998): 1858–64.

28. Jacklitsch et al., *Occupational Exposure to Heat and Hot Environments*.

29. Jacklitsch et al., *Occupational Exposure to Heat and Hot Environments*.

30. Loris Borghi, Tiziana Meschi, Ferdinando Amato, Almerico Novarini, Alessandro Romanelli, and Ferdinando Cigala, "Hot Occupation and Nephrolithiasis," *Journal of Urology* 150, no. 6 (1993): 1757–60.

31. Peter A. Hancock and Ioannis Vasmatzidis, "Effects of Heat Stress on Cognitive Performance: The Current State of Knowledge," *International Journal of Hyperthermia* 19, no. 3 (2003): 355–72.

32. Edward James Walter and Mike Carraretto, "The Neurological and Cognitive Consequences of Hyperthermia," *Critical Care* 20, no. 1 (2016): 199.

33. Michelle A. Cleary, Lori A. Sweeney, Zebulon V. Kendrick, and Michael R. Sitler, "Dehydration and Symptoms of Delayed-Onset Muscle Soreness in Hyperthermic Males," *Journal of Athletic Training* 40, no. 4 (2005): 288.

34. Lisa R. Leon and Abderrezak Bouchama, "Heat Stroke," *Comprehensive Physiology* 5, no. 2 (2011): 611–47.

35. G. Patrick Lambert, "Intestinal Barrier Dysfunction, Endotoxemia, and Gastrointestinal Symptoms: The 'Canary in the Coal Mine' during Exercise–Heat Stress?," in *Thermoregulation and Human Performance: Physiological and Biological Aspects*, ed. F. E. Marino (Basel: Karger Publishers, 2008), 61–73.

36. Jacklitsch et al., *Occupational Exposure to Heat and Hot Environments*.

37. Abderrezak Bouchama and James P. Knochel, "Heat Stroke," *New England Journal of Medicine* 346, no. 25 (2002): 1978–88.

38. Yoram Epstein and William O. Roberts, "The Pathophysiology of Heat Stroke: An Integrative View of the Final Common Pathway," *Scandinavian Journal of Medicine and Science in Sports* 21, no. 6 (2011): 742–48.

39. Lisa R. Leon, "Heat Stroke and Cytokines," *Progress in Brain Research* 162 (2007): 481–524.

40. Epstein and Roberts, "The Pathophysiology of Heat Stroke."

41. Nannette M. Lugo-Amador, Todd Rothenhaus, and Peter Moyer, "Heat-Related Illness," *Emergency Medicine Clinics of North America* 22, no. 2 (2004): viii, 315–27.

42. M. Royburt, Y. Epstein, Z. Solomon, and J. Shemer, "Long-Term Psychological and Physiological Effects of Heat Stroke," *Physiology and Behavior* 54, no. 2 (1993): 265–67.

43. *ISO 7243: 1989. Hot Environments—Estimation of the Heat Stress on Working Man, Based on the WBGT-Index (Wet Bulb Globe Temperature)* (Geneva: International Organization for Standardization, 1989).

44. Francesca R. d'Ambrosio Alfano, Jacques Malchaire, Boris Igor Palella, and Giuseppe Riccio, "WBGT Index Revisited after 60 Years of Use," *Annals of Occupational Hygiene* 58, no. 8 (2014): 955–70.

45. *ISO 7243: 2017. Ergonomics of the Thermal Environment—Assessment of Heat Stress Using the WBGT (Wet Bulb Globle Temperature) Index* (Geneva: International Standards

Organization, 2017); Ken Parsons, "Heat Stress Standard ISO 7243 and Its Global Application," *Industrial Health* 44, no. 3 (2006): 368–79.

46. *ISO 7243: 2017. Erganomics of the Thermal Environment*; Parsons, "Heat Stress Standard ISO 7243."

47. Climate CHIP, "Your Weather: Today."

48. Graham P. Bates and John Schneider, "Hydration Status and Physiological Workload of UAE Construction Workers: A Prospective Longitudinal Observational Study," *Journal of Occupational Medicine and Toxicology* 3, no. 1 (2008): 21; Habibolah Dehghan, Seyed Bagher Mortazavi, Mohammad J. Jafari, and Mohammad R. Maracy, "Evaluation of Wet Bulb Globe Temperature Index for Estimation of Heat Strain in Hot/Humid Conditions in the Persian Gulf," *Journal of Research in Medical Sciences: The Official Journal of Isfahan University of Medical Sciences* 17, no. 12 (2012): 1108; Pongjan Yoopat, Pornkamon Toicharoen, Thirayudh Glinsukon, Kamiel Vanwonterghem, and Veikko Louhevaara, "Ergonomics in Practice: Physical Workload and Heat Stress in Thailand," *International Journal of Occupational Safety and Ergonomics* 8, no. 1 (2002): 83–93; Vidhya Venugopal, Jeremiah Chinnadurai, Rebekah Lucas, and Tord Kjellstrom, "Occupational Heat Stress Profiles in Selected Workplaces in India," *International Journal of Environmental Research and Public Health* 13, no. 1 (2016): 89.

49. Robert Byard, "Heat-Related Deaths," *Forensic Science Medical Pathology* 2013, no. 9 (2013): 469–70.

50. Thomas E. Bernard, Christina L. Luecke, Skai K. Schwartz, K. Scott Kirkland, and Candi D. Ashley, "WBGT Clothing Adjustments for Four Clothing Ensembles under Three Relative Humidity Levels," *Journal of Occupational and Environmental Hygiene* 2, no. 5 (2005): 251–56; Parsons, "Heat Stress Standard ISO 7243."

51. Linda Nash, *Inescapable Ecologies: A History of Environment, Disease, and Knowledge* (Berkeley: University of California Press, 2006).

52. Christopher C. Sellers, *Hazards of the Job: From Industrial Disease to Environmental Health Science* (Chapel Hill: University of North Carolina Press, 1997); David Rosner and Gerald E. Markowitz, *Dying for Work: Workers' Safety and Health in Twentieth-Century America* (Bloomington: Indiana University Press, 1987).

53. David Rosner and Gerald Markowitz, *Deadly Dust: Silicosis and the Politics of Occupational Disease in Twentieth-Century America* (Princeton, NJ: Princeton University Press, 1994); Ronald Johnston and Arthur J. McIvor, *Lethal Work: A History of the Asbestos Tragedy in Scotland* (Edinburgh: John Donald, 2000).

54. Richard A. Pollock, Ted W. Brown Jr., and David M. Rubin, "'Phossy Jaw' and 'Bisphossy Jaw' of the 19th and 21st Centuries: The Diuturnity of John Walker and the Friction Match," *Craniomaxillofacial Trauma and Reconstruction* 8, no. 3 (2015): 262–70, accessed November 30, 2020, https://doi.org/10.1055/s-0035-1558452; Sven Hernberg, "Lead Poisoning in a Historical Perspective," *American Journal of Industrial Medicine* 38, no. 3 (2000): 244–54; Eva Hnizdo and Val Vallyathan, "Chronic Obstructive Pulmonary Disease Due to Occupational Exposure to Silica Dust: A Review of Epidemiological and Pathological Evidence," *Occupational and Environmental Medicine* 60, no. 4 (2003): 237–43.

55. Geoffrey Tweedale, *Magic Mineral to Killer Dust: Turner and Newall and the Asbestos Hazard* (Oxford: Oxford University Press, 2000).

56. Jianjun Xiang, Peng Bi, Dino Pisaniello, and Alana Hansen, "Health Impacts of Workplace Heat Exposure: An Epidemiological Review," *Industrial Health* 52, no. 2 (2014): 91–101; Elizabeth G. Hanna, Tord Kjellstrom, Charmian Bennett, and Keith Dear, "Climate Change and Rising Heat: Population Health Implications for Working People in Australia," *Asia Pacific Journal of Public Health* 23, no. 2 (2011): 14S–26S; Larry L. Jackson and Howard R. Rosenberg, "Preventing Heat-Related Illness among Agricultural Workers," *Journal*

of Agromedicine 15, no. 3 (2010): 200–215; Kjellstrom et al., "Heat, Human Performance, and Occupational Health"; Paul A. Schulte, A. Bhattacharya, C. R. Butler, Heekyoung K. Chun, Brenda Jacklitsch, T. Jacobs, Max Kiefer, et al., "Advancing the Framework for Considering the Effects of Climate Change on Worker Safety and Health," *Journal of Occupational and Environmental Hygiene* 13, no. 11 (2016): 847–65, accessed November 30, 2020, https://doi.org/10.1080/15459624.2016.1179388.

57. Ramón García-Trabanino, Emmanuel Jarquín, Catharina Wesseling, Richard J. Johnson, Marvin González-Quiroz, Ilana Weiss, Jason Glaser, et al., "Heat Stress, Dehydration, and Kidney Function in Sugarcane Cutters in El Salvador—A Cross-Shift Study of Workers at Risk of Mesoamerican Nephropathy," *Environmental Research* 142 (2015): 746–55; David H. Wegman, Jenny Apelqvist, Matteo Bottai, Ulf Ekström, Ramón García-Trabanino, Jason Glaser, Christer Hogstedt, et al., "Intervention to Diminish Dehydration and Kidney Damage among Sugarcane Workers," *Scandinavian Journal of Work, Environment and Health* 44, no. 1 (2018): 16–24; Payel Acharya, Bethany Boggess, and Kai Zhang, "Assessing Heat Stress and Health among Construction Workers in a Changing Climate: A Review," *International Journal of Environmental Research and Public Health* 15, no. 2 (2018): 247; Chuansi Gao, Kalev Kuklane, Per-Olof Östergren, and Tord Kjellstrom, "Occupational Heat Stress Assessment and Protective Strategies in the Context of Climate Change," *International Journal of Biometeorology* 62, no. 3 (2018): 359–71; Steve Rowlinson, Andrea YunyanJia, Baizhan Li, and Carrie ChuanjingJu, "Management of Climatic Heat Stress Risk in Construction: A Review of Practices, Methodologies, and Future Research," *Accident Analysis and Prevention* 66 (2014): 187–98; Ariane Adam-Poupart, Audrey Smargiassi, Marc-Antoine Busque, Patrice Duguay, Michel Fournier, Joseph Zayed, and France Labrèche, "Effect of Summer Outdoor Temperatures on Work-Related Injuries in Quebec (Canada)," *Occupational and Environmental Medicine* 72, no. 5 (2015): 338–45; Sarah Bronwen Horton, *They Leave Their Kidneys in the Fields: Illness, Injury, and Illegality among US Farmworkers* (Berkeley: University of California Press, 2016).

58. Nash, *Inescapable Ecologies*, 13.

59. Nash, *Inescapable Ecologies*, 13.

60. Human Rights Watch, "Qatar: Take Urgent Action to Protect Construction Workers," September 27, 2017, accessed November 10, 2020, https://www.hrw.org/news/2017/09/27/qatar-take-urgent-action-protect-construction-workers#.

61. Qatar Ministry of the Municipality and Environment, *Qatar Construction Specifications of 2010* (Doha 2010).

62. Weather Underground, "Doha, Qatar Weather History," 2020, accessed February 16, 2020, https://www.wunderground.com/history/daily/OTBD/date.

63. Sellers, *Hazards of the Job*.

64. Rosner and Markowitz, *Dying for Work*.

65. Andrea Boggio, *Compensating Asbestos Victims: The Dark Side of Industrialization* (New York: Routledge, 2016); Oluf Dimitri Røe and Giulia Maria Stella, "Malignant Pleural Mesothelioma: History, Controversy, and Future of a Man-Made Epidemic," in *Asbestos and Mesothelioma*, ed. Joseph R. Testa (New York: Springer, 2017), 73–101.

66. Garry C. Gray, "The Responsibilization Strategy of Health and Safety: Neo-Liberalism and the Reconfiguration of Individual Responsibility for Risk," *British Journal of Criminology* 49, no. 3 (2009): 326–42.

67. Susan S. Silbey, "Taming Prometheus: Talk about Safety andCulture," *Annual Review of Sociology* 35 (2009): 341–69.

68. Sidney W. A. Dekker, "The Bureaucratization of Safety," *Safety Science* 70 (2014): 348–57; Teemu Reiman and Carl Rollenhagen, "Does the Concept of Safety Culture Help or Hinder Systems Thinking in Safety?," *Accident Analysis and Prevention* 68 (2014): 5–15;

Johann Weichbrodt, "Safety Rules as Instruments for Organizational Control, Coordination and Knowledge: Implications for Rules Management," *Safety Science* 80 (2015): 221–32.

69. Linda M. Goldenhar, Stacey Kohler Moran, and Michael Colligan, "Health and Safety Training in a Sample of Open-Shop Construction Companies," *Journal of Safety Research* 32, no. 2 (2001): 237–52; Tuula Laukkanen, "Construction Work and Education: Occupational Health and Safety Reviewed," *Construction Management and Economics* 17, no. 1 (1999): 53–62.

70. Marion Gillen, Davis Baltz, Margy Gassel, Luz Kirsch, and Diane Vaccaro, "Perceived Safety Climate, Job Demands, and Coworker Support among Union and Nonunion Injured Construction Workers," *Journal of Safety Research* 33, no. 1 (2002): 33–51; Amotz Perlman, Rafael Sacks, and Ronen Barak, "Hazard Recognition and Risk Perception in Construction," *Safety Science* 64 (2014): 22–31; Riza Yosia Sunindijo and Patrick X. W. Zou, "The Roles of Emotional Intelligence, Interpersonal Skill, and Transformational Leadership on Improving Construction Safety Performance," *Construction Economics and Building* 13, no. 3 (2013): 97–113.

71. Sara A. Quandt, Melinda F. Wiggins, Haiying Chen, Werner E. Bischoff, and Thomas A. Arcury, "Heat Index in Migrant Farmworker Housing: Implications for Rest and Recovery from Work-Related Heat Stress," *American Journal of Public Health* 103, no. 8 (2013): e24–e26.

72. Karin Lundgren, Kalev Kuklane, Chuansi Gao, and Ingvar Holmer, "Effects of Heat Stress on Working Populations When Facing Climate Change," *Industrial Health* 51, no. 1 (2013): 3–15.

73. Lundgren et al., "Effects of Heat Stress"; Valerie Vi Thien Mac and Linda A. McCauley, "Farmworker Vulnerability to Heat Hazards: A Conceptual Framework," *Journal of Nursing Scholarship* 49, no. 6 (2017): 617–24, accessed December 1, 2020, https://doi .org/10.1111/jnu.12327.

Chapter 6. Earth: How the Politics of Skill Shape Responses to Climate Change

1. Qatar Planning and Statistics Authority, *Annual Bulletin Labor Force Survey, 2010 and 2015*.

2. Mainul Ahsan and Md. Mizanur Rahman Bhuiyan, "Soil and Water Salinity: Their Management in Relation to Climate Changes in Coastal Areas of Bangladesh," *Khulna University Studies* (2010): 31–42.

3. Robert J. Nicholls, Craig W. Hutton, A. N. Lázár, Andrew Allan, W. Neil Adger, Helen Adams, Judith Wolf, et al., "Integrated Assessment of Social and Environmental Sustainability Dynamics in the Ganges-Brahmaputra-Meghna Delta, Bangladesh," *Estuarine, Coastal and Shelf Science* 183 (2016): 370–81.

4. Md. Arif Chowdhury, Yahya Khairun, Md. Salequzzaman, and Md. Mizanur Rahman, "Effect of Combined Shrimp and Rice Farming on Water and Soil Quality in Bangladesh," *Aquaculture International* 19, no. 6 (2011): 1193–206.

5. Md. Monirul Islam, Arifa Jannat, Aurup Ratan Dhar, and Tofael Ahamed, "Factors Determining Conversion of Agricultural Land Use in Bangladesh: Farmers' Perceptions and Perspectives of Climate Change," *GeoJournal* (2019): 1–20.

6. Chowdhury et al., "Effect of Combined Shrimp and Rice Farming."

7. Joyce J. Chen and Valerie Mueller, "Coastal Climate Change, Soil Salinity and Human Migration in Bangladesh," *Nature Climate Change* 8, no. 11 (2018): 981–85, accessed December 2, 2020, https://doi.org/10.1038/s41558-018-0313-8.

8. Reazul Ahsan, Jon Kellett, and Sadasivam Karuppannan, "Climate Migration and Urban Changes in Bangladesh," in *Urban Disasters and Resilience in Asia*, ed. Rajib

Shaw, Atta-ur-Rahman, Akhilesh Surjan, and Gulsan Parvin (Amsterdam: Elsevier, 2016), 293–316; Clark L. Gray and Valerie Mueller, "Natural Disasters and Population Mobility in Bangladesh," *Proceedings of the National Academy of Sciences* 109, no. 16 (2012): 6000–6005; Mohammad Moniruzzaman and Margaret Walton-Roberts, "Migration, Debt and Resource Backwash: How Sustainable Is Bangladesh-Gulf Circular Migration?," *Migration and Development* 7, no. 1 (2017): 85–103, accessed December 2, 2020, https://doi.org/10.1080/21632324.2017.1358799.

9. Md. Habibur Rahman and Md. Sakhawat Hossain, "Convergence in Per Capita Income across Regions in Bangladesh," *Bangladesh Development Studies* 32, no. 1 (2009): 45–60, accessed December 2, 2020, https://bids.org.bd/uploads/publication/BDS/32/32-1/03_Rahman%20&%20Hossain.pdf.

10. Education Policy Data Center, "EDPC Spotlight on Bangladesh," FHI 360, 2012, accessed December 2, 2020, https://www.epdc.org/sites/default/files/documents/Bangladesh_coreusaid.pdf.

11. Andrew Gardner, Silvia Pessoa, Abdoulaye Diop, Kaltham Al-Ghanim, Kien Le Trung, and Laura Harkness, "A Portrait of Low-Income Migrants in Contemporary Qatar," *Journal of Arabian Studies* 3, no. 1 (2013): 1–17, accessed December 2, 2020, https://doi.org/10.1080/21534764.2013.806076; Md. Mizanur Rahman, "Migrant Indebtedness: Bangladeshis in the GCC Countries," *International Migration* 53, no. 6 (2015): 205–19, accessed December 2, 2020, https://doi.org/10.1111/imig.12084.

12. Matthew Adams, Victoria Burrows, and Stephen Richardson, *Bringing Embodied Carbon Upfront* (London: World Green Building Council, 2019), accessed December 2, 2020, https://www.worldgbc.org/sites/default/files/WorldGBC_Bringing_Embodied_Carbon_Upfront.pdf.

13. Hannah Ritchie and Max Roser, "CO_2 Country Profile: Qatar and the United States,"Our World in Data, accessed January 5, 2020, https://ourworldindata.org/co2/country/qatar?country=~QAT. This is a website, so no single date of publication is indicated.

14. World Bank, *Groundswell: Preparing for Internal Climate Migration*, (March 19, 2018), accessed December 2, 2020, https://www.worldbank.org/en/news/infographic/2018/03/19/groundswell-preparing-for-internal-climate-migration.

15. Amnesty International, *Qatar: The Dark Side of Migration: Spotlight on Qatar's Construction Sector Ahead of the World Cup* (London: Amnesty International, 2013), accessed November 10, 2020, https://www.amnesty.org/en/documents/MDE22/010/2013/en/; Amnesty International, *Nepal: False Promises: Exploitation and Forced Labor of Nepalese Migrant Workers* (London: Amnesty International, 2011), accessed December 2, 2020, https://www.amnesty.org/en/documents/asa31/007/2011/en/; Amnesty International, *Nepal: Turning People into Profits: Abusive Recruitment, Trafficking and Forced Labor of Nepali Migrant Workers* (London: Amnesty International, 2017), accessed December 2, 2020, https://www.amnesty.org/en/documents/asa31/6206/2017/en/; Amnesty International, *The Ugly Side of the Beautiful Game: Exploitation of Migrant Workers on a Qatar 2022 World Cup Site* (London: Amnesty International, 2016), accessed November 12, 2020, https://www.amnesty.org/download/Documents/MDE2235482016ENGLISH.PDF; Priyanka Motaparthy, *Building a Better World Cup: Protecting Migrant Workers in Qatar Ahead of FIFA 2022* (New York: Human Rights Watch, 2012), accessed November 12, 2020, https://www.hrw.org/sites/default/files/reports/qatar0612webwcover_0.pdf; Declan Croucher, "A Way Forward for Qatar?," *Verité*, December 14, 2017, accessed December 2, 2020, https://www.verite.org/way-forward-qatar/.

16. Amnesty International, *Qatar: The Dark Side of Migration*; Motaparthy, *Building a Better World Cup*; Ray Jureidini, *Migrant Labour Recruitment to Qatar* (Doha: Bloomsbury Qatar Foundation Journals, 2014).

17. Amnesty International, *Nepal: False Promises.*

18. Jureidini, *Migrant Labour Recruitment to Qatar.*

19. Isaku Endo and Gabi G. Afram, *The Qatar-Nepal Remittance Corridor: Enhancing the Impact and Integrity of Remittance Flows by Reducing Inefficiencies in the Migration Process* (Washington, DC: World Bank, 2011).

20. Gardner et al., "A Portrait of Low-Income Migrants."

21. Motaparthy, *Building a Better World Cup*, 3.

22. Motaparthy, *Building a Better World Cup*, 53.

23. Impactt Limited, *Annual External Compliance Report of the Supreme Committee for Delivery and Legacy's Workers' Welfare Standards* (London: Impactt Limited, April 2017), accessed December 2, 2020, https://impacttlimited.com/wp-content/uploads/2017/01/SC-Annual-Report-Issue-3.2.pdf.

24. Anthony Harwood, "Migrant Stadium Workers to Be Refunded Recruitment Fees by Qatar," *New Vision* (UK), March 16, 2018, accessed December 2, 2020, https://www.newvision.co.ug/new_vision/news/1473429/migrant-stadium-workers-refunded-recruitment-fees-qatar.

25. "Qatar to Reimburse Recruitment Fees to 30,000 Workers; Global Trade Union Body Hails Decision," *Peninsula Qatar* (Doha), March 18, 2018, accessed December 2, 2020, https://www.thepeninsulaqatar.com/article/18/03/2018/Qatar-to-reimburse-recruitment-fees-to-30,000-workers-Global-trade-union-body-hails-decision.

26. Adriana Kemp and Rebeca Raijman, "Bringing in State Regulations, Private Brokers, and Local Employers: A Meso-Level Analysis of Labor Trafficking in Israel," *International Migration Review* 48, no. 3 (2018), accessed December 2, 2020, https://doi.org/10.1111/imre.12109.

27. Sophie Cranston, "Calculating the Migration Industries: Knowing the Successful Expatriate in the Global Mobility Industry," *Journal of Ethnic and Migration Studies* 44, no. 4 (2018): 626–43; Thomas Gammeltoft-Hansen and Ninna Nyberg Sorensen, *The Migration Industry and the Commercialization of International Migration* (Abingdon, UK: Routledge, 2013); Rubén Hernández-León, *Metropolitan Migrants: The Migration of Urban Mexicans to the United States* (Berkeley: University of California Press, 2008); David McCollum and Allan Findlay, "Oiling the Wheels? Flexible Labour Markets and the Migration Industry," *Journal of Ethnic and Migration Studies* 44, no. 4 (2018): 558–74, accessed December 2, 2020, https://doi.org/10.1080/1369183x.2017.1315505.

28. Jennifer Gordon, "Regulating the Human Supply Chain," *Iowa Law Review* 102 (2016): 450.

29. Nicola Phillips, "Unfree Labour and Adverse Incorporation in the Global Economy: Comparative Perspectives on Brazil and India," *Economy and Society* 42, no. 2 (2013): 171–96, accessed December 2, 2020, https://doi.org/10.1080/03085147.2012.718630; Nicola Phillips and Fabiola Mieres, "The Governance of Forced Labour in the Global Economy," *Globalizations* 12, no. 2 (2014): 244–60, accessed December 2, 2020, https://doi.org/10.1080/14747731.2014.932507; Genevieve LeBaron, "Reconceptualizing Debt Bondage: Debt as a Class-Based Form of Labor Discipline," *Critical Sociology* 40, no. 5 (2014): 763–80, accessed December 2, 2020, https://doi.org/10.1177/0896920513512695.

30. Hernández-León, *Metropolitan Migrants*, 154; Bassina Farbenblum and Justine Nolan, "The Business of Migrant Worker Recruitment: Who Has the Responsibility and Leverage to Protect Rights?," *Texas International Law Journal* 52, no. 1 (2017): 18–26.

31. Manolo I. Abella, "The Role of Recruiters in Labor Migration," in *International Migration: Prospects and Policies in a Global Market*, ed. Douglas S. Massey and J. Edward Taylor (Oxford: Oxford University Press, 2004), 203; Jureidini, *Migrant Labour Recruitment to Qatar*, 30; Ray Jureidini, "Wage Protection Systems and Programmes in the GCC," in

Migration to the Gulf: Policies in Sending and Receiving Countries, ed. Philippe Fargues and Nasra M. Shah (Cambridge, UK: Gulf Research Centre, 2017), 9–33; Nguyen Quynh Phuong and Sundar Venkatesh, "Does 'Buyer Beware' Work in Migration? Contracting between Brokers and Migrants in Vietnam," *International Migration* 54, no. 6 (2016): 94–108.

32. Michelle Buckley, Adam Zendel, Jeff Biggar, Lia Frederiksen, and Jill Wells, *Migrant Work and Employment in the Construction Sector* (Geneva: International Labour Organization, 2016); Froilan T. Malit Jr. and George Naufal, "Asymmetric Information under the Kafala Sponsorship System: Impacts on Foreign Domestic Workers' Income and Employment Status in the GCC Countries," *International Migration* 54, no. 5 (2016): 76–90.

33. Bassina Farbenblum, "Governance of Migrant Worker Recruitment: A Rights-Based Framework for Countries of Origin," *Asian Journal of International Law* 7, no. 1 (2017): 152–84; David Segall and Sarah Labowitz, *Making Workers Pay: Recruitment of the Migrant Labor Force in the Gulf Construction Industry* (New York: NYU Stern Center for Business and Human Rights, 2017).

34. Elizabeth Frantz, "Jordan's Unfree Workforce: State-Sponsored Bonded Labour in the Arab Region," *Journal of Development Studies* 49, no. 8 (2013): 1072–87, accessed December 2, 2020, https://doi.org/10.1080/00220388.2013.780042; Julia O'Connell Davidson, "Troubling Freedom: Migration, Debt, and Modern Slavery," *Migration Studies* 1, no. 2 (2013): 176–95, accessed December 2, 2020, https://dx.doi.org/10.1093/migration/mns002.

35. Farbenblum and Nolan, "The Business of Migrant Worker Recruitment."

36. Gordon, "Regulating the Human Supply Chain," 451.

37. Siobhán McGrath, "Fuelling Global Production Networks with Slave Labour?: Migrant Sugar Cane Workers in the Brazilian Ethanol GPN," *Geoforum* 44 (2013): 32–43, accessed December 2, 2020, https://doi.org/10.1016/j.geoforum.2012.06.011.

38. Genevieve LeBaron and Nicola Phillips, "States and the Political Economy of Unfree Labour," *New Political Economy* 24, no. 1 (2018): 1–21, accessed December 2, 2020, https://doi.org/10.1080/13563467.2017.1420642; Sverre Molland, "Safe Migration, Dilettante Brokers and the Appropriation of Legality: Lao-Thai 'Trafficking' in the Context of Regulating Labour Migration," *Pacific Affairs* 85, no. 1 (2012): 117–36, accessed December 2, 2020, https://doi.org/10.5509/2012851117.

39. Dovelyn Rannveig Agunias, "What We Know about Regulating the Recruitment of Migrant Workers," *Policy Brief* 6 (2013): 1–11; Patricia Pittman, "Alternative Approaches to the Governance of Transnational Labor Recruitment," *International Migration Review* 50, no. 2 (2018): 269–314, accessed December 2, 2020, https://doi.org/10.1111/imre.12164.

40. Gordon, "Regulating the Human Supply Chain," 475.

41. Johan Lindquist, Biao Xiang, and Brenda S. A. Yeoh, "Opening the Black Box of Migration: Brokers, the Organization of Transnational Mobility and the Changing Political Economy in Asia," *Pacific Affairs* 85, no. 1 (2012): 7–19, accessed December 2, 2020, https://doi.org/10.5509/20128517.

42. Michele Ford, Lenore Lyons, and Willem van Schendel, "Labour Migration and Human Trafficking: An Introduction," in *Labour Migration and Human Trafficking in Southeast Asia: Critical Perspectives*, ed. Michele Ford, Lenore Lyons, and Willem van Schendel (London: Routledge, 2012), 1–22; Gordon, "Regulating the Human Supply Chain"; Jureidini, *Migrant Labour Recruitment to Qatar*; Ray Jureidini, *Ways Forward in Recruitment of Low-Skilled Migrant Workers in the Asia-Arab States Corridor* (Geneva: International Labour Organization, 2016).

43. Nasser Al Jurf and Salwa Beheiry, "Factors Affecting Cost and Schedule in Qatar's Residential Compounds Projects," *International Journal of Engineering Management and*

Economics 2 3, no. 1–2 (2012): 117–34; Ahmed Senouci, Alaa Ahmad Ismail, and Neil Eldin, "Time and Cost Overrun in Public Construction Projects in Qatar" (paper presented at the Creative Construction Conference, Budapest, 2016).

44. This informal step is also omitted in documentary reports on labor recruitment for Qatar. See, for example, Jureidini, *Migrant Labour Recruitment to Qatar.*

45. Kunniparampil Curien Zachariah and Sebastian Irudaya Rajan, *Kerala's Gulf Connection, 1998–2011: Economic and Social Impact of Migration* (Telangana, India: Orient Blackswan, 2012).

46. The Department of Foreign Employment did not require that Nepali citizens migrating to India secure a labor permit.

47. Government of Nepal, Ministry of Labour and Employment, *Labour Migration for Employment: A Status Report for Nepal: 2015/2016–2016/2017* (Kathmandu: Government of Nepal, Ministry of Labour and Employment, 2017), accessed December 3, 2020, https://asiafoundation.org/wp-content/uploads/2018/05/Nepal-Labor-Migration-status-report-2015-16-to-2016-17.pdf.

48. Sarah Paoletti, Eleanor Taylor-Nicholson, Bandita Sijapati, and Bassina Farbenblum, *Migrant Workers' Access to Justice at Home: Nepal* (New York: Open Society Foundations, 2014).

49. International Labor Organization, *Promoting Informed Policy Dialogue on Migration, Remittance, and Development in Nepal* (Kathmandu: International Labor Organization, 2016).

50. Paoletti et al., *Migrant Workers' Access to Justice at Home.*

51. Asia Foundation, *Labour Migration Trends and Patterns: Bangladesh, India, and Nepal 2013* (Kathmandu: Asia Foundation, 2013).

52. Alice Kern and Ulrike Müller-Böker, "The Middle Space of Migration: A Case Study on Brokerage and Recruitment Agencies in Nepal," *Geoforum* 65 (2015): 158–69, accessed December 4, 2020, https://doi.org/10.1016/j.geoforum.2015.07.024; Paoletti et al., *Migrant Workers' Access to Justice at Home.*

53. Gardner et al., "A Portrait of Low-Income Migrants"; Amnesty International, *Nepal: False Promises.*

54. International Labor Organization, *Promoting Informed Policy Dialogue.*

55. P. Krishna. Krishnamurthy, C. Hobbs, A. Matthiasen, S. R. Hollema, R. J. Choularton, K. Pahari, and M. Kawabata, "Climate Risk and Food Security in Nepal—Analysis of Climate Impacts on Food Security and Livelihoods," CCAFS Working Paper No. 48, 2013.

56. Andreas Schild, "ICIMOD's Position on Climate Change and Mountain Systems: The Case of the Hindu Kush–Himalayas," *Mountain Research and Development* 28, no. 3 (2008): 328–31.

57. Rahul Karki and Anup Gurung, "An Overview of Climate Change and Its Impact on Agriculture: A Review from Least Developing Country, Nepal," *International Journal of Ecosystem* 2, no. 2 (2012): 19–24.

58. Sunal Ojha, Koji Fujit, Katsuhiko Asahi, Akiko Sakai, Damodar Lamsal, Takayuki Nuimara, and Hiroto Nagai, "Glacier Area Shrinkage in Eastern Nepal Himalaya since 1992 Using High-Resolution Inventories from Aerial Photographs and ALOS Satellite Images," *Journal of Glaciology* 62, no. 233 (2016): 512–24.

59. Samjwal Ratna Bajracharya, Pradeep Kumar Mool, and Basanta Raj Shrestha, *Impact of Climate Change on Himalayan Glaciers and Glacial Lakes: Case Studies on GLOF and Associated Hazards in Nepal and Bhutan* (Lalitpur, Nepal: International Centre for Integrated Mountain Development, 2007).

60. Binod P. Heyojoo, Nabin K. Yadav, and Rajan Subedi, "Assessments of Climate Change Indicators, Climate-Induced Disasters, and Community Adaptation Strategies: A

Case from High Mountain of Nepal," in *Land Cover Change and Its Eco-Environmental Responses in Nepal*, ed. Ainong Li, Wei Deng, and Wei Zhao (New York: Springer, 2017), 203–22.

61. Bishal Nath, Subodh Dhakal, Tara Nidhi Bhattargai, Bassanta Raj Adhikari, Samjwal Ratna Bajarcharya, and Masaru Yoshida, "Climate Change Impact on Glacier Retreat and Local Community in the Langtang Valley, Central Nepal," *Journal of Development Innovations* 1, no. 1 (2017): 45–59.

62. Binod Chapagain and Popular Gentle, "Withdrawing from Agrarian Livelihoods: Environmental Migration in Nepal," *Journal of Mountain Science* 12, no. 1 (2015): , accessed December 4, 2020, https://doi.org/10.1007/s11629-014-3017-1: 1–13; Mina Nath Paudel, "Consequences of Climate Change in Agriculture and Ways to Cope Up Its Effect in Nepal," *Agronomy Journal of Nepal* 4 (2016): 25–37.

63. Gokarna Jung Thapa, Eric Wikramanayake, and Jessica Forrest, *Climate-Change Impacts on the Biodiversity of the Terai Arc Landscape and the Chitwan-Annapurna Landscape* (Kathmandu: Hariyo Ban, 2015).

64. Krishna Raj Tiwari, S. Rayamajhi, Ridish K. Pokharel, and M. K. Balla, "Determinants of the Climate Change Adaptation in Rural Farming in Nepal Himalaya," *International Journal of Multidisciplinary and Current Research* 2 (2014): 234–40.

65. Ryan Bartlett, Luna Bharati, Dhruba Pant, Heather Hosterman, and Peter G. McCornick, *Climate Change Impacts and Adaptation in Nepal*, International Water Management Institute Working Paper 139, 2010; G. Malla, "Climate Change and Its Impact on Nepalese Agriculture," *Journal of Agriculture and Environment* 9 (2008): 62–71.

66. Niranjan Devkota and Ram Kumar Phuyal, "Climatic Impact on Wheat Production in Terai of Nepal," *Journal of Development and Administrative Studies* 23, no. 1–2 (2015): 1–2.

67. Chapagain and Gentle, "Withdrawing from Agrarian Livelihoods"; Paudel, "Consequences of Climate Change."

68. Thapa, Wikramanayake, and Forrest, "Climate-Change Impacts"; Tiwari et al., "Determinants of the Climate Change Adaptation in Rural Farming"; Ryan Bartlett et al., *Climate Change Impacts and Adaptation*; Malla, "Climate Change and Its Impact"; Devkota and Phuyal, "Climatic Impact on Wheat Production"; Rajendra P. Shrestha and Namita Nepal, "An Assessment by Subsistence Farmers of the Risks to Food Security Attributable to Climate Change in Makwanpur, Nepal," *Food Security* 8, no. 2 (2016): 415–25.

69. Uttam Khanal, Clevo Wilson, Viet-Ngu Hoang, and Boon Lee, "Farmers' Adaptation to Climate Change, Its Determinants and Impacts on Rice Yield in Nepal," *Ecological Economics* 144 (2018): 139–47; Fraser Sugden, "A Mode of Production Flux: The Transformation and Reproduction of Rural Class Relations in Lowland Nepal and North Bihar," *Dialectical Anthropology* 41, no. 2 (2017): 129–61.

70. Andrew Nelson, *The Mobility of Permanence: The Process of Relocating to Kathmandu* (Kathmandu: Center for the Study of Labor and Mobility, 2013).

71. Roshan Sharma, Bhagawat Rial, Nigel Stork, Himlal Baral, and Maheshwar Dhakal, "Spatial Assessment of the Potential Impact of Infrastructure Development on Biodiversity Conservation in Lowland Nepal," *ISPRS International Journal of Geo-Information* 7, no. 9 (2018): 365.

72. Devendra Chhetry, "Understanding Rural Poverty in Nepal" (paper presented at the Asia and Pacific Forum on Poverty: Reforming Policies and Institutions for Poverty Reduction, 2001).

73. Keshav Lall Maharjan and Niraj Prakash Joshi, "Effect of Climate Variables on Yield of Major Food-Crops in Nepal: A Time-Series Analysis," in *Climate Change, Agriculture and Rural Livelihoods in Developing Countries* (New York: Springer, 2013).

74. Sharma et al., *State of Migration in Nepal*.

75. Kindie Tesfave, Pramod K. Aggarwal, Fasil Mequanint, Paresh B. Shirsath, Clare M. Stirling, Arun Khatri-Chhetri, and Dil Bahadur Rahut, "Climate Variability and Change in Bihar, India: Challenges and Opportunities for Sustainable Crop Production," *Sustainability* 9, no. 1 (2017): 1998.

76. Chitta Prasad Sinha, "Climate Change and Its Impacts on the Wetlands of North Bihar, India," *Lakes and Reservoirs: Research and Management* 16, no. 2 (2011): 109–11.

77. Sugden, "A Mode of Production Flux."

78. Wesley M. Cohen and Daniel A. Levintha, "Absorptive Capacity: A New Perspective on Learning and Innovation," *Administrative Science Quarterly* 35, no. 1 (1990): 128–52.

79. Dipak Duvey, "Comparison of Socio Economic Development of Tarai and Nepal," *Research Nepal Journal of Development Studies* 3 (2020): 67–76, accessed December 7, 2020, https://doi.org/10.3126/rnjds.v3i1.29653.

80. Shiva Lohani, Ram Balak Singh, and Jeevan Lohani, "Universal Primary Education in Nepal: Fulfilling the Right to Education," *PROSPECTS* 40, no. 3 (2010): 355–74, accessed December 7, 2020, https://doi.org/10.1007/s11125-010-9162-6.

81. Laurent Bossavie and Anastasiya Denisova, *Youth Labor Migration in Nepal*, Jobs Working Paper, No. 13 (Washington, DC: World Bank, 2018), figure 7.

82. Prakriti Thami and Ashim Bhattarai, *Labor Migration and Skills Training* (Kathmandu: Centre for the Study of Labour and Mobility, 2015), 6, 9, accessed December 7, 2020, https://ceslam.org/index.php?pageName=publication&pid=44.

83. Emanuela Di Gropello, *Skills for the Labor Market in the Philippines* (Washington, DC: World Bank, 2010).

84. "Typhoon Haiyan: Philippines Battles to Bring Storm Aid," BBC, November 10, 2013, accessed December 29, 2020, https://www.bbc.com/news/world-asia-24887746.

85. Betsy Hartmann, "Rethinking Climate Refugees and Climate Conflict: Rhetoric, Reality and the Politics of Policy Discourse," *Journal of International Development: The Journal of the Development Studies Association* 22, no. 2 (2010): 233–46; Luisa Veronis, Bonnie Boyd, Reiko Obokata, and Brittany Main, "Environmental Change and International Migration: A Review," in *Routledge Handbook of Environmental Displacement and Migration*, ed. Robert McLeman and François Gemenne (Abingdon, UK: Routledge, 2018), 42–70.

86. Douglas K. Bardsley and Graeme J. Hugo, "Migration and Climate Change: Examining Thresholds of Change to Guide Effective Adaptation Decision-Making," *Population and Environment* 32, no. 2–3 (2010): 238–62; Kathleen Hermans-Neumann, Joerg Priess, and Martin Herold, "Human Migration, Climate Variability, and Land Degradation: Hotspots of Socio-Ecological Pressure in Ethiopia," *Regional Environmental Change* 17, no. 5 (2017): 1479–92.

Conclusion

1. Pete Pattisson and Roshan Sendhai, "COVID-19 Lockdown Turns Qatar's Largest Migrant Camp into 'Virtual Prison,'" *Guardian*, March 20, 2020, accessed March 20, 2020, https://www.theguardian.com/global-development/2020/mar/20/covid-19-lockdown-turns-qatars-largest-migrant-camp-into-virtual-prison.

2. "Revealed: How Coronavirus Outbreak Is Shining a Light on Violations Inside Qatar's Labor Camps," *Arab News*, April 5, 2020, accessed April 20, 2020, https://www.arabnews.com/node/1653741/middle-east.

3. Chandan Kumar Mandal, "Nepalis in Qatar Live in Overcrowded and Squalid Conditions Even during Pandemic," *Kathmandu Post*, March 26, 2020, accessed April 5, 2020,

https://kathmandupost.com/2/2020/03/26/nepalis-in-qatar-live-in-overcrowded-and
-squalid-conditions-even-during-pandemic.

4. Human Rights Watch, "COVID-19: Unblock Voice Over IP Platforms in Gulf,"
April 7, 2020, accessed April 20, 2020, https://www.hrw.org/news/2020/04/07/covid-19
-unblock-voice-over-ip-platforms-gulf#; Mariam Kiparoidze, "Foreign Workers in the Gulf
Still Can't Call home," *Coda*, July 21, 2020, accessed July 26, 2020, https://www.codastory
.com/authoritarian-tech/gulf-foreign-workers/.

5. Sophie Cousins, "Migrant Workers Can't Afford a Lockdown," *Foreign Policy*, April 8,
2020, accessed April 20, 2020, https://foreignpolicy.com/2020/04/08/qatar-south-asian
-migrant-workers-cant-afford-coronavirus-lockdown-world-cup-2022/; WDR, "Gefangen in Katar—Corona und die Fußball-WM 2022, April 6, 2020, accessed April 20, 2020,
https://www1.wdr.de/mediathek/video/sendungen/sport-inside/video-gefangen-in-katar
---corona-und-die-fussball-wm----100.html.

6. WDR, "Gefangen in Katar."

7. Laith J. Abu-Raddad, Hiam Chemaitelly, Houssein H. Ayoub, Zaina Al Kanaani,
Abdullatif Al Khal, Einas Al Kuwari, Adeel A. Butt, et al., "Characterizing the Qatar
Advanced-Phase SARS-CoV-2 Epidemic." medRxiv, 2020.

8. "Coronavirus World Map: Tracking the Global Outbreak," *New York Times*, July 27,
2020, accessed December 24, 2020, https://www.nytimes.com/interactive/2020/world
/coronavirus-maps.html?action=click&module=Top%20Stories&pgtype=Homepage.

9. Natasha Iskander, "Qatar, the Coronavirus, and Cordons Sanitaires: Migrant Workers and the Use of Public Health Measures to Define the Nation," *Medical Anthropology
Quarterly*, December 4, 2020, accessed December 8, 2020, https://pubmed.ncbi.nlm.nih
.gov/33274452/.

10. Natasha Iskander, "On Detention and Skill: Reflections on Immigrant Incarceration, Bodying Practices, and the Definition of Skill," *American Behavioral Scientist* 63,
no. 9 (2019): 1370–88.

Postscript

1. "British Researchers 'Missing' in Qatar," BBC News, September 4, 2014, accessed
December 8, 2020, https://www.bbc.com/news/uk-29058534.

2. Associated Press, "Qatar Admits Detaining British Human Rights Workers," *Guardian*, September 7, 2014, accessed December 8, 2020, https://www.theguardian.com/world
/2014/sep/07/qatar-detains-humn-rights-british-workers.

3. Cahal Milmo, "British Human Rights Investigator Detained by Qatari Authorities for Two Weeks Speaks Out," *Independent*, September 22, 2014, accessed December 8,
2020, https://www.independent.co.uk/news/world/middle-east/british-human-rights
-investigator-detained-by-qatari-authorities-for-two-weeks-speaks-out-9749426.html.

4. Raziye Akkoc, "BBC Journalist Arrested for Filming Qatar World Cup 2022 Workers," *Telegraph*, May 18, 2015, accessed February 13, 2020, https://www.telegraph.co.uk
/news/worldnews/middleeast/qatar/11612216/BBC-journalist-arrested-for-filming-Qatar
-World-Cup-2022-workers.html.

5. Mark Lobel, "Arrested for Reporting on Qatar's World Cup Labourers," BBC News,
May 18, 2015, accessed December 8, 2020, https://www.bbc.com/news/world-middle-east
-32775563.

6. Marlies Glasius, "What Authoritarianism Is . . . and Is Not: A Practice Perspective,"
International Affairs 94, no. 3 (2018): 515–33.

7. Konstantin Belousov, Tom Horlick-Jones, Michael Bloor, Yakov Gilinskiy, Valentin Golbert, Yakov Kostikovsky, Michael Levi, and Dmitri Pentsov, "Any Port in a Storm:

Fieldwork Difficulties in Dangerous and Crisis-Ridden Settings," *Qualitative Research* 7, no. 2 (2007): 155–75; Daniel Fuchs, Patricia Fuk-Ying Tse, and Xiaojun Feng, "Labour Research under Coercive Authoritarianism: Comparative Reflections on Fieldwork Challenges in China," *Economic and Industrial Democracy* 40, no. 1 (2019): 132–55; J. Paul Goode and Ariel I. Ahram, "Special Issue Editors' Introduction: Observing Autocracies from the Ground Floor," *Social Science Quarterly* 97, no. 4 (2016): 823–33; Helen Sampson, "'Fluid Fields' and the Dynamics of Risk in Social Research," *Qualitative Research* (2017): 131–47.

8. Marlies Glasius et al., *Research, Ethics and Risk in the Authoritarian Field* (New York: Springer, 2017), 9.

9. Andreas Schedler, *The Politics of Uncertainty: Sustaining and Subverting Electoral Authoritarianism* (Oxford: Oxford University Press, 2013); Glasius et al., *Research, Ethics and Risk*, 9.

10. Glasius et al., *Research, Ethics and Risk*, 9.

11. Michael Burawoy, "Critical Sociology: A Dialogue between Two Sciences," *Contemporary Sociology* 27, no. 1 (1998): 15.

12. Michael Gentile, "Meeting the 'Organs': The Tacit Dilemma of Field Research in Authoritarian States," *Area* 45, no. 4 (2013): 426–32.

Abella, Manolo I. "The Role of Recruiters in Labor Migration." In *International Migration: Prospects and Policies in a Global Market,* edited by Douglas S. Massey and J. Edward Taylor, 201–11. Oxford: Oxford University Press, 2004.

Abu-Raddad, Laith J., Hiam Chemaitelly, Houssein H. Ayoub, Zaina Al Kanaani, Abdullatif Al Khal, Einas Al Kuwari, Adeel A. Butt, et al. "Characterizing the Qatar Advanced-Phase SARS-CoV-2 Epidemic." medRxiv, 2020.

Acharya, Payel, Bethany Boggess, and Kai Zhang. "Assessing Heat Stress and Health among Construction Workers in a Changing Climate: A Review." *International Journal of Environmental Research and Public Health* 15, no. 2 (2018): 247.

Acker, Joan. "Hierarchies, Jobs, Bodies: A Theory of Gendered Organizations." *Gender and Society* 4, no. 2 (1990): 139–58.

Adam-Poupart, Ariane, Audrey Smargiassi, Marc-Antoine Busque, Patrice Duguay, Michel Fournier, Joseph Zayed, and France Labrèche. "Effect of Summer Outdoor Temperatures on Work-Related Injuries in Quebec (Canada)." *Occupational and Environment Medicine* 72, no. 5 (2015): 338–45.

Adams, Matthew, Victoria Burrows, and Stephen Richardson. *Bringing Embodied Carbon Upfront.* London: World Green Building Council, 2019. Accessed December 2, 2020. https://www.worldgbc.org/sites/default/files/WorldGBC_Bringing_Embodied_Carbon _Upfront.pdf.

Addleton, J. "The Impact of the Gulf War on Migration and Remittances in Asia and the Middle East." *International Migration* 29, no. 4 (1991): 509–26.

Adham, Khaled. "Rediscovering the Island: Doha's Urbanity from Pearls to Spectacle." In *The Evolving Arab City: Tradition, Modernity and Urban Development,* edited by Yasser Elsheshtawy, 218–57. London: Routledge, 2008.

AECOM. *Property and Construction Handbook: Middle East.* Los Angeles: AECOM, 2019. Accessed November 20, 2020. https://www.aecom.com/ae/wp-content/uploads/2018 /10/Construction-Handbook-2018_19.pdf.

Aguilar, Joey. "Qatar Mega Marathon 2015 Set for March 27." *Gulf Times,* February 4, 2015. Accessed February 13, 2020. https://desktop.gulf-times.com/story/425911/Qatar-Mega -Marathon-2015-set-for-March-27.

Agunias, Dovelyn Rannveig. "What We Know about Regulating the Recruitment of Migrant Workers." *Policy Brief* 6 (2013): 1–11.

Ahmadi, Ameena. "The Urban Core of Doha: Spacial Structure and the Experienced Center." MA thesis, University College London, 2008.

Ahmed, Sherif M., Hassan H. Emam, and Peter Farrell. "Barriers to BIM/4D Implementation in Qatar." Paper presented at the First International Conference of the CIB Middle East and North Africa Research Network, 2014.

Ahsan, Mainul, and Md. Mizanur Rahman Bhuiyan. "Soil and Water Salinity: Their Management in Relation to Climate Changes in Coastal Areas of Bangladesh." *Khulna University Studies* (2010): 31–42.

Ahsan, Reazul, Jon Kellett, and Sadasivam Karuppannan. "Climate Migration and Urban Changes in Bangladesh." In *Urban Disasters and Resilience in Asia,* edited by Rajib Shaw, Atta-ur-Rahman, Akhilesh Surjan, and Gulsan Parvin, 293–316. Amsterdam: Elsevier, 2016.

Akkoc, Raziye. "BBC Journalist Arrested for Filming Qatar World Cup 2022 Workers." *Telegraph*, May 18, 2015. Accessed February 13, 2020. https://www.telegraph.co.uk/news/worldnews/middleeast/qatar/11612216/BBC-journalist-arrested-for-filming-Qatar-World-Cup-2022-workers.html.

Al Jurf, Nasser, and Salwa Beheiry. "Factors Affecting Cost and Schedule in Qatar's Residential Compounds Projects." *International Journal of Engineering Management and Economics* 2 3, no. 1–2 (2012): 117–34.

Al-Maani, Abed Al-Razzak, and Saleh Alsharari. "Pearl Trade in the Persian Gulf during the 19th Century." *Asian Culture and History* 6, no. 1 (2014): 43–52.

al-Othman, Nasser. *With Their Bare Hands: The Story of the Oil Industry in Qatar*. Translated by Ken Whittingham. London: Longman, 1984.

Alsudairi, Mohammed, and Rogaia Mustafa Abusharaf. "Migration in Pre-Oil Qatar: A Sketch." *Studies in Ethnicity and Nationalism* 15, no. 3 (2015): 511–21.

Al-Thani, Ahmed bin Ali. "Act No. (3) for the Year 1963 Governing Aliens Entry and Residence in Qatar." Qatar: National Legislative Bodies / National Authorities, February 16, 1963. Accessed November 17, 2020. https://www.refworld.org/docid/3fb9f96f2.html.

———. "Law No. 2 of 1961 on the Qatari Nationality (Repealed)." Al Meezan: Qatar Legal Portal, 1961. Accessed November 17, 2020. http://www.almeezan.qa/LawView.aspx?opt&LawID=2578&language=en.

Al-Thani, Hamad bin Khafila. "Law No. 13 of 1988 on the Temporary Expropriation and Appropriation of Real Estate for the Public Benefit." Al Meezan: Qatar Legal Portal, 2018. Accessed November 18, 2020. http://www.almeezan.qa/LawPage.aspx?id=3957&language=en.

Al-Thani, Jassim bin Hamad. "Law No. 13 of 2000 Regulation of the Investment of Non-Qatari Capital in the Economic Activity 13/2000." Edited by Council of Ministers. 2000. Accessed November 20, 2020. https://ticaret.gov.tr/data/5b8882ec13b87615b0eea9d7/Law%20No%2013%20of%202000%20Regulation%20of%20the%20Investment%20of%20Non-Qatari%20Capital%20in%20the%20Economic%20Activity.pdf.

Al-Thani, Khalifa bin Hamad. "Law No. 3 of 1984 Regulating the Sponsorship of Residence and Departure of Foreigners (Repealed)." Al Meezan: Qatar Legal Portal, January 1, 1984. Accessed November 17, 2020. http://www.almeezan.qa/LawView.aspx?opt&LawID=292&language=en.

Al-Thani, Tamim bin Hamad. "Law No. 1 of 2014 Regulating the Activities of Nursery Schools." Al Meezan: Qatar Legal Portal, January 30, 2014. Accessed November 18, 2020. http://www.almeezan.qa/LawPage.aspx?id=6115&language=en.

———. "Law No. 4 of 2009 regarding Regulation of the Expatriates Entry, Departure, Residence, and Sponsorship." Al Meezan: Qatar Legal Portal, 2009. Accessed November 17, 2020. http://www.almeezan.qa/LawView.aspx?opt&LawID=2611&language=en.

Amanpour, Christiane. "Full Interview: Emir of Qatar." *CNN World*, 2014. Accessed November 12, 2020. https://www.cnn.com/videos/world/2014/09/25/intv-amanpour-qatar-emir-tamim-bin-hamad-al-thani-full.cnn.

American FactFinder. 2020. Accessed February 21, 2020. https://factfinder.census.gov/faces/tableservices/jsf/pages/productview.xhtml?src=bkmk.

Amnesty International. *All Work, No Pay: The Struggle of Qatar's Migrant Workers for Justice*. London: Amnesty International, 2019. Accessed November 10, 2020. https://www.amnesty.at/media/6034/amnesty_all-work-no-pay-the-struggle-of-qatars-migrant-workers-for-justice_bericht-september-2019.pdf.

———. *Nepal: False Promises: Exploitation and Forced Labor of Nepalese Migrant Workers*. London: Amnesty International, 2011. Accessed December 2, 2020. https://www.amnesty.org/en/documents/asa31/007/2011/en/.

———. *Nepal: Turning People into Profits: Abusive Recruitment, Trafficking and Forced Labor of Nepali Migrant Workers.* London: Amnesty International, 2017. Accessed December 2, 2020. https://www.amnesty.org/en/documents/asa31/6206/2017/en/.

———. *Qatar: Migrant Workers Unpaid for Months of Work by Company Linked to World Cup Host City.* London: Amnesty International, 2018. Accessed November 10, 2020. https://www.amnestyusa.org/reports/qatar-migrant-workers-unpaid-for-months-of -work-by-company-linked-to-world-cup-host-city/.

———. *Qatar: The Dark Side of Migration: Spotlight on Qatar's Construction Sector Ahead of the World Cup.* London: Amnesty International, 2013. Accessed November 10, 2020. https://www.amnesty.org/en/documents/MDE22/010/2013/en/.

———. *Qatar: Unpaid Migrant Construction Workers Left to Go Hungry.* December 18, 2013. Accessed November 26, 2020. https://www.amnesty.org/en/latest/news/2013/12/qatar -unpaid-migrant-construction-workers-left-go-hungry/.

———. *The Ugly Side of the Beautiful Game: Exploitation of Migrant Workers on a Qatar 2022 World Cup Site.* London: Amnesty International, 2016. Accessed November 12, 2020. https://www.amnesty.org/download/Documents/MDE2235482016ENGLISH .PDF.

"Analysis: Qatar Projects Market Forcast and Review H1 2019." MEED: Middle East Business Intelligence, 2019.

Anderson, Michael L. "Embodied Cognition: A Field Guide." *Artificial Intelligence* 149, no. 1 (2003): 91–130.

Anscombe, Frederick F. *The Ottoman Gulf: The Creation of Kuwait, Saudi Arabia, and Qatar.* New York: Columbia University Press, 1997.

Arendt, Hannah. *The Human Condition.* Chicago: University of Chicago Press, 2013.

Asi, A'. "The Arab/Persian Gulf: Oil on Troubled Waters." *MERIP Reports* (1971): 1–8.

Asia Foundation. *Labour Migration Trends and Patterns: Bangladesh, India, and Nepal 2013.* Kathmandu: Asia Foundation, 2013.

Associated Press. "AP Interview: Qatar Labor Chief Criticizes Migrant Worker Housing, Vows to Improve Their Lives." Fox News, December 2, 2015, World. Accessed November 18, 2020. https://www.foxnews.com/world/ap-interview-qatar-labor-chief-criticizes -migrant-worker-housing-vows-to-improve-their-lives.

———. "Qatar Admits Detaining British Human Rights Workers." *Guardian*, September 7, 2014. Accessed December 8, 2020. https://www.theguardian.com/world/2014/sep/07 /qatar-detains-humn-rights-british-workers.

Attewell, Paul. "The Deskilling Controversy." *Work and Occupations* 14, no. 3 (1987): 323–46.

———. "What Is Skill?" *Work and Occupations* 17, no. 4 (1990): 422–48.

Aziz, Omer, and Murtaza Hussain. "Qatar's World Cup Must Not Become a Monument to Slavery." Opinion, *Globe and Mail*, December 18, 2013. Accessed November 18, 2020. https://www.theglobeandmail.com/opinion/qatars-world-cup-must-not-become-a -monument-to-slavery/article16027180/.

Badger, Sam, and Giorgio Cafiero. "Kingdom of Slaves." Foreign Policy in Focus, September 12, 2014. Accessed January 2, 2020. https://fpif.org/kingdom-slaves/.

Bajracharya, Samjwal Ratna, Pradeep Kumar Mool, and Basanta Raj Shrestha. *Impact of Climate Change on Himalayan Glaciers and Glacial Lakes: Case Studies on GLOF and Associated Hazards in Nepal and Bhutan.* Lalitpur, Nepal: International Centre for Integrated Mountain Development, 2007.

Barandiaran, Xabier E. "Autonomy and Enactivism: Towards a Theory of Sensorimotor Autonomous Agency." *Topoi* 36, no. 3 (September 1, 2017): 409–30. Accessed November 23, 2020. https://doi.org/10.1007/s11245-016-9365-4.

Bardsley, Douglas K., and Graeme J. Hugo. "Migration and Climate Change: Examining Thresholds of Change to Guide Effective Adaptation Decision-Making." *Population and Environment* 32, no. 2–3 (2010): 238–62.

Barley, Stephen R., and Gideon Kunda. "Bringing Work Back In." *Organization Science* 12, no. 1 (2001): 76–95.

Barsalou, Lawrence W., Paula M. Niedenthal, Aron K. Barbey, and Jennifer A. Ruppert. "Social Embodiment." *Psychology of Learning and Motivation* 43 (2003): 43–92.

Bartlett, Ryan, Luna Bharati, Dhruba Pant, Heather Hosterman, and Peter G. McCornick. *Climate Change Impacts and Adaptation in Nepal.* International Water Management Institute Working Paper 139. 2010.

Bates, Graham P., and John Schneider. "Hydration Status and Physiological Workload of UAE Construction Workers: A Prospective Longitudinal Observational Study." *Journal of Occupational Medicine and Toxicology* 3, no. 1 (2008): 21.

Bechky, Beth A. "Sharing Meaning across Occupational Communities: The Transformation of Understanding on a Production Floor." *Organization Science* 14, no. 3 (2003): 312–30.

Belousov, Konstantin, Tom Horlick-Jones, Michael Bloor, Yakov Gilinskiy, Valentin Golbert, Yakov Kostikovsky, Michael Levi, and Dmitri Pentsov. "Any Port in a Storm: Fieldwork Difficulties in Dangerous and Crisis-Ridden Settings." *Qualitative Research* 7, no. 2 (2007): 155–75.

Berkeley Earth. "Regional Climate Change: Qatar." 2015. Accessed February 13, 2020. http://berkeleyearth.lbl.gov/regions/qatar.

Bernard, Thomas E., Christina L. Luecke, Skai K. Schwartz, K. Scott Kirkland, and Candi D. Ashley. "WBGT Clothing Adjustments for Four Clothing Ensembles under Three Relative Humidity Levels." *Journal of Occupational and Environmental Hygiene* 2, no. 5 (2005): 251–56.

Bernstein, Richard J. *Praxis and Action: Contemporary Philosophies of Human Activity.* Philadelphia: University of Pennsylvania Press, 2011.

Bird, Allan. "Careers as Repositories of Knowledge: A New Perspective on Boundaryless Careers." *Journal of Organizational Behavior* 15, no. 4 (1994): 325–44.

Birks, J. Stace, Ian J. Seccombe, and Clive A. Sinclair. "Labour Migration in the Arab Gulf States: Patterns, Trends and Prospects." *International Migration* 26, no. 3 (1988): 267–86.

Blake, Heidi, and Jonathan Calvert. *The Ugly Game: The Qatari Plot to Buy the World Cup.* New York: Simon and Schuster, 2015.

Blanton, C. D. "Abstract in Concrete: Brutalism and Modernist Half-Life." In *The Contemporaneity of Modernism: Literature, Media, Culture,* edited by Michael D'Arcy and Mathias Nilges, 17–30. New York: Routledge, 2015.

Boggio, Andrea. *Compensating Asbestos Victims: The Dark Side of Industrialization.* New York: Routledge, 2016.

Booth, Robert. "Qatar World Cup 2022: 70 Nepalese Workers Die on Building Sites." *Guardian* (Qatar), October 1, 2013. Accessed November 29, 2020. https://www.theguardian.com/world/2013/oct/01/qatar-world-cup-2022-nepalese-die-building-sites.

Borghi, Loris, Tiziana Meschi, Ferdinando Amato, Almerico Novarini, Alessandro Romanelli, and Ferdinando Cigala. "Hot Occupation and Nephrolithiasis." *Journal of Urology* 150, no. 6 (1993): 1757–60.

Bose, Sugata. *A Hundred Horizons: The Indian Ocean in the Age of Global Empire.* Cambridge, MA: Harvard University Press, 2006.

Bossavie, Laurent, and Anastasiya Denisova. *Youth Labor Migration in Nepal.* Jobs Working Paper, No. 13. Washington, DC: World Bank, 2018.

Bouchama, Abderrezak, and James P. Knochel. "Heat Stroke." *New England Journal of Medicine* 346, no. 25 (2002): 1978–88.

"British Researchers 'Missing' in Qatar." BBC News, September 4, 2014. Accessed December 8, 2020. https://www.bbc.com/news/uk-29058534.

Buckley, Michelle. "Construction Work, 'Bachelor' Builders and the Intersectional Politics of Urbanization in Dubai." In *Transit States: Labour, Migration and Citizenship in the Gulf*, edited by Abdulhadi Khalaf, Omar AlShehabi, and Adam Hanieh, 132–52. London: Pluto Press, 2015.

———. "Locating Neoliberalism in Dubai: Migrant Workers and Class Struggle in the Autocratic City." *Antipode* 45, no. 2 (2013): 256–74.

Buckley, Michelle, Adam Zendel, Jeff Biggar, Lia Frederiksen, and Jill Wells. *Migrant Work and Employment in the Construction Sector*. Geneva: International Labour Organization, 2016.

Burawoy, Michael. "Critical Sociology: A Dialogue between Two Sciences." *Contemporary Sociology* 27, no. 1 (1998): 12–20.

———. *Manufacturing Consent: Changes in the Labor Process under Monopoly Capitalism*. Chicago: University of Chicago Press, 1982.

———. "Revisits: An Outline of a Theory of Reflexive Ethnography." *American Sociological Review* (2003): 645–79.

Buret, Stéphanie. "Lusail: Sleek New City Offers Glimpse of Qatar's Post-Oil Future." *Guardian*, July 11, 2019. Accessed November 20, 2020. https://www.theguardian.com/cities/2019/jul/11/lusail-sleek-new-city-offers-glimpse-of-qatar-post-oil-future.

Business Monitor International. *Qatar Infrastructure Report Q1 2015*. London: Business Monitor International, 2015.

Butler, Judith. "Bodily Vulnerability, Coalitions, and Street Politics." *Critical Studies* 37 (2014): 99–119.

Byard, Robert. "Heat-Related Deaths." *Forensic Science Medical Pathology* 2013, no. 9 (2013): 469–70.

Central Intelligence Agency. "Country Comparison: Natural Gas—Proved Reserves." World Factbook. Accessed February 13, 2020. https://www.cia.gov/library/publications/the-world-factbook/rankorder/2253rank.html.

Chalcraft, John. "Migration and Popular Protest in the Arabian Peninsula and the Gulf in the 1950s and 1960s." *International Labor and Working-Class History* 79, no. 1 (2011): 28–47.

Chant, Seung-Ik. "Overseas Construction Expected to Be 'Dollar Box.'" *Korea Times*, March 2, 1975.

Chapagain, Binod, and Popular Gentle. "Withdrawing from Agrarian Livelihoods: Environmental Migration in Nepal." *Journal of Mountain Science* 12, no. 1 (2015): 1–13. Accessed December 4, 2020. https://doi.org/10.1007/s11629-014-3017-1.

Chavaillaz, Yann, Philippe Roy, Antti-Ilari Partanen, Laurent Da Silva, Émilie Bresson, Nadine Mengis, Diane Chaumont, and H. Damon Matthews. "Exposure to Excessive Heat and Impacts on Labour Productivity Linked to Cumulative CO_2 Emissions." *Scientific Reports* 9, no. 1 (2019): 13711. Accessed November 29, 2020. https://doi.org/10.1038/s41598-019-50047-w.

Chen, Joyce J., and Valerie Mueller. "Coastal Climate Change, Soil Salinity and Human Migration in Bangladesh." *Nature Climate Change* 8, no. 11 (2018): 981–85. Accessed December 2, 2020. https://doi.org/10.1038/s41558-018-0313-8.

Cheng, Way Lee, Ayman Saleem, and Reza Sadr. "Recent Warming Trend in the Coastal Region of Qatar." *Theoretical and Applied Climatology* 128, no. 1 (2017): 193–205. Accessed November 10, 2020. https://doi.org/10.1007/s00704-015-1693-6.

Chhetry, Devendra. "Understanding Rural Poverty in Nepal." Paper presented at the Asia and Pacific Forum on Poverty: Reforming Policies and Institutions for Poverty Reduction, 2001.

Choo, Chun Wei. "The Knowing Organization: How Organizations Use Information to Construct Meaning, Create Knowledge and Make Decisions." *International Journal of Information Management* 16, no. 5 (1996): 329–40.

Chowdhury, Md. Arif, Yahya Khairun, Md. Salequzzaman, and Md. Mizanur Rahman. "Effect of Combined Shrimp and Rice Farming on Water and Soil Quality in Bangladesh." *Aquaculture International* 19, no. 6 (2011): 1193–206.

Cleary, Michelle A., Lori A. Sweeney, Zebulon V. Kendrick, and Michael R. Sitler. "Dehydration and Symptoms of Delayed-Onset Muscle Soreness in Hyperthermic Males." *Journal of Athletic Training* 40, no. 4 (2005): 288.

Climate CHIP. "Your Weather: Today." 2020. Accessed February 16, 2020. https://www .climatechip.org/your-area-climate-data.

Cohen, Wesley M., and Daniel A. Levintha. "Absorptive Capacity: A New Perspective on Learning and Innovation." *Administrative Science Quarterly* 35, no. 1 (1990): 128–52.

"Coll 30/231 'Annual Political Review of Events in the Persian Gulf' [12r] (24/33)." IOR/L/PS/12/3973. British Library: India Office Records and Private Papers, Qatar Digital Library. Accessed November 15, 2020. https://www.qdl.qa/archive/81055/vdc _100060870618.0x000019.

"Coll 54/2 'Middle East (Official) Committee: Working Party.'" IOR/L/PS/12/4758. British Library: India Office Records and Private Papers, Qatar Digital Library. Accessed November 14, 2020. https://www.qdl.qa/en/archive/81055/vdc_100000000691.0x0001dd.

Collins, Ben. "Slaves Forced to Run Marathon Shoeless in Qatar." *Daily Beast*, April 14, 2017. Accessed February 13, 2020. https://www.thedailybeast.com/slaves-forced-to-run -marathon-shoeless-in-qatar.

Collins, Jane L. *Threads: Gender, Labor, and Power in the Global Apparel Industry.* Chicago: University of Chicago Press, 2009.

Connell, John, Jenny Wang, A. K. Tripathi, and V. B. Bhatt. "Distant Victims? The Impact of the Gulf War on International Migration to the Middle East from Asia." In *Changing Environmental Ideologies*, edited by A. K. Tripathi and V. B. Bhatt, 131–64. New Delhi: Ashish Publishing House, 1992.

"Construction Risky Business in Qatar." *MEED: Middle East Economic Digest* 59, no. 20 (2015): 56.

Contu, Alessia. "On Boundaries and Difference: Communities of Practice and Power Relations in Creative Work." *Management Learning* 45, no. 3 (2014): 289–316.

Contu, Alessia, Christopher Grey, and Anders Örtenblad. "Against Learning." *Human Relations* 56, no. 8 (2003): 931–52.

Coole, Diana. "Rethinking Agency: A Phenomenological Approach to Embodiment and Agentic Capacities." *Political Studies* 53, no. 1 (2005): 124–42.

Cooper, Frederick. "Conflict and Connection: Rethinking Colonial African History." *American Historical Review* 99, no. 5 (1994): 1516–45.

"Coronavirus World Map: Tracking the Global Outbreak." *New York Times*, July 27, 2020. Accessed December 24, 2020. https://www.nytimes.com/interactive/2020/world /coronavirus-maps.html?action=click&module=Top%20Stories&pgtype=Homepage.

Cousins, Sophie. "Migrant Workers Can't Afford a Lockdown." *Foreign Policy*, April 8, 2020. Accessed April 20, 2020. https://foreignpolicy.com/2020/04/08/qatar-south-asian -migrant-workers-cant-afford-coronavirus-lockdown-world-cup-2022/.

Cranston, Sophie. "Calculating the Migration Industries: Knowing the Successful Expatriate in the Global Mobility Industry." *Journal of Ethnic and Migration Studies* 44, no. 4 (2018): 626–43.

Croucher, Declan. "A Way Forward for Qatar?" *Verité*, December 14, 2017. Accessed December 2, 2020. https://www.verite.org/way-forward-qatar/.

Crystal, Jill. *Oil and Politics in the Gulf: Rulers and Merchants in Kuwait and Qatar*. Vol. 24. Cambridge: Cambridge University Press, 1995.

CW Guest Columnist. "Beyond the Numbers." *Construction Week*, December 6, 2014. Accessed November 20, 2020. https://www.constructionweekonline.com/article-31516 -beyond-the-numbers.

———. "Fast-track to Delay." *Construction Week*, September 15, 2016. Accessed November 20, 2020. https://www.constructionweekonline.com/article-40900-fast-track-to-delay.

d'Ambrosio Alfano, Francesca R., Jacques Malchaire, Boris Igor Palella, and Giuseppe Riccio. "WBGT Index Revisited after 60 Years of Use." *Annals of Occupational Hygiene* 58, no. 8 (2014): 955–70.

Davidson, Julia O'Connell. "Troubling Freedom: Migration, Debt, and Modern Slavery." *Migration Studies* 1, no. 2 (2013): 176–95. Accessed December 2, 2020. https://dx.doi .org/10.1093/migration/mns002.

Dawood, Nashwan, and Vladimir Vukovic. "Whole Lifecycle Information Flow Underpinned by BIM: Technology, Process, Policy and People." Paper presented at the Second International Conference on Civil and Building Engineering Informatics, 2015.

"Death and Servitude in Qatar." Editorial, *New York Times*, 2013. Accessed November 18, 2020. https://www.nytimes.com/2013/11/02/opinion/death-and-servitude-in-qatar.html.

Dehghan, Habibolah, Seyed Bagher Mortazavi, Mohammad J. Jafari, and Mohammad R. Maracy. "Evaluation of Wet Bulb Globe Temperature Index for Estimation of Heat Strain in Hot/Humid Conditions in the Persian Gulf." *Journal of Research in Medical Sciences: The Official Journal of Isfahan University of Medical Sciences* 17, no. 12 (2012): 1108.

De Jaegher, Hanne, and Ezequiel Di Paolo. "Participatory Sense-Making." *Phenomenology and the Cognitive Sciences* 6, no. 4 (2007): 485–507.

De Jaegher, Hanne, Barbara Pieper, Daniel Clénin, and Thomas Fuchs. "Grasping Intersubjectivity: An Invitation to Embody Social Interaction Research." *Phenomenology and the Cognitive Sciences* 16, no. 3 (2017): 491–523.

Dekker, Sidney W. A. "The Bureaucratization of Safety." *Safety Science* 70 (2014): 348–57.

de Vega, Manuel, Arthur M. Glenberg, and Arthur C. Graesser. *Symbols and Embodiment: Debates on Meaning and Cognition*. Oxford: Oxford University Press, 2012.

Devkota, Niranjan, and Ram Kumar Phuyal. "Climatic Impact on Wheat Production in Terai of Nepal." *Journal of Development and Administrative Studies* 23, no. 1–2 (2015): 1–22.

Di Gropello, Emanuela. *Skills for the Labor Market in the Philippines*. Washington, DC: World Bank, 2010.

DLA Piper. *The A-Z of Construction Law in Qatar*. London: DLA Piper, 2016. Accessed November 20, 2020. www.dlapiper.com.

———. *Migrant Labor in the Construction Sector in the State of Qatar*. London: DLA Piper UK LLP, April 2014.

Doeringer, Peter B., and Michael J. Piore. *Internal Labor Markets and Manpower Analysis*. Armonk, NY: M. E. Sharpe, 1985.

Dovas. "People Make Anti-Logos to Urge Sponsors to Withdraw from Qatar 2022 World Cup." 2016. Accessed November 29, 2020. https://www.boredpanda.com/qatar-2022 -world-cup-human-rights-sponsor-anti-advertisement/.

Downey, Greg. *Learning Capoeira: Lessons in Cunning from an Afro-Brazilian Art*. Oxford: Oxford University Press, 2005.

———. "Scaffolding Imitation in Capoeira: Physical Education and Enculturation in an Afro Brazilian Art." *American Anthropologist* 110, no. 2 (2008): 204–13.

Dreyfus, Hubert L. "Intelligence without Representation—Merleau-Ponty's Critique of Mental Representation: The Relevance of Phenomenology to Scientific Explanation." *Phenomenology and the Cognitive Sciences* 1, no. 4 (2002): 367–83.

Dunne, John P., Ronald J. Stouffer, and Jasmin G. John. "Reductions in Labour Capacity from Heat Stress under Climate Warming." *Nature Climate Change* 3, no. 6 (2013): 563.

Duvey, Dipak. "Comparison of Socio Economic Development of Tarai and Nepal." *Research Nepal Journal of Development Studies* 3 (2020): 67–76. Accessed December 7, 2020. https://doi.org/10.3126/rnjds.v3i1.29653.

Education Policy Data Center. "EDPC Spotlight on Bangladesh." FHI 360. 2012. Accessed December 2, 2020. https://www.epdc.org/sites/default/files/documents/Bangladesh _coreusaid.pdf.

El Mallakh, Ragaei. *Qatar: Energy and Development.* London: Croom Helm, 1985.

Elsheshtawy, Yasser. *Dubai: Behind an Urban Spectacle.* Abingdon, UK: Routledge, 2009.

———. *Planning Middle Eastern Cities: An Urban Kaleidoscope.* London: Routledge, 2004.

Elson, Diane, and Ruth Pearson. "Nimble Fingers Make Cheap Workers: An Analysis of Women's Employment in Third World Export Manufacturing." *Feminist Review* 7, no. 1 (1981): 87–107.

Endo, Isaku, and Gabi G. Afram. *The Qatar-Nepal Remittance Corridor: Enhancing the Impact and Integrity of Remittance Flows by Reducing Inefficiencies in the Migration Process.* Washington, DC: World Bank, 2011.

Epstein, Yoram, and William O. ORoberts. "The Pathophysiology of Heat Stroke: An Integrative View of the Final Common Pathway." *Scandinavian Journal of Medicine and Science in Sports* 21, no. 6 (2011): 742–48.

Erfani, Azadeh. "Kicking Away Responsibility: FIFA's Role in Response to Migrant Worker Abuses in Qatar's 2022 World Cup." *Jeffrey S. Moorad Sports LJ* 22 (2015): 623.

Erickson, Frederick. "What Makes School Ethnography 'Ethnographic'?" *Anthropology and Education Quarterly* 15, no. 1 (1984): 51–66.

Errichiello, Gennaro. "Foreign Workforce in the Arab Gulf States (1930–1950): Migration Patterns and Nationality Clause." *International Migration Review* 46, no. 2 (2012): 389–413.

"Face to Face: Amr Belal, Powergreen." *Construction Week*, June 1, 2016. Accessed November 20, 2020. https://www.constructionweekonline.com/article-39318-face-to-face-amr -belal-powergreen.

"Face-to-Face: Jason Morris, AECOM." *Construction Week*, October 10, 2016. Accessed November 20, 2020. https://www.constructionweekonline.com/article-41164-face-to -face-jason-morris-aecom.

"Face to Face: Mark Ainger, Faithful+Gould." *Construction Week*, March 3, 2016. Accessed November 20, 2020. https://www.constructionweekonline.com/article-37765-face-to -face-mark-ainger-faithfulgould.

"Face to Face: Mihir Shah, KPMG." *Construction Week*, May 8, 2016. Accessed November 20, 2020. https://www.constructionweekonline.com/article-38884-face-to-face-mihir-shah -kpmg.

Farbenblum, Bassina. "Governance of Migrant Worker Recruitment: A Rights-Based Framework for Countries of Origin." *Asian Journal of International Law* 7, no. 1 (2017): 152–84.

Farbenblum, Bassina, and Justine Nolan. "The Business of Migrant Worker Recruitment: Who Has the Responsibility and Leverage to Protect Rights?" *Texas International Law Journal* 52, no. 1 (2017): 18–26.

Farnsworth-Alvear, Ann. *Dulcinea in the Factory: Myths, Morals, Men, and Women in Colombia's Industrial Experiment, 1905–1960.* Durham, NC: Duke University Press, 2000.

Fernandez, Bina. "Cheap and Disposable? The Impact of the Global Economic Crisis on the Migration of Ethiopian Women Domestic Workers to the Gulf." *Gender and Development* 18, no. 2 (2010): 249–62.

Field, Michael. *The Merchants: The Big Business Families of Saudi Arabia and the Gulf States*. New York: Overlook Press, 1985.

"'File 3/21 Political Officer, Qatar and Political Affairs, Qatar' [13r] (25/94)." IOR/R/15/2/2000. British Library: India Office of Records and Private Papers, Qatar Digital Library. Accessed November 15, 2020. https://www.qdl.qa/en/archive/81055/vdc_100026682295.0x00001a.

"'File 10/3 III Qatar Oil Concession' [108r] (323/470)." IOR/R/15/2/412. British Library: India Office Records and Private Papers, Qatar Digital Library. Accessed November 14, 2020. http://www.qdl.qa/en/archive/81055/vdc_100023550520.0x000021.

"'File 10/3 III Qatar Oil Concession' [136r] (293/470)." IOR/R/15/2/412. British Library: India Office Records and Private Papers, Qatar Digital Library. Accessed November 14, 2020. http://www.qdl.qa/en/archive/81055/vdc_100023550520.0x00005e.

"'File 10/3 III Qatar Oil Concession' [179r] (382/470)." IOR/R/15/2/412. British Library: India Office Records and Private Papers, Qatar Digital Library. Accessed November 14, 2020. http://www.qdl.qa/en/archive/81055/vdc_100023550520.0x0000b7.

"'File 28/39 Roster of Petroleum Concessions Limited Employees' [43r] (85/180)." IOR/R/15/2/1736. British Library: India Office Records and Private Papers, Qatar Digital Library. Accessed November 15, 2020. http://www.qdl.qa/en/archive/81055/vdc_100023548254.0x000056.

"'File 82/27 VII F 91 Qatar Oil' [37r] (82/468)." IOR/R/15/1/633. British Library: India Office of Records and Private Papers, Qatar Digital Library. Accessed November 14, 2020. https://www.qdl.qa/en/archive/81055/vdc_100023800656.0x000054.

Fineman, Mark. "Lines in the Sand Drawing Gulf Nationals into Disputes; It's Not Just Iraq." *Los Angeles Times*, October 13, 1992.

Finn, Tom. "'Bachelor Ban' in Qatar Tests Relations with Migrant Workers." Reuters (Al Khor, Qatar), May 17, 2016, World News. Accessed November 19, 2020. https://www.reuters.com/article/us-qatar-labour-bachelors-idUSKCN0Y81H4.

Finnie, David. "Recruitment and Training of Labor: The Middle East Oil Industry." *Middle East Journal* (1958): 127–43.

Finnie, David H. *Desert Enterprise: The Middle East Oil Industry in Its Local Environment*. Vol. 1. Cambridge, MA: Harvard University Press, 1958.

Fitch Solutions. *Qatar Infrastructure Report Q1*. London: Fitch Solutions, 2019.

———. *Qatar Infrastructure Report Q4 2018*. London: Fitch Solutions, 2018.

Ford, Michele, Lenore Lyons, and Willem van Schendel. "Labour Migration and Human Trafficking: An Introduction." In *Labour Migration and Human Trafficking in Southeast Asia: Critical Perspectives*, edited by Michele Ford, Lenore Lyons, and Willem van Schendel, 1–22. London: Routledge, 2012.

Fox, Kit. "Problems Abundant at Qatar Mega Marathon." *Runner's World*, April 6, 2015. Accessed February 13, 2020. https://www.runnersworld.com/news/a20783965/problems-abundant-at-qatar-mega-marathon/.

Frader, Laura Levine. "From Muscles to Nerves: Gender, 'Race' and the Body at Work in France, 1919–1939." *International Review of Social History* 44, no. S7 (1999): 123–47.

Frantz, Elizabeth. "Jordan's Unfree Workforce: State-Sponsored Bonded Labour in the Arab Region." *Journal of Development Studies* 49, no. 8 (2013): 1072–87. Accessed December 2, 2020. https://doi.org/10.1080/00220388.2013.780042.

Freire, Paulo. *Pedagogy of the Oppressed*. New York: Bloomsbury Publishing USA, 2018.

Frings, Mary. "Financial Times Survey: Qatar—Economy—Heavy Reliance on State Spending." *Financial Times* (London), July 9, 1984.

Fuchs, Daniel, Patricia Fuk-Ying Tse, and Xiaojun Feng. "Labour Research under Coercive Authoritarianism: Comparative Reflections on Fieldwork Challenges in China." *Economic and Industrial Democracy* 40, no. 1 (2019): 132–55.

Fuchs, Thomas. *Ecology of the Brain: The Phenomenology and Biology of the Embodied Mind.* Oxford: Oxford University Press, 2017.

Gallagher, Shaun, and Robb Lindgren. "Enactive Metaphors: Learning through Full-Body Engagement." *Educational Psychology Review* 27, no. 3 (2015): 391–404.

Gamboa, Erasmo. *Mexican Labor and World War II: Braceros in the Pacific Northwest, 1942–1947.* Seattle: University of Washington Press, 2000.

Gammeltoft-Hansen, Thomas, and Ninna Nyberg Sorensen. *The Migration Industry and the Commercialization of International Migration.* Abingdon, UK: Routledge, 2013.

Gao, Chuansi, Kalev Kuklane, Per-Olof Östergren, and Tord Kjellstrom. "Occupational Heat Stress Assessment and Protective Strategies in the Context of Climate Change." *International Journal of Biometeorology* 62, no. 3 (2018): 359–71.

García-Trabanino, Ramón, Emmanuel Jarquín, Catharina Wesseling, Richard J. Johnson, Marvin González-Quiroz, Ilana Weiss, Jason Glaser, et al. "Heat Stress, Dehydration, and Kidney Function in Sugarcane Cutters in El Salvador—A Cross-Shift Study of Workers at Risk of Mesoamerican Nephropathy." *Environmental Research* 142 (2015): 746–55.

Gardner, Andrew, Silvia Pessoa, Abdoulaye Diop, Kaltham Al-Ghanim, Kien Le Trung, and Laura Harkness. "A Portrait of Low-Income Migrants in Contemporary Qatar." *Journal of Arabian Studies* 3, no. 1 (2013): 1–17. Accessed December 2, 2020. https://doi.org/10.1080/21534764.2013.806076.

Gardner, Andrew M., Silvia Pessoa, and Laura M. Harkness. *Labour Migrants and Access to Justice in Contemporary Qatar.* LSE Middle East Centre, November 2014.

General Secretariat for Development Planning. *Qatar National Vision 2030.* Doha: General Secretariat for Development Planning, July 2008. Accessed November 18, 2020. https://www.gco.gov.qa/wp-content/uploads/2016/09/GCO-QNV-English.pdf.

Gentile, Michael. "Meeting the 'Organs': The Tacit Dilemma of Field Research in Authoritarian States." *Area* 45, no. 4 (2013): 426–32.

Ghani, Faras. "Minimum Wage, No NOC: Qatar Announces Changes to Labour Law." Al Jazeera, August 30, 2020. Accessed December 27, 2020. https://www.aljazeera.com/economy/2020/8/30/minimum-wage-no-noc-qatar-announces-changes-to-labour-law.

Gillan, Kevin. "Social Movements, Protest, and Practices of Social Change." In *The Wiley Blackwell Companion to Sociology,* edited by George Ritzer and Wendy Wiedenhoft Murphy (Hoboken, NJ: John Wiley and Sons, 2019): 301–18.

Gillen, Marion, Davis Baltz, Margy Gassel, Luz Kirsch, and Diane Vaccaro. "Perceived Safety Climate, Job Demands, and Coworker Support among Union and Nonunion Injured Construction Workers." *Journal of Safety Research* 33, no. 1 (2002): 33–51.

Gilmore, Ruth Wilson. *Golden Gulag: Prisons, Surplus, Crisis, and Opposition in Globalizing California.* Berkeley: University of California Press, 2007.

Glasius, Marlies. "What Authoritarianism Is . . . and Is Not: A Practice Perspective." *International Affairs* 94, no. 3 (2018): 515–33.

Glasius, Marlies, Meta De Lange, Jos Bartman, Emanuela Dalmasso, Aofei Lv, Adele Del Sordi, Marcus Michaelsen, and Kris Ruijgrok. *Research, Ethics and Risk in the Authoritarian Field.* New York: Springer, 2017.

Glenberg, Arthur M. "Few Believe the World Is Flat: How Embodiment Is Changing the Scientific Understanding of Cognition." *Canadian Journal of Experimental Psychology / Revue canadienne de psychologie expérimentale* 69, no. 2 (2015): 165.

Glenberg, Arthur M., Jessica K. Witt, and Janet Metcalfe. "From the Revolution to Embodiment: 25 Years of Cognitive Psychology." *Perspectives on Psychological Science* 8, no. 5 (2013): 573–85.

Glenn, Evelyn Nakano. "From Servitude to Service Work: Historical Continuities in the Racial Division of Paid Reproductive Labor." *Signs: Journal of Women in Culture and Society* 18, no. 1 (1992): 1–43.

GlobalData Energy. "Qatar North Field Expansion to Increase LNG Export Capacity by 43%." August 7, 2019. Accessed January 19, 2020. https://www.offshore-technology.com/comment/qatar-north-field-expansion-to-increase-lng-export-capacity-by-43/.

Gold, Russell. "Power Play: In Qatar, Oil Firms Make Huge Bet on Alternative Fuel; Supporters Say New Diesel Is Cleaner, More Efficient; Untested on Large Scale; 'It Was Just Like Water.'" *Wall Street Journal*, February 15, 2005, A1.

Goldenhar, Linda M., Stacey Kohler Moran, and Michael Colligan. "Health and Safety Training in a Sample of Open-Shop Construction Companies." *Journal of Safety Research* 32, no. 2 (2001): 237–52.

Goode, J. Paul, and Ariel I. Ahram. "Special Issue Editors' Introduction: Observing Autocracies from the Ground Floor." *Social Science Quarterly* 97, no. 4 (2016): 823–33.

Goodman, Joshua, Michael Hurwitz, Jisung Park, and Jonathan Smith. "Heat and Learning." National Bureau of Economic Research Working Paper No. 24639, 2019. Accessed December 9, 2020. https://www.nber.org/papers/w24639.

Gordon, Jennifer. "Regulating the Human Supply Chain." *Iowa Law Review* 102 (2016): 450.

Government of Nepal, Ministry of Labour and Employment. *Labour Migration for Employment: A Status Report for Nepal: 2015/2016–2016/2017.* Kathmandu: Government of Nepal, Ministry of Labour and Employment, 2017. Accessed December 3, 2020. https://asiafoundation.org/wp-content/uploads/2018/05/Nepal-Labor-Migration-status-report-2015-16-to-2016-17.pdf.

Gray, Clark L., and Valerie Mueller. "Natural Disasters and Population Mobility in Bangladesh." *Proceedings of the National Academy of Sciences* 109, no. 16 (2012): 6000–6005.

Gray, Garry C. "The Responsibilization Strategy of Health and Safety: Neo-Liberalism and the Reconfiguration of Individual Responsibility for Risk." *British Journal of Criminology* 49, no. 3 (2009): 326–42.

Gregory, Sean. "Major FIFA Sponsors Don't Want to Talk about Qatar, Either." *Time*, May 29, 2015. Accessed November 29, 2020. https://time.com/3900357/fifa-sponsors-coke-visa-adidas/.

Grose, Michael, and Ramiz Shlah. "Construction Law in Qatar and the United Arab Emirates: Key Differences." *Turkish Commercial Law Review* 1 (2015): 189.

Guillén, Mauro F. *The Taylorized Beauty of the Mechanical: Scientific Management and the Rise of Modernist Architecture.* Princeton, NJ: Princeton University Press, 2006.

"Gulf States: Qatar." OxResearch Daily Brief Service. Oxford, 1989.

Hamzeh, A Nizar. "Qatar: The Duality of the Legal System." *Middle Eastern Studies* 30, no. 1 (1994): 79–90.

Han, Kon-ju. "Arab Nations Interested in Learning Technology." *Korea Times*, February 11, 1982.

Hancock, Peter A., and Ioannis Vasmatzidis. "Effects of Heat Stress on Cognitive Performance: The Current State of Knowledge." *International Journal of Hyperthermia* 19, no. 3 (2003): 355–72.

Hanieh, Adam. *Money, Markets, and Monarchies: The Gulf Cooperation Council and the Political Economy of the Contemporary Middle East.* Cambridge: Cambridge University Press, 2018.

Hanna, Elizabeth G., Tord Kjellstrom, Charmian Bennett, and Keith Dear. "Climate Change and Rising Heat: Population Health Implications for Working People in Australia." *Asia Pacific Journal of Public Health* 23, no. 2 (2011): 14S–26S.

Hartmann, Betsy. "Rethinking Climate Refugees and Climate Conflict: Rhetoric, Reality and the Politics of Policy Discourse." *Journal of International Development: The Journal of the Development Studies Association* 22, no. 2 (2010): 233–46.

Harwood, Anthony. "Migrant Stadium Workers to Be Refunded Recruitment Fees by Qatar." *New Vision* (UK), March 16, 2018. Accessed December 2, 2020. https://www.newvision .co.ug/new_vision/news/1473429/migrant-stadium-workers-refunded-recruitment -fees-qatar.

Hashem, Nadeem, and Perumal Balakrishnan. "Change Analysis of Land Use / Land Cover and Modelling Urban Growth in Greater Doha, Qatar." *Annals of GIS* 21, no. 3 (2015): 233–47. Accessed November 19, 2020. https://doi.org/10.1080/19475683.2014.992369.

Hassabou, Abdelhakim Mohamed, and Moazzam Ali Khan. "Energy Efficient and Sustainable Buildings: Integration with Solar Air-conditioning Technology in Qatar—A Step towards Grid Free Zero Carbon Living." *International Solar Energy Society* (2018). Accessed November 11, 2020. http://proceedings.ises.org/paper/eurosun2018 /eurosun2018-0090-Khan.pdf.

Hay, Rupert. "The Impact of the Oil Industry on the Persian Gulf Shaykhdoms." *Middle East Journal* 9, no. 4 (1955): 361–72.

———. *The Persian Gulf States.* London: Middle East Institute, 1959.

Hayman, Mark. "Inducement and Coercion on the Trucial Coast: The First Oil Agreements." *Journal of Imperial and Commonwealth History* 38, no. 2 (2010): 261–78.

Health and Safety Executive. *Construction Statistics in Great Britain, 2019.* 2019. Accessed November 29, 2020. https://www.hse.gov.uk/statistics/industry/construction.pdf.

Hermans-Neumann, Kathleen, Joerg Priess, and Martin Herold. "Human Migration, Climate Variability, and Land Degradation: Hotspots of Socio-Ecological Pressure in Ethiopia." *Regional Environmental Change* 17, no. 5 (2017): 1479–92.

Hernández-León, Rubén. *Metropolitan Migrants: The Migration of Urban Mexicans to the United States.* Berkeley: University of California Press, 2008.

Hernberg, Sven. "Lead Poisoning in a Historical Perspective." *American Journal of Industrial Medicine* 38, no. 3 (2000): 244–54.

Heyojoo, Binod P., Nabin k. Yadav, and Rajan Subedi. "Assessments of Climate Change Indicators, Climate-Induced Disasters, and Community Adaptation Strategies: A Case from High Mountain of Nepal." In *Land Cover Change and Its Eco-Environmental Responses in Nepal,* edited by Ainong Li, Wei Deng, and Wei Zhao, 203–22. New York: Springer, 2017.

Himalayan News Service. "Qatar World Cup Workers Unpaid for Months: AI." *Himalayan Times,* September 27, 2018. Accessed February 13, 2020. https://thehimalayantimes.com /kathmandu/qatar-world-cup-workers-unpaid-for-months-amnesty-international/.

Hnizdo, Eva, and Val Vallyathan. "Chronic Obstructive Pulmonary Disease Due to Occupational Exposure to Silica Dust: A Review of Epidemiological and Pathological Evidence." *Occupational and Environmental Medicine* 60, no. 4 (2003): 237–43.

Holston, James. *The Modernist City: An Anthropological Critique of Brasília.* Chicago: University of Chicago Press, 1989.

Homewood, Brian. "Blatter Calls Qatar Labor Situation 'Unacceptable.'" Reuters, November 20, 2013, Sports News. Accessed November 18, 2020. https://www.reuters.com /article/us-soccer-qatar-labour/blatter-calls-qatar-labor-situation-unacceptable -idUSBRE9AJ0V620131120.

———. "Soccer-FIFA Warned to Make Sure Qatar Respects Workers Rights." *Reuters,* November 16, 2011. Accessed February 19, 2020. https://uk.reuters.com/article /soccer-fifa-workers/soccer-fifa-warned-to-make-sure-qatar-respects-workers-rights -idUKB18866220111116.

Hopper, Matthew S. "East Africa and the End of the Indian Ocean Slave Trade." *Journal of African Development* 13, no. 1 (2011): 39–65.

———. *Slaves of One Master: Globalization and Slavery in Arabia in the Age of Empire*. New Haven, CT: Yale University Press, 2015.

Horton, Sarah Bronwen. *They Leave Their Kidneys in the Fields: Illness, Injury, and Illegality among US Farmworkers*. Berkeley: University of California Press, 2016.

Hosea, Leana. "Inside Qatar's Squalid Labour Camps." *BBC World News*, 2014. Accessed November 12, 2020. https://www.bbc.com/news/world-middle-east-26482775.

Hostetter, Autumn B., and Martha W. Alibali. "Visible Embodiment: Gestures as Simulated Action." *Psychonomic Bulletin and Review* 15, no. 3 (2008): 495–514.

Howard, Arthur. "Selling Jewels to Multimillionaires: The Duchess of Montrose's Necklace." *McClure's Magazine*, July 1913, 56–65.

Human Rights Watch. "COVID-19: Unblock Voice Over IP Platforms in Gulf." April 7, 2020. Accessed April 20, 2020. https://www.hrw.org/news/2020/04/07/covid-19-unblock-voice-over-ip-platforms-gulf#.

———. "Qatar: Take Urgent Action to Protect Construction Workers." September 27, 2017. Accessed November 10, 2020. https://www.hrw.org/news/2017/09/27/qatar-take-urgent-action-protect-construction-workers#.

Humphrey, Steven. *Qatar Construction Market Outlook 2017–2030*. Crossville, TN: Plateau Group, June 2017.

Hutto, Daniel D., and Erik Myin. *Radicalizing Enactivism: Basic Minds without Content*. Cambridge, MA: MIT Press, 2012.

Hutzell, Kelly, Rami el Samahy, and Adam Himes. "Inexhaustible Ambition: Two Eras of Planning in Doha, Qatar." *Architectural Design* 85, no. 1 (2015): 80–91.

Ibrahim, Ibrahim, and Frank Harrigan. "Qatar's Economy: Past, Present and Future." *QScience Connect*, no. 1 (2012): 9.

Impactt Limited. *Annual External Compliance Report of the Supreme Committee for Delivery and Legacy's Workers' Welfare Standards*. London: Impactt Limited, 2017. Accessed December 2, 2020. https://impacttlimited.com/wp-content/uploads/2017/01/SC-Annual-Report-Issue-3.2.pdf.

Ingold, Tim. "Five Questions of Skill." *Cultural Geographies* 25, no. 1 (2018): 159–63.

International Labor Organization. *Complaint concerning Non-Observance by Qatar of the Forced Labour Convention, 1930 (No. 29), and the Labour Inspection Convention, 1947 (No. 81), Made by Delegates to the 103rd Session (2014) of the International Labour Conference under Article 26 of the ILO Constitution* (Geneva: International Labor Organization, March 17, 2016). Accessed November 18, 2020. https://www.ilo.org/wcmsp5/groups/public/---ed_norm/---relconf/documents/meetingdocument/wcms_459148.pdf.

———. *Promoting Informed Policy Dialogue on Migration, Remittance, and Development in Nepal*. Kathmandu: International Labor Organization, 2016.

International Monetary Fund. *IMF Country Report No 19/146*. Washington, DC: International Monetary Fund, June 2019. Accessed November 20, 2020. www.imf.org.

International Trade Union Confederation. *Hidden Faces of the Gulf Miracle*. May 5, 2011. Accessed November 12, 2020. https://www.ituc-csi.org/hidden-faces-of-the-gulf-miracle-9144.

"In the Crosshairs: Could the Construction Sector Be Facing a Slowdown, Lead by Sharq Crossing's Shelving?" *Construction Week*, March 3, 2015. Accessed November 19, 2020. https://www.constructionweekonline.com/article-32744-in-the-crosshairs.

Iskander, Natasha. "On Detention and Skill: Reflections on Immigrant Incarceration, Bodying Practices, and the Definition of Skill." *American Behavioral Scientist*, 63, no. 9 (2019): 1370–88.

Iskander, Natasha. "Qatar, the Coronavirus, and Cordons Sanitaires: Migrant Workers and the Use of Public Health Measures to Define the Nation." *Medical Anthropology Quarterly*, December 4, 2020. Accessed December 8, 2020. https://pubmed.ncbi.nlm.nih.gov /33274452/.

Iskander, Natasha, and Nichola Lowe. "Hidden Talent: Tacit Skill Formation and Labor Market Incorporation of Latino Immigrants in the United States." *Journal of Planning Education and Research* 30, no. 2 (2010): 132–46.

Islam, Md. Monirul, Arifa Jannat, Aurup Ratan Dhar, and Tofael Ahamed. "Factors Determining Conversion of Agricultural Land Use in Bangladesh: Farmers' Perceptions and Perspectives of Climate Change." *GeoJournal* (2019): 1–20.

ISO 7243: 1989. Hot Environments—Estimation of the Heat Stress on Working Man, Based on the WBGT-Index (Wet Bulb Globe Temperature). Geneva: International Organization for Standardization, 1989.

ISO 7243: 2017. Erganomics of the Thermal Environment—Assessment of Heat Stress Using the WBGT (Wet Bulb Globle Temperature) Index. Geneva: International Standards Organization, 2017.

Jacklitsch, Brenda, W. John Williams, Kristin Musolin, Aitor Coca, Jung-Hyun Kim, and Nina Turner. *Occupational Exposure to Heat and Hot Environments, Revised Criteria 2016.* Department of Health and Human Services, Centers for Disease Control and Prevention, National Institute for Occupational Safety and Health, February 2016. Accessed November 30, 2020. https://www.cdc.gov/niosh/docs/2016-106/pdfs/2016-106.pdf.

Jackson, Larry L., and Howard R. Rosenberg. "Preventing Heat-Related Illness among Agricultural Workers." *Journal of Agromedicine* 15, no. 3 (2010): 200–215.

Jain, Sarah S. Lochlann. *Injury: The Politics of Product Design and Safety Law in the United States.* Princeton, NJ: Princeton University Press, 2006.

Jansen, Robert S. *Revolutionizing Repertoires: The Rise of Populist Mobilization in Peru.* Chicago: University of Chicago Press, 2017.

Jarkas, Abdulaziz M., and Theodore C. Haupt. "Major Construction Risk Factors Considered by General Contractors in Qatar." *Journal of Engineering, Design and Technology* 13, no. 1 (2015): 165–94.

Jarkas, Abdulaziz M., and Jamal H. Younes. "Principle Factors Contributing to Construction Delays in the State of Qatar." *International Journal of Construction Project Management* 6, no. 1 (2014): 39.

Johnson, Richard J., Laura Gabriela Sánchez-Lozada, Lee Scott Newman, Miguel A. Lanaspa, Henry F. Diaz, Jay Lemery, Bernardo Rodriguez-Iturbe, et al. "Climate Change and the Kidney." *Annals of Nutrition and Metabolism* 74 (Suppl. 3), no. 3 (2019): 38–44. Accessed November 29, 2020. https://doi.org/10.1159/000500344.

Johnston, Ronald, and Arthur J. McIvor. *Lethal Work: A History of the Asbestos Tragedy in Scotland.* Edinburgh: John Donald, 2000.

Joyce, Miriam. *Ruling Shaikhs and Her Majesty's Government, 1960–1969.* London: Psychology Press, 2003.

"J.P. Morgan Gives Pearls to Bride." *New York Times*, January 3, 1909.

Juarrero, Alicia. "Dynamics in Action: Intentional Behavior as a Complex System." *Emergence* 2, no. 2 (2000): 24–57.

"Jung Woo Boasts Hi-Fi Skills." *Korea Times*, June 23, 1981.

Jureidini, Ray. *Migrant Labour Recruitment to Qatar.* Doha: Bloomsbury Qatar Foundation Journals, 2014.

———. "Wage Protection Systems and Programmes in the GCC." In *Migration to the Gulf: Policies in Sending and Receiving Countries*, edited by Philippe Fargues and Nasra M. Shah, 9–33. Cambridge, UK: Gulf Research Centre, 2017.

———. *Ways Forward in Recruitment of Low-Skilled Migrant Workers in the Asia-Arab States Corridor*. Geneva: International Labour Organization, 2016.

Kale, Madhavi. *Fragments of Empire: Capital, Slavery, and Indian Indentured Labor in the British Caribbean*. Philadelphia: University of Pennsylvania Press, 2010.

Kalleberg, Arne L. *Good Jobs, Bad Jobs: The Rise of Polarized and Precarious Employment Systems in the United States, 1970s–2000s*. New York: Russell Sage Foundation, 2011.

Kanchana, Radhika. "Is the Kafala Tradition to Blame for the Exploitative Work Conditions in the Arab-Gulf Countries?" In *South Asian Migration in the Gulf: Causes and Consequences*, edited by Mehdi Chowdhury and S. Irudaya Rajan, 61–79. New York: Springer, 2018.

Karki, Rahul, and Anup Gurung. "An Overview of Climate Change and Its Impact on Agriculture: A Review from Least Developing Country, Nepal." *International Journal of Ecosystem* 2, no. 2 (2012): 19–24.

Katodrytis, George, and Kevin Mitchell. *UAE and the Gulf: Architecture and Urbanism Now*. London: John Wiley and Sons, 2015.

Kemp, Adriana, and Rebeca Raijman. "Bringing in State Regulations, Private Brokers, and Local Employers: A Meso-Level Analysis of Labor Trafficking in Israel." *International Migration Review* 48, no. 3 (2018). Accessed December 2, 2020. https://doi.org/10.1111/imre.12109.

Kern, Alice, and Ulrike Müller-Böker. "The Middle Space of Migration: A Case Study on Brokerage and Recruitment Agencies in Nepal." *Geoforum* 65 (2015): 158–69. Accessed December 4, 2020. https://doi.org/10.1016/j.geoforum.2015.07.024.

Kerr, Simeon. "Qatar's Slowing Economy Puts World Cup Spending in Spotlight." *Financial Times* (London), March 1, 2017. Accessed November 20, 2020. https://www.ft.com/content/048e5762-f9a4-11e6-bd4e-68d53499ed71.

Khan, Azfar, and Hélène Harroff-Tavel. "Reforming the Kafala: Challenges and Opportunities in Moving Forward." *Asian and Pacific Migration Journal* 20, no. 3–4 (2011): 293–313.

Khanal, Uttam, Clevo Wilson, Viet-Ngu Hoang, and Boon Lee. "Farmers' Adaptation to Climate Change, Its Determinants and Impacts on Rice Yield in Nepal." *Ecological Economics* 144 (2018): 139–47.

Kim, Sooyong. "Labor Migration from Korea to the Middle East: Its Trend and Impact on the Korean Economy." In *Asian Labor Migration*, edited by Fred Arnold and Nasra M. Shah, 163–75. Boulder, CO: Westview Press, 1986.

Kiparoidze, Mariam. "Foreign Workers in the Gulf Still Can't Call Home." *Coda*, July 21, 2020. Accessed July 26, 2020. https://www.codastory.com/authoritarian-tech/gulf-foreign-workers/.

Kjellstrom, Tord. "Impact of Climate Conditions on Occupational Health and Related Economic Losses: A New Feature of Global and Urban Health in the Context of Climate Change." *Asia Pacific Journal of Public Health* 28, no. 2 (2016): 28S–37S. Accessed November 29, 2020. https://doi.org/10.1177/1010539514568711.

Kjellstrom, Tord, David Briggs, Chris Freyberg, Bruno Lemke, Matthias Otto, and Olivia Hyatt. "Heat, Human Performance, and Occupational Health: A Key Issue for the Assessment of Global Climate Change Impacts." *Annual Review of Public Health* 37, no. 1 (2016): 97–112. Accessed November 29, 2020. https://doi.org/10.1146/annurev-publhealth-032315-021740.Kovessy, Peter. "Qatar Answers Call for Better Housing with New 'Labor City.'" *Doha News*, November 5, 2015.

Krane, Jim. "Gas Bubble Creates Economic Boom." Associated Press, April 25, 2005.

Krishnamurthy, P. Krishna, C. Hobbs, A. Matthiasen, S. R. Hollema, R. J. Choularton, K. Pahari, and M. Kawabata. "Climate Risk and Food Security in Nepal—Analysis of Climate Impacts on Food Security and Livelihoods." CCAFS Working Paper No. 48, 2013.

Kunz, George Frederick, and Charles Hugh Stevenson. *The Book of the Pearl: The History, Art, Science and Industry of the Queen of Gems* (1908; repr., Mineola, NY: Dover Publications, 1993).

"The Labour Law No. 3 of 1962." Al Meezan: Qatar Legal Portal, 1962. Accessed November 17, 2020. http://almeezan.qa/LawView.aspx?opt&LawID=2599&language=en.

LaFayette, Bill, Wayne Curtis, Denise Bedford, and Seema Iyer. "Learning and the Knowledge Capacity of Organizations." *Knowledge Economies and Knowledge Work (Working Methods for Knowledge Management)* (2019): 171–209.

Lambert, G. Patrick. "Intestinal Barrier Dysfunction, Endotoxemia, and Gastrointestinal Symptoms: The 'Canary in the Coal Mine' during Exercise–Heat Stress?" In *Thermoregulation and Human Performance: Physiological and Biological Aspects*, edited by F. E. Marino, 61–73. Basel: Karger Publishers, 2008.

LaPorte, Robert. "The Ability of South and East Asia to Meet the Labor Demands of the Middle East and North Africa." *Middle East Journal* 38, no. 4 (1984): 699–711. Accessed November 17, 2020. http://ezproxy.library.nyu.edu:2105/stable/4326924.

"Late Payments Challenge Qatar Construction Sector." *Construction Week*, March 3, 2016. Accessed November 20, 2020. https://www.constructionweekonline.com/article-37759-late-payments-challenge-qatar-construction-sector.

Latzka, William A., Michael N. Sawka, Scott J. Montain, Gary S. Skrinar, Roger A. Fielding, Ralph P. Matott, and Kent B. Pandolf. "Hyperhydration: Tolerance and Cardiovascular Effects during Uncompensable Exercise-Heat Stress." *Journal of Applied Physiology* 84, no. 6 (1998): 1858–64.

Laukkanen, Tuula. "Construction Work and Education: Occupational Health and Safety Reviewed." *Construction Management and Economics* 17, no. 1 (1999): 53–62.

Lave, Jean. *Apprenticeship in Critical Ethnographic Practice.* Chicago: University of Chicago Press, 2011.

———. "The Culture of Acquisition and the Practice of Understanding." *Situated Cognition: Social, Semiotic, and Psychological Perspectives* (1997): 63–82.

———. "Situating Learning in Communities of Practice." *Perspectives on Socially Shared Cognition* 2 (1991): 63–82.

Lave, Jean, and Etienne Wenger. *Situated Learning: Legitimate Peripheral Participation.* Cambridge: Cambridge University Press, 1991.

"Law No. 14 on the Promulgation of Labour Law." Al Meezan: Qatar Legal Portal, July 7, 2004. Accessed November 17, 2020. http://www.almeezan.qa/LawView.aspx?opt&LawID=3961&language=en.

"Law No. 15 of 2010 Prohibition of Workers Camps within Family Residential Areas." In *15*. Al Meezan: Qatar Legal Portal, August 19, 2010. Accessed November 19, 2020. http://www.almeezan.qa/LawView.aspx?opt&LawID=2510&language=en.

"Law No. 21 of 2015 Regulating the Entry and Exit of Expatriates and Their Residence." Official Gazette, October 27, 2015. Accessed November 18, 2020. https://www.ilo.org/dyn/natlex/natlex4.detail?p_lang=en&p_isn=102231.

LeBaron, Genevieve. "Reconceptualizing Debt Bondage: Debt as a Class-Based Form of Labor Discipline." *Critical Sociology* 40, no. 5 (2014): 763–80. Accessed December 2, 2020. https://doi.org/10.1177/0896920513512695.

LeBaron, Genevieve, and Nicola Phillips. "States and the Political Economy of Unfree Labour." *New Political Economy* 24, no. 1 (2018): 1–21. Accessed December 2, 2020. https://doi.org/10.1080/13563467.2017.1420642.

Le Deist, Françoise Delamare, and Jonathan Winterton. "What Is Competence?" *Human Resource Development International* 8, no. 1 (2005): 27–46.

Leitan, Nuwan D., and Lucian Chaffey. "Embodied Cognition and Its Applications: A Brief Review." *Sensoria: A Journal of Mind, Brain and Culture* 10, no. 1 (2014): 3–10.

Leon, Lisa R. "Heat Stroke and Cytokines." *Progress in Brain Research* 162 (2007): 481–524.

Leon, Lisa R., and Abderrezak Bouchama. "Heat Stroke." *Comprehensive Physiology* 5, no. 2 (2011): 611–47.

Lewis, Ben. "Digitally Designed—Qatar Faculty of Islamic Studies." *Structural Engineer: Journal of the Institution of Structural Engineer* 94, no. 3 (2016): 69–76.

Lindquist, Johan, Biao Xiang, and Brenda S. A. Yeoh. "Opening the Black Box of Migration: Brokers, the Organization of Transnational Mobility and the Changing Political Economy in Asia." *Pacific Affairs* 85, no. 1 (2012): 7–19. Accessed December 2, 2020. https://doi.org/10.5509/20128517.

Lobel, Mark. "Arrested for Reporting on Qatar's World Cup Labourers." BBC News, May 18, 2015. Accessed December 8, 2020. https://www.bbc.com/news/world-middle-east -32775563.

Locke, Richard M. *The Promise and Limits of Private Power: Promoting Labor Standards in a Global Economy.* New York: Cambridge University Press, 2013.

Lohani, Shiva, Ram Balak Singh, and Jeevan Lohani. "Universal Primary Education in Nepal: Fulfilling the Right to Education." *PROSPECTS* 40, no. 3 (2010): 355–74. Accessed December 7, 2020. https://doi.org/10.1007/s11125-010-9162-6.

Longhurst, Henry. *Adventure in Oil: The Story of British Petroleum.* London: Sidgwick and Jackson, 1959.

Longva, Anh Nga. *Walls Built on Sand: Migration, Exclusion, and Society in Kuwait.* Boulder, CO: Westview Press, 1999.

López-Sánchez, José Ignacio, and PA Hancock. "Thermal Effects on Cognition: A New Quantitative Synthesis." *International Journal of Hyperthermia* 34, no. 4 (2018): 423–31.

Lorimer, John Gordon. *Gazetteer of the Persian Gulf, Oman, and Central Arabia.* Calcutta: Superintendent Government Printing, 1915. Accessed November 13, 2020. http://catalog .hathitrust.org/Record/011590480.

Lugo-Amador, Nannette M. Todd Rothenhaus, and Peter Moyer. "Heat-Related Illness." *Emergency Medicine Clinics of North America* 22, no. 2 (2004): viii, 315–27.

Lundgren, Karin, Kalev Kuklane, Chuansi Gao, and Ingvar Holmer. "Effects of Heat Stress on Working Populations When Facing Climate Change." *Industrial Health* 51, no. 1 (2013): 3–15.

Lusail City. "The Vision Is Taking Shape." Accessed January 17, 2020. http://www.lusail.com /who-we-are/the-vision-is-taking-shape/.

Mabag, Arturo. "Qatar Mega Marathon 2015." YouTube, March 28, 2015. Accessed February 13, 2020. https://www.youtube.com/watch?v=Arlrl Ha30ME&t=116s.

Mac, Valerie Vi Thien, and Linda A. McCauley. "Farmworker Vulnerability to Heat Hazards: A Conceptual Framework." *Journal of Nursing Scholarship* 49, no. 6 (2017): 617–24. Accessed December 1, 2020. https://doi.org/10.1111/jnu.12327.

Macrotrends. "Qatar GDP 1970–2020." Macrotrends. 2010–20. Accessed November 17, 2020. https://www.macrotrends.net/countries/QAT/qatar/gdp-gross-domestic-product.

MacShane, Denis. "Gulf Slaves." *New Statesman and Society*, 1991, 15–16.

Maharjan, Keshav Lall, and Niraj Prakash Joshi. "Effect of Climate Variables on Yield of Major Food-Crops in Nepal: A Time-Series Analysis." In *Climate Change, Agriculture and Rural Livelihoods in Developing Countries.* New York: Springer, 2013.

Malhotra, Yogesh. "Why Knowledge Management Systems Fail: Enablers and Constraints of Knowledge Management in Human Enterprises." In *Handbook on Knowledge Management 1*, edited by Clyde Holsapple, 577–99. New York: Springer, 2004.

Malit, Froilan T., Jr., and George Naufal. "Asymmetric Information under the Kafala Sponsorship System: Impacts on Foreign Domestic Workers' Income and Employment Status in the GCC Countries." *International Migration* 54, no. 5 (2016): 76–90.

Malla, G. "Climate Change and Its Impact on Nepalese Agriculture." *Journal of Agriculture and Environment* 9 (2008): 62–71.

Mandal, Chandan Kumar. "Nepalis in Qatar Live in Overcrowded and Squalid Conditions Even during Pandemic." *Kathmandu Post*. March 26, 2020. Accessed April 5, 2020. https://kathmandupost.com/2/2020/03/26/nepalis-in-qatar-live-in-overcrowded-and -squalid-conditions-even-during-pandemic.

Mangera Yvars Architects. "Qatar Faculty of Islamic Studies." Architonic, 2015. Accessed January 18, 2020. https://www.architonic.com/en/project/mangera-yvars-architects -qatar-faculty-of-islamic-studies/5105543.

Manning, Patrick. *Slavery and African Life: Occidental, Oriental, and African Slave Trades.* Vol. 67. Cambridge: Cambridge University Press, 1990.

Marchand, Trevor H. J. "Making Knowledge: Explorations of the Indissoluble Relation between Minds, Bodies, and Environment." *Journal of the Royal Anthropological Institute* 16 (2010): S1–S21.

———. *Making Knowledge: Explorations of the Indissoluble Relation between Mind, Body and Environment.* London: John Wiley and Sons, 2011.

Marhaba Qatar Destination Guide. "QFIS Building Wins Award at World Architecture Festival." Marhaba: Qatar's Premier Information Guide, November 10, 2015. Accessed January 18, 2020. https://www.marhaba.qa/qfis-building-wins-award-at-world-architecture -festival/.

MarketWatch. "Sysorex Announces $2.5 Milliion AirPatrol Contract." July 1, 2015. Accessed November 21, 2020. https://www.marketwatch.com/press-release/sysorex-announces -25-million-airpatrol-contract-2015-07-01.

Marx, Karl. *Economic and Philosophic Manuscripts of 1844.* Mineola, NY: Dover Publications, Inc., 2007.

Mauritius. *Labor Laws of Mauritius or a Collection of the Laws Specially Relating to Masters and Servants at Mauritius Including the Acts of the Government of India on Emigration to That Colony.* Oxford: L. Channell's Steam Printing Establishment, 1869.

McAdam, Doug, Sidney Tarrow, and Charles Tilly. "Comparative Perspectives on Contentious Politics." In *Comparative Politics: Rationality, Culture, and Structure*, edited by Mark Irving Lichbach and Alan S. Zuckerman, 260–90. Cambridge: Cambridge University Press, 2009.

McCollum, David, and Allan Findlay. "Oiling the Wheels? Flexible Labour Markets and the Migration Industry." *Journal of Ethnic and Migration Studies* 44, no. 4 (2018): 558–74. Accessed December 2, 2020. https://doi.org/10.1080/1369183x.2017.1315505.

McGrath, Siobhán. "Fuelling Global Production Networks with Slave Labour?: Migrant Sugar Cane Workers in the Brazilian Ethanol GPN." *Geoforum* 44 (2013): 32–43. Accessed December 2, 2020. https://doi.org/10.1016/j.geoforum.2012.06.011.

McKeown, Adam M. *Melancholy Order: Asian Migration and the Globalization of Borders.* New York: Columbia University Press, 2013.

McMurray, David. "Recent Trends in Middle Eastern Migration." *Middle East Report*, no. 211 (1999): 16–19. Accessed November 17, 2020. https://doi.org/10.2307/3013329.

Melamed, Jodi. "Racial Capitalism." *Critical Ethnic Studies* 1, no. 1 (2015): 76–85.

Miers, Suzanne. "Slavery and the Slave Trade as International Issues, 1890–1939." *Slavery and Abolition* 19, no. 2 (1998): 16–37.

———. *Slavery in the Twentieth Century: The Evolution of a Global Problem.* Walnut Creek, CA: Rowman and Littlefield, 2003.

Migiakis, Constantine Emmanouil. "The Qatar Faculty of Islamic Studies." July 11, 2015. Accessed November 22, 2020. http://eeme.ntua.gr/proceedings/7th/003.pdf.

Milmo, Cahal. "British Human Rights Investigator Detained by Qatari Authorities for Two Weeks Speaks Out." *Independent*, September 22, 2014. Accessed December 8, 2020. https://www.independent.co.uk/news/world/middle-east/british-human-rights -investigator-detained-by-qatari-authorities-for-two-weeks-speaks-out-9749426.html.

"Ministry of Civil Service Affairs and Housing Decree No. 17 of 2005 on Workers' Living Quarters." Qatar, December 29, 2005. Accessed November 19, 2020. https://gulfmigration.org/ministry-of-civil-service-affairs-and-housing-decree-no-17-of-2005-on-workers-living-quarters/.

Ministry of Development Planning and Statistics. *First Section: Population and Social Statistics, Chapter 1: Population.* 2016. Accessed November 19, 2020. https://www.psa.gov.qa/en/statistics/Statistical%20Releases/Population/Population/2016/Population_social_1_2016_AE.pdf.

———. *First Section: Population and Social Statistics, Chapter II: Labour Force.* 2015. Accessed November 11, 2020. https://www.psa.gov.qa/en/statistics/Statistical%20Releases/Social/LaborForce/2015/Labour_force_2_2015_AE.pdf.

Ministry of Municipal Affairs and Civil Planning. "Qatar: Ministry of Municipal Affairs and Civil Planning Decree No. 83 regarding Family Residential Areas." Al Meezan: Qatar Legal Portal, August 25, 2011.

Ministry of Municipality and Environment. "Doha Mun Family Zone." 2019. Accessed February 18, 2020. http://www.mme.gov.qa/cui/view.dox?id=1182&contentID=1425&siteID=2.

Mirchandani, Kiran. "Challenging Racial Silences in Studies of Emotion Work: Contributions from Anti-Racist Feminist Theory." *Organization Studies* 24, no. 5 (2003): 721–42.

Mirincheva, Velina. "The Qatar Faculty of Islamic Studies by Mangera Yvars Is a Process of Continuous Learning and Enlightenment." *Architectural Review*, March 7, 2017. Accessed November 22, 2020. https://www.architectural-review.com/buildings/the-qatar-faculty-of-islamic-studies-by-mangera-yvars-is-a-process-of-continuous-learning-and-enlightenment/10017755.article.

Mishra, D., and P. Koirala. "Status of Chronic Kidney Disease Patients Registered in National Kidney Center, Banasthali, Kathmandu." *Journal of Manmohan Memorial Institute of Health Sciences* 1, no. 4 (2015): 19–23.

Molland, Sverre. "Safe Migration, Dilettante Brokers and the Appropriation of Legality: Lao-Thai 'Trafficking' in the Context of Regulating Labour Migration." *Pacific Affairs* 85, no. 1 (2012): 117–36. Accessed December 2, 2020. https://doi.org/10.5509/2012851117.

Molotch, Harvey, and Davide Ponzini. *The New Arab Urban: Gulf Cities of Wealth, Ambition, and Distress.* New York: NYU Press, 2019.

Mongia, Radhika. *Indian Migration and Empire: A Colonial Genealogy of the Modern State.* Durham, NC: Duke University Press, 2018.

Moniruzzaman, Mohammad, and Margaret Walton-Roberts. "Migration, Debt and Resource Backwash: How Sustainable Is Bangladesh-Gulf Circular Migration?" *Migration and Development* 7, no. 1 (2017): 85–103. Accessed December 2, 2020. https://doi.org/10.1080/21632324.2017.1358799.

Morris, Aldon D. "Birmingham Confrontation Reconsidered: An Analysis of the Dynamics and Tactics of Mobilization." *American Sociological Review* (1993): 621–36.

Moss, Phillip, and Chris Tilly. *Stories Employers Tell: Race, Skill, and Hiring in America.* New York: Russell Sage Foundation, 2001.

Motaparthy, Priyanka. *Building a Better World Cup: Protecting Migrant Workers in Qatar Ahead of FIFA 2022.* New York: Human Rights Watch, 2012. Accessed November 12, 2020. https://www.hrw.org/sites/default/files/reports/qatar0612webwcover_0.pdf.

Moubaydeen, Safwan, Julian Pope, Julie Tuck, Matthew Walker, and Natalie Mackay. "Construction and Projects in Qatar: Overview." In *Construction and Projects Multi-Jurisdictional Guide (2013/2014), Qatar: Dentons and Co.* 2013.

Mufson, Steven. "Facing Unbearable Heat, Qatar Has Begun to Air-condition the Outdoors." *Washington Post* (Doha), October 16, 2019. Accessed November 11, 2020. https://www.washingtonpost.com/graphics/2019/world/climate-environment/climate-change-qatar-air-conditioning-outdoors/.

Municipality Designates Areas for Bachelor Living (Alraya, Doha, October 3, 2011).

Nafi, Zuhair Ahmed. *Economic and Social Development in Qatar*. London: Bloomsbury Academic, 1983.

Nafukho, Fredrick Muyia, Nancy Hairston, and Kit Brooks. "Human Capital Theory: Implications for Human Resource Development." *Human Resource Development International* 7, no. 4 (2004): 545–51.

Nagi, Mostafa H. "Migration of Asian Workers to the Arab Gulf: Policy Determinants and Consequences." *Journal of South Asian and Middle Eastern Studies* 9, no. 3 (1986): 19.

Nagy, Sharon. "Dressing up Downtown: Urban Development and Government Public Image in Qatar." *City and Society* 12, no. 1 (2000): 125–47.

Nash, Linda. *Inescapable Ecologies: A History of Environment, Disease, and Knowledge*. Berkeley: University of California Press, 2006.

Needham, Steve. "End of Exit Permits for Most Migrant Workers in Qatar Welcomed." International Labor Organization, September 4, 2018. Accessed November 18, 2020. https://www.ilo.org/global/about-the-ilo/newsroom/news/WCMS_638754/lang--en/index.htm.

Nelson, Andrew. *The Mobility of Permanence: The Process of Relocating to Kathmandu*. Kathmandu: Center for the Study of Labor and Mobility, 2013.

"New Exit Permit Law Comes into Effect." *Gulf Times*, October 29, 2018, Qatar. Accessed November 18, 2020. https://www.gulf-times.com/story/611068/New-exit-permit-law-comes-into-effect.

Newman, Dylan. "Qatari Soccer Team Forces Migrant Workers to Run Half-Marathon in Flip Flops without Water." *Soccer Politics*, April 3, 2015. Accessed February 13, 2020. https://sites.duke.edu/wcwp/2015/04/03/qatari-soccer-team-forces-migrant-workers-to-run-half-marathon-in-flip-flops-without-water/.

Nicholls, Robert J., Craig W. Hutton, A. N. Lázár, Andrew Allan, W. Neil Adger, Helen Adams, Judith Wolf, Munsur Rahman, and Mashfiqus Salehin. "Integrated Assessment of Social and Environmental Sustainability Dynamics in the Ganges-Brahmaputra-Meghna Delta, Bangladesh." *Estuarine, Coastal and Shelf Science* 183 (2016): 370–81.

Noë, Alva. *Action in Perception*. Cambridge, MA: MIT Press, 2004.

Nonaka, Ikujirō, and Hirotaka Takeuchi. "The Knowledge-Creating Company." *Harvard Business Review* 85, no. 7–8 (2007): 162.

"North Field Expansion Project." NS Energy Business. Accessed January 19, 2020. https://www.nsenergybusiness.com/projects/north-field-expansion-project/.

Northrup, David. *Indentured Labor in the Age of Imperialism, 1834–1922*. Cambridge: Cambridge University Press, 1995.

Occupational Safety and Health Administration. "Commonly Used Statistics." United States Department of Labor. Accessed February 15, 2020. https://www.osha.gov/oshstats/commonstats.html.

"Oil in the Persian Gulf: Qatar Peninsula Terminals." *Times* (London), December 30, 1952.

Ojha, Sunal, Koji Fujit, Katsuhiko Asahi, Akiko Sakai, Damodar Lamsal, Takayuki Nuimara, and Hiroto Nagai. "Glacier Area Shrinkage in Eastern Nepal Himalaya since 1992 Using High-Resolution Inventories from Aerial Photographs and ALOS Satellite Images." *Journal of Glaciology* 62, no. 233 (2016): 512–24.

Orlikowski, Wanda J. "Using Technology and Constituting Structures: A Practice Lens for Studying Technology in Organizations." *Organization Science* 11, no. 4 (2000): 404–28.

Orr, Julian. *Talking about Machines: An Ethnography of a Modern Job*. Ithaca, NY: Cornell University Press, 1996.

Osterman, Paul. "Choice of Employment Systems in Internal Labor Markets." *Industrial Relations: A Journal of Economy and Society* 26, no. 1 (1987): 46–67.

Paap, Kris. *Working Construction: Why White Working-Class Men Put Themselves—and the Labor Movement—in Harm's Way*. Ithaca, NY: Cornell University Press, 2006.

Pal, Jeremy S., and Elfatih A. B. Eltahir. "Future Temperature in Southwest Asia Projected to Exceed a Threshold for Human Adaptability." *Nature Climate Change* 6, no. 2 (2016): 197–200. Accessed November 29, 2020. https://doi.org/10.1038/nclimate2833.

Paoletti, Sarah, Eleanor Taylor-Nicholson, Bandita Sijapati, and Bassina Farbenblum. *Migrant Workers' Access to Justice at Home: Nepal*. New York: Open Society Foundations, 2014.

Parreñas, Rhacel. *Servants of Globalization: Migration and Domestic Work*. Palo Alto, CA: Stanford University Press, 2015.

Parsons, Ken. "Heat Stress Standard ISO 7243 and Its Global Application." *Industrial Health* 44, no. 3 (2006): 368–79.

Pattisson, Pete. "Qatar's 'Families Only' Zones Entrench Segregation of Migrant Workers." *Guardian* (Doha), April 13, 2016, accessed November 19, 2020, https://www.theguardian.com/global-development/2016/apr/13/qatar-families-only-zones-entrench-segregation-of-migrant-workers.

———. "Revealed: Qatar's World Cup 'Slaves.'" *Guardian* (Kathmandu and Doha), September 25, 2013. Accessed November 12, 2020. https://www.theguardian.com/world/2013/sep/25/revealed-qatars-world-cup-slaves.

Pattisson, Pete, and Roshan Sedhai. "COVID-19 Lockdown Turns Qatar's Largest Migrant Camp into 'Virtual Prison.'" *Guardian*, March 20, 2020. Accessed March 20, 2020. https://www.theguardian.com/global-development/2020/mar/20/covid-19-lockdown-turns-qatars-largest-migrant-camp-into-virtual-prison.

Paudel, Mina Nath. "Consequences of Climate Change in Agriculture and Ways to Cope Up Its Effect in Nepal." *Agronomy Journal of Nepal* 4 (2016): 25–37.

Payne, Marissa. "Bill Clinton Reportedly Smashed a Mirror after Hearing Qatar Won the 2022 World Cup Bid." *Washington Post*, June 3, 2014. Accessed January 2, 2020. https://www.washingtonpost.com/news/early-lead/wp/2014/06/03/bill-clinton-reportedly-smashed-a-mirror-after-hearing-qatar-won-the-2022-world-cup-bid/?utm_term=.fo6ae74d38ca.

PBS NewsHour. "FIFA Announces Russia, Qatar as World Cup Hosts for 2018, 2022 (Full Presentation)." YouTube, December 2, 2010. Accessed January 2, 2020. https://www.youtube.com/watch?v=YfyPi5MnPSY.

"Pearls Growing Scarce: Rich Are Buying Them." *New York Times*, September 14, 1906.

Perlman, Amotz, Rafael Sacks, and Ronen Barak. "Hazard Recognition and Risk Perception in Construction." *Safety Science* 64 (2014): 22–31.

Petryna, Adriana. *Life Exposed: Biological Citizens after Chernobyl*. Princeton, NJ: Princeton University Press, 2013.

Phillips, Nicola. "Unfree Labour and Adverse Incorporation in the Global Economy: Comparative Perspectives on Brazil and India." *Economy and Society* 42, no. 2 (2013): 171–96. Accessed December 2, 2020. https://doi.org/10.1080/03085147.2012.718630.

Phillips, Nicola, and Fabiola Mieres. "The Governance of Forced Labour in the Global Economy." *Globalizations* 12, no. 2 (2014): 244–60. Accessed December 2, 2020. https://doi.org/10.1080/14747731.2014.932507.

Phuong, Nguyen Quynh, and Sundar Venkatesh. "Does 'Buyer Beware' Work in Migration? Contracting between Brokers and Migrants in Vietnam." *International Migration* 54, no. 6 (2016): 94–108.

Piore, Michael J. "Thirty Years Later: Internal Labor Markets, Flexibility and the New Economy." *Journal of Management and Governance* 6, no. 4 (2002): 271–79.

Pittman, Patricia. "Alternative Approaches to the Governance of Transnational Labor Recruitment." *International Migration Review* 50, no. 2 (2018): 269–314. Accessed December 2, 2020. https://doi.org/10.1111/imre.12164.

Planning and Statistics Authority. *Window on Economic Statistics of Qatar.* July 2019. Accessed November 20, 2020. https://www.psa.gov.qa/en/statistics/Statistical%20 Releases/Economic/GeneralEconomicStatistics/windowonstatistics/2019/Q1 /WinEconomicStat_28th_Issue_Q1_2019_AE.pdf.

Planning Council. *Population and Housing Census (1997), QSA,* 1997.

———. *Population and Housing Census (2004), QSA,* 2004.

"PM Inaugurates Largest Labour City in Gulf Region." *Gulf Times* (Doha), November 1, 2015. Accessed November 21, 2020. https://www.gulf-times.com/story/461159/PM -inaugurates-largest-Labour-City-in-Gulf-region.

Polanyi, Michael. *The Tacit Dimension.* London: Routledge, 1966.

Pollock, Richard A., Ted W. Brown Jr., and David M. Rubin. "'Phossy Jaw' and 'Bis-phossy Jaw' of the 19th and 21st Centuries: The Diuturnity of John Walker and the Friction Match." *Craniomaxillofacial Trauma and Reconstruction* 8, no. 3 (2015): 262–70. Accessed November 30, 2020. https://doi.org/10.1055/s-0035-1558452.

Pradhan, Bandana, Tord Kjellstrom, Dan Atar, Puspa Sharma, Birendra Kayastha, Gita Bhandari, and Pushkar K. Pradhan. "Heat Stress Impacts on Cardiac Mortality in Nepali Migrant Workers in Qatar." *Cardiology* 143, no. 1 (2019): 37–48.

Press Association. "FIFA's Sepp Blatter Dismisses Fears over 2022 World Cup in Qatar." *Guardian,* December 13, 2010. Accessed November 13, 2020. https://www.theguardian .com/football/2010/dec/13/fifa-sepp-blatter-discrimination-qatar-2022.

Qafisheh, Mutaz M. "Restorative Justice in the Islamic Penal Law: A Contribution to the Global System." *International Journal of Criminal Justice Sciences* 7, no. 1 (2012): 487–507.

"Qatar Abolishes Controversial 'Kafala' Labour System." BBC News, December 13, 2016, Middle East. Accessed November 18, 2020. https://www.bbc.com/news/world-middle -east-38298393.

Qatar Country Study Guide. Washington, DC: International Business Publications, 2006.

Qatar Foundation. *QF Mandatory Standards of Migrant Workers' Welfare for Contractors and Sub-Contractors.* Doha: Qatar Foundation, 2013.

"Qatar GDP—Gross Domestic Product," Countryeconomy.com, 2009, accessed February 19, 2020, https://countryeconomy.com/gdp/qatar?year=2009.

Qatar Ministry of the Municipality and Environment. *Qatar Construction Specifications of 2010.* Doha, 2010.

Qatar National Vision and Ministry of Development Planning and Statistics. *Qatar Second National Development Strategy, 2018–2022.* Doha: Planning and Statistics Authority, 2019. Accessed November 18, 2020. https://www.psa.gov.qa/en/knowledge/Documents /NDS2Final.pdf.

"Qatar Opens 'Labour City' for 70000 Migrant Workers." *New Arab,* November 2, 2015. Accessed November 21, 2020. https://www.alaraby.co.uk/english/news/2015/11/2/qatar -opens-labour-city-for-70000-migrant-workers.

Qatar Planning and Statistics Authority. *Annual Bulletin Labor Force Survey, 2010 and 2015.*

———. *Bulletin Labor Force Statistics, 2015.* Qatar: Government of Qatar, 2015.

———. *Population and Social Statistics—Quarterly Bulletin (2000–2018).* Doha: State of Qatar, 2018.

"Qatar to Open Doors to More ROK Builders." *Korea Times,* May 4, 1982.

"Qatar to Reimburse Recruitment Fees to 30,000 Workers; Global Trade Union Body Hails Decision." *Peninsula Qatar* (Doha), March 18, 2018. Accessed December 2, 2020. https:// www.thepeninsulaqatar.com/article/18/03/2018/Qatar-to-reimburse-recruitment-fees -to-30,000-workers-Global-trade-union-body-hails-decision.

"Qatar 2022 World Cup Risks 4000 Lives, Warns International Trade Union Confederation." ITUC CSI IGB, September 27, 2013. Accessed February 15, 2020. https://www.ituc-csi .org/qatar-2022-world-cup-risks-4000.

"Qatar 2022 World Cup Stadiums: All You Need to Know." Al Jazeera, September 18, 2019, News/Football. Accessed November 19, 2020. https://www.aljazeera.com/news/2018 /10/qatar-2022-world-cup-stadiums-181025142408471.html.

"Qatar World Cup: 'Squalid' Conditions for Migrant Workers." *Channel 4 News*, 2015. Accessed November 12, 2020. https://www.channel4.com/news/qatar-world-cup -squalid-conditions-for-migrant-workers.

"Qatar's 'Bachelor Ban' Makes Life Laborious for Blue-collar Workers." New Arab, 2016. Accessed November 19, 2020. https://www.alaraby.co.uk/english/blog/2016/5/20/qatars -bachelor-ban-makes-life-laborious-for-blue-collar-workers.

"Qatar's Reliance on Unskilled Workers Reduced." *Construction Week*, June 26, 2016. Accessed November 21, 2020. https://www.constructionweekonline.com/article-39733 -qatars-reliance-on-unskilled-workers-reduced.

"The QFIS Challenges: Astutely Addressed by ASTAD." *Special Integration Asia* 156, no. 2 (2017): 72–77.

"QPMC Contracts Ensure Materials Supply." *Construction Week*, October 13, 2015. Accessed November 20, 2020. https://www.constructionweekonline.com/article-35877-qpmc -contracts-ensure-materials-supply.

Quandt, Sara A., Melinda F. Wiggins, Haiying Chen, Werner E. Bischoff, and Thomas A. Arcury. "Heat Index in Migrant Farmworker Housing: Implications for Rest and Recovery from Work-Related Heat Stress." *American Journal of Public Health* 103, no. 8 (2013): e24–e26.

Quirke, Joe. "Samsung and OHL Fired from $1.4bn Qatar Rail Contract." *Global Construction Review*, May 9, 2016. Accessed November 20, 2020. http://www.globalconstructionreview .com/news/samsung-and-ohl-fired-14bn-qat7ar-ra7il-contr7act/.

Rabi, Uzi. "Qatar." In *Middle East Contemporary Survey 1991*, edited by Ami Ayalon, 605–12. Boulder, CO: Westview Press, 1993.

Rahman, Khondker. "The Qatar National Master Plan." *Sustainable Development: An Appraisal from the Gulf Region* 19 (2014): 82.

Rahman, Md. Habibur, and Md. Sakhawat Hossain. "Convergence in Per Capita Income across Regions in Bangladesh." *Bangladesh Development Studies* 32, no. 1 (2009): 45–60. Accessed December 2, 2020. https://bids.org.bd/uploads/publication/BDS/32/32-1/03 _Rahman%20&%20Hossain.pdf.

Rahman, Md. Mizanur. "Migrant Indebtedness: Bangladeshis in the GCC Countries." *International Migration* 53, no. 6 (2015): 205–19. Accessed December 2, 2020. https://doi .org/10.1111/imig.12084.

Rai, Om Astha. "A Mysterious Rash of Kidney Failures." *Nepali Times*, April 7–13, 2017. Accessed November 29, 2020. http://archive.nepalitimes.com/article/Nepali-Times -Buzz/A-mysterious-rash-of-kidney-failures,3639.

"Revealed: How Coronavirus Outbreak Is Shining a Light on Violations Inside Qatar's Labor Camps." *Arab News*. April 5, 2020. Accessed April 20, 2020. https://www.arabnews.com /node/1653741/middle-east.

Reilly, Benjamin. *Slavery, Agriculture, and Malaria in the Arabian Peninsula*. Athens: Ohio University Press, 2015.

Reilly, Benjamin J. "A Well-Intentioned Failure: British Anti-Slavery Measures and the Arabian Peninsula, 1820–1940." *Journal of Arabian Studies* 5, no. 2 (2015): 91–115.

Reiman, Teemu, and Carl Rollenhagen. "Does the Concept of Safety Culture Help or Hinder Systems Thinking in Safety?" *Accident Analysis and Prevention* 68 (2014): 5–15.

Reuters. "Nepal Envoy Recalled after Qatar 'Open Jail' Remarks." September 26, 2013. Accessed February 15, 2020. https://www.reuters.com/article/us-nepal-qatar-ambassador/nepal -envoy-recalled-after-qatar-open-jail-remarks-idUSBRE98P10O20130926.

Reuters. "Qatar Slashes Healthcare Spending, World Cup Escapes Cuts." *Arabian Business Global*, May 25, 2016. Accessed November 20, 2020. https://www.arabianbusiness.com /qatar-slashes-healthcare-spending-world-cup-escapes-cuts-632971.html.

Rizzo, Agatino. "Metro Doha." *Cities* 31 (2013): 533–43.

———. "Rapid Urban Development and National Master Planning in Arab Gulf Countries: Qatar as a Case Study." *Cities* 39 (2014): 50–57.

Robinson, Cedric J. *Black Marxism: The Making of the Black Radical Tradition*. Chapel Hill: University of North Carolina Press, 2000.

Røe, Oluf Dimitri, and Giulia Maria Stella. "Malignant Pleural Mesothelioma: History, Controversy, and Future of a Man-Made Epidemic." In *Asbestos and Mesothelioma*, , edited by Joseph R. Testa, 73–101. New York: Springer, 2017.

Roscoe, Andrew. "Qatar Primary Materials Company." *MEED: Middle East Economic Digest* 57, no. 49 (2013): 26–27.

Rosner, David, and Gerald Markowitz. *Deadly Dust: Silicosis and the Politics of Occupational Disease in Twentieth-Century America*. Princeton, NJ: Princeton University Press, 1994.

Rosner, David, and Gerald E. Markowitz. *Dying for Work: Workers' Safety and Health in Twentieth-Century America*. Bloomington: Indiana University Press, 1987.

Rowlinson, Steve, Andrea YunyanJia, Baizhan Li, and Carrie ChuanjingJu. "Management of Climatic Heat Stress Risk in Construction: A Review of Practices, Methodologies, and Future Research." *Accident Analysis and Prevention* 66 (2014): 187–98.

Royburt, M., Y. Epstein, Z. Solomon, and J. Shemer. "Long-Term Psychological and Physiological Effects of Heat Stroke." *Physiology and Behavior* 54, no. 2 (1993): 265–67.

Russell, Sharon Stanton. "International Migration and Political Turmoil in the Middle East." *Population and Development Review* 18, no. 4 (1992): 719–27. Accessed November 17, 2020. https://doi.org/10.2307/1973761.

Salama, Ashraf M., and Florian Wiedmann. *Demystifying Doha: On Architecture and Urbanism in an Emerging City*. Abingdon, UK: Routledge, 2016.

Sampson, Helen. "'Fluid Fields' and the Dynamics of Risk in Social Research." *Qualitative Research* (2017): 131–47.

Sarmadi, Behzad. "'Bachelor' in the City: Urban Transformation and Matter Out of Place in Dubai." *Journal of Arabian Studies* 3, no. 2 (2013): 196–214.

Satija, Bhanvi. "Why Were These Immigrant Workers Made to Run a Marathon, Shoeless, in Qatar?" *Youth Ki Awaaz*, April 15, 2015. Accessed February 13, 2020. https://www .youthkiawaaz.com/2015/04/qatar-mega-marathon/.

Schär, Christoph. "Climate Extremes: The Worst Heat Waves to Come." *Nature Climate Change* 6, no. 2 (2016): 128–29. Accessed November 29, 2020. https://doi.org/10.1038 /nclimate2864. https://doi.org/10.1038/nclimate2864.

Schedler, Andreas. *The Politics of Uncertainty: Sustaining and Subverting Electoral Authoritarianism*. Oxford: Oxford University Press, 2013.

Schild, Andreas. "ICIMOD's Position on Climate Change and Mountain Systems: The Case of the Hindu Kush–Himalayas." *Mountain Research and Development* 28, no. 3 (2008): 328–31.

Schulte, Paul A., A. Bhattacharya, C. R. Butler, Heekyoung K. Chun, Brenda Jacklitsch, T. Jacobs, Max Kiefer, et al. "Advancing the Framework for Considering the Effects of Climate Change on Worker Safety and Health." *Journal of Occupational and Environmental Hygiene* 13, no. 11 (2016): 847–65. Accessed November 30, 2020. https://doi.org /10.1080/15459624.2016.1179388.

Scott, James C. *Seeing Like a State: How Certain Schemes to Improve the Human Condition Have Failed*. New Haven, CT: Yale University Press, 1998.

Seccombe, Ian J. "Labour Migration to the Arabian Gulf: Evolution and Characteristics, 1920–1950." *British Journal of Middle Eastern Studies* 10, no. 1 (1983): 3–20.

Seccombe, Ian J., and Richard I. Lawless. "Foreign Worker Dependence in the Gulf, and the International Oil Companies: 1910–50." *International Migration Review* (1986): 548–74.

———. "The Gulf Labour Market and the Early Oil Industry: Traditional Structures and New Forms of Organisation." In *The Gulf in the Early 20th Century: Foreign Institutions and Local Responses*, edited by Richard I. Lawless, 91–124. Durham, NC: Center for Middle Eastern and Islamic Studies, 1986.

———. "Work Camps and Company Towns: Settlement Patterns and the Gulf Oil Industry." Working paper, University of Durham, Centre for Middle Eastern and Islamic Studies, 1987.

Segall, David, and Sarah Labowitz. *Making Workers Pay: Recruitment of the Migrant Labor Force in the Gulf Construction Industry*. New York: NYU Stern Center for Business and Human Rights, 2017.

Sellers, Christopher C. *Hazards of the Job: From Industrial Disease to Environmental Health Science*. Chapel Hill: University of North Carolina Press, 1997.

Sennett, Richard. *The Craftsman*. New Haven, CT: Yale University Press, 2008.

Senouci, Ahmed, Ahmed Alsarraj, Murat Gunduz, and Neil Eldin. "Analysis of Change Orders in Qatari Construction Projects." *International Journal of Construction Management* 17, no. 4 (2017): 280–92.

Senouci, Ahmed, Alaa Ahmad Ismail, and Neil Eldin. "Time and Cost Overrun in Public Construction Projects in Qatar." Paper presented at the Creative Construction Conference, Budapest, 2016.

Serageldin, Ismail, James A. Socknat, J. Stace Birks, Bob Li, and Clive A. Sinclair. *Manpower and International Labor Migration in the Middle East and North Africa*, edited by World Bank. Washington, DC: Oxford University Press, 1983.

Shahdad, Ibrahim. "الحراك الشعبيفيقطر 1950–1963 دراسة تحليلية" [Popular movements, 1950–1963, analytic study]." Kuwait City: Gulf Center for Development Policies, 2012.

Shakespeare, Ananda. "Building Boom Gathers Pace in Qatar." MEED: Middle East Business Intelligence, May 13, 2014. Accessed November 19, 2020. https://www.meed.com /building-boom-gathers-pace-in-qatar/.

Shandas, Vivek, Yasuyo Makido, and Salim Ferwati. "Rapid Urban Growth and Land Use Patterns in Doha, Qatar: Opportunities for Sustainability." *European Journal of Sustainable Development Research* 1, no. 2 (2017): 1–13.

Shapiro, Lawrence. *Embodied Cognition*. Abingdon, UK: Routledge, 2019.

Sharma, Roshan, Bhagawat Rial, Nigel Stork, Himlal Baral, and Maheshwar Dhakal. "Spatial Assessment of the Potential Impact of Infrastructure Development on Biodiversity Conservation in Lowland Nepal." *ISPRS International Journal of Geo-Information* 7, no. 9 (2018): 365.

Sharma, Sanjay, Shibani Pandey, Dinesh Pathak, and Bimbika Sijapati-Basnett. *State of Migration in Nepal*. Kathmandu: Centre for the Study of Labour and Mobility, 2014.

Sharma, Sanjib Kumar, Subodh Dhakal, Lekhjung Thapa, Anup Ghimire, Rikesh Tamrakar, Satdal Chaudhary, Rajib Deo, et al. "Community-Based Screening for Chronic Kidney Disease, Hypertension and Diabetes in Dharan." *Journal of the Nepal Medical Association* 52, no. 189 (2013): 205–12.

Shepherd, Craig, Sean Whitham, and Herbert Freehills. *Construction Arbitration: Qatar*. 2018. November 20, 2020. https://globalarbitrationreview.com/jurisdiction/1005078/qatar.

Shirras, G. Findlay. "Indian Migration." In *International Migrations, Volume II: Interpretations*, edited by Walter F. Willcox. Cambridge, MA: National Bureau of Economic Research, 1931.

Shrestha, Rajendra P., and Namita Nepal. "An Assessment by Subsistence Farmers of the Risks to Food Security Attributable to Climate Change in Makwanpur, Nepal." *Food Security* 8, no. 2 (2016): 415–25.

Shulz, Markus S. "Collective Action across Borders: Opportunity Structures, Network Capacities, and Communicative Praxis in the Age of Advanced Globalization." *Sociological Perspectives* 41, no. 3 (1998): 587–616.

Silbey, Susan S. "Taming Prometheus: Talk about Safety and Culture." *Annual Review of Sociology* 35 (2009): 341–69.

Silvey, Rachel. "Consuming the Transnational Family: Indonesian Migrant Domestic Workers to Saudi Arabia." *Global Networks* 6, no. 1 (2006): 23–40.

Sinha, Chitta Prasad. "Climate Change and its Impacts on the Wetlands of North Bihar, India." *Lakes and Reservoirs: Research and Management* 16, no. 2 (2011): 109–11.

Sinha, Mrinalini. "Premonitions of the Past." *Journal of Asian Studies* 74, no. 4 (2015): 821–41.

Smart, John E., Virginia A. Teodosio, and Carol J. Jimenez. "Skills and Earnings: Issues in the Developmental Impact on the Philippines of Labor Export to the Middle East." In *Asian Labor Migration*, edited by Fred Arnold and Nasra M. Shah, 101–24. Boulder, CO: Westview Press, 1986.

Smith, Matt. "Qatar Building Boom Proves a Challenge for Foreign Construction Firms." Reuters (Dubai), June 23, 2015. Accessed November 20, 2020. https://www.reuters.com/article/qatar-construction-idUSL5N0YU1BK20150623.

Snoj, Jure. "Population of Qatar by Nationality—2019." *Priya Dsouza Communications*, no. In Our Perspectives, Our Expertise (August 15, 2019). Accessed February 13, 2020. http://priyadsouza.com/population-of-qatar-by-nationality-in-2017/.

Spencer, Richard. "Asian Labourers Press Ganged into Joining Qatar Marathon Record Attempt." *Telegraph*, March 30, 2015. Accessed February 13, 2020. https://www.telegraph.co.uk/news/worldnews/middleeast/qatar/11503669/Asian-labourers-press-ganged-into-joining-Qatar-marathon-record-attempt.html.

Spong, Rebecca. "Airport Delay Affecting National Airline." *MEED: Middle East Economic Digest* 57, no. 19 (May 10, 2013): 42–43.

State of Qatar. Census of Population and Housing and Establishments 2010. 2010. Accessed November 17, 2020. https://www.psa.gov.qa/en/statistics/Statistical%20Releases/General/Census/Population_Households_Establishment_QSA_Census_AE_2010_1.pdf.

Steinberg, Ronnie J., and Deborah M. Figart. "Emotional Labor Since: The Managed Heart." *Annals of the American Academy of Political and Social Science* 561, no. 1 (1999): 8–26.

Sturman, Rachel. "Indian Indentured Labor and the History of International Rights Regimes." *American Historical Review* 119, no. 5 (2014): 1439–65.

Sugden, Fraser. "A Mode of Production Flux: The Transformation and Reproduction of Rural Class Relations in Lowland Nepal and North Bihar." *Dialectical Anthropology* 41, no. 2 (2017): 129–61.

Sunindijo, Riza Yosia, and Patrick X. W. Zou. "The Roles of Emotional Intelligence, Interpersonal Skill, and Transformational Leadership on Improving Construction Safety Performance." *Construction Economics and Building* 13, no. 3 (2013): 97–113.

Supreme Committee for Delivery and Legacy. *SC Workers' Welfare Standards: A Lasting Legacy of Human and Social Development*. Doha: Supreme Committee for Delivery and Legacy, 2014.

Tarrow, Sidney. "Cycles of Collective Action: Between Moments of Madness and the Repertoire of Contention." *Social Science History* 17, no. 2 (1993): 281–307.

———. "Social Movements in Contentious Politics: A Review Article." *American Political Science Review* 90, no. 4 (1996): 874–83.

Taylor, Joseph, and Elizabeth Strack. *Pearl Production*. Amsterdam: Elsevier, 2008.

Tesfave, Kindie, Pramod K. Aggarwal, Fasil Mequanint, Paresh B. Shirsath, Clare M. Stirling, Arun Khatri-Chhetri, and Dil Bahadur Rahut. "Climate Variability and Change in Bihar, India: Challenges and Opportunities for Sustainable Crop Production." *Sustainability* 9, no. 1 (2017): 1998.

Tetzlaff, Stefan. "Entangled Boundaries: British India and the Persian Gulf Region during the Transition from Empires to Nation States, c. 1880–1935." MA thesis., Humboldt Universitat zu Berlin, 2009.

Thami, Prakriti, and Ashim Bhattarai. *Labor Migration and Skills Training*. Kathmandu: Centre for the Study of Labour and Mobility, 2015. Accessed December 7, 2020. https:// ceslam.org/index.php?pageName=publication&pid=44.

Thapa, Gokarna Jung, Eric Wikramanayake, and Jessica Forrest. *Climate-Change Impacts on the Biodiversity of the Terai Arc Landscape and the Chitwan-Annapurna Landscape*. Kathmandu: Hariyo Ban, 2015.

Tilly, Charles. "Contentious Repertoires in Great Britain, 1758–1834." *Social Science History* 17, no. 2 (1993): 253–80.

———. *Popular Contention in Great Britain, 1758-1834*. London: Routledge, 2015.

———. *Regimes and Repertoires*. Chicago: University of Chicago Press, 2010.

———. "Social Movements as Historically Specific Clusters of Political Performances." *Berkeley Journal of Sociology* 38 (1993): 1–30.

Tiwari, Krishna Raj, S. Rayamajhi, Ridish K. Pokharel, and M. K. Balla. "Determinants of the Climate Change Adaptation in Rural Farming in Nepal Himalaya." *International Journal of Multidisciplinary and Current Research* 2 (2014): 234–40.

Toth, Anthony. "Qatar." In *Persian Gulf States: Country Studies*, edited by Helen Chapin Metz, 147–96. Washington, DC: Federal Research Division, Department of the Army, 1994.

Traugott, Mark. *Repertoires and Cycles of Collective Action*. Durham, NC: Duke University Press, 1995.

Truss, Catherine, Edel Conway, Alessia d'Amato, Gráinne Kelly, Kathy Monks, Enda Hannon, and Patrick C. Flood. "Knowledge Work: Gender-Blind or Gender-Biased?" *Work, Employment and Society* 26, no. 5 (2012): 735–54.

Tweedale, Geoffrey. *Magic Mineral to Killer Dust: Turner and Newall and the Asbestos Hazard*. Oxford: Oxford University Press, 2000.

Upreti, Bishal Nath, Subodh Dhakal, Tara Nidhi Bhattargai, Bassanta Raj Adhikari, Samjwal Ratna Bajarcharya, and Masaru Yoshida. "Climate Change Impact on Glacier Retreat and Local Community in the Langtang Valley, Central Nepal." *Journal of Development Innovations* 1, no. 1 (2017): 45–59.

Urban Times. "Carbon Heavy Qatar Roars Ahead in Green Building Innovation." *Smart Cities Dive*. Accessed November 11, 2020. https://www.smartcitiesdive.com/ex /sustainablecitiescollective/qatar-green-building-innovation/122191/.

Van Maanen, John. "Ethnography as Work: Some Rules of Engagement." *Journal of Management Studies* 48, no. 1 (2011): 218–34.

Van Manen, Max. "Phenomenological Pedagogy." *Curriculum Inquiry* 12, no. 3 (1982): 283–99.

Varela, Francisco J. *Ethical Know-how: Action, Wisdom, and Cognition*. Palo Alto, CA: Stanford University Press, 1999.

Varela, Francisco J., Eleanor Rosch, and Evan Thompson. *The Embodied Mind: Cognitive Science and Human Experience*. Cambridge, MA: MIT Press, 2017.

Venugopal, Vidhya, Jeremiah Chinnadurai, Rebekah Lucas, and Tord Kjellstrom. "Occupational Heat Stress Profiles in Selected Workplaces in India." *International Journal of Environmental Research and Public Health* 13, no. 1 (2016): 89.

Veronis, Luisa, Bonnie Boyd, Reiko Obokata, and Brittany Main. "Environmental Change and International Migration." *Routledge Handbook of Enviromental Displacement and Migration*, edited by Robert McLeman and François Gemenne, 42–70. Abingdon, UK: Routledge, 2018.

Walter, Edward James, and Mike Carraretto. "The Neurological and Cognitive Consequences of Hyperthermia." *Critical Care* 20, no. 1 (2016): 199.

Walton, Gregory. "Qatar to End Controversial Migrant Worker Restrictions." *AFP International Text Wire in English* (Washington, DC), October 16, 2019.

WDR. "Gefangen in Katar—Corona und die Fußball-WM 2022." April 6, 2020. Accesed April 20, 2020. https://www1.wdr.de/mediathek/video/sendungen/sport-inside/video -gefangen-in-katar---corona-und-die-fussball-wm----100.html.

Weather Underground. "Doha, Qatar Weather History." 2020. Accessed February 16, 2020. https://www.wunderground.com/history/daily/OTBD/date.

Weaver, Mary Anne. "Democracy by Decree." *New Yorker*, November 20, 2000, 54–61.

Wegman, David H., Jenny Apelqvist, Matteo Bottai, Ulf Ekström, Ramón García-Trabanino, Jason Glaser, Christer Hogstedt, et al. "Intervention to Diminish Dehydration and Kidney Damage among Sugarcane Workers." *Scandinavian Journal of Work, Environment and Health* 44, no. 1 (2018): 16–24.

Weichbrodt, Johann. "Safety Rules as Instruments for Organizational Control, Coordination and Knowledge: Implications for Rules Management." *Safety Science* 80 (2015): 221–32.

Wiedmann, Florian, and Ashraf M. Salama. "From Pre-Oil Settlement to Post-Oil Hub: The Urban Transformation of Doha." *Archnet-IJAR: International Journal of Architectural Research* 7, no. 2 (2013): 146–59.

William L. Pereira Associates. *New Doha Planning Studies: Concept Plan.* Los Angeles: William L. Pereira Associates, 1975.

Willmott, Hugh. "From Knowledge to Learning." In *Managing Knowledge: Critical Investigations of Work and Learning*, edited by Craig Prichard, Richard Hull, Mike Chumer, and Hugh Willmott, 216–22. London: Macmillan, 2000.

Wilson, Margaret. "Six Views of Embodied Cognition." *Psychonomic Bulletin and Review* 9, no. 4 (2002): 625–36.

Winckler, Onn. "The Immigration Policy of the Gulf Cooperation Council (GCC) States." *Middle Eastern Studies* 33, no. 3 (1997):.

Wolkowitz, Carol. *Bodies at Work.* London: Sage, 2006.

World Bank. *Groundswell: Preparing for Internal Climate Migration.* March 19, 2018. Accessed December 2, 2020. https://www.worldbank.org/en/news/infographic/2018 /03/19/groundswell---preparing-for-internal-climate-migration.

———. "Qatar: Oil Revenue." TheGlobalEconomy.com. 2019. Accessed November 17, 2020. https://www.theglobaleconomy.com/Qatar/oil_revenue/.

"World Economic Outlook Database, April 2019." International Monetary Fund, April 12, 2019.

Xiang, Jianjun, Peng Bi, Dino Pisaniello, and Alana Hansen. "Health Impacts of Workplace Heat Exposure: An Epidemiological Review." *Industrial Health* 52, no. 2 (2014): 91–101.

Xue, Pengfei, and Elfatih A. B. Eltahir. "Estimation of the Heat and Water Budgets of the Persian (Arabian) Gulf Using a Regional Climate Model." *Journal of Climate* 28, no. 13 (2015): 5041–62.

Yakhlef, Ali. "The Corporeality of Practice-Based Learning." *Organization Studies* 31, no. 4 (2010): 409–30.

Yoopat, Pongjan, Pornkamon Toicharoen, Thirayudh Glinsukon, Kamiel Vanwonterghem, and Veikko Louhevaara. "Ergonomics in Practice: Physical Workload and Heat Stress in Thailand." *International Journal of Occupational Safety and Ergonomics* 8, no. 1 (2002): 83–93.

Zachariah, Kunniparampil Curien, and Sebastian Irudaya Rajan. *Kerala's Gulf Connection, 1998–2011: Economic and Social Impact of Migration*. Telangana, India: Orient Blackswan, 2012.

Zahlan, Rosemarie Said. *The Creation of Qatar*. London: Croon Helm, 1979.

———. "The Impact of the Early Oil Concessions in the Gulf States." In *The Gulf in the Early 20th Century: Foreign Institutions and Local Responses*, edited by Richard I. Lawless. Durham, NC: Center for Middle Eastern and Islamic Studies, 1986.

Zdanowski, Jerzy. *Slavery and Manumission: British Policy in the Red Sea and the Persian Gulf in the First Half of the 20th Century*. Reading, UK: Ithaca Press, 2013.

———. *Speaking with Their Own Voices: The Stories of Slaves in the Persian Gulf in the 20th Century*. Cambridge: Cambridge Scholars Publishing, 2014.

Zolberg, Aristide R. "Moments of Madness." *Politics and Society* 2, no. 2 (1972): 183–207.

A NOTE ON THE TYPE

{⸺⸻}

THIS BOOK has been composed in Miller, a Scotch Roman typeface designed by Matthew Carter and first released by Font Bureau in 1997. It resembles Monticello, the typeface developed for The Papers of Thomas Jefferson in the 1940s by C. H. Griffith and P. J. Conkwright and reinterpreted in digital form by Carter in 2003.

Pleasant Jefferson ("P. J.") Conkwright (1905–1986) was Typographer at Princeton University Press from 1939 to 1970. He was an acclaimed book designer and AIGA Medalist.

The ornament used throughout this book was designed by Pierre Simon Fournier (1712–1768) and was a favorite of Conkwright's, used in his design of the *Princeton University Library Chronicle*.

GPSR Authorized Representative: Easy Access System Europe - Mustamäe tee
50, 10621 Tallinn, Estonia, gpsr.requests@easproject.com

www.ingramcontent.com/pod-product-compliance
Ingram Content Group UK Ltd.
Pitfield, Milton Keynes, MK11 3LW, UK
UKHW041833130425
457319UK00003B/430